March of America Facsimile Series

Number 54

History of the Late War in the Western Country

Robert Breckinridge McAfee

History of the Late War
in the Western Country

by Robert Breckinridge McAfee

ANN ARBOR

UNIVERSITY MICROFILMS, INC.

A Subsidiary of Xerox Corporation

Foreword

In the period leading up to the War of 1812 the western regions of the United States produced some of the most vociferous advocates of war with Great Britain. The western "war hawks" feared above all else an Indian alliance with the British which would jeopardize American control over the area. The War of 1812 helped allay those fears. The Indian menace in the Old Northwest was greatly reduced and settlement proceeded thereafter with relatively little bloodshed. Fewer complaints were heard about the encroachments of British fur traders on unoccupied American territory. Furthermore many American soldiers from other parts of the country who fought in the West returned to settle there after the war, accelerating development of the region. A number of military heroes from the western campaigns received public acclaim—men like William Henry Harrison, Zachary Taylor, and Andrew Jackson—and later turned their popularity to political advantage. Robert McAfee, a Kentuckian who had participated in some of the battles in the West, provided the American public with the first thoroughgoing account of the war in the West with his *History of the Late War in the Western Country*, published in 1816.

McAfee's parents had been among the first to settle in Kentucky and he was thoroughly western in his outlook. He admitted that almost all of the information for his history came from the American side and that what little he had come across from the British side he regarded as "notoriously false." As one who had "lost many of his friends in the Indian wars, during the first settling of this country," he had "necessarily imbibed an abhorrence of those principles and practices of the savages, and their British allies, by which the western settlements have suffered so much in both wars." In spite of McAfee's obvious bias, he provided valuable information about the campaigns in the West. General Harrison and other prominent figures in the war gave him access to their papers. These he supplemented with verbal accounts from his acquaintances in the army.

McAfee's history begins with William Henry Harrison's successful repulse of the Indian Confederation at the Battle of Tippecanoe in 1811, which occurred before the war with England had actually begun. He describes the exaltation of Tecumseh's brother, the "Prophet," who "kept himself secure, on an adjacent eminence, singing a war song" and urging his followers into battle against the Americans. McAfee closes his history with Andrew Jackson's defense of New Orleans against British attack.

A biographical sketch of Robert McAfee is given by the *Dictionary of American Biography*. To check McAfee's *History* with the results of modern scholarship on the war in the West, see Alec R. Gilpin, *The War of 1812 in the Old Northwest* (East Lansing, 1958).

History of the Late War
in the Western Country

HISTORY

OF THE

LATE WAR

IN THE

WESTERN COUNTRY,

COMPRISING A FULL ACCOUNT OF ALL THE TRANSACTIONS IN
THAT QUARTER, FROM THE COMMENCEMENT OF HOSTILITIES
AT TIPPECANOE, TO THE TERMINATION OF THE CONTEST
AT NEW ORLEANS ON THE RETURN OF PEACE.

LEXINGTON, K.

PUBLISHED BY WORSLEY & SMITH.

1816.

PREFACE.

THE AUTHOR of the following history will not detain the reader with many prefatory remarks. It was written during those hours of leisure, which he was able occasionally to reserve from other necessary occupations; and he therefore wishes it to be regarded, as not advancing any lofty pretensions to literary merit. His object has chiefly been, to give a plain and correct statement of facts, and to make only such reflections upon them, as they would obviously authorize; and he can conscientiously say, that he has in no case intentionally distorted or concealed any thing. He has no private friendships or enmities to gratify—nothing but a rational attachment to his country, and hostility to her enemies according to their deserts. Being a native of Kentucky, and having lost many of his friends in the Indian wars, during the first settling of this country, he has necessarily imbibed an abhorrence of those principles and practices of the savages, and their British allies, by which the western settlements have suffered so much in both wars. If any of his expressions should be deemed too acrimonious and intemperate for dignified and impartial history, the reader will excuse them on this account, together with the consideration, that the feelings excited by the occurrences described are still fresh and vigorous in his bosom. He believes however, that he has said nothing which is not *strictly true and just*, though perhaps not entirely agreeable to the taste of every reader.

In procuring materials for this work, the author is greatly indebted to general Harrison and governor Shelby for the many valuable documents they furnished, particularly their correspondence with the war department and with each other. He is also indebted to governor Edwards for his correspondence, but it unfortunately arrived too late to be of use. Colonels Croghan and Todd, with many other officers of the northwestern army, have also laid him under great obligations by the cheerfulness with which they furnished, and assisted him in collecting, all the information within their power. To the latter he is indebted for the journal of colonel Wood of the engineers, who justly attained a lofty character for military genius and services before his untimely but glorious fall. Most of these papers will remain in the possession of colonel C. S. Todd, subject to be examined by any person, who may wish to see the authorities on which any statement in this history is founded.

In preparing this work for the press, I have to acknowledge the assistance I received from doctor Joseph Buchanan, who first undertook its publication. He carefully examined and compared all the materials from which it has been compiled, and in fact attentively revised it in every respect. In some instances he has made alterations, on the propriety of which I have differed with him in opinion : however there is no material fact, which I am not satisfied is correctly stated ; and as for reflections, the reader will no doubt judge for himself.

The transactions in the Illinois and Missouri territories are imperfectly detailed, because many important documents did not reach me before the work had gone to press—hence I have not been able to do justice to governors Howard and Edwards and colonel Russell for the arduous services they performed. The mounted expedition conducted by general Hopkins is also very briefly narrated, owing to delays of a similar nature. These imperfections can be remedied hereafter, should the patronage of the work ever call for another edition. The author will also gratefully receive and admit any other corrections or additions, which may be shewn on good authority to be necessary. He at first intended to notice a greater number of meritorious individuals by name ; but in revising the work for the press, it was found necessary to abridge it in this respect, and to omit the army list and names of subscribers, to bring it within the limits of a single volume. It still exceeds the size prescribed for it, and promised in the prospectus.

In describing the operations against the Creek Indians, I have had to rely chiefly on official reports, which however correct, are insufficient in fulness for a complete history.—As to the campaign at New Orleans, besides the common sources of information, I have had recourse to major Thomas Curry, and I acknowledge with pleasure the assistance he has given me. He served in the Kentucky militia on that campaign, and was able as an eye witness to furnish much important matter.

In justice to our late enemies, as well as to myself, it may be proper to add, that my information with respect to them has unavoidably been very imperfect ; and hence I may have made erroneous statements respecting them in many instances. Their own official reports which they published, are so notoriously false, that no reliance can be placed upon them ; and the inofficial anonymous reports which circulated in our public prints concerning them, were not much better authority. But with respect to our own operations, I have authentic documents, or the evidence of highly respectable witnesses, to substantiate every statement I have made.

ROBERT B. M'AFEE.

CONTENTS.

HISTORY

OF THE

LATE WAR IN THE WESTERN COUNTRY.

─────────────

CHAPTER I.

Preliminary views....Causes of the War....Battle of Tippecanoe.

AT the close of the American revolution, many persons in England entertained an opinion, that the American colonies were not irretrievably lost to the mother country. They hoped that Great Britain would be able, at some favorable moment, to regain the sovereignty of these states ; and in this hope it is highly probable the British ministry participated.

From calculations and sentiments like these, as well as from the irritation caused by the failure of their arms, may have proceeded their unjustifiable conduct, on the interior frontiers of the new states. The military posts of Niagara, Detroit, and Mackinaw, were detained under various pretences, for many years, in violation of the treaty of peace. The Indian tribes on our borders, were at the same time supplied with munitions of war, and instigated to commit depredations and hostilities on the frontiers of Kentucky, and the settlements northwest of the Ohio. This fact is fully established by the letters of colonel M'Kee, the British commandant of fort Miami at the foot of the

Rapids, written previous to the visit of general Wayne to that place in '94, and published during the late war in the American journals, the originals having then fallen into the hands of our government.

This unwarrantable interference with the Indians, residing within the limits of the United States, was continued by the British from the peace of '83, quite down to the commencement of the late war. During a great part of that time, they kept the Indians in hostility with our western settlements : and when the probability of a new war between the two countries, became very strong, they so excited the savages, as to make a battle with them the necessary prelude to general hostilities. Although this interference with the Indians, was not an obvious and ostensible cause of the war ; yet it may fairly be considered as a very efficient cause. Much of that resentment against the British, which prevailed so strongly in the western states, the principal advocates for the war, may fairly be attributed to this source.

President Washington was apprised of the intrigues of the English agents, and endeavored by negotiation to obtain redress : and nothing but the exhausted state of the country after the revolutionary war, prevented that great man from resorting to arms to punish British perfidy. His policy however was wise ; it was consistent with the genius of our government, and the condition of our country. It would certainly have been hazardous, to venture on a new war, so soon after we had established our independence, and instituted an untried form of government.

Several campaigns however, were conducted against the Indians northwest of the Ohio. General Harmer commanded one, in the year 1790, against the Miami village, at the junction of the rivers St. Marys and St. Josephs, where fort Wayne was subsequently built. It eventuated in burning the town ; and afterwards in the defeat of several detachments of his army, with the loss of many of his men.

In the following year another army was conducted in the same direction, from Kentucky and the back parts of Pennsylvania and Virginia, by general Arthur St. Clair. The object of this expedition, was to destroy the Miami and Shawanoe settlements, on the Auglaize and Miami rivers : but it was late in the season before the necessary arrangements were made, and the Indians having received intelligence of his march, and anticipating his views, advanced and met him near the place where fort Recovery now stands. On the 7th of November, they attacked his army in its encampment, when a total rout ensued, and the greater part of the army was destroyed. The Indian mode of warfare was not well understood by this general, and the panic produced by the savage yells in the time of action, threw the whole into confusion.

For several years previous to this disastrous campaign, the people of Kentucky had remonstrated against the manner in which the general government was conducting the war against the Indians : and President Washington had so far regarded their representations, as to authorise certain eminent citizens, Messrs. Scott, Innes, Brown, Logan, and Shelby, to send expeditions against the Indians in their own way. Accordingly in the spring and summer preceding the defeat of general St. Clair, two expeditions of volunteer militia from the district of Kentucky, were sent by those gentlemen against the Indians on the Wabash— the first under the command of general Charles Scott, and the other under general James Wilkinson. They were both completely successful. The Indian country was laid waste, many lives were destroyed, and many prisoners were taken, without much loss on the part of the Kentuckians. Yet in the autumn of the same year, the old method of sending regulars, under a general unskilled in savage warfare, was again employed in the case of St. Clair's campaign, with the disastrous consequence of a total defeat.

After this disaster, affairs with the Indians wore a
gloomy aspect. It was extremely difficult to procure
supplies, from the scattered settlements of the frontiers,
to subsist a regular army sufficient to humble the savages.   General Washington hence determined to attempt a negotiation with them ; and colonel Hardin
was accordingly sent to them with a flag. All that is
known about him after his departure, is that he was
met and massacred by the Indians. A predatory, skirmishing warfare was then continued for several years,
without any important and decisive action being
fought, until in the year '94 a formidable and successful expedition was conducted against the savages by
general Anthony Wayne, a distinguished revolutionary officer from Pennsylvania, who was then commander in chief of the American army. He was accompanied by generals Wilkinson and Scott of the same
character from Kentucky. The principal part of the
troops were assembled at Cincinnati in the month of
June, and thence marched by the way of forts Hamilton, Greenville, Recovery, Adams, and Defiance, which
had been built by the regulars under Wayne, during
several preceding years of preparation for this decisive campaign.

In the mean time, the British commandant at Detroit, had seized a commanding spot, in the American territory, on the north side of the Miami of the
lakes, below the Rapids, where he had erected a strong
fort, from which the Indians were notoriously fed and
supplied with ammunition, under the pretence of paying them annuities. They also were secretly counsel-
led, in relation to their management of the war. The
following extracts from the letters of colonel M'Kee,
the superintendant of Indian affairs for the districts of
Detroit and Mackinaw, which were addressed from
this fort to colonel England, the military commandant
at Detroit, are worthy to be preserved as evidence of
the conduct of the British government in this case.

The letters were written from one *British officer* to another, and were endorsed "*on his Majesty's service.*"

'*Rapids, July 2d, '94.*'

' By the same channel I learn that a large body of troops, supposed to be 3000, with wagons &c. crossed the Ohio some days ago and marched towards the forts in the Indian country.

' I am much pressed for tobacco and ammunition *(for the Indians)* which I hope I may receive by the return of the boat.'

'*Rapids, July 5th, '94.*'

'Sir—I send this by a party of Saganas, who returned yesterday from fort Recovery, where the whole body of Indians, except the Delawares, who had gone another route, imprudently attacked the fort on Monday the 30th of last month, and lost 16 or 17 men, besides a good many wounded.

' Every thing had been settled, prior to their leaving the Fallen Timber, and it had been agreed upon to confine themselves to taking convoys, and attacking at a distance from the forts, if they should have the address to entice *the enemy out*; but the impetuosity of the Mackinaw Indians, and their eagerness to begin with the nearest, prevailed with the others to alter their system, the consequences of which, from the present appearance of things, may most materially injure the interest of these people; both the Mackinaw and Lake Indians seeming resolved on going home again, having completed the belts they carried with scalps and prisoners, and having no provision there, or at the Glaze to subsist upon; so that his *Majesty's post* will derive *no security* from the late great *influx of Indians* into this part of the country, should they persist in their resolution of returning so soon.

' Capt. Elliott writes that they are immediately to hold a council at the Glaze, in order to try if they can *prevail on the Lake Indians to remain; but without provisions, ammunition &c. being sent to that place, I conceive it will be extremely difficult to keep them together.*'

'*Rapids, August 13th, '94.*'

Sir—I was honored last night with your letter of the 11th, and am extremely glad to find you are making *such exertions to supply the Indians with provisions.*

' Capt. Elliott arrived yesterday ; *what he has brought will greatly relieve us,* having been obliged all day yesterday to take the corn and flour which the traders had there.'

' Scouts are sent up to view the situation of the army, *and we now muster* 1000 *Indians.* All the Lake Indians from Sagana downwards *should not loose one moment in joining their bre-thren*, as every accession of strength is an addition to their spirits.'

' *Camp near Fort Miami, August* 30, '94.

' SIR, I have been employed several days *in endeavoring to fix the Indians*, (who have been driven from their villages and corn fields) between the fort and the bay. Swan creek is generally agreed upon, and will be a very convenient place for the delivery of provisions &c.'

As general Wayne advanced, the Indians retired, leaving their villages and corn, on the Miami and Auglaize rivers, to be burnt and destroyed. Through the medium of his spies, the general often tendered them terms of peace, which they as often rejected. They at length determined on making a stand about two miles above the British garrison to give Wayne battle. An engagement accordingly took place on the 20th of August, '94—the result was a complete discomfiture of the Indians. A number of British Canadians fought with the Indians in this battle. On the next day, the general reconnoitred the British fort, and demanded in peremptory terms the reasons for their intrusion. The British officer commanding, replied that he was there by the orders of his government, and would abandon the place as soon as he was ordered to do so by his superiors; and that he hoped the general would not proceed to extremities till their respective governments were consulted. General Wayne then retired up the Miami and erected fort Wayne.

This victory over the Indians laid the foundation of a general peace with them. They had believed, that the British would protect them; but they found themselves deceived; for the gates of the British fort were shut against them as they retreated after the battle. In the following year, '95, general Wayne held a general council, with all the Indians northwest of the Ohio, at Greenville, which eventuated in a treaty, by which they ceded us an extensive tract of country, as an indemnity for past injuries, and in consideration of annuities to be paid to them by the United States.

In the year '94, a treaty was also negotiated by Mr. Jay with the British government. It was signed on the 19th November, a few months after Wayne's battle with the Indians. In pursuance of this treaty, in the year '96, all the military posts, held by the British, on the American side of the lakes, were given up to the American authorities.

These treaties and events secured our interior frontiers from the active hostility of the Indians, and promoted the commercial enterprise of our citizens on the ocean. Our western settlements in consequence, rapidly advanced in population and the improvement of their country, while our Atlantic citizens were fast accumulating wealth by their trade with foreign nations. This prosperity however, was not permitted to advance uninterrupted by British aggressions. The British continued their intercourse with the Indians within our limits, so as to keep them attached to British interests, and hostile in their feelings towards the United States. But the evils we experienced on the ocean, were now infinitely more intolerable than those of the interior.

The war in Europe, which had originally been instigated by the British against the revolution in France, continued to rage with unabated violence. England and France, the leading parties in the war, used every species of artifice and violence, to involve all other nations in the contest. Orders and decrees were published, by which the maritime rights of neutral nations were infringed, and extensive coasts declared in a state of blockade, without any adequate means of enforcement. By the British orders in council, our vessels were required, under the penalty of being liable to capture, to call at a British port, on their way to any place belonging to France and her allies. By way of retaliation, Bonaparte decreed, that all vessels which had submitted to this British regulation, should be

subject to capture by his cruisers. And thus no vessel
of the United States could sail, either to Britain or
France, or to any of their allies including all Europe,
without being subject to capture by one or the other of
the belligerents. At the same time the British naval
officers carried on the practice of impressing American
seamen, in a manner so extensive and vexatious, as to
cause much distress among our seafaring people, and
much inconvenience and risk to our merchants.

An endless course of negotiation was pursued, on
these different subjects of complaint, without the prospect of success becoming any brighter. The American government could obtain in this way neither indemnity for the past nor security for the future. No
alternative was left, but a resort to arms, to vindicate
our honor and our rights, and to protect our interests
on the ocean. Our losses by captures and impress-
ments nearly equalled the expenses of a war in men
and money. A formal declaration of war was accordingly made on the 18th of June, 1812. But previous
to this declaration, hostilities had commenced with the
Indians, and the battle of Tippecanoe had been fought.

A preliminary view of Indian affairs will enable us
to understand this commencement of the war. By the
combined counsels and schemes of the British agents,
and some of the principal chiefs among the Indians,
the seeds of hostility were sown among them soon after the peace of Greenville, and were gradually nur-
tured into war. At that time, Little Turtle and Blue
Jacket were the leading chiefs among the northwestern
tribes. They had disagreed about the manner of
opposing Wayne's army. The plan of Blue Jacket
was adopted, and eventuated in the total defeat of the
Indians, as predicted by the other. After this event,
Little Turtle continued friendly to the United States.
He was of opinion, that the Indian tribes were unable
to contend against the Americans; that no material aid
would be furnished them by the British: and that war

would only be the means of their losing more of their lands. Blue Jacket had more confidence in the British; he thirsted for revenge against the Americans; and he wished to regain the lands which had been ceded by the treaty of Greenville. His influence increased, whilst the Little Turtle became unpopular. He found in Tecumseh, a Shawanoese Indian, whom he associated with him in his views and projects, an able and persevering coadjutor. The leading principles in their policy were, to combine all the tribes together in one confederacy; to prevent the sale of their lands by any single tribe; and to join the British in the event of war, with a view to revenge and the recovery of their lands. They contended, that by the treaty of Greenville, the United States had acknowledged the right to their lands to reside jointly in all the tribes; and that of course the United States had no right to purchase lands from any single tribe, without the consent of the others. Blue Jacket did not live to execute his schemes; but they were diligently pursued by Tecumseh, in which he was encouraged and supported by the British agents.

The various tribes, who were in the habit of visiting Detroit and Sandwich, were annually subsidised by the British. When the American agent at Detroit gave one dollar by way of annuity, the British agent on the other side of the river Detroit would give them ten. This course of iniquity had the intended effect: the Indians were impressed with a great aversion for the Americans; and disregarding the treaty of Greenville, they desired to recover the lands which they had ceded, and for which they had annually received the stipulated annuity. They wished also to try their strength again with the "Big Knife." as they called the Kentuckians, in order to wipe away the disgrace of their defeat by general Wayne. And they were still promised the aid of the British, in the event of a war between the British and Americans. Their na-

B

tural temper for war was thus inflamed, and they were held in readiness at any moment to commence the contest.

About the year 1804, a Shawanoese Indian, the brother of Tecumseh, proclaimed himself a Prophet, alleging that he had been commanded, by the Great Spirit, who made the red people, and who was not the same that made the white people, and whom the latter worshipped, to inform his red children, that the misfortunes which had fallen upon them, proceeded from their having abandoned the mode of life which he had prescribed for them, and adopted the manners and dress of the white people : and that he was commanded to tell them, that they must return to their former habits, leave off the use of whiskey, and as soon as possible clothe themselves in skins instead of blankets.

The Prophet fixed himself at Greenville, the spot which had been so noted from the cantonment of general Wayne's army, and from the treaty made by him with the Indian tribes at that place in the year 1795. The fame of the Prophet spread through the surrounding Indian tribes, and he soon found himself at the head of a considerable number of followers, composed principally however of the most abandoned of the young men of the Shawanoese. Delawares, Wyandots, Potawatamies, Ottowas, Chippewas and Kickapoos. Besides these he was visited by an immense concourse of men, women and children from the tribes of the Mississippi and Lake Superior. The most absurd stories were told, and believed by the Indians, of his power to perform miracles, and no fatigue or suffering was thought too great to be endured to get a sight of him. The people of Ohio became much alarmed at the great assemblage of the Indians upon their frontier; and a mission was sent by the governor to insist upon their removal. The United States' agent at fort Wayne also joined in the remonstrance, against his forming a permanent settlement at Greenville, which was within the boun-

dary of the United States.   Accordingly, in 1808, he
removed to the Wabash, and fixed his residence on
the north bank of that river, near the mouth of the
Tippecanoe.   This land was the property of the Miami tribe, who made strong remonstrances against it,
but were not strong enough to effect his removal by
force, as he had collected around him a considerable
body of the most daring and unprincipled young men,
of all the neighbouring tribes.   The chiefs of the latter were almost unaminously opposed to him, as they
discovered that he was constantly endeavouring to destroy their influence, or to prevail on the warriors to
take the authority into their own hands.   Several of the
most influential chiefs were put to death by the young
men, under the pretence of their practising magic.   Te-
teboxke, the venerable chief of the Delawares, with
several of his friends, were condemned to the flames.
The loss of their chiefs began however to be regretted,
and those that survived made a common cause, in opposing the extension of the Prophet's influence.   He
was only able to retain about 40 warriors of his own
tribe, the chiefs of which hated him most cordially.
In the year 1809, he had not more than 250 or 300
warriors with him.   They had suffered much for provisions, and the greater part of them perhaps would
have perished, if they had not been supplied with
corn by governor Harrison, from Vincennes.   In September, 1809, a treaty was made at fort Wayne, by the
governor, as commissioner upon the part of the United
States, for the extinguishment of the title to a considerable tract of land, extending about 60 miles up the
Wabash above Vincennes.   The Delawares, Miamies
and Potawatamies were parties to this treaty ; but the
Prophet and his followers were not invited ; because,
as the governor says in his address to the legislature of
Indiana, "it never had been suggested, that they could
plead even the title of occupancy to the lands which
were then conveyed to the United States," and it was

well known they were the rightful property of the Miamies, who had possessed them from the time of the
first arrival of the white people among them. The
Shawanoese tribe made no pretensions to those lands.
Their principal chief attended the treaty, and recommended to the Miami chiefs to make the cession. About
the time that the treaty was made, the affairs of the Prophet were at a low ebb. In the course of the succeeding winter, however, the intrigues and negotiations of
his brother Tecumseh, procured a large accession of
strength. They were joined by a considerable number of Winnebagoes or Puants, the greater part of the
Kickapoo tribe, and some of the Wyandots. Although the affairs were managed in the name of the
Prophet, Tecumseh was in fact the director of every
thing. This extraordinary man had risen into consequence, subsequently to the treaty of Greenville in the
year 1795. He had been considered an active warrior in the war which was terminated by that treaty,
but possessed no considerable influence. The principal object of his labors, by which he obtained distinction, was to unite all the tribes upon the continent in
one grand confederacy for the purpose of opposing
the encroachments of the whites. Tecumseh was on a
mission for this purpose, when the treaty was concluded in 1809. Upon his return, he threatened to kill
the chiefs who had signed it, and declared his determination to prevent the lands from being surveyed and
settled.

Governor Harrison, upon being informed of his proceedings, sent him a message, informing him "that any
claims he might have to the lands which had been ceded, were not affected by the treaty; that he might
come to Vincennes and exhibit his pretensions, and if
they were found to be solid, that the land would either
be given up, or an ample compensation made for it."
Accordingly in the month of August, 1810, he came
down to Vincennes, attended by several hundred war-

riors. A day was appointed to hear his statement, which it took him many hours to make. He asserted, that the Great Spirit had made the continent for the use of the Indians exclusively—that the white people had no right to come here, and take it from them—that no particular part of it was given to any tribe, but that the whole was the common property of all; and that any sale of lands, made without the consent of all, was not valid. In his answer, the governor observed, that the Indians, like the white people, were divided into different tribes or nations, and that the Great Spirit never intended that they should form but one nation, or he would not have taught them to speak different languages, which put it out of their power to understand each other—and that the Shawanoese, who emigrated from Georgia, could have no claim to the lands on the Wabash, which had been occupied far beyond the memory of man by the Miamies. The governor having proceeded thus far, sat down for the purpose of giving the interpreters time to explain what he had said, to the different tribes that were present. As soon as it was interpreted in Shawanoese, Tecumseh interrupted the interpreter, and said that it was all false, and giving a signal to his warriors, they seized their tomahawks and war clubs and sprang upon their feet.

For some minutes the governor was in the most imminent danger: he preserved his presence of mind however, and disengaging himself from an arm-chair in which he was sitting, seized his sword to defend himself. A considerable number of the citizens of Vincennes were present, all unarmed. At a little distance however, there was a guard of a sergeant and 12 men, who were immediately brought up by an officer. The governor then told Tecumseh, that he was a bad man, and he would have no further intercourse with him; and directed him to retire to his camp and set out immediately on his return home. As the Indians with Tecumseh greatly outnumbered the citizens of the town, and the regular troops there, two companies of militia were brought in during the night, and a large number the next day.   Early however on the following morning, Tecumseh sent for the interpreter, made an apology for his conduct, and earnestly requested that he might have another conference with the governor.   His request was at length granted; but the governor took care to be attended by a number of his friends, well armed, and to have the troops in the town ready for action.   In his speech Tecumseh said, that he had been advised by some white persons, to act as he had done; but that it was not his intention to offer any violence to the governor.   The latter then inquired; whether he had any other grounds for claiming the lands, that had been ceded to the United States, but those which he had stated; and he answered in the *negative*.   The governor then observed to him, that so great a warrior should disdain to conceal his intentions, and desired to know whether he really intended to make war upon the United States, if the lately purchased lands were not relinquished by them.   He answered that it was decidedly his determination, and that he would never rest, until he brought all the tribes upon the continent, to unite in one confederacy.   The activity and perseverance, which he manifested in the prosecution of this scheme, are most wonderful.   He visited all the tribes west of the Mississippi, and on lakes Superior, Huron, and Erie repeatedly, before the year 1811.   So sanguine were his followers about this time, and so much were they encouraged by the British agents, that in the event of a war between England and America, they believed the confederated tribes, with the aid of the British, would be able to drive the Americans over the Ohio river to the south side, and thus regain all the country on the northwest of that river :   And from the *sine qua non*, advanced by the British commissioners in the negotiation at

Ghent, it would appear, that the British ministry had indulged a delusion not much less extravagant.

It was the intention of Tecumseh, to avoid hostilities with the whites, until he should effect a combination strong enough to resist them, or until the expected war with Great Britain should commence. Whether the British were really the authors of this plan, for forming a general confederacy amongst the tribes, or whether the scheme originated with Blue Jacket and Tecumseh themselves, is not certain; but from the papers found in the baggage of the British army taken on the Thames, it appears more than probable, that the former was the case—at least it is certain, that an intimate communication was kept up, between the Prophet and Tecumseh, and the British Indian department, from their first establishment at Greenville; and that they were constantly supplied with arms, ammunition and clothing, from the King's stores at Malden. In the winter and spring of the year 1811, many depredations and several murders were committed upon the inhabitants of the frontiers of the Indiana, Illinois, and Missouri territories. The perpetrators were demanded of the respective chiefs, but no satisfaction could be obtained. A militia officer was sent by governor Harrison to demand the delivery of some horses, that had been stolen from the settlements, and which were discovered with the Indians: no satisfaction was however obtained; and Tecumseh and his brother informed the officer, that they would pay a visit in person to the governor. They were told that they would be well received, provided they came with not more than 30 followers. This was acceded to. The governor however caused their motions to be watched, and was soon informed, that they were descending the river with several hundred warriors. The same officer was dispatched to meet them, and to forbid their approach to Vincennes with that body. Compliance was again promised, and Tecumseh came on with a few canoes only, but was soon followed by all the rest, who joined and encamped with him a mile from the town of Vincennes. The inhabitants were much alarmed, and there is little doubt, but that it was the intention of the Indians, to surprise and plunder the town. The governor was however on his guard. The militia of the town were kept under arms, and some companies were brought in from the country. Tecumseh demanded an interview. The governor agreed to it, and asked whether it was the intention of the Indians to come armed to the council. Tecumseh replied that he would be governed by the conduct of the white people; if they attended the council armed, his warriors would be armed also, but if the white people would come unarmed, his would come in the same way. The governor informed him, that he would be attended by a troop of dragoons, dismounted, who would have only side arms, and that the Indians might bring their war clubs, tomahawks, and knives. The meeting took place in a large arbour, on one side of which were placed the dragoons, 80 in number, seated in rows; on the other side, the Indians. Besides their swords, the dragoons had their pistols stuck in their belts. The Indians were evidently alarmed, and when the governor, who was seated in front of the front row of dragoons, began to address them, Tecumseh complained that he could not hear him, and desired him to remove his seat to a open space near himself. The governor complied. In his speech he complained of the constant depredations, which were committed by the Indians of Tippecanoe. The refusal on their part to give satisfaction—and the constant accumulation of force at that place, for the avowed purpose of obliging the United States to give up lands, which they had fairly purchased of the rightful owners. In his answer Tecumseh denied that he had taken the murderers under his protection; but admitted his design of forming a grand confederacy of all the nations and tribes of Indians upon the continent, for the purpose of putting a stop to the encroachments of the white people.   He said, that " the policy which the United States pursued, of purchasing their lands from the Indians, he viewed as a *mighty water*, ready to overflow his people, and that the confederacy which he was forming among the tribes, to prevent any individual tribe from selling without the consent of the others, was the *dam* he was erecting to resist this mighty water." And he added, "your great father may sit over the mountains and drink his wine, but if he continues this policy, you and I will have to fight it out." He admitted, that he was then on his way to the Creek nation for the purpose of bringing them over to his measures; and he actually did, two days afterwards, set out on this journey with 12 or 15 of his warriors. Having visited the Creeks, Choctaws, and Chickasaws, he crossed the Mississippi and continued his course northwardly, as high as the river Demoins. Having obtained, it is believed, the promise of assistance from all the tribes in that direction, he returned to the Wabash by land, across the heads of the Illinois river. In his absence his affairs had sustained a sad reverse. His town was consumed, his large deposit of provisions destroyed, his bravest followers killed, and the rest dispersed. Upon his departure to visit the southern Indians, the Prophet his brother, was left in charge of the temporal as well as spiritual concerns of the establishment. It is believed that he received from Tecumseh, positive instructions to avoid coming to extremities with the white people, and to restrain his followers from committing depredations, which might lead to the commencement of hostilities before his plans were ripe. The Prophet however wanted the inclination as well as the authority necessary to follow the direction. Murders and other depredations followed in quick succession; no redress could be obtained; the people upon the frontiers became exceedingly alarmed, as well as the citizens of Vincennes, at which place a large

C

meeting was held, which passed a number of resolutions indicating their sense of the danger they were in, and warmly approbating the measures, which had been taken by the governor for their defence. These resolutions, with a strong remonstrance against the propriety of suffering this banditti to continue their depredations, were forwarded to the President of the United States. They produced the desired effect, and the 4th regiment commanded by colonel Boyd, which was at that time at Pittsburgh, was ordered to repair immediately to Vincennes, and was placed under the command of governor Harrison. The governor was also directed to add to them a body of militia, to take measures for the defence of the citizens, and as a last resort to remove the Prophet and his followers by force.

As soon as it was known in Kentucky, that Harrison was authorized to march with an army against the Indians, a number of volunteers went over to join his standard. Many of them were men of high standing at home, as military, civil, and literary characters. Of this number were Samuel Wells, a major general of the militia, who had been an active soldier in former wars with the Indians—Joseph H. Daveiss esq. a very eminent attorney, who had great military ambition—Col. Abraham Owen, a veteran in Indian warfare—and Col. Keiger, who raised a small company of young men near Louisville, including among them Messrs. Croghan, O'Fallon, Shipp, Chum and Edwards, who afterwards distinguished themselves as officers in the army of the United States.

In the latter part of September, the governor commenced his march up the Wabash, with a force of about *nine hundred effective men*, composed of the 4th regiment, a body of militia, and about 130 volunteer dragoons. The 4th regiment had been raised for some time, and was well trained and well officered. The militia too, who were all volunteers, had been trained with great assiduity by the governor, in those particu-

lar evolutions which had been practised by general
Wayne's army, and which had been found useful in a
covered country, and operating against Indians. Conformably to his orders from the president, the governor
halted within the boundary of the United States, and
endeavoured by the intervention of the Delaware and
Miami tribes, to induce the Prophet to deliver up the
murderers and the stolen horses. These messengers
of peace were received and treated with great insolence, and the demands made by them rejected with
disdain by the Prophet and his council. To put an
end to all hopes of accommodation, a small war party
was detached for the purpose of commencing hostilities. Finding no stragglers about the camp, they fired
upon one of the sentinels, and wounded him severely ;
the Delaware chiefs informed the governor of the object of the party, and that it was in vain to expect, that
any thing but force could obtain either satisfaction for the
injuries done, or security for the future. He learned
also from the same source, that the strength of the Prophet was daily increasing by the ardent and giddy
young men from every tribe, and particularly from the
tribes on and beyond the Illinois river. The governor
was at this time busily engaged, in erecting a fort on
the southeast side of the Wabash, some miles within
the boundary of the United States, and in preparing
ammunition, and disciplining his men for the expected
conflict, which from the character of the enemy, he
knew would be a desperate one. His little army had
been much weakened by sickness, the effect of fresh
food without vegetables and a sufficient quantity of
bread. The governor finding his flour growing short,
had early in October put the troops upon half allowance of that article—this regulation extended to the officers of every rank, and was rigidly conformed to in
the family of the general. The sick having been deposited in the fort ; which the officers, in compliment to
their commander, had requested might be called Fort

Harrison ; and the weak and convalescent being drawn out to form the garrison ; the troops on the 29th of October took up the line of march : the infantry in two columns in single file on each side of the trace, and capable by a single conversion, of being formed into two lines, to receive the enemy on any point he might attack, or of being reduced into a hollow square.

The country through which the army passed was occasionally open, beautiful prairie, intersected by thick woods, deep creeks, and ravines. The cavalry and mounted riflemen, of the latter of which there were two companies, covered the advance, the flanks and the rear, and were made to exchange positions with each other, as the ground varied—so as to keep them upon that which best suited the mode of fighting which they respectively practised. The Indians being perfectly master of the art of ambuscading, every precaution was used to guard against surprise, and prevent the army from being attacked in a disadvantageous position. At some distance above fort Harrison, two routes for approaching the Prophet's town presented themselves to the choice of the governor. The one passing up the south side of the Wabash, was much shorter than the other, but it led through an uneven woody country. To the north of the river, the prairies are very extensive, affording few situations for the kind of warfare peculiar to the savages. To deceive the enemy, the governor caused the route to be reconnoitred on the south side and a wagon road laid out, and having advanced upon it a short distance, he suddenly changed his direction and gained the right bank of the Wabash, by crossing it above the mouth of Racoon creek. Here the army was joined by some of the volunteers from Kentucky, amongst whom were major general Wells, and colonels Owen and Keiger. To general Wells the command of the mounted riflemen was assigned with the rank of major. Colonel Owen was appointed aid-de-camp to the governor ; and the rest of the volunteers with a detachment of the Indiana militia under major Beck were formed into a company, and placed under the command of colonel Keiger as captain. To colonel Daveiss the command of the dragoons had been given with the rank of major. In passing the large prairies, the army was frequently halted, and made collectively to perform the evolutions, which they had been taught in smaller bodies, during their stay at fort Harrison, at which place, the governor had manœuvred the relieving guards every day in person, and had required the attendance of the field officers on those occasions.

The Indians not expecting the army on the north side of the river, no signs of them were seen, until it approached Pine creek, a very dangerous pass, where a few men might successfully oppose a whole army. The appearance of this creek forms a singular exception to the other water courses of this country. It runs for the distance of 15 or 20 miles above its mouth, between immense cliffs of rock, upon whose summits are found considerable quantities of pine and red cedar, the former of which is rare, and the latter no where else to be found near the Wabash. The ordinary crossing place, to which the trace led that the army was pursuing, was represented by the traders, who served as guides, to be extremely difficult, if not impassable for wagons, and that it was no doubt the spot where the Indians would make their attack, if they had determined to meet the army in the field. It had been twice selected by them for that purpose—once in the year 1780, when general Clarke undertook a campaign against the Indians of the Wabash; but their design was then frustrated by a mutiny of a part of his troops 70 or 80 miles above Vincennes—and a second time in the year 1790, when colonel Hamtramack penetrated with a small force as high as the Vermillion, to make a diversion in favor of general Harmer's expedition to the Miami of the Lake. The governor had no inten-

tion of encountering the enemy in a place like this.
He accordingly, in the course of the night preceding
his approach to the creek, dispatched captain Prince,
of the Indiana militia, with an escort of forty men,
to reconnoitre the creek some miles above, and endeavour to find a better fording.   About 10 o'clock next
day, this excellent officer met the army in its advance,
and informed the general, that at the distance of six or
eight miles, he had found a trace, used by the Illinois
Indians in travelling to Tippecanoe, which presented
an excellent ford, at a place where the prairie skirted
the creek.   This prairie which they were now crossing, excited the admiration and astonishment of the
officers and soldiers, who had never been on the north
west side of the Wabash.   To the north and west the
prospect was unbounded—from the highest eminence no
limit was to be seen, and the guides asserted, that the
prairie extended to the Illinois river.   On the evening
of the 5th November, the army encamped at the distance of nine or ten miles from the Prophet's town.
It was ascertained that the approach of the army had
been discovered before it crossed Pine creek.   The
traces of reconnoitring parties were very often seen,
but no Indians were discovered until the troops arrived
within 5 or 6 miles of the town on the 6th November.
The interpreters were then placed with the advanced
guard, to endeavour to open a communication with
them.   The Indians would however return no answer
to the invitations that were made to them for that purpose, but continued to insult our people by their gestures.   Within about three miles of the town, the
ground became broken by ravines and covered with
timber.   The utmost precaution became necessary, and
every difficult pass was examined by the mounted riflemen before the army was permitted to enter it. The
ground being unfit for the operation of the squadron
of dragoons, they were thrown in the rear.   Through
the whole march, the precaution had been used of

changing the disposition of the different corps, that each might have the ground best suited to its operations. Within about two miles of the town, the path descended a steep hill, at the bottom of which was a small creek running through a narrow wet prairie, and beyond this a level plain partially covered with oak timber, and without under-brush. Before the crossing of the creek, the woods were very thick and intersected by deep ravines. No place could be better calculated for the savages to attack with a prospect of success, and the governor apprehended that the moment the troops descended into the hollow, they would be attacked. A disposition was therefore made of the infantry, to receive the enemy on the left and rear. A company of mounted riflemen was advanced a considerable distance from the left flank to check the approach of the enemy ; and the other two companies were directed to turn the enemy's flanks, should he attack from that direction. The dragoons were ordered to move rapidly from the rear and occupy the plain in advance of the creek, to cover the crossing of the army from an attack in front. In this order the troops were passed over; the dragoons were made to advance to give room to the infantry, and the latter having crossed the creek, were formed to receive the enemy in front in one line, with a reserve of three companies—the dragoons flanked by mounted riflemen forming the first line. During all this time, Indians were frequently seen in front and on the flanks. The interpreters endeavoured in vain to bring them to a parley. Though sufficiently near to hear what was said to them, they would return no answer, but continued by gestures to menace and insult those who addressed them. Being now arrived within a mile and a half of the town, and the situation being favorable for an encampment, the governor determined to remain there and fortify his camp, until he could hear from the friendly chiefs, whom he had dispatched from fort Harrison, on the day he had left it, for the purpose of making another attempt to prevent the recurrence to hostilities. Those chiefs were to have met him on the way, but no intelligence was yet received from them. Whilst he was engaged in tracing out the lines of the encampment, major Daveiss and several other field officers approached him, and urged the propriety of immediately marching upon the town. The governor answered that his instructions would not justify his attacking the Indians, as long as there was a probability of their complying with the demands of the government, and that he still hoped to hear something in the course of the evening from the friendly Indians, whom he had dispatched from fort Harrison.

To this it was observed, that as the Indians seen hovering about the army, had been frequently invited to a parley by the interpreters, who had proceeded some distance from the lines for the purpose; and as these overtures had universally been answered by menace and insult, it was very evident that it was their intention to fight; that the troops were in high spirits and full of confidence; and that advantage ought to be taken of their ardour to lead them immediately to the enemy. To this the governor answered, that he was fully sensible of the eagerness of the troops; and admitting the determined hostility of the Indians, and that their insolence was full evidence of their intention to fight, yet he knew them too well to believe, that they would ever do this, but by surprsie, or on ground which was entirely favorable to their mode of fighting. He was therefore determined not to advance with the troops, until he knew precisely the situation of the town, and the ground adjacent to it, particularly that which intervened between it and the place where the army then was—that it was their duty to fight when they came in contact with the enemy—it was his to take care that they should not engage in a situation where their valor would be useless, and where a corps upon which he placed great reliance would be unable

to act—that the experience of the last two hours ought
to convince every officer, that no reliance ought to be
placed upon the guides, as to the topography of the
country—that relying on their information, the troops had
been led into a situation so unfavorable, that but for
the celerity with which they changed their position, a
few Indians might have destroyed them : he was
therefore determined not to advance to the town, until he had previously reconnoitred, either in person, or
by some one, on whose judgment he could rely.   Major Daveiss immediately replied, that from the right of
the position of the dragoons, which was still in front,
the opening made by the low grounds of the Wabash
could be seen ; that with his adjutant D. Floyd, he
had advanced to the bank, which descends to the low
grounds, and had a fair view of the cultivated fields
and the houses of the town ; and that the open woods,
in which the troops then were, continued without in-
terruption to the town.   Upon this information, the governor said he would advance, provided he could get
any proper person to go to the town with a flag.   Captain T. Dubois of Vineennes having offered his services, he was dispatched with an interpreter to the Prophet, desiring to know whether he would now comply
with the terms, that had been so often proposed to him.
The army was moved slowly after in order of battle. In
a few moments a messenger came from captain Dubois,
informing the governor that the Indians were near him
in considerable numbers, but that they would return
no answer to the interpreter, although they were sufficiently near to hear what was said to them, and that
upon his advancing, they constantly endeavored to cut
him off from the army.   Governor Harrison during
this last effort to open a negotiation, which was sufficient to shew his wish for an accommodation, resolved
no longer to hesitate in treating the Indians as enemies.
He therefore recalled captain Dubois, and moved on
with a determination to attack them.   He had not

D

proceeded far however before he was met by three Indians, one of them a principal counsellor to the Prophet.   They were sent, they said, to know why the
army was advancing upon them—that the Prophet
wished if possible to avoid hostilities ; that he had
sent a pacific message by the Miami and Potawatamie
chiefs, who had come to him on the part of the govern-
or—and that those chiefs had unfortunately gone down
on the south side of the Wabash.   A suspension of
hostilities was accordingly agreed upon ; and a meeting was to take place the next day between Harrison
and the chiefs, to agree upon the terms of peace.   The
governor further informed them, that he would go on
to the Wabash, and encamp there for the night.   Upon marching a short distance further he came in view
of the town, which was seen at some distance up the
river upon a commanding eminence.   Major Daveiss
and adjutant Floyd had mistaken some scattered
houses in the fields below, for the town itself.   The
ground below the town being unfavorable for an encampment, the army marched on in the direction of
the town, with a view to obtain a better situation beyond it.   The troops were in an order of march, calculated by a single conversion of companies, to form
the order of battle, which it had last assumed,
the dragoons being in front.   This corps however
soon became entangled in ground, covered with brush
and tops of fallen trees.   A halt was ordered, and
major Daveiss directed to change position with Spencer's rifle corps, which occupied the open fields adjacent to the river.   The Indians seeing this manœuvre,
at the approach of the troops towards the town, supposed that they intended to attack it, and immediately
prepared for defence.   Some of them sallied out, and
called to the advanced corps to halt.   The governor
upon this rode forward, and requested some of the Indians to come to him, assured them, that nothing was
farther from his thoughts, than to attack them—that

the ground below the town on the river, was not calculated for an encampment, and that it was his intention to search for a better one above. He asked if there was any other water convenient beside that which the river afforded ; and an Indian with whom he was well acquainted, answered, that the creek, which had been crossed two miles back, ran through the prairie to the north of the village. A halt was then ordered, and some officers sent back to examine the creek, as well as the river above the town. In half an hour, brigade major Marston Clarke and major Waller Taylor returned, and reported that they had found on the creek, every thing that could be desirable in an encampment—an elevated spot, nearly surrounded by an open prairie, with water convenient, and a sufficiency of wood for fuel. An idea was propagated by the enemies of governor Harrison, after the battle of Tippecanoe, that the Indians had forced him to encamp on a place, chosen by them as suitable for the attack they intended. The place however was chosen by majors Taylor and Clark, after examining all the environs of the town : and when the army of general Hopkins was there in the following year, they all united in the opinion, that a better spot to resist Indians, was not to be found in the whole country.

The army now marched to the place selected, and encamped late in the evening, on a dry piece of ground, which rose about ten feet above the level of a marshy prairie in front towards the town, and about twice as high above a similar prairie in the rear ; through which, near the bank, ran a small stream clothed with willows and brush wood. On the left of the encampment, this bench of land became wider; on the right it gradually narrowed, and terminated in an abrupt point, about 150 yards from the right flank. The two columns of infantry occupied the front and rear. The right flank, being about eighty yards wide, was filled with captain Spencer's company of eighty men. The left flank, about 150 yards in extent, was composed of three companies of mounted riflemen, under major general Wells, commanding as a major. The front line was composed of one battalion of United States' infantry, under the command of major Floyd, flanked on the right by two companies of militia infantry, and on the left by one company of the same troops. The rear line consisted of a battalion of United States infantry, under captain Baen, commanding as a major ; and four companies of militia infantry, under lieut. colonel Decker ; the regulars being stationed next the riflemen under Wells, and the militia on the other end of the line adjoining Spencer's company. The cavalry under Daveiss were encamped in the rear of the front line and the left flank. The encampment was not more than three fourths of a mile from the town.

The order given to the army, in the event of a night attack, was for each corps to maintain its ground at all hazards till relieved. The dragoons were directed in such a case, to parade dismounted, with their swords on and their pistols in their belts, and to wait for orders. The guard for the night consisted of two captains' commands of 42 men and 4 non-commissioned officers each ; and two subalterns' guards of twenty men and non-commissioned officers—the whole under the command of a field officer of the day.

The night was dark and cloudy : the moon rose late, and after midnight there was a drizzling rain. Many of the men appeared to be much dissatisfied : they were anxious for a battle, and the most ardent regretted, that they would have to return without one. The army generally had no expectation of an attack ; but those who had experience in Indian affairs suspected some treachery. Colonel Daveiss was heard to say, he had no doubt but that an attack would be made before morning.

It was the constant practice of governor Harrison to call up the troops an hour before day, and keep them under arms till it was light.   After 4 o'clock in the morning, the governor, general Wells, colonel Owen, and colonel Daveiss had all risen, and the governor was going to issue his orders for raising the army; when the treacherous Indians had crept up so near the sentries, as to hear them challenge when relieved. They intended to rush upon the sentries and kill them before they could fire : but one of them discovered an Indian creeping towards him in the grass, and fired. This was immediately followed by the Indian yell, and a desperate charge upon the left flank.   The guard in that quarter gave way, and abandoned their officer without making any resistance. Capt. Barton's company of regulars and capt. Keiger's company of mounted riflemen, forming the left angle of the rear line, received the first onset.   The fire there was excessive ; but the troops who had lain on their arms, were immediately prepared to receive, and gallantry resist the furious savage assailants.   The manner of the attack was calculated to discourage and terrify the men ; yet as soon as they could be formed and posted, they maintained their ground with desperate valor, though but very few of them had ever before been in battle.   The fires in the camp were extinguished immediately, as the light they afforded was more serviceable to the Indians than to our men.

As soon as the governor could mount his horse, he proceeded towards the point of attack, and finding the line much weakened there, he ordered two companies from the centre of the rear line to march up and form across the angle in the rear of Barton's and Keiger's companies.   General Wells immediately proceeded to the right of his command ; and colonel Owen, who was with him, was proceeding directly to the point of attack, when he was shot on his horse near the lines, and thus bravely fell among the first victims of savage perfidy.   A heavy fire now commenced all along the left flank, upon the whole of the front and right flank, and on a part of the rear line.

In passing through the camp, towards the left of the front line, the governor met with colonel Daveiss and the dragoons. The colonel informed him that the Indians, concealed behind some trees near the line, were annoying the troops very severely in that quarter; and he requested permission to dislodge them, which was granted. He immediately called on the first division of his cavalry to follow him, but the order was not distinctly heard, and but few of his men charged with him. Among those who charged, were two young gentlemen who had gone with him from Kentucky, Messrs. Meade and Sanders, who were afterwards distinguished as captains in the United States' service. They had not proceeded far out of the lines, when Daveiss was mortally wounded by several balls and fell. His men stood by him, and repulsed the savages several times, till they succeeded in carrying him into camp.

In the mean time the attack on Spencer's and Warwick's companies on the right, became very severe. Captain Spencer and his lieutenants were all killed, and captain Warwick was mortally wounded. The governor in passing towards that flank, found captain Robb's company near the centre of the camp. They had been driven from their post; or rather, had fallen back without orders. He sent them to the aid of captain Spencer, where they fought very bravely, having seventeen men killed during the battle. Capt. Prescott's company of United States' infantry had filled up the vacancy caused by the retreat of Robb's company. Soon after colonel Daveiss was wounded, captain Snelling at the head of his company charged on the same Indians and dislodged them with considerable loss. The battle was now maintained on all sides with desperate valor. The Indians advanced and retreated by a rattling noise made with deer hoofs:

they fought with enthusiasm, and seemed determined on victory or death.

As soon as day light appeared, captain Snelling's company, captain Posey's, under lieutenant Albright, and captain Scott's, were drawn from the front line, and Wilson's from the rear, and formed on the left flank ; while Cook's and Baen's companies were ordered to the right. General Wells took command of the corps formed on the left, and with the aid of some dragoons, who were now mounted and commanded by captain Parke, made a successful charge on the enemy in that direction, driving them into an adjoining swamp through which the cavalry could not pursue them. At the same time Cook's and lieutenant Laribiè's companies, with the aid of the riflemen and militia on the right flank, charged on the Indians and put them to flight in that quarter, which terminated the battle.

During the time of this contest, the Prophet kept himself secure, on an adjacent eminence, singing a war song. He had told his followers, that the Great Spirit would render the army of the Americans unavailing, and that their bullets would not hurt the Indians, who would have light, while their enemies were involved in thick darkness. Soon after the battle commenced, he was informed that his men were falling. He told them to fight on, it would soon be as he had predicted, and then began to sing louder.

Colonel Boyd commanded as a brigadier general in this engagement ; and the governor in his letter to the war department, speaks highly of him and his brigade, and of Clarke and Croghan who were his aids. Col. Decker is also commended for the good order in which he kept his command : and of general Wells, it is said, that he sustained the fame which he had acquired in almost every campaign since the first settlement of Kentucky.

The officers and soldiers generally, performed their duties well. They acted with a degree of coolness,

bravery and good order, which was not to be expected
from men unused to carnage, and in a situation so well
calculated to produce terror and confusion. The fortune of war necessarily put it in the power of some officers and their men, at the expense of danger, wounds
and death, to render more service and acquire more
honor than others : but to speak of their particular merits, would be to detail again the operations of the conflict.

Of colonels Owen and Daveiss, the governor speaks
in the highest terms. Owen joined him as a private in
Keiger's company at fort Harrison, and accepted the
place of volunteer aid. He had been a representative
in the legislature of Kentucky. His character was
that of a good citizen and a brave soldier. He left a
wife and a large family of children, to add the poig-
nancy of domestic grief to the public regret for his
loss.

Colonel Daveiss also joined the army as a private,
and was promoted on the recommendation of the officers of the dragoons ; his conduct as their commander
fully justified their choice. Never was there an officer possessed of more military ardor, nor more zeal
to discharge all his duties with punctilious propriety :
and never perhaps did any man, who had not been
educated for the profession of arms, possess a richer
fund of military information at his entrance on a military life. All that books and study could furnish, all
the preparation the closet could make for the field, was
his. He was a man of great talents—of genius—and
indefatigable industry. In Kentucky he stood among
the foremost in the profession of the law. His elocu-
tion was singularly attractive and forcible. Wit and
energy, acuteness and originality of thought, were the,
characteristics of his eloquence. But as an orator he
was very unequal. Some times he did not rise above
mediocrity, whilst some of his happiest efforts were
never surpassed in America—never perhaps in any age

or country. Such at least was the opinion of men, whose talents, acquirements and taste, had qualified them to judge. He had much eccentricity in his manners and his dress. In his disposition he was generous; and in his friendship he was ardent. His person was about six feet high, well formed and robust—his countenance open and manly. He had acquired fortune and fame by his own exertions—neither his patrimony nor his education having been very ample. Being in the prime of life, and possessing great military ambition and acquirements, he was destined perhaps, had he lived, to become one of the first military characters of America. He died a few hours after the battle had closed. As soon as he was informed, that the Indians were repulsed, and the victory was complete, he observed, he could die satisfied—that he had fallen in defence of his country. He left a wife but no children.

Capt. Baen, who fell early in the action, had the character of an able officer and a brave soldier. Capt. Spencer was wounded in the head—he exhorted his men to fight on. He was then shot through both thighs and fell—still he continued to encourage his men. He was then raised up, and received a ball through his body which immediately killed him. His lieuts. M'Mahan and Berry, fell bravely encouraging their men. Warwick was shot through the body, and was taken to the surgery to be dressed: as soon as it was over, being a man of much bodily strength and still able to walk, he insisted on going back to his post, though it was evident, he had but a few hours to live. Col. White, formerly U. S. agent at the Saline, was also killed in the action. The whole number killed, with those who died soon of their wounds, was upwards of fifty: the wounded were about double that number. Governor Harrison himself narrowly escaped, the hair on his head being cut by a ball.

The Indians left 38 warriors dead on the field, and buried several others in the town, which with those

E

who must have died of their wounds, would make
their loss at least as great as that of the Americans.
The troops under the command of governor Harrison
of every description, amounted on the day before the
battle, to something more than 800. The ordinary
force, that had been at the Prophet's town, through the
preceding summer, was about 450. But they were
joined a few days before the action, by all the Kickapoos of the Prairie, and by many bands of Potawatamies from the Illinois river, and the St. Josephs of
Lake Michigan. They estimated their number after
the battle, to have been 600; but the traders who had
a good opportunity of knowing, made them at least
800, and some as many as 1000. However it is certain, that no victory was ever before obtained over
the northern Indians, where the numbers were any
thing like equal. The number of killed too was greater, than was ever before known. It is their custom
always to avoid a close action, and from their dexteri-
ty in hiding themselves, but few of them can be killed,
even when they are pouring destruction into the ranks
of their enemy. It is believed that there were not ten
of them killed at St. Clair's defeat, and still fewer at
Braddock's. At Tippecanoe, they rushed up to the
bayonets of our men, and in one instance, related by
capt. Snelling, an Indian adroitly put the bayonet of
a soldier aside, and clove his head with his war club,
an instrument on which there is fixed a triangular
piece of iron, broad enough to project several inches
from the wood. Their conduct on this occasion, so
different from what it usually is, was attributed to the
confidence of success, with which their prophet had
inspired them, and to the distinguished bravery of the
Winebago warriors.

The Indians did not determine to attack the American camp till late at night. The plan that was formed the evening before, was to meet the governor in
council the next day, and agree to the terms he pro-

posed.   At the close of the council, the chiefs were to
retire to the warriors, who were to be placed at a convenient distance.   The governor was then to be killed
by two Winebagoes, who had devoted themselves to
certain death to accomplish this object.   They were
to loiter about the camp, after the council had broken
up; and their killing the governor and raising the
war whoop, was to be the signal for a general attack.
The Indians were commanded by White Loon, Stone
Eater, and Winemac, a Potawatamie chief, who had
been with the governor on his march, and at fort Harrison, making great professions of friendship.

The 4th regiment was about 250 strong, and there
were about 60 volunteers from Kentucky in the army.
The rest of the troops were volunteers from the Indiana militia.   Those from the neighbourhood of Vincennes had been trained for several years by the governor, and had become very expert in the manœuvres
which he had adopted for fighting the Indians.   The
greater part of the territorial troops followed him as
well from personal attachment as from a sense of duty.   Indeed a greater degree of confidence and personal attachment has rarely been found in any army towards its commander, than existed in this; nor has
there been many battles in which the dependence of
the army on its leader was more distinctly felt.   During the whole action the governor was constantly on
the lines, and always repaired to the point which was
most hardly pressed.   The reinforcements drawn occasionally from the points most secure, were conducted
by himself and formed on the spot, where their services were most wanted.   The officers and men who
believed that their ultimate success depended on his
safety, warmly remonstrated against his so constantly
exposing himself.   Upon one occasion as he was approaching an angle of the line, against which the Indians were advancing with horrible yells, lieut. Em-
merson of the dragoons seized the bridle of his horse,

and earnestly entreated that he would not go there; but the governor putting spurs to his horse, pushed on to the point of attack, where the enemy were received with firmness and driven back.

The army remained in camp on the 7th and 8th November, to bury the dead and dress the wounded; and to make preparations for returning. During this time, gen. Wells was permitted with the mounted riflemen to visit the town, which he found evacuated by all, except a chief whose leg was broke. The general burnt their houses, destroyed their corn and brass kettles, and returned to camp unmolested. The town was well prepared for an attack, and no doubt but the Indians fully expected it; for they had determined to agree to no terms which could be offered. The wounds of the chief being dressed, and provision made for him, he was left with instructions to tell his companions, that if they would abandon the Prophet and return to their respective tribes, they should be forgiven.

On the 9th November the return of the army was commenced. It marched slowly, on account of the wounded, the difficulty of transportation, and some apprehensions of another attack. As the army had come up the river, a block house had been built on its bank, where some boats and heavy baggage had been left. The wounded were now put in the boats as the army returned, and were taken to fort Harrison and Vincennes by water. Capt. Snelling and his company were left at fort Harrison; and the governor arrived at Vincennes on the 18th, having been met and welcomed back by a concourse of two hundred citizens.

The battle of Tippecanoe has been the subject of much speculation, both as to its object, and the manner of its execution and final issue. Gov. Harrison was censured by some, for not making an attack upon the Indians, on the evening of the 6th November, and for not fortifying his camp with a breast work. It was erroneously said by some, that indulging a false security, he had suffered his camp to be surprised. He was also blamed by the friends of col. Daveiss, for directing him with his dragoons only, to dislodge the Indians, who were sheltered near the line, and doing much execution in safety. Many other complaints of less magnitude were also made by men, who were wise after the transaction was over. There were indeed more able generals in the United States, who could tell what ought to have been done after the battle was fought, than the governor had soldiers in his army to fight it. Col. Boyd who commanded the regulars, wishing to monopolize all the honor to himself and his regiment, concluded the governor had not sufficiently noticed him in his report; and he therefore made a separate communication to the war department; and also made many round assertions respecting the conduct of the militia—which was promptly explained, and the charges in general disproved by governor Harrison. Col. Boyd however had his partizans, and some of them still persist in attributing the salvation of the army to him; though all the troops, regulars as well as militia, with the exception of only three or four individuals, united in attributing the victory to the governor. Most of the officers publickly united in attesting his merits. Without intending to impeach col. Boyd with any dereliction of duty, we can positively aver, that he did not give a single order, nor perform a single act, that contributed in any perceptible way to the issue of the contest. All the arrangements and orders before the action and during its continuance, came direct from gov. Harrison.

After much altercation, by which the battle of Tippecanoe was fought over again and fully investigated, in all the public circles of the western country, the public opinion preponderated greatly in favor of the governor. All the material accusations of his enemies were disproved; and after all the testimony had been heard, the common opinion seemed to be, that the ar-

my had been conducted with prudence, and that the
battle had been fought as well as it could have been
by any general, considering the time and manner of
the attack. If the governor had made the attack himself on the evening of the 6th, after a chief had informed him, that the Indians were desirous of an accommodation, and had sent a messenger three days
before to meet him for that purpose, his conduct would
have had the appearance of rashness and cruelty.
His enemies and the opposition in general, would have
vilified him and the executive as murderers, who had
first provoked, and then massacred those "*innocent
people*" in their own dwellings. Hence a regard for
his own character and for the dictates of humanity required, that he should not make an attack while any
prospect of accommodation remained. The principal
error consisted in not fortifying his camp, when so
near the enemy and so likely to be attacked ; but this
he excuses by stating, that the army had scarcely a
sufficient number of axes to procure firewood. It is
not the object of this history however to justify or con-
demn, but to relate facts correctly and leave the reader
to judge for himself.

In December, the month after the battle, the legislature of Kentucky, on the motion of J. H. Hawkins
esq. went into mourning for the loss of cols. Daveiss,
Owen, and others, who had fallen at Tippecanoe; and
in the same session, while this battle was the subject
of much discussion, the following resolution, moved
by J. J. Crittenden esq. was adopted with only two
or three dissenting votes—"Resolved &c. That in
the late campaign against the Indians on the Wabash,
governor W. H. Harrison has, in the opinion of this legislature, behaved like a hero, a patriot, and a general ; and that for his cool, deliberate, skillful and gallant conduct in the late battle of Tippecanoe, he well
deserves the warmest thanks of the nation."

The veteran soldier, governor Charles Scott, approved this resolution, which at once gave tone to the po-

pularity of Harrison, effectually turning the tide in his
favor, and reducing the clamor of his enemies to private murmurs.

On the 22d November, the annual meeting of the
Indians to receive their annuities took place at fort
Wayne, where several of those who had fought in the
battle, had the effrontery to present themselves and
claim their respective portions.   They had the address
completely to deceive our Indian agent at that place,
John Johnson esq.   They represented, that the Prophet's party had him in confinement and were determined to kill him; that they blamed him for all their
misfortunes; with many other deceptive stories, which
induced Mr. Johnson to inform the government, that
the Indians were all inclined for peace, and that no
further hostilities should be committed against them.
Yet at this very time, in most of the nations there assembled, a British faction was boiling to the brim, and
ready to overflow on our devoted frontiers, whenever
the perfidious British agents might think proper to increase the fire of their hostility.   The Prophet instead
of being in confinement, was at perfect liberty at Mississineway, a village about 70 miles southwest from
fort Wayne.   Previous to the battle, the Governor General of the Canadas, had given our government information, that some of the Indians were hostile to the U.
States: but this was evidently done to remove suspicion,
and to render the British more secure and successful
in their intrigues with the savages.

The Indians, assembled at this place, were the
chiefs and head men of the Delawares, Miamies, Potawatamies, and Shawanoese.   The agent delivered
them a speech, in which he explained to them, that
the President wished to live in peace and friendship
with them, and promised pardon to any of the hostile
Indians who would lay down their arms.   An answer
was returned on the part of all the tribes present, by
Black-Hoof a Shawanoe chief, in which they professed

the strongest desire to live in peace and friendship with the United States. The profession was sincere on the part of the Shawanoese, and a great majority of the Delawares; but the Potawatamies and Miamies had no intention to be peaceable after receiving their annuities. The Little Turtle of the Miamies, now in the decline of life and of influence, was the strenuous advocate of peace, but the majority of his people followed the counsels of Tecumseh.

On the Wabash, after the battle of Tippecanoe, the Indians remained quiet, and in a few days many of them returned to their towns. Before Christmas, Stone Eater, with two Winebagoes, one Kickapoo, and a Piankishaw, came to fort Harrison, and delivered a talk to capt. Snelling, in which they professed much contrition for what had happened, with a desire to be at friendship. The same fellow had defended the cause of Tecumseh in a council at Vincennes, shortly before the march of the expedition ; and he now wished to go there again, to make deceptious offers of friendship to the governor. He pretended, that the Prophet was despised, and had escaped from them to the Huron Indians. After receiving orders from governor Harrison, capt. Snelling permitted them to go on to Vincennes, where they renewed their professions of friendship, and promised to punish the Prophet, or deliver him to the U. States, as soon as they could catch him. They returned once more to their own country, determined not to commit hostilities again— till a favorable opportunity should occur.

During the winter 1811–12, a number of Indians from various tribes came to fort Harrison and Vincennes ; but Tecumseh, the Prophet, and others known to be the most hostile, staid behind—hence little reliance could be placed on the professions of those who came in. After Tecumseh returned from the south, he visited fort Wayne, and was still haughty, and obstinate in the opinions he had embraced. He made bitter reproaches against Harrison; and at the same time had the presumption to demand ammunition from the commandant, which was refused him. He then said he would go to his British father, who would not deny him—he appeared thoughtful a while, then gave the war whoop and went off.

Early in the spring 1812, Tecumseh and his party began to put their threats into execution. Small parties began to commit depredations on the frontiers of the Indiana and Illinois Territories, and part of Ohio. Twenty scalps were taken in the Indiana alone before the 1st June. The people were thus compelled to protect themselves by going into forts along the frontiers. Volunteer companies of militia were organised, and the marauders were frequently pursued, but generally without success, as they fled immediately after doing mischief. Governor Harrison requested permission from the war department, to raise a mounted force and penetrate to their towns to chastise them. They occupied Tippecanoe, and had commenced raising corn. But the governor was not permitted to march against them, and the frontiers continued to suffer in every direction. Had a strong mounted army been permitted to scour the Wabash as far as Mississineway, the settlements of the savages would have been completely destroyed, and their depredations would have ceased. The government appears to have pursued a mistaken policy of forbearance, lest the Indians should join the British in the expected war. But this forbearance only inspired them with a belief, that we were weak and pusillanimous, and tended to ensure their alliance with the British, had any thing been necessary for that purpose. By vigorous measures we might easily have beaten them into peaceable deportment and respect. Mr. Secretary Eustis of the war department, thought differently; and while he was attempting to soothe them with good words, they were laughing at his credulity. To maintain peace with an

F

Indian, it is necessary to adopt his own principles and punish every aggression promptly, and thus convince him that you are a *man* and not a *squaw*.

In May governor Harrison made considerable arrangements towards organising a corps of mounted volunteers, to chastise the Indians on the Wabash. A company of mounted volunteers was raised in Franklin county, Ky. containing about 70 gentlemen of respectability, under the command of Capt. John Arnold, and Col. Anthony Crocket, who had distinguished themselves not only in the revolution, but in most of the Indian wars at an early period in Kentucky. This company remained at Vincennes only 10 days; during which time several parties made excursions up the Wabash, and protected the inhabitants while planting their corn. The governor being disappointed in receiving orders for the expedition from the war department, the company was dismissed; and all measures for offensive operations being abandoned, the Indians pursued their course of robbery and murder on the frontiers unresisted.

It will no doubt be interesting to the reader, to conclude the present chapter with the following letter from general Harrison to the war department, respecting the northwestern Indians. It contains, says the general, in a different letter to the secretary—"a sketch of the situation of each of the tribes bordering on this frontier; and an abstract of the policy, which has been pursued in the negotiations, which have been conducted by me, for the extinguishment of their title to lands, since the year 1801; and which you could only otherwise obtain, by wading through a most voluminous correspondence in the archives of your office." It will further explain the causes of Indian hostility, and enable the reader to understand more correctly many parts in the following history.

H. Q. Cincinnati, March 22nd, 1814.

SIR—The tribes of Indians upon this frontier and east of the Mississippi, with whom the U. S. have been connected by treaty, are the Wyandots, Delawares, Shawanoese, Miamies, Potawatamies, Ottawas, Chippewas, Piankashaws, Kaskaskias, and Sacs. All but the two last were in the confederacy. which carried on the former Indian war against the United States, that was terminated by the peace of Greenville. The Kaskaskias were parties to the treaty, but they had not been in the war. The Wyandots are admitted by the others to be the leading tribe. They hold the grand *calumet*, which unites them and kindles the council fire. This tribe is nearly equally divided between the *Crane* at Sandusky, who is the grand Sachem of the nation, and Walk-in-the-Water at Brownstown near Detroit. They claim the lands, bounded by the settlements of this state, southwardly and eastwardly; and by lake Erie, the Miami river, and the claim of the Shawanoese upon the Auglaize, a branch of the latter. They also claim the lands they live on near Detroit, but I am ignorant to what extent.

The Wyandots of Sandusky have adhered to us through the war. Their chief, the Crane, is a venerable, intelligent, and upright man. Within the tract of land claimed by the Wyandots a number of Senecas are settled. They broke off from their own tribe six or eight years ago, but receive a part of the annuity granted that tribe by the U. States, by sending a deputation for it to Buffaloe. The claim of the Wyandots to the lands they occupy, is not disputed, that I know of, by any other tribe. Their residence on it however, is not of long standing, and the country was certainly once the property of the Miamies.

Passing westwardly from the Wyandots, we meet with the Shawanoese settlement at Stony creek, a branch of the big Miami, and at Wapockaunata on the Auglaize. These settlements were made immediately after the treaty of Greenville, and with the consent of the Miamies, whom I consider the real owners of those lands. The chiefs of this band of Shawanoese, Blackhoof, Wolf, and Lewis, are attached to us from principle as well as interest—they are all honest men.

The Miamies have their principal settlements at the forks of the Wabash, thirty miles from fort Wayne; and at Mississineway, thirty miles lower down. A band of them under the name of Weas, have resided on the Wabash sixty miles above Vincennes; and another under the Turtle on Eel river, a branch of the Wabash, twenty miles northwest of fort Wayne. By an artifice of the Little Turtle, these three bands were passed on general Wayne as distinct tribes, and an annuity was granted to each. The Eel river and Weas however to this day call themselves Miamies, and are recognised as such by the Mississineway band. The Miamies, Maumees, or Tewicktovies, are the undoubted proprietors of all that beautiful country which is watered by the Wabash and its branches; and there is as little doubt, that their claim extended at least as far east as the Scioto. They have no tradition of removing from any other quarter of the country; whereas all the neighboring tribes, the Piankishaws, excepted, who are a branch of the Miamies, are either intruders upon them, or have been permitted to settle in their country. The Wyandots emigrated first from lake Ontario, and subsequently from lake Huron—the Delawares, from Pennsylvania and Maryland—the Shawanoese from Georgia—the Kickapoos and Potawatamies from the country between lake Michigan and the Mississippi—and the Ottawas and Chippewas from the peninsula formed by the lakes Michigan, Huron, and St. Clair, and the streight connecting the latter with Erie. The claims of the Miamies were bounded on the north and west by those of the Illinois confederacy, consisting originally of five tribes, called Kaskaskias, Cahokias, Peorians, Michiganians, and Temarois, speaking the Miami language, and no doubt branches of that nation.

When I was first appointed governor of Indiana Territory, these once powerful tribes were reduced to about thirty warriors, of whom twenty-five were Kaskaskias, four Peorians, and a single Michiganian. There was an individual lately alive at St. Louis, who saw the enumeration made of them by the Jesuits in the year 1745, making the number of their warriors four thousand. A furious war between them and the Sacs and Kickapoos, reduced them to that miserable remnant, which had taken refuge amongst the white people of the towns of Kaskaskia and St. Genevieve. The Kickapoos had fixed their principal village at Peoria, upon the south bank of the Illinois river, whilst the Sacs remained masters of the country to the north.

During the war of our revolution, the Miamies had invited the Kickapoos into their country to assist them against the whites, and a considerable village was formed by that tribe on the Vermillion river near its junction with the Wabash. After the treaty of Greenville, the Delawares had with the approbation of the Miamies, removed from the mouth of the Auglaize to the head waters of White river, a large branch of the Wabash—and the Potawatamies without their consent had formed two villages upon the latter river, one at Tippecanoe, and the other at Chippoy twenty-five miles below.

The Piankishaws lived in the neighbourhood of Vincennes, which was their ancient village, and claimed the lands to the mouth of the Wabash, and to the north and west as far as the Kaskaskians claimed. Such was the situation of the tribes, when I received the instructions of President Jefferson, shortly after his first election, to make efforts for extinguishing the Indian claims upon the Ohio, below the mouth of the Kentucky river, and to such other tracts as were necessary to connect and consolidate our settlements. It was at once determined, that the community of interests in the lands amongst the Indian tribes, which seemed to be recognised by the treaty of Greenville, should be objected to; and that each individual tribe should be protected in every claim that should appear to be founded in reason and justice. But it was also determined, that as a measure of policy and liberality, such tribes as lived upon any tract of land which it would be desirable to purchase, should receive a portion of the compensation, although the title might be exclusively in another tribe. Upon this principle the Delawares, Shawanoese, Potawatamies, and Kickapoos were admitted as parties to several of the treaties. Care was taken however, to place the title to such tracts as it might be desirable to purchase hereafter, upon a footing that would facilitate the procuring of them, by getting the tribes who had no claim themselves, and who might probably interfere, to recognise the titles of those who were ascertained to possess them.

This was particularly the case with regard to the lands watered by the Wabash, which were declared to be the property of the Miamies, with the exception of the tract occupied by the Delawares on White river, which was to be considered the joint property of them and the Miamies. This arrangement was very much disliked by Tecumseh, and the banditti that he had assembled at Tippecanoe. He complained loudly, as well of the sales that had been made, as of the principle of considering a particular tribe as the exclusive proprietors of any part of the country, which he said the Great Spirit had given to all his red children. Besides the disaffected amongst the neighboring tribes, he had brought together a considerable number of Winebagoes and Folsovoins from the neighborhood of Green Bay, Sacs from the Mississippi, and some Ottawas and Chippewas from Abercrosh on lake Michigan. These people were better pleased with the climate and country of the Wabash, than with that they had left.

The Miamies resisted the pretensions of Tecumseh and his followers for some time, but a system of terror was adopted, and the young men were seduced by eternally placing before them a picture of labor, and restriction as to hunting, to which the system adopted would inevitably lead. The Potawatamies and other tribes inhabiting the Illinois river and south of lake Michigan, had been for a long time approaching gradually towards the Wabash. Their country, which was never abundantly stocked with game, was latterly almost exhausted of it. The fertile regions of the Wabash still afforded it. It was represented, that the progressive settlements of the whites upon that river, would soon deprive them of their only resource, and indeed would force the Indians of that river upon them, who were already half starved.

It is a fact, that for many years the current of emigration, as to the tribes east of the Mississippi, has been from north to south. This is owing to two causes: the diminution of those animals from which the Indians procure their support; and the pressure of the two great tribes, the Chippewas and Sioux to the north and west. So long ago as the treaty of Greenville, the Potawatamies gave notice to the Miamies, that they intended to settle upon the Wabash. They made no pretensions to the country, and their only excuse for the intended aggression, was that "they were tired of eating fish, and wanted meat." It has been already observed that the Sacs had extended themselves to the Illinois river, and that the settlement of the Kickapoos at the Peorias was of modern date. Previously to the commencement of the present war, a considerable number had joined their brethren upon the Wabash. The Tawas from the Des Moins river have twice made attempts to get a footing there.

From these facts it will be seen, that it will be nearly impossible to get the Indians south of the Wabash to go beyond the Illinois river. The subject of providing an outlet to such of the tribes as it might be desirable to remove, has been under consideration for many years. There is but one. It was long since discovered by the Indians themselves, and but for the humane policy, which has been pursued by our government, the Delawares, Kickapoos, and Shawanoese would long since have been out of our way. The country claimed by the Osages abounds with every thing that is desirable to a savage. The Indians of the tribes above mentioned have occasionally intruded upon them—a war was the consequence, which would soon have given a sufficient opening for emigration. But our government interfered and obliged the hostile tribes to make peace.

I was afterwards instructed to endeavour to get the Delawares to join that part of their tribe, which is settled on the west side of the Mississippi near Cape Girardeau. The attempt was unsuccessful at the time. I have no doubt however, that they could be prevailed on to move; but it ought not in my opinion to be attempted in a general council of the tribes.

The question of the title to the lands south of the Wabash has been thoroughly examined: every opportunity was afforded to Tecumseh and his party to exhibit their pretensions, and they were found to rest upon no other basis, than that of their being the common property of all the Indians. The Potawatamies and Kickapoos have unequivocally acknowledged the Miami and Delaware title. The latter as I before observed can

I think be induced to remove. It may take a year or eighteen months to effect it. The Miamies will not be in our way. They are a poor, miserable, drunken set, diminishing every year. Becoming too lazy to hunt, they feel the advantage of their annuity. The fear of the other Indians has alone prevented them from selling their whole claim to the United States; and as soon as there is peace, or the British can no longer intrigue, they will sell. I know not what inducements can be held out to the Wyandots to remove; they were not formerly under my superintendence, but I am persuaded that a general council would not be the place to attempt it.

I have the honor &c. &c.

WM. H. HARRISON.

Hon. J. ARMSTRONG,
   Secretary of war.

From this able and interesting review of Indian settlements, rights, and politics—the result of an intimacy, for 20 years, with those affairs—we are enabled to judge of the justice of the cause advocated by Tecumseh. His scheme of policy was certainly well calculated to secure and promote the best interests of the Indians as savages; but to render it just in theory, and efficient in practice, it was necessary that it should receive the undivided sanction and support of all the tribes concerned. This, all the talents and persevering industry of Tecumseh, aided by the intrigues and bribes of the British, were unable to effect. To form a confederacy out of so many and such various tribes, required a degree of civilisation to which the Indians had not attained. If such a union were actually effected, it is improbable that any purchase of lands could ever afterwards be accomplished by the United States. The consent of all the tribes in a general council, to the cession of any part of their country, was considered by the advocates of the scheme as a thing unattainable. On the contrary, while no such confederacy existed *in fact*, had our government acknowledged the principle of Tecumseh, that a community of interest in their lands was a matter of *natural right*, we should have been subjected to great inconvenience in the extension of our settlements. As soon as one tribe had sold us a parcel of land, other hordes might settle on it in succession, and by the mere temporary occupancy of the soil, compel our government to purchase it again twenty times over.

It is doubtless true, that scarcely any tribe has lands appropriated to itself by exact and special boundaries. Its villages and the lands immediately around them, may be considered as clearly its exclusive property; but the remote wilderness, between the more distant settlements of the different tribes, is not partitioned with any precision, except where nature may have done it, by a water course or some such striking limit. The wandering nature of their occupation renders a more exact appropriation impracticable. This vagueness of their claims however, is no foundation for the doctrine of a common property. The Miamies appear to have been the original occupants and real owners of all the lands northwest of the Ohio; but other tribes have gradually intruded, and formed settlements with or without their consent, till they are at last reduced to narrow limits and insignificance themselves.

CHAPTER II.

Declaration of war—Hull's campaign.

DURING those transactions with the Indians, which have been described in the preceding chapter, affairs between the United States and Great Britain were fast approaching to a crisis. In April an embargo was laid by Congress on all the shipping in the ports and harbors of the United States. An act authorizing the President to detach one hundred thousand militia for six months was passed and carried into execution : several others authorizing a regular army to be raised were also passed ; and the people in general expected that a declaration of war would soon take place.

In April the President made a requisition on the state of Ohio for twelve hundred militia, and ordered the 4th regiment from Vincennes to Cincinnati, under the command of col. Miller, to be joined with the militia. Boyd, in the mean time, having gone to Washington City, had been promoted to the rank of brigadier general. In obedience to the requisition, governor Meigs of Ohio, issued orders to the major generals of the middle and western divisions of that state, for their respective proportions of men, to rendezvous on the 29th April at Dayton, a town at the mouth of Mad river on the Big Miami. The corps was raised without difficulty—the people of Ohio, with an ardent love of country and zeal for its interests, voluntarily tendered their services to the government of their choice. In a few days, more than the number wanted came forward. Citizens of the first respectability enroled themselves and prepared for the dangers of the

G

field, contending with each other who should go first into the service of their country. The troops being collected, they proceeded to choose their field officers, when Duncan M'Arthur was elected colonel of the first regiment, and James Denny and William A. Trimble, majors—for the 2d regiment, James Findley, colonel, and Thomas Moore and Ths. B. Vanhorne, majors—for the 3rd, Lewis Cass, colonel, and Robert Morrison and J. R. Munson, majors.

No accommodations having been prepared for the troops, they were obliged to camp without tents or other equipage ; and having been hurried from home very suddenly, they had to encounter many difficulties without being prepared to meet them. Most of them had never been in a camp before, and were entirely unacquainted with the necessary equipments. It was the middle of May before blankets and camp equipage arrived from Pittsburgh by the way of Cincinnati.

William Hull esq. governor of the Michigan Territory, having been appointed a brigadier general in the army of the United States, was destined to command these troops. He arrived at Dayton about the 20th of May, and appointed his son, capt. A. F. Hull, and Robert Wallace jr. his aids—lieut. Ths. S. Jessup, his brigade major—and doctor Ab. Edwards, his hospital surgeon. General James Taylor of Kentucky, also accompanied this army as quarter master general. The organization of the troops into regiments being completed, governor Meigs proceeded as directed by the Secretary at war, to surrender the command to general Hull. The 25th of May, being selected for this ceremony, the army was formed in close column, and addressed by the governor in a speech full of patriotic sentiments and good advice. He congratulated them on being placed under general Hull, a distinguished officer of revolutionary experience ; and who, being superintendent of Indian affairs, and governor of the Territory to which they were destined, would

thence be able more effectually to provide for their
comfort and convenience.   Colonel Cass also delivered an appropriate address, which was received with
much applause.   General Hull being invested with
the command, then addressed the troops in flattering
and animated terms.   After commending their patriotism and recommending discipline, he proceeded, " In
marching through a wilderness memorable for savage
barbarity, you will remember the causes, by which
that barbarity has been heretofore excited.   In viewing the ground stained with the blood of your fellow
citizens, it will be impossible to suppress the feelings
of indignation.   Passing by the ruins of a fortress,
erected in our territory by a foreign nation, in times
of profound peace, and for the express purpose of exciting the savages to hostility, and supplying them
with the means of conducting a barbarous war, must
remind you of that system of oppression and injustice,
which that nation has continually practised, and which
the spirit of an indignant people can no longer endure."

The delivery of this speech by the general animated every breast, and great expectations were formed
of his prowess and abilities.   His manners were familiar and his appearance prepossessing.   The frost of
time had given him a venerable aspect, and the idea
of his revolutionary services inspired the troops with
confidence.   Such were the auspicious circumstances
under which general Hull took command of the army.
Those who were induced by their discernment, or their
intimate acquaintance with the general, to doubt his
abilities to lead an invading army, hesitated to express
their sentiments, and were silent before the voice of
public admiration.

On the first of June, the army marched up the Miami to Staunton, a small village on the east bank.
Here they waited for the boats in which the baggage
was coming up the river.   They intended to ascend

Lorimies river 18 miles, then march by Piqua to the Auglaize, and then descend that river. But on the 6th of June, they were informed, that the water was too low for the boats to ascend—they were then ordered by the general to march to Urbanna, a village about 30 miles to the east of Staunton. Here they were informed on the morning of the 8th, by a general order, that they would be met that day on parade, by the governor accompanied by many distinguished citizens and some Indian chiefs. On the following day, governor Meigs and general Hull held a council with 12 chiefs, of the Shawanoe, Mingoe, and Wyandot nations, to obtain leave from them to march the army through their territory, and to erect such forts as might be deemed necessary; which was promptly granted by them, and every assistance, which they could give the army in the wilderness was promised. Governor Meigs had held a council with these Indians on the 6th, in which it was agreed to adhere to the treaty of Greenville.

At these councils, the just and humane policy of our government, was exhibited in fair-dealing with the Indians, and in exhorting them to peace and neutrality. It forms a striking contrast to the conduct of the British, who were using every insidious means to engage the Indians in their service, and to excite them to massacre our innocent women and children.

On the 10th of June, the 4th regiment with colonel Miller at its head. arrived at Urbanna. They were met about a mile from town, by cols. M'Arthur, Cass, and Findley, at the head of their respective regiments, by whom they were escorted into camp, through a triumphal arch, adorned with an eagle, and inscribed with the words, TIPPECANOE—GLORY. On this occasion the general issued a congratulatory order to his troops to excite their emulation.

' *H. Q. Urbanna, June* 10, 1812.

' The general congratulates the army on the arrival of
the 4th U. S. regiment.   The first army of the state of Ohio
will feel a pride in being associated with a regiment so distinguished for its valor and discipline.   The general is persuaded,
that there will be no other contention in this army, but who will
most excel in discipline and bravery.   Whatever the rank of
the regiment, or to whatever description it belongs, it will in
reality consider itself the first regiment in the army.   The patriots of Ohio, who yield to none in spirit and patriotism, will
not be willing to yield to any in discipline and valor.

' Ths. S. JESSUP, *Brig. Maj.*'

On the next day general M'Arthur was detached
with his regiment, to cut a road for the army as far as
the Scioto river, which rises northwest of the head
branches of the Big Miami.   The whole army having
moved as far as King's creek, three miles from Urbanna, another general order was issued on the 16th
June, from which the following are extracts.   "In the
honor of this army the general feels the deepest interest.   He sincerely hopes, that nothing will take place
during the campaign, to tarnish the fame it has already
acquired : its glory however is not yet complete.   Bare
professions of patriotism do not establish the character
of a patriot.   It is necessary for this army to meet
with a cheerful and manly fortitude, the fatigues and
dangers it may be called to encounter, before it can
be entitled to the honorable appellation of a patriotic
army.   It is easy to boast of patriotism : it is hard to
perform the duties it requires.   The general retains
the highest confidence in the honorable motives of this
army, and he assures the officers and soldiers, that
while on the one hand he will do all in his power for
their comfort and convenience, on the other hand he
expects a ready submission to his orders and a punctual discharge of all their duties."

On the day this order was issued, col. M'Arthur's
regiment had opened the road as far as the Scioto, and
had begun to build two block houses on the south bank

of the river, which is there but 40 or 50 feet wide. These houses were strengthened by stockades, and in honor of the colonel, the whole was called Fort M'Arthur. At this place, Peter Vassar, a Frenchman, while on guard deliberately shot a brother sentry by the name of Joseph England, and wounded him badly, but he afterwards recovered and returned home. Vassar was put under guard, and a general order was issued, prohibiting sutlers from selling liquor to any non-commissioned officer or private, without a written permit from his commanding officer.

The whole army having arrived here on the 19th, col. Findley was ordered to proceed with his regiment on the 21st, and cut the road as far as Blanchard's fork of the Auglaize ; and on the 22nd, the whole army followed, except a part of capt. Dill's company, which was left to keep the fort and take care of the sick. It now rained for several days excessively, so as to render the road almost impassable for wagons. After marching only 16 miles, the army halted again, in the midst of a swampy country, in which the water courses, both of the Ohio and the lakes, have their sources. A block house was erected here, which was honored with the name of *Fort* Necessity. The mud was deep, and from every appearance the whole army was likely to stick in the swamps. The horses and oxen were put on short allowance ; and every man who could make a pack saddle was detailed on that business. The general intended to transport his baggage on pack horses ; but as soon as a sufficient number of saddles were made, the order was rescinded, and they were deposited in the block house.

The general's first order of march was given, it is believed, on the 20th June, at fort M'Arthur : but he seems to have entirely forgotten to give his army an order of battle—perhaps he did not deem it necessary, intending to do all the fighting himself on paper. The following was the order of march : " The 4th

U. S. regiment on the right; col. M'Arthur on the left; col. Findley on the left of the 4th; and col. Cass on the right of M'Arthur; the cavalry on the right of the whole. In marching, the riflemen of the respective regiments, will form the flank guards, and on the day the army marches, they will be excused from any other duty."

When the army was ready to march from fort Necessity, they were met by general Robert Lucas and Mr. Wm. Denny, who had been sent by general Hull from Dayton, with despatches for Mr. Atwater, the acting governor at Detroit. Their report was not the most favorable. Gen. Lucas had been present at several councils, held by Mr. Atwater with the chiefs of the Ottawa and Chippewa tribes, and the Wyandots of Brownstown. They all expressed a disposition to be friendly, except Walk-in-the-Water, of the Wyandots, who declared that the American government was acting improperly in sending an army into their country, which would cut off their communication with Canada. He said the Indians were their own masters and would trade where they pleased; and that the disturbance on the Wabash was the fault of governor Harrison entirely. Gen. Lucas had also ascertained, that the British had collected a considerable body of Indians at Malden, who were fed and supplied with arms and ammunition, and were ready to fight the Americans at the first signal from their employers. It was represented that Detroit was in a bad state of defence, and that the citizens generally were much elated at the approach of an army for their protection. General Lucas had no opportunity of visiting fort Malden; but from every information, it was believed to be in a much worse situation than Detroit, one side of it being entirely open.

The weather having become more favorable, the army at last marched from fort Necessity, and arrived in three days at Blanchard's fork, where col. Findley

had built block houses and stockading on the southwest side, which was called fort Findley.   On the 26th
June, col. Dunlap arrived in camp as an express from
Chilicothe, with dispatches from the war department
for general Hull.   They were confidential; but it was
believed, that they contained certain and official intelligence of the declaration of war against England, as
the general ordered all the heavy camp equipage to be
left at this fort, and determined to commence a forced
march.   Col. Cass was sent with his regiment to cut
the remainder of the road to the Rapids; and the balance of capt. Dill's company being left at the fort, the
army proceeded, but not with more speed than usual,
and in a few days encamped on the banks of the Miami of the Lake, opposite the battle ground of general
Wayne, and in view of a small village at the foot of
the rapids.   Here the army was cheered with a view
of civilized habitations, after a tedious march through
a dreary wilderness.   Having delayed here a day,
they marched down through the village in regular order, and encamped just below the ruins of the old
British fort Miami, from which the Indians were supplied by the British, previous to their battle with
Wayne on the 20th August '94.

   At this place, a small schooner, belonging to a capt.
Chapin, was employed to carry a quantity of baggage
to Detroit, about 30 officers and privates being put on
board for its protection.   It being the last of the month,
complete muster rolls of every company in the brigade,
were made out and deposited in a trunk, which was
put on board this vessel.   An open boat with the sick,
was also sent in company with capt. Chapin.   It was
here represented to general Hull, by capt. M'Pherson
of Cincinnati, that war must have been declared, and
that the schooner would certainly be captured at Malden.   Notwithstanding this suggestion, and the general's own knowledge on the subject, he persisted in
sending the vessel.

Lieutenant Davidson with 25 men being left here to build a block house, the army again marched on the 1st July, after considerable time spent in preparation as usual.   Their route was through an open country, interspersed with thin groves of oak, and scattering settlements of French.   When they arrived at the river Raisin, on which there is a handsome village of French inhabitants, information was received, that the schooner, in attempting to pass Malden with the baggage, had been captured by the British, and the whole crew and passengers made prisoners, the enemy having previously received intelligence of the declaration of war which was made on the 18th June by the American government.   Though general Hull had certainly received some intimation of this act of the government by col. Dunlap, yet the troops had not been informed of it, till the evening before they reached the river Raisin, at which time the baggage had been captured.   The colonels having on that evening informed their men of the declaration of war, and that the situation of the army required strict subordination, firmness, and bravery to ensure success; and each man being supplied with ten rounds of ammunition and an extra flint; every heart beat warm in the cause of the country, and new life and animation beamed in every countenance.

A day was spent at the river Raisin; and a day and a half in marching fifteen miles to the river Huron. Here the 4th of July was spent in erecting a bridge over the river, which is but 40 feet wide, but very deep. The road crosses about half a mile from the lake; from which place the army had a full view of the Canada shore below Malden, and a delightful prospect of Lake Erie to the east.   A large vessel, supposed to be the Queen Charlotte, with troops on board, was seen going towards Malden, where the firing of cannon was distinctly heard.   An attack from the British

H

and Indians was expected at this place, and the army, anxiously desiring it, was kept under arms the whole day.

On the 5th the army marched early, and having passed the villages of Brownstown and Maguaga, and the rivers De Corce and Roach, it arrived at Spring-wells, the lower end of the Detroit settlement, and but two miles from the town. Here is a handsome emi-nence on the river Detroit, well calculated for a fort, which would command the town of Sandwich on the Canada shore, the river being about three quarters of a mile wide. The following extract from a general order issued at this place, will shew in what manner general Hull informed the northwestern posts of the declaration of war. "The garrisons of Detroit, Mi-chilimacinac, Chicago and fort Wayne, being placed by the President of the U. States, under the command of general Hull, the commanding officers of those gar-risons are informed, that congress have declared war against Great Britain ; and they will immediately place their garrisons in the best possible state of de-fence, and make a return to brigade major Jessup at Detroit, of the quantity of provisions the contractor has on hand at their respective posts, the number of officers and men, ordnance and military stores of eve-ry kind, and the public property of all kinds." When this general order, containing a variety of other mat-ters trivial and local, had issued from the pen of the general, it was left to find a conveyance to Chicago and Macinaw, in the best way it could, no human means being employed by the general for that purpose.

On the morning of the 6th col. Cass was sent with a flag of truce to Malden, which was commanded at that time by colonel St. George. The object was to demand the baggage and prisoners captured in the schooner. When he arrived there, he was blind-fold-ed, and his demands were refused : he then returned to camp with capt. Burbanks of the British army. In this instance general Hull betrayed his ignorance of military diplomacy, in sending col. Cass with a flag to an equal, if not an inferior in rank. But perhaps there was some greater object in view than simply to demand the baggage.

Five pieces of artillery were brought down from the fort on the 7th and placed on the bank in front of the army, in a situation to annoy the enemy at Sandwich. On the same day the general held a council with the principal chiefs of the Wyandot, Shawanoe, Potawatamie, Seneca and Mohawk nations, which ended in their professing to be our friends. On the next day the general became alarmed, lest the enemy should bombard his camp from the upper side of Sandwich: he therefore removed into the rear of Detroit to be out of the reach of danger.

The town of Detroit contains about 160 houses and 700 inhabitants. It is handsomely situated on the west side of the river Detroit, about nine miles below lake St. Clair, the opening of which can be seen from the town. Fort Detroit stands on an elevated spot of ground, in the rear of the town, and about 250 yards from the bank of the river. It is a square, containing near two acres of ground. It is surrounded with a double row of pickets, the outside row being set in the ditch, and the other obliquely in the bank, which is thrown up against the walls of the fort, and which is so high, that at some distance from the fort, the interior buildings cannot be seen. The ground gradually declines from the fort in every direction. It is badly situated to command the river; but it is a place of great strength, and could not be injured by any battery on the same side of the river. The inhabitants about Detroit are mostly descendents of the old French settlers, professing the catholic religion. The Territory can raise between six and seven hundred militia.

Preparations were now made for the invasion of
Canada; arms were repaired and carriages made for
the cannon; and the officers endeavoured to inspire
their men with ardor, a willingness to obey, and a determination to avenge the wrongs of their country, by
invading the territories of her enemy. The night of
the 10th was appointed for crossing into Canada; but
it was prevented by the disorderly conduct of some
individuals, who kept firing their guns by one of
whom major Munson was severely wounded. But
few of the enemy were to be seen on the opposite
shore: it was deemed necessary however to use some
precaution in landing. On the evening of the 11th
the regiment of col. M'Arthur, accompanied by some
boats, was marched down to the Springwells, to decoy the enemy. The British were thus induced to
believe, that a descent would be made from that point;
and that an attack would immediately be made upon
Malden; which ought to have been done before this
time. They accordingly drew all their forces to that
place. Next morning the army marched about a mile
above Detroit, where boats had been taken in the
night. The regiments of cols. Miller and Cass embarked at once, and in fifteen minutes landed on the
Canada shore without opposition. General Hull was
among the last to embark, and as his boat reached the
shore, he was heard to exclaim "The critical moment
draws near!" The American flag was unfurled, and
the huzzas of the front, were answered by the rear,
and the citizens of Detroit. An encampment was
formed in the farm of colonel Baubee, a British officer;
the quarters of the general being fixed in a brick house
near the centre of the camp, and not far from the bank
of the river. On the same day the general issued his
famous proclamation, as follows:

BY WILLIAM HULL, brigadier general, commanding the American Northwestern Army.

INHABITANTS OF CANADA! After thirty years of peace and prosperity, the United States have been driven to arms. The injuries and aggressions, the insults and indignities of Great Britain, have once more left them no alternative but manly resistance or unconditional submission. The army under my command has invaded your country, and the standard of the union now waves over the Territory of Canada. To the peaceable, unoffending inhabitant, it brings neither danger nor difficulty. I come to find enemies, not to make them. I come to protect, not to injure you—separated by an immense ocean and an extensive wilderness from Great Britain, you have no participation in her councils, no interest in her conduct. You have felt her tyranny; you have seen her injustice; but I do not ask you to avenge the one or to redress the other. The United States are sufficiently powerful to afford every security, consistent with their rights or your expectations. I tender you the invaluable blessings of civil, political and religious liberty, and their necessary results, individual and general prosperity—that liberty which gave decision to our counsels, and energy to our conduct, in a struggle for independence; and which conducted us safely and triumphantly through the stormy period of the Revolution—that liberty which has raised us to an elevated rank among the nations of the world; and which has afforded us a greater measure of peace and security, of wealth and improvement, than ever fell to the lot of any other people.

In the name of my country, and by the authority of my government, I promise you protection to your persons, property and rights. Remain at your homes; pursue your peaceful and customary avocations; raise not your hands against your brethren. Many of your fathers fought for the freedom and independence we now enjoy. Being children therefore of the same family with us, and heirs to the same heritage, the arrival of an army of friends, must be hailed by you with a cordial welcome. You will be emancipated from tyranny and oppression, and restored to the dignified station of free-men. Had I any doubt of eventual success, I might ask your assistance; but I do not; I come prepared for every contingency. I have a *force, which will look down all opposition*; and that force is but the vanguard of a much greater! If contrary to your own interests and the just expectations of my country, you should take part in the approaching contest, you will be considered and treated as enemies, and the horrors and calamities of war will stalk before you. If the barbarous and savage policy of Great Britain be pursued, and the savages are let loose to murder our citizens, and

butcher our women and children, this war will be a war of extermination. The first stroke of the tomahawk, the first attempt with the scalping knife, will be the signal for one indiscriminate scene of desolation. No white man found fighting by
the side of an Indian will be taken prisoner. Instant destruction will be his lot. If the dictates of reason, duty, justice and
humanity, cannot prevent the employment of a force, which
respects no rights, or knows no wrongs, it will be prevented by
a severe and relentless system of retaliation. I doubt not your
courage and firmness; I will not doubt your attachment to liberty. If you tender your services voluntarily, they will be
accepted readily. The United States offer you peace, liberty,
and security : your choice lies between these and war. Choose
then, but choose wisely—and may HE who knows the justice of
our cause, and who holds in his hands the fate of nations, guide
you to a result the most compatible with your rights, and your
interests.

                                    WILLIAM HULL.
        By the general,
    A. F. HULL, *capt. 13th U. S. regiment and aid.*
    Sandwich, July 12, 1812.

This proclamation had a tendency to recall the greater part of the inhabitants of Sandwich and the adjacent country to their dwellings. They had fled to the
woods on the approach of the Americans, as if an army of cannibals had invaded their country. The
British officers had used every means to induce the
people to believe, that the Americans were worse than
savages.

The Territory of Upper Canada, which was thus
invaded by general Hull, is a very extensive country.
From southeast to northwest it is more than 1000 miles
long; and from Lake Erie northward it is upwards of
500 miles across : but in general its breadth is less
than 300 miles. The population in 1806 was estimated at 80,000.

On the 13th capt. Ulry with 40 men was sent down
towards Malden to reconnoitre. At a bridge over
Turkey creek, about 9 miles from camp, he discovered where a party of near 200 Indians had been lying

in ambush to cut off any detachment, that might cross the bridge, which had been partly destroyed. A Canadian farmer informed the captain, that there were a great many Indians in the neighbourhood; and not considering it prudent to risk a battle with superior numbers he returned to camp. This infornation and an alarm, which occurred at night in the camp, induced the general next day to fortify his camp with a breast work, except the side next the river which was defended by cannon.

On the 14th a detachment from capt. Sloan's cavalry was sent up the river to reconnoitre. At 8 o'clock in the evening two of them returned with information, that a body of Indians had gone up the river about sunset. Col. M'Arthur was ordered to pursue them with 100 men from his own regiment, and a rifle corps from col. Findley's. At half after 9, he marched without blankets or provisions, accompanied by the reconnoitring party, which in the mean time had returned. They went but 8 miles that night, expecting to overtake the Indians early next morning in a wood before them. They did not however come up with the Indians, till they had reached Ruskin river, about twenty-four miles above Sandwich; and here the savages received information of their approach soon enough to escape into the woods, in which the mounted men could not pursue them for logs and brush.

Capt. Smith of the Detroit dragoons now overtook them, with orders for the party to go on to the river Thames or Trench, to procure provisions. Having reached that river, they encamped about half a mile from the mouth, opposite the house of Mr. Isaac Hull, a nephew of the general's, where a corporal and six militia men of the enemy were stationed as a guard to his family. The colonel disarmed them and sent them home on parole. Next day they marched some distance up the river, and on their return collected all the boats they could find, in which they brought off near two hundred barrels of flour, 400 blankets, a number of guns, and a considerable quantity of military stores, most of which was public property; but the colonel gave receipts for all, as if it had been private property, and paid for the provisions they consumed out of his own funds. They arrived at camp on the evening of the 17th, having penetrated upwards of sixty miles into the province unmolested, the inhabitants having received them in a friendly manner.

Deserters from Malden, and inhabitants of the country, now came into the camp daily to obtain protections from the American commander, many of whom were known to return immediately to the fort with all the information they could collect. On the 16th col. Cass and lieut. col. Miller were sent down towards Malden with a detachment, the object and the result of which will be understood from the following report of colonel Cass :

'Sir—In conformity with your instructions, I proceeded with a detachment of 280 men to reconnoitre the enemy's advanced posts. We found them in possession of a bridge over the Aux Kanards river, at the distance of 4 miles from Malden. After examining their position I left one company of riflemen, to conceal themselves near the bridge, and upon our appearance on the opposite side of the river, to commence firing upon the enemy. I then proceeded with the remainder of the detachment about five miles up, to a ford across the Kanards, and down on the southern bank of the river. About sunset we arrived in sight of the enemy. Being entirely destitute of guides, we marched too close to the bank of the river, and found our progress checked by a creek which was impassible. We were then compelled to march a mile up the creek in order to effect a passage. This gave the enemy time to make his arrangements and prepare for defence. On coming down the creek, we found them formed. They commenced a distant fire of musquetry. The riflemen of our detachment were formed upon the wings, and the two companies of infantry in the centre. The men moved on with great spirit and alacrity. After the first discharge the British retreated. We continued advancing. Three times they formed and as often retreated. We drove them about half a mile, when it became so dark, that we were obliged to relinquish the pursuit. Two privates of the 41st regiment were wounded and taken prisoners. We learn from deserters, that nine or ten were wounded, and some killed. We could gain no certain information of the number opposed to us. It consisted of a considerable detachment from the 41st regiment, some militia, and a body of Indians. The guard at the bridge consisted of 50 men. Our riflemen stationed at the bridge, on this side the Kanards, discovered the enemy reinforcing the whole afternoon. There is no doubt, but their numbers exceeded ours. Lieut. col. Miller conducted in the most spirited and able manner. I have every reason to be satisfied with the conduct of the whole detachment.'

Next morning captain Brown of the 4th U. States regiment went down to Malden, without the knowledge of col. Cass; but there is no doubt of his mission being known to gen. Hull: the object of it has never yet been developed. Presently a reinforcement of our troops arrived, consisting of the balance of the 4th regiment, and a piece of artillery under the command of lieut. Eastman. A council of officers was now convened, a majority of whom insisted on leaving the bridge. Col. Cass and capt. Snelling insisted on holding it, as it would be of the utmost importance in marching the army to Malden. Their opinion being overruled, and no order to hold the bridge being received from the general, the whole detachment marched back to camp. The abandonment of this bridge, which had been gained so easy, and which in the possession of the enemy would be the chief obstruction to the advance of the army, was a most fatal error. It was sufficient itself to develope the character of the general; and I can scarcely restrain my indignation sufficiently while writing, to mention the event in deliberate terms. The officers from this occurrence began to distrust the views of the general, and their opinion of his abilities began to dwindle into contempt. It was evident to every person, that the possession of the bridge was important to the success of the enterprise; and had the army marched immediately to Malden, that fortress must have fallen an easy conquest. The command of the

I

river, and security to the upper country, would have
been the consequences.   Col. Cass's orders were, to
reconnoitre the advance posts of the enemy, but not to
hold any posi.ion he might conquer.

In the evening a report prevailed, that the Queen
Charlotte was sailing up the straits, and committing
depredations on the American side; and that the British had again occupied the bridge.   Col. Findley in
consequence went down to the bridge with a small party to reconnoitre.   He found it torn up, and a breast
work of timber erected on the south side, to defend
the pass.   The Queen Charlotte also occupied a station convenient to aid in its defence.   Col. Findley having returned next day, another small party under capt.
Snelling, went down in the evening as a corps of observation.   Gen. Hull for his part staid close in his
quarters at Sandwich;   but to induce his officers to
believe, that he really intended to attack Malden, he
issued the following general order, by way of retaliation for the capture of his baggage; the execution of it
would have placed our army on a level with the disgraceful conduct of the British.

" Whereas the private property, consisting principally of the necessary clothing of the officers and soldiers of this army, has been seized by the British force,
and is detained at Malden or its dependencies, notwithstanding application has been made for the resti-
tution of it—In order to remunerate those officers and
soldiers who have suffered, the general directs that all
personal property of officers now serving in the British
army, at the aforesaid post, shall be taken under special orders from the general, and delivered to the quarter master general for safe keeping, until the orders of
the government are known on the subject.   One hundred and fifty men properly officered, will be detached
for command to-morrow morning at 5 o'clock from col.
M'Arthur's regiment.   Colonel M'Arthur will command, and will call at head quarters for instructions."

In pursuance of this order, col. M'Arthur was sent down to relieve capt. Snelling, who was found at the Petit Cote settlement about a mile above the bridge. From this place to the bridge, the country is a dry, level prairie. About 300 yards from the Kanards, there is a small ridge across the road about 8 feet high, which is covered towards the west with small oak and hazle bushes. From the ridge to the river the prairie is somewhat marshy and covered with long grass. The river is about 25 yards wide and very deep, and on the south side a thick wood commences at a short distance from the bridge. Col. M'Arthur was instructed to ascertain the situation of the bridge and the position of the Queen Charlotte; but not to go within reach of her guns, nor attempt to pass the bridge. This information the general had already received from the other parties repeatedly, and of course was merely amusing his men and spending time by this conduct.

Colonel M'Arthur left his men at the Petit Cote settlement, and went with adjutant Puthuff and a few riflemen to the top of the ridge to reconnoitre. He found the plank had been torn off the bridge, and that a battery had been erected at the south end of it, near which there were about 60 regulars, 150 Canadian militia, 25 dragoons and 50 Indians. Some firing occurred between the riflemen and the Indians, some of whom came over the bridge; and as the colonel rode down to view the Queen Charlotte, he was fired on by a gun boat which accompanied her, and which had approached him unperceived, under the bank of the river. They now all retreated uninjured to the main detachment: but the colonel not yet being satisfied, returned to the ridge again with a few others, to make further observations. They were there fired on again by some Indians who in the mean time had concealed themselves in the brushwood. The whole detachment immediately came up to their relief, and drove the Indians back over the bridge: but as they retired *Tecumseh* followed them

with a considerable force, when a halt was called and
another skirmish ensued. Ammunition becoming scarce,
the colonel sent an express to camp to inform the general
of all the circumstances; and at the same time concluded to return to camp with the detachment. When
the express arrived, col. Cass pushed down with 150
men, and a six pounder, to reinforce M'Arthur. About
sun set they met at Turkey creek bridge, nine miles
from camp; and immediately returned to the Petit Cote
settlement where they encamped for the night. Next
morning on reconnoitring the enemy, he was found to
be considerably reinforced both in men and artillery.
At the desire of col. Cass, the whole detachment marched down near the bridge, and with the six pounder
exchanged a few shot with the battery. The whole
detachment then marched back to camp, hungry and
fatigued, without having effected any thing valuable.

Tecumseh who was very conspicuous among the
Indians for his influence, and for his bravery and skill
in Indian warfare, was about this time said to be appointed a brigadier general by the British.

The whole army now began to lose all confidence in
gen. Hull. His sending detachments to contend for
the bridge; and when it was taken, his failing to hold
it, or to march immediately to Malden; and afterwards
sending party after party to reconnoitre and skirmish;
were strong, irresistible proofs of incapacity or of
treachery; which must have convinced even the British
themselves, that he either did not intend to attack their
fort, or that he had neither courage nor skill to execute
such an enterprise. The distrust of the army was still
more confirmed, by his leaving them and going over
to Detroit on the 21st July, where he remained till the
26th under a variety of frivolous pretexts. While he
was thus wasting his time and resources, the government entertained the most favorable opinion of his
firmness and ability. His proclamation was read
throughout the union, and highly applauded as the pro-

duction of superior talents; and great expectations were formed by an admiring and sanguine people. A peace of nearly thirty years duration, under a popular, deliberative form of government, had accustomed the people to judge the abilities of public men, by the fine things they were able to say; and hence men the best qualified *to act,* were overlooked and neglected for those who were only qualified *to speak and write.*

The British forces at Malden were in the mean time daily augmented; and the greatest exertions were made night and day to strengthen that post by entrenchments and picketing.

By the absence of general Hull at Detroit, the command devolved on col. M'Arthur, who immediately dispatched capt. M'Cullough, with the rangers and spies, to examine whether a road could not be made, to cross the Kanards above the bridge, so as to avoid the battery, and the guns of the Queen Charlotte. The captain reported, that a road for the artillery was impracticable, on account of swamps and morasses.

It being reported, that the Indians came above the Aux Kanards in considerable numbers, col. M'Arthur sent major Denny with three companies of militia, making 117 men, to oppose them. He marched on the night of the 24th with instructions to form an ambuscade at some place where the Indians were expected to pass, and thus cut them off, unless they were too powerful; in which case he was to be situated so as to have a retreat in his power. He formed an ambuscade next morning in the Petit Cote settlement, and caught a Frenchman, with his three sons, who said he was going to reap his harvest. He proved to be the captain of a company of militia, then in service at Malden, from which place he had been sent out as a spy. Major Denny then marched his party in view of the enemy; and having again retired, and stopped about noon to rest in the shade, a small party of Indians came along very near his men. Having discoved them, he ordered his men to charge and fire well; which they executed so as to kill many of the Indians. The remainder were pursued by some of the men, about half a mile, before they returned. The fugitives meeting with a strong reinforcement, returned also to renew the contest. Major Denny endeavoured to gain an advantageous position in a point of woods, but was anticipated by the Indians; and after a short conflict, a part of his line gave way, and he was obliged to retreat in confusion. He was pursued about two miles and a half by the Indians, till they had reached near Turkey creek bridge. The major endeavored in vain to rally his men before they crossed the bridge and met general Lucas with a reinforcement. He lost but six killed, and two wounded: the loss of the British and Indians was at least double that number.

Reports of an unfavorable nature, respecting the conduct of major Denny in this affair, being circulated in the camp, he requested a court of inquiry, which was granted by colonel M'Arthur. After full investigation he was honorably acquitted; and the sentence of the court was approved by general Hull.

On the 28th July, intelligence was received in camp, that fort Macinaw had surrendered on the 17th. This event arrested all the offensive operations of gen. Hull in Upper Canada, nothing more being done by the army after this date, except the building of an inconsiderable fort, in a disadvantageous place about half a mile below camp, round the house of Mr. Gowies. The surrender of Macinaw alarmed general Hull excessively. He declared " The whole northern hordes of Indians will be let loose upon us." His anticipations no doubt were just: the loss of that fort must have injured our cause very much among the savages; and it is to be recorded with regret, that the government itself neglected a post so important, in not ordering more men for its defence; while the officer immediately in command was perhaps in some degree

culpable, in not placing it in the most defensible condition; and gen. Hull still more so, in neglecting to
apprize him of the declaration of war. The general
government were certainly well acquainted with the
situation and importance of the place. The legislature of Kentucky had particularly called the attention
of the war department to this point. In its neglected
state, with only a lieutenant to defend it, the enemy
found it an easy conquest. The following is the report of lieut. P. Hanks, who was its commander,
to gen. Hull, after his arrival at Detroit, 4th August.

"SIR—I take the earliest opportunity to acquaint
your excellency, with the surrender of the garrison of
Macinaw, under my command, to his Britannic Majesty's forces, under the command of captain Roberts,
on the 17th July, the particulars of which are as follows: on the 16th I was informed by the Indian interpreter, that he had discovered from an Indian, that
the several nations of Indians, then at St. Josephs,
(a British garrison distant about 40 miles) intended to
make an immediate attack on Macinaw. I was inclined from the coolness I had discovered in some of
the principal chiefs of the Ottawa and Chippewa nations, who had but a few days before professed the
greatest friendship for the United States, to place confidence in this report. I immediately called a meeting
of the American gentlemen at that time on the Island,
in which it was thought proper to dispatch a confidential person to St. Josephs, to watch the motions of the
Indians. Capt. Daurman of the militia was thought
the most suitable person for this service. He embarked about sunset, and met the British forces within ten
or 15 miles of the Island, by whom he was made a
prisoner, and put on his parole of honor. He was
landed on the Island at day break, with positive instructions to give me no intelligence whatever. He was
also instructed to take the inhabitants of the village

indiscriminately to a place on the west side of the Island, where their persons and property would be protected by a British guard : but should they go to the fort, they would be subject to a general massacre by the savages, which would be inevitable if the garrison fired a gun. This information I received from Dr. Day, who was passing through the village, when every person was flying for refuge to the enemy. Immediately on being informed of the approach of the enemy, I placed ammunition &c. in the block houses, and made every preparation for action. About nine o'clock, I could discover that the enemy were in possession of the heights that commanded the fort, with one piece of artillery directed to the most defenceless part of the garrison. The Indians were to be seen at this time in great numbers in the edge of the woods. At half past 11, the enemy sent in a flag of truce, demanding the surrender of the fort and Island to his Britannic Majesty's forces. This sir, was the first intimation I had of the declaration of war. I however had anticipated it, and was as well prepared to meet such an event, as I possibly could have been with the force under my command, amounting to 57 effective men, including officers. The American gentlemen who were prisoners were permitted to accompany the flag : from them I ascertained the strength of the enemy to be from 900 to 1000 men, consisting of regular troops, Canadians and savages; that they had two pieces of artillery, and were provided with ladders and ropes for the purpose of scaling the works if necessary. After I had obtained this information, I consulted my officers, and also the American gentlemen present; the result of which was, that it was impossible for the garrison to hold out against such superior force. In this opinion I fully concurred, from a conviction that it was the only measure that could prevent a general massacre. The fort and garrison were accordingly surrendered."

The report concludes with requesting a court of inquiry. By the articles of capitulation the garrison was to march out with the honors of war, and to be paroled and conveyed to the United States : private property was to be held sacred : and all citizens, who would not take the oath of allegiance to the British government, were to depart within a month. The army to which lieut. Hanks surrendered, was ascertained after the capitulation, to consist of 46 regulars, 260 Canadian militia, and 715 Indians, making an army of more than a thousand men.

Early in August, an express arrived at the army of gen. Hull, with information that capt. Henry Brush, with a company of volunteers, was near the river Raisin with provisions for the army ; and that he wanted an escort, as it was ascertained that the British and Indians had crossed from Malden to Brownstown, which is opposite on the American side, with a view to intercept the mail and convoys of provisions. The colonels of the Ohio militia applied to gen. Hull for leave to take a detachment, and open the communication with capt. Brush, and conduct the provisions in safety to Detroit : but the general would not grant their request, and seemed indifferent about the fate of capt. Brush and his provisions. At length however he consented, that major Vanhorne might go as an escort to the mail and join capt. Brush at the river Raisin. The major crossed the Detroit river on the 4th August, and marched that evening as far as the river De Corce. Here they lay on their arms in the bushes till morning, when they marched again, with 4 spies before them. Having passed the Maguaga village, capt. M'Cullough of the spies unfortunately missed his way. and as he was passing round a cornfield was fired on by 10 or 12 Indians, who were lying in ambush. He fell, and was tomahawked and scalped by the savages. His loss was severely felt by the army, for he was brave, intrepid and skilful in the department of spies.   K

Soon after this occurrence, a number of mounted militia, and some gentlemen who wished to go to the river Raisin, joined the detachment: and a Frenchman informed major Vanhorne, that three or four hundred Indians and some British were lying in ambush near Brownstown, for the purpose of intercepting his party. Accustomed to hear false reports from the French he did not sufficiently respect this information; but marched on with his front guard of 24 men divided into two columns, each preceded by three dragoons, and the main party in the same order, the mail with an escort of horsemen being placed in the centre. Where the ground would permit, the columns marched a hundred yards apart. Having arrived near Brownstown, the road passes through a narrow prairie, skirted by thick woods, with the creek, which runs by Brownstown, on the right. The woods on the creek come to a point towards the town, through which point the road passes to the ford. On the left are several small Indian cornfields, and thickets of thorn bushes; so that the columns of the party had to approach near each other at the creek. As they entered the open ground of the town, the Indians commenced a heavy fire on the right column from the opposite side of the creek, and on the left from the bushes on that side. The suddenness of the attack threw the troops into some confusion: and the major, apprehensive that he would be surrounded, immediately ordered a retreat. The detachment was halted several times, and fired on the enemy who pursued them some distance. The retreat was continued to the river De Corce—seventeen killed and several wounded being left behind. Among the killed were captains Ulry, Gilchrist, Boersler, lieut. Pents, and ensign Rubey. The loss of so many officers was caused by their attempting to rally their men. The loss of the enemy was nearly as great as ours.

On this occasion the force of the enemy was greatly exaggerated, as it was in many other instances. Major Vanhorne, though a gentleman and a soldier, was certainly not entitled to the praise bestowed upon him by some of his countrymen. Being warned of his danger, he should have taken care to prevent a surprise; and had he done so, he would doubtless have been victorious. The enemy had a great advantage in the ground; but in point of numbers he was not superior. I do not wish to detract from the real merits of maj. Vanhorne; but at Detroit in October 1813, I was informed by an American gentleman of high standing, who had made particular enquiry, that the force of the enemy in this case did not exceed forty British and seventy Indians : and this statement is corroborated by the recollection, that the main army was still in Canada, and the British being in daily expectation of an attack on Malden, would not send a large detachment to the American side. The practice, so common among the officers in Hull's army, of estimating extravagantly the numbers of British and Indians opposed to them in skirmishes, was calculated to have an injurious effect on our affairs. It had a tendency to discourage their men, to cover their own mismanagement, and to alarm the general, whose susceptibility of fear, did not require any extraordinary impressions.

On the 6th the colonels again solicited leave from the general, to march a detachment of 500 men to Brownstown, for the purpose of burying the dead and attempting again to open a communication with capt. Brush, who had arrived at the river Raisin with the provisions. The general would not permit more than 100 men to go, which was entirely too few, considering the late defeat and the prevailing opinion of the enemy's numbers. The project was therefore abandoned for the want of men.

A council being convened at head quarters, consisting of the field officers, with capt. Dyson and lieut. Eastman of the artillery, it was agreed by all except the two last, to make an immediate attack upon Malden. In consequence of this decision the following general order was issued :

'*Sandwich, August 7, 1812.*

' Doctor Edwards will take charge of the medical and surgical departments until farther orders, and will immediately make every preparation to take the field against the enemy. All the tents and baggage not necessary will be immediately sent to Detroit. The boats not necessary for the movement of the army will be sent to Detroit. An officer and 25 convalescents will be left at the fort at Gowies, with a boat sufficient to carry them across the river if necessary. All the artillery not taken by the army will be sent immediately to Detroit. The army will take seven days provision. Three days provisions will be drawn to-morrow morning and will be cooked ; the residue will be taken in wagons. Pork will be drawn for the meat part of the ration. One hundred axes, fifty spades, and twenty pick-axes will be taken for the army ; and a raft of timber and plank suitable for bridges, will be prepared and floated down with the batteries. Only one days whiskey will be drawn each day, and twelve barrels will be taken in wagons. All the artificers, and all men on any kind of extra duty, will immediately join their regiments.

(Signed) ' WM. HULL, *Brig. Gen. Com.*'

On the receipt of this order, the army in the hope of making an immediate attack upon Malden, were animated with new life and activity. Every preparation was industriously made, and every countenance was bright with joy. But how shall I name with deliberation the order which followed! The whole army was immediately ordered, to recross to Detroit and encamp in the rear of the fort, and thus relinquish all offensive operations in Canada! With what deep contempt was this order heard! with what sullen murmuring was it executed! A few weeks before, the army had landed triumphantly in the enemy's country ; and now without any ostensible cause, was ordered to return in the most disgraceful manner. What feelings of indignation filled every true American bosom; and what anguish was felt by a number of the poor inhabitants, who confiding in gen. Hull's promises of protection, had made themselves obnoxious to the vengeance of their own government!

The whole army now recrossed the river in sullen procession and indignant contempt, and encamped once more behind fort Detroit. Major Denny was left in the stockade work at Gowies, with a hundred and thirty convalescents, and lieut. Anderson's corps of artillerists. He was ridiculously instructed " to hold possession of this part of Upper Canada, and afford all possible protection to the well disposed inhabitants." He was to defend the post to the last extremity against musquetry; but if overpowered by artillery he was authorized to retreat.

On the same day after the army had re-crossed, col. Miller, with majors Vanhorne and Morrison of the Ohio volunteers, was sent with a detachment to make another attempt to open the communication with capt. Brush at the river Raisin. The only account of their operations which has been published, is that by gen. Hull, which follows:

"The main body of the army having recrossed the river Detroit, on the night and morning of the 8th August, six hundred men were immediately detached under the command of lieut. col. Miller, to open the communication with the river Raisin and protect the provisions. This detachment consisted of the 4th U. S. regiment and two small detachments under the command of lieut. Stansbury and ensign M'Abe, of the 1st regiment: detachments from the Ohio and Michigan volunteers; a corps of artillerists with one six pounder and a howitzer under the command of lieut. Eastman; a part of capt. Smith's and Sloan's cavalry commanded by capt. Sloan of the Ohio volunteers.

Lieut. col. Miller marched from Detroit on the afternoon of the 8th August, and on the 9th in the afternoon about 4 o'clock, the front guard commanded by capt. Snelling of the 4th U. S. regiment, was fired on by an extensive line of British and Indians, about two miles below Maguaga village, where there had been a small opening on the bank of Detroit river, surrounded with thick brush and white oak timber, and about 14 miles from Detroit. At this time the main body was marching in two lines, and capt. Snelling maintained his position in a most gallant manner, under a very heavy fire, until the line was formed and advanced to the ground he occupied, when the whole except the rear guard was brought into action. The enemy were formed behind a temporary breast work of logs, with the Indians extending in a thick wood on their left. Lieutenant colonel Miller ordered his whole line to advance, and when within a small distance of the enemy, made a general fire upon them, and immediately followed it up with charged bayonets, when the whole British line and Indians commenced a retreat. They were pursued in a most vigorous manner about two miles, and the pursuit only discontinued on account of the fatigue of the men, the approach of evening, and the necessity of returning to take care of the wounded. The judicious arrangements made by lieutenant colonel Miller, and the gallant manner in which they were executed, justly entitles him to the highest honor. From the moment the line commenced the fire, it continually moved on, and the enemy maintained their position until forced at the point of the bayonet. The Indians on the left under the command of Tecumseh fought with great obstinacy, but were continually forced, and compelled to retreat. The victory was complete in every part of the line; but the success would have been more brilliant, had the cavalry charged the enemy on their retreat, when a most favorable opportunity presented. Although orders were given for that purpose, unfortunately they were not executed. Majors Vanhorne and Morrison were associated with colonel Miller as field officers in this command, and were highly distinguished by their exertions in forming the line, and the firm intrepid manner they led their respective commands to action."

At the commencement colonel Miller was thrown from his horse, and remained on foot through the rest of the battle: of course the most active part of the command devolved on majors Vanhorne and Morrison, who certainly deserve great credit for their conduct in this affair. The officers and men generally behaved very well, with the exception only of captain Sloan of the cavalry, and captain A. F. Hull. The 4th regiment lost ten killed and 32 wounded: The Ohio and Michigan militia, 8 killed and 28 wounded.

The British were commanded by major Muir of the 41st regiment. His force comprised about four hundred regulars and Canadian militia, with a large body of Indians under Tecumseh. Forty Indians were found dead on the field; fifteen regulars were killed and wounded, and 4 taken prisoners; the loss of the Canadian militia and volunteers, was never ascertained, but as they were in the hottest part of the action, it must have been great. Muir and Tecumseh were both wounded.

Colonel Miller sent an express to general Hull with information of his success, and a request for a supply of provisions. About ten o'clock at night, colonel M'Arthur was ordered, to take a hundred men from his regiment, and proceed down the river in boats, with 600 rations for colonel Miller's detachment, and to bring up the wounded to Detroit. Colonel M'Arthur immediately applied to David Baird the contractor, who was strongly suspected of being a British agent in disguise, but could not prevail on him to issue the rations before 2 o'clock in the morning. As soon

as he received them, he embarked in nine boats, and
arrived safe at colonel Miller's encampment two miles
above Brownstown.   He had to pass the Queen Charlotte and brig Hunter in the river, but in consequence
of a heavy rain they did not perceive him.   As soon
as he could deliver the provisions and place the wounded in his boats, he commenced his return in obedi-
en c to his orders; but having permitted as many of
his men as desired, to join colonel Miller, his boats
were so poorly manned that he had to row one himself, while it was steered by a wounded soldier.   He
had but just left the camp, which was not far below
the head of the Island between Malden and Brownstown, when signal guns were fired at the former place,
and answered by the Queen Charlotte and Hunter.
When the boats arrived near the head of the Island,
those vessels were seen sailing up, on the other side
of the river.   The men immediately put to shore, and
all who were able ran across a marsh into the woods,
leaving the wounded in the boats.   But the energy of
the colonel saved them from the enemy; he followed
his men to the woods, and with some difficulty prevailed on them to return to their duty.   Having a bar-
rel of whiskey on board, he invited them to fill their
canteens, while he told them the story of the Indian,
who stuck to his bottle of rum, while descending the
falls of Niagara.   They now proceeded up to a place,
where the woods were nigher to the river, and carried
out the wounded, the colonel encouraging the men by
his own exertions.   The brig Hunter in the mean
time had anchored above the head of the Island, to
prevent the boats from ascending the river.   An express was immediately sent to Detroit, to inform the
general of their situation, and for wagons to carry
up the wounded.   The colonel however, having fore-
seen the difficulties of the voyage, had previously requested colonel Godfrey and captains Sibby and
Knaggs of the Michigan militia, to meet him with

wagons. They had complied, and the express soon returned with the pleasing intelligence of their approach. The nearest they could come, was a quarter of a mile above the boats on the bank of the river; which rendered it necessary to re-embark the wounded and carry them up in boats. This was done under a constant, but wholly ineffectual fire from the brig Hunter, which lay opposite the wagons. Colonel Cass who was always ready for any service, met them with a detachment, and hastened down to secure the boats; but the enemy had taken them before he could arrive.

Colonel Miller had intended to march on for the river Raisin, as soon as he was supplied and relieved of the wounded; but he was prevented by indisposition; and an express was sent to general Hull with this information, and with a request for more provision. This was a critical moment in the enterprise. It is plain, that colonel Miller should have marched on, even if it had been necessary to carry him in a litter; for he was not more than 22 miles from captain Brush, who had 150 men, and plenty of provisions. If he had been too sick to proceed in any manner, one of the other colonels should have been sent in his place, without waiting for more supplies from Detroit. The detachment having beaten the enemy, could have reached the river Raisin with safety in a day, and without suffering much for provisions. When colonel Cass, several miles below the river De Corce, was informed of colonel Miller's situation, he addressed this laconic note to general Hull: "Sir, colonel Miller is sick, may I relieve him? L. CASS." No answer being given to this note, he returned to Detroit; and colonel Miller had called a council of his officers to deliberate on the course he should take, when an express arrived from the general with positive orders for the detachment to return to Detroit. Thus the favorable moment for opening the communication with

L

the river Raisin, was lost for the want of a little energy
and decision. The enterprise was made to miscarry,
after the principal difficulties to be apprehended, had
actually been surmounted. The general is the soul of
an army, and if he has not the requisite qualifications,
no matter what may be the talents of his officers—they
will do but little good. The responsibility of a military commander, like his power, is unlimited—there is
no legal excuse for his failures but impossibility.

From the manner in which our flags had been treated by the enemy, it was expected, that no more would
be sent; but to the surprise of the whole army, on the
12th a boat was seen descending with a white flag
from Detroit to Sandwich, where it was known that
general Brock had arrived with the 41st regiment.
Colonels M'Arthur, Cass, and Findley, with some
warmth and indignation, immediately repaired to head
quarters, and inquired of the general why a flag of
truce had been sent to Sandwich. The general denied having any knowledge of it; and the colonels then
expressed their determination to inquire into the affair,
and have the offender punished. The general seemed
to be somewhat disconcerted, and observed that he
would inquire of captain Hickman, his volunteer aid,
whether he had authorized any person to take a flag
to the enemy's camp. He went to the captain, and
after a few minutes returned and said, that captain
Hickman had conversed with captain Rough on the
subject, but did not wish him to consider himself permitted to take a flag, but that the captain had probably considered himself authorized. The colonels
then left their general in disgust, and extended their
inquiries no farther on the subject, but strongly suspected his fidelity to the country. He had for several days been an object of general contempt, having
frequently been intoxicated, and apparently lost to all
sense of honor, and even decency. He was sullen in
his deportment and wavering in his orders.

A conversation now took place, between the colonels of the Ohio Volunteers and general J. Taylor of Kentucky, respecting the abilities and fidelity of the general. They were unanimously of the opinion, that if he continued in the command of the army, it would be surrendered to the enemy. They came therefore to a determination to deprive him of the command, and solicited colonel Miller to assume it. He refused, but declared he would unite with them in giving it to M'Arthur. A faint hope remaining, that they might yet be relieved from the state of Ohio, the project was abandoned, and colonel Cass immediately addressed the following letter to the governor of Ohio:

'*Detroit, August* 12, 1812.

'DEAR SIR—From causes not fit to be put on paper, but which I trust I shall live to communicate to you, this army has been reduced to a critical and alarming situation. We have wholly left the Canadian shore, and have abandoned the miserable inhabitants, who depended on our will and our power to protect them, to their fate. Unfortunately the general and our principal officers could not view our situation and our prospects in the same light. That Malden might easily have been reduced, I have no doubt. That the army were in force and in spirits enough to have done it, no one doubts. But the precious opportunity has fled; and instead of looking back, we must now look forward. The letter from the secretary of war to you, a copy of which I have seen, authorizes you to preserve and keep open the communication from the state of Ohio to Detroit. It is all important that it should be kept open; our very existence depends upon it. Our supplies must come from our state. This country does not furnish them. In the existing state of things, nothing but a large force of 2,000 men at least, will effect the object. It is the unanimous wish of the army, that you should accompany them. Every exertion that can, must be made. If this reaches you safely by Murray, he will tell you more than I can or ought here to insert.

'I am &c. LEWIS CASS.'

This letter having been written and shewn to the other officers, they were induced from the appearance

of the British in the mean time at Sandwich, to add
the following endorsement:

'Since the other side of this letter was written, new circumstances have arisen. The British force is opposite, and our situation has nearly reached its crisis. Believe all the bearer
will tell you. Believe it, however it may astonish you! as
much as if told by one of us. Even a c * * * * is talked of by
the * * * * *! The bearer will supply the vacancy. On you
we depend.'

    Signed by—CASS, FINDLEY, M'ARTHUR,
       TAYLOR & E. BRUSH.

The intention was, if governor Meigs could arrive
in time to relieve them, to divest general Hull of the
command and confer it on the governor, who had the
confidence of the army.

Major Denny now evacuated the fortification at Gowies, having previously set fire to the works, which
unfortunately communicated to the house and burnt
it down.   On the 13th the British were seen marching
up from Sandwich to a place opposite fort Detroit,
within point blank shot of our batteries; yet the general would not suffer lieutenants Dalaby and Anderson to fire on them with our 24 pounders, and they
were permitted unmolested to erect their batteries opposite Detroit.

On the evening of the 14th a detachment of 300
men, was sent under the command of *two colonels*,
M'Arthur and Cass, to endeavor again by a circuitous
route to open the communication with the river Raisin.
Colonel M'Arthur remonstrated against sending them
without provisions; upon which the general promised
to send provisions after them on pack horses; but he
failed in the end to do it.   This detachment after
marching about 24 miles, having passed the rivers
Rouge and De Corce some distance, got into a marsh
and could go no farther without provisions. Being
still a great distance from the river Raisin, on account

of their circuitous route, a council of officers was held, which judged it expedient to return. But in the mean time affairs at Detroit had been brought to a crisis.

On the morning of the 15th general Hull pitched his markee in the centre of the camp with red and blue stripes painted on its top. This was the first time he had erected a tent in camp since the 4th of July. It was remarked with astonishment by every person; and about one o'clock two British officers arrived from Sandwich with a flag of truce, and a letter from general Brock demanding the surrender of fort Detroit to His Britannic Majesty's forces. The following is a copy:

'*H. Q. Sandwich, August 15th, 1812.*

'Sir—The force at my disposal authorizes me to require of you the surrender of fort Detroit. It is far from my inclination to join in a war of extermination; but you must be aware, that the numerous body of Indians, who have attached themselves to my troops, will be beyond my control the moment the contest commences. You will find me disposed to enter into such conditions as will satisfy the most scrupulous sense of honor. Lieutenant colonel M'Donnell, and major Glegg are fully authorized to conclude any arrangement that may prevent the unnecessary effusion of blood.

'I have the honor to be. your most obedient servant,
'ISAAC BROCK, *Maj. Gen.*'
'His excellency brigadier general Hull,
Commanding at Detroit.'

The British were at this time engaged in pulling down a house opposite Detroit, behind which they had erected a battery: and lieutenants Dalaby and Anderson were busily engaged in completing a battery on our side. When the troops were informed, that the British had demanded a surrender of the fort, they laughed at the idea and seemed to be inspired with new vigor. The general himself seemed to be actuated by contending passions. At one moment he seemed to be determined to make an obstinate defence, and save his army from disgrace and his Territory from invasion; then again he would discover symptoms of the greatest fear and pusillanimity. His conversation with his officers was of the most dispiriting nature, exaggerating the force of the enemy &c. The absence of colonels M'Arthur and Cass was deeply deplored by the army, and was a cause of increasing the suspicions against the general. The threat of the British commander, to let loose the Indians to massacre and exterminate the people, excited the most indignant contempt towards a nation, which pretending to be civilized, could associate with savages in a war of the most horrible nature. General Hull after a considerable struggle in his own mind, which was observed in his countenance by the British officers, at last returned the following reply to the demand they had brought:

'H. Q. Detroit, August 15, 1812.

'Sir—I have received your letter of this date. I have no other reply to make, than to inform you that I am ready to meet any force which may be at your disposal, and any consequences which may result from its execution in any way you may think proper to use it.

'I avail myself of this opportunity to inform you, that the flag of truce, under the direction of captain Brown, proceeded contrary to the orders, and without the consent of colonel Cass, who commanded the troops who attacked your picket near the river Kanard bridge. I likewise take this occasion to inform you, that Gowies' house was set on fire contrary to my orders; and it did not take place, till after the evacuation of the fort. From the best information I have been able to obtain on the subject, it was set on fire by some of the inhabitants on the other side of the river.

'I am very respectfully your excellency's
most obedient servant,
Wm. HULL, Brig. Gen.
Commanding N. W. Army
of the United States.'

'His excellency, major general Brock,
Commanding His Britannic Majesty's
forces in Upper Canada.'

This letter being written and delivered to the British officers, general Hull immediately retired into the fort with every appearance of alarm; and no sooner had they landed in Sandwich, than the British armed vessels appeared in sight, and the battery on the opposite shore began to play upon the fort. The fire was returned from our batteries and the fort, and one of the enemy's guns was silenced in a few minutes. As soon as the firing commenced, all the troops, except colonel Findley's regiment, were crowded into the fort and posts assigned to as many as could be employed. Colonel Findley was stationed three hundred yards from the fort on the northwest.

Previous to the opening of the batteries, brigade major Jessup and quarter master Dugan, rode down the river to Springwells to view the enemy at Sandwich; and from the position of the Queen Charlotte, they concluded, that the enemy intended to effect a landing at that place. Having ascertained a position for a battery, which would be secure from the fire of her guns, the major returned to Head Quarters, and requested that a 24 pounder might be sent down to sink that vessel. The general told him, that he had consulted his artillery officers, and they were of opinion, that a bridge over which it must pass, was not strong enough to bear the weight of a 24 pounder. The major informed him, that there was plenty of timber near it, to make it stronger; to which remark the general made no reply. Major Jessup then returned to the Springwells, where he found captain Snelling with a few men and a brass 6 pounder. Observing that the principal part of the British forces were at Sandwich, he returned again to general Hull and requested permission to cross the river with 150 men, and spike the enemy's cannon on the battery opposite Detroit. The general said he could not spare that number. He then asked for one hundred, in which he was joined by captain Snelling. The general replied "I will think of it." The enemy still kept up a constant fire from the battery; from which they did not desist until 10 o'clock at night: and at day light next morning the 16th, they commenced again; but their fire had very little effect. Our batteries returned it with promptitude till near 11 o'clock, having in the mean time silenced two of their guns.

The British had by this time effected a landing at Springwells with their whole force, consisting of about thirty royal artillerists, 300 regulars, 400 militia, and about 600 Indians, with three 6, and two 3 pounders. They advanced towards the fort without any opposition, the militia and regulars being on the margin of the river, and the Indians next the woods on the west of the town. When they had arrived within three quarters of a mile from the fort, two 24 pounders, loaded with grape shot, were levelled at them under the direction of captain Forsythe and lieutenant Anderson; but just as the artillerists were applying the matches, captain Dyson the senior officer of the artillery, came up and drew his sword, and swore that the first man who attempted to fire on the enemy should be cut to pieces.

General Hull had taken refuge on the east side of the fort under the wall, where he was sure the balls of the enemy could not hit him—yet he seemed to be stupified and nearly torpid with fear. A ball from the British battery, which now kept up a constant fire, struck in the fort and killed captain Hanks, lieutenant Sibley, Dr. Reynolds, and wounded Dr. Blood. Another passed through the gate, and killed two soldiers in the barracks. Two men were also killed on the outside. The general had crowded so many men into the fort, together with the women and children, who had come there for protection, that it was almost impossible for a ball to strike in the fort, without killing some person. Very little injury however was experienced from the shells of the enemy: though well directed, they generally burst too soon.

Under these circumstances, which excited in the general the most terrible apprehensions, an officer of the Michigan militia came into the fort and inquired, whether general Hull expected colonel Brush to defend the city with two or three hundred men? He stated that the British forces were at the tanyard below the town : upon which information general Hull stept into a room in the barracks, and returning in a few minutes, handed a note to his son, who immediately hoisted a white flag on a pike staff, and inquired whether he should say any thing in addition to the note—being answered in the negative, he went out and proceeded to meet general Brock. When he returned from the enemy, he was accompanied by colonel M'Donnell and major Glegg. It was now evident to every person, that the general had tendered a capitulation ; and white flags in the mean time being hoisted on the walls in different places, the firing from the British batteries was discontinued. General Hull now called upon general Taylor of Kentucky, major Jessup, and several others, to assist in drawing up the articles of capitulation ; but they all indignantly refused their assistance. However the business was soon arranged between the general and the British officers ; who then immediately returned to the tanyard, where the British forces had halted. Our troops in the mean time were ordered to stack their arms ; colonel Findley with his regiment being ordered into the fort for the same purpose. It is impossible to describe the indignation which was felt and expressed by the officers on this occasion. The men very generally shed tears, and the common expression as they indignantly dashed down their arms, often breaking them to pieces, was " *damn such a general.*"

The Indians soon began their devastations by killing the cattle and sheep in the commons. About 12 o'clock the British forces, with general Brock at their head marched into the fort : the Americans were marched out, and put into an adjoining garden : the American flag was pulled down, and the British hoisted in its place. The firing of their cannon, with the yelling of the savages, and the discharging of their guns in the air, closed the scene and proclaimed their joy at their success. The following are the articles of capitulation :

' *Camp at Detroit, August* 16, 1812.

' Capitulation for the surrender of fort Detroit, entered into between major general Brock commanding his Britannic majesty's forces on the one part, and brigadier general Hull commanding the northwestern army of the United States, on the other part :

' 1. Fort Detroit with all the troops regulars as well as militia, will be immediately surrendered to the British forces under the command of major general Brock, and will be considered prisoners of war, with the exception of such of the militia of the Michigan Territory as have not joined the army.

' 2. All public stores, arms, and all public documents, including every thing else of a public nature, will be immediately given up.

' 3. Private persons and property of every description will be respected.

' 4. His excellency brigadier general Hull having expressed a desire, that a detachment from the state of Ohio, on its way to join the army, as well as one sent from Detroit under the command of colonel M'Arthur, shall be included in the above capitulation, it is accordingly agreed to : it is however to be understood, that such part of the Ohio militia as have not joined the army will be permitted to return to their homes, on condition that they will not serve during the war. Their arms however will be delivered up, if belonging to the public.

' 5. The garrison will march out at the hour of 12 o'clock this day, and the British forces will take immediate possession of the fort.

' J. M'Donnell, lt. col. mil. p. a. d c.

' J. B. Glegg, maj. a. d o.

' J. Miller, lt. col. 4th regt. u. s. inft.

' E. Brush, col. 1st regt. Mich. mil.

' Approved,

' Wm. Hull. Brig. Gen. Com. N. W. Army.

' Isaac Brock, Maj. Gen.'

To these articles, two additional ones were added, to which general Brock says "certain considerations induced him to agree." They were not known to the troops at the time.

'*Detroit, 16th August, 1812.*

' It is agreed, that the officers and soldiers of the Ohio militia, shall be permitted to proceed to their respective homes, on this condition, that they are not to serve during the present war, unless they are exchanged.

'WM. HULL, Brig. Gen.
'ISAAC BROCK, Maj. Gen.'

The other additional article places the Michigan militia and volunteers under major Wetherell on the same principles with the Ohio militia.

Colonel M'Arthur with his detachment, being ignorant of these transactions, was hastening back, with all possible dispatch; having had no provisions except a few green pumpkins and potatoes from Friday morning till Sunday evening, when he arrived within a mile of the fort, he was informed of its surrender, and immediately ordered his men back to the river Rouge. There he found an ox, which being killed and divided among his men was eaten half raw. After some consultation with his officers, he sent captain Mansfield with a flag of truce to the fort. On his way he was robbed of his horse and his arms by the Indians, and in the evening returned to the detachment, in company with majors Dixon and Givens of the British army. Captain Elliott arrived about the same time and handed colonel M'Arthur the articles of capitulation. The colonel struck his sword in the ground and broke it to pieces, while tears of indignation stood in his eyes. The detachment then marched to the fort, and stacked their arms in the citadel. Colonels M'Arthur and Cass both remonstrated against surrendering rifles, which were private property, but without success. They then observed, that they had already surrendered the muskets, or they would *contend* for the rifles.

While the troops were stationed in the ordnance yard, the British guard pulled off their knapsacks, and took their knives from their scabbards; the Indians at the same time being employed in robbing the citizens of their property and taking the horses from the dragoons.

Several pieces of brass cannon, which had been surrendered on the 16th August, '76, by colonel Baum to the American general Stark, were viewed with the greatest pleasure by the British officers, some of whom saluted them with kisses.

The troops who had surrendered in the fort, were escorted by the British guards to their vessels, which were lying in the river, and being stowed aboard, they were floated down to Springwells. The Michigan militia were liberated. Colonel M'Arthur's detachment was embarked next morning; and they all descended the river, the 4th regiment being destined for Quebec, and the militia for the state of Ohio, in which they were landed at different places on the shores of Lake Erie. They returned home dejected and spiritless, the issue of the campaign having proved so very different from the anticipations with which they commenced it. General Hull being landed from Lake Erie, made the best of his way to Massachusetts, his former place of residence, consigned to eternal infamy, with the curses of his country lowering over his head.

To prove, that the fort was not surrendered for the want of ammunition and provisions, it is only necessary to state the facts, on the authority of private and official information. For the 24 pounders, there were six hundred rounds of fixed ammunition, prepared for use, of which two hundred were grape shot; the same quantity was ready for the six pounders, and two hundred rounds for the four pounders. The number of shells was very considerable. For the muskets 75

thousand cartridges were made up, besides 24 rounds
a piece in each man's box. In the magazine there
were sixty barrels of powder, and 150 tons of lead.
In the contractor's store there was at least 25 days
provision, and in the Territory a considerable quantity of wheat, and a sufficiency of windmills to grind
it.   To this stock might have been added captain
Brush's escort of 150 horse loads of flour, and 300
beeves at the river Raisin. The whole would have
enabled the fort to stand a siege, if the enemy had
been strong enough to besiege it, until the governor of
Ohio could have relieved them. But cowardice had
conspired with fate to produce a different result.

There were nearly *two thousand four hundred* stand
of arms surrendered to the enemy, besides those in
the arsenal; and the following is the British official
return of the ordnance :

Iron,		*Brass,*	
9	24 pounders,	3	6 pounders,
5	9 ditto,	4	2 ditto,
3	6 ditto,	3	1 ditto,
		1	8 inch howitzer
		1	5½ do. do.

17 iron pieces.   12 brass pieces.
12 brass pieces.

29 total.

From this account of the arms surrendered; from
the preceding statement of the British force; and from
the description of troops which composed each army;
it is abundantly evident, that the American force under
general Hull, was at least doubly as efficient as that
to which he surrendered: and in addition to this
great superiority of force, he had the advantage of a
strong fortress which might have been defended against
numbers vastly superior.

If general Hull had made a bold and vigorous attack upon Malden, when he first crossed into Canada,

though he had even then lost much precious time, there cannot be a doubt, but that the fort would have surrendered without much loss on our part, and all the British forces in that quarter would have fallen into our hands. But it is doubtful whether the British, having the command of the Lake, would not have soon compelled him to abandon it. Fortifications might have been erected on the Island of Bois Blanc opposite Malden, which would have commanded the river Detroit still more effectually : but it would have been very expensive to maintain an army there, sufficient with these advantages only, to hold the country against the command of the Lake, the importance of which had been duly appreciated by the British government. The fall of Malden however, would doubtless have awed the savages, into a temporary neutrality at least, which would have greatly relieved our frontier settlements.

The administration of the general government exhibited great want of foresight, in sending general Hull into Canada, without having taken the necessary measures to obtain the command of Lake Erie : and unless it had been determined to hold Upper Canada, during the war at least, and thus to cut off all communication between the British and Indians, the invasion of that territory was wholly unnecessary and improper. Although the foregoing account of the operations of general Hull, clearly proves *his* incapacity to conduct any species of warfare, yet we ought not to conceal the errors of others in relation to the affairs he had to manage. It is a fact that general Hull, while governor of Michigan, previous to his being appointed a brigadier in the army, and as early as the 6th of March 1812, in a memorial which he laid before the war department, did suggest the propriety of having a superior naval force on lake Erie, as an auxiliary in the reduction of Upper Canada, without which it would be impossible to effect that object ; and he

pointed out the various difficulties which must attend
a different course. In another communication on the
11th of April, after he had received his appointment
in the army, he recommended in strong and explicit
terms, the erection of a navy on the lakes. The United States had then but one old transport vessel on
lake Erie, which was repairing, and was not even
launched for a month after the declaration of war.
He represented to the government, that unless the
northwestern army was strengthened by addition to its
numbers, and followed by detachments to keep open
the communication, and ensure supplies from the state
of Ohio; and without the aid of a superior naval force
on lake Erie; it would be impossible for that army to
carry on offensive operations in Upper Canada, or
even to maintain its position at Detroit. But the war
department disregarded these suggestions, and expected general Hull to get command of the lakes, with the
forces placed at his disposal. Nothing could be more
chimerical, unless general Dearborn had been ready
to co-operate with a powerful army on the Niagara
strait. By the capture of Malden with all the British
forces in that quarter; and by an efficient invasion at
the same time from Niagara so as to cut off the communication of the British with lake Erie and the upper country; the objects of the government might
have been effected, without the expense of a navy on
lake Erie. But general Dearborn was not even ready to make an *attempt* at invasion, before the unfortunate affair at Queenstown on the 12th of October.
While Hull was invading Upper Canada, he was lying at his ease at Greenbush; and on the 9th of August he concluded an armistice with the governor general of the Canadas, which was not to extend above
fort Erie on the Niagara. This measure was proposed by governor Prevost, in consequence of intelligence
that the orders in council were repealed. By excluding general Hull from the benefit of this arrangement,

his opponent general Brock would have been able in a short time to bring all the British forces against him. This forms no excuse however for the surrender of Detroit, for the armistice below was unknown to general Hull, till he was informed of it after the capitulation by general Brock. In this instance general Dearborn acted very imprudently, in suffering himself to be lulled by an armistice, which was disapproved by the President, when it was his duty to co-operate with the northwestern army, by *threatening* an invasion at least, which would prevent general Brock from pressing with all his force against Hull. Thus in the catalogue of our early failures, we discover many blunders and causes of miscarriage, besides those for which the commander of the northwestern army has to answer.

No sooner was general Brock in full possession of Detroit, than he issued the following proclamation :

' Whereas the Territory of Michigan was this day ceded by capitulation to the arms of his Britannic Majesty, without any other condition than the protection of private property ; and wishing to give an early proof of the moderation and justice of the government, I do hereby announce to all the inhabitants of the said Territory, that the laws heretofore in existence shall continue in force, until his majesty's pleasure be known, or so long as the peace and safety of the said Territory will admit thereof. And I do hereby also declare and make known to the inhabitants, that they shall be protected in the full exercise and enjoyment of their *religion,* of which all persons both civil and military will take notice, and govern themselves accordingly. All persons having in their possession, or having any knowledge of any public property, shall forthwith deliver in the same. Officers of the militia will be held responsible, that all arms in the possession of the militiamen, be immediately delivered up ; and all individuals whatever, who have in their possession arms of any kind, will deliver them up without delay. Given under my hand at Detroit, 16th of August, 1812, and in the 52d year of his majesty's reign. ' ISAAC BROCK, G. C.'

This proclamation was executed in a few days, by the delivery or seizure of all the arms in the hands of the citizens, whether public or private property. Having garrisoned Detroit with 250 men, the general left it under the command of colonel Proctor, and retired to Malden, where he learnt, that the President of the United States had disapproved the armistice negotiated with general Dearborn, and that preparations would be made to invade Canada on the Niagara strait. The greater part of his troops were in consequence sent down to forts George and Erie, to which places he soon followed them, having previously planned an expedition to be conducted by major Muir against fort Wayne.

In concluding my account of this disastrous campaign, it may not be amiss to state the final result in relation to general Hull. He requested an investigation of his conduct; and a court martial was ordered by the executive of the United States, of which general Dearborn was president. This court met on the 3rd of January 1814, in the city of Albany, New-York, before which general Hull appeared, and was charged with two crimes, 1st, Treason, 2nd, Cowardice. He plead *not guilty*. The court after a patient and impartial investigation finally pronounced their decision on the 26th March. They acquitted him on the charge of treason, as not properly coming before them; but found him guilty of cowardice, and sentenced him to be *shot to death:* at the same time they recommended him to the mercy of the President, on account of his age and his revolutionary services. The President approved the sentence on the 25th of April, and remitted its execution. On the same day the following general order was issued :

‘ *Washington City, April 25th,* 1814.

‘ ‘The rolls of the army are to be no longer disgraced by having upon them the name of brigadier general Wm. Hull. The general court martial, of which general Dearborn is president, is hereby dissolved.

By order, ‘ J. B. WALBACH, *Adjt. Gen.*’

N

CHAPTER III.

Proceedings at Chicago—organization and march of troops from Kentucky and Ohio—siege and relief of fort Wayne—mounted expeditions &c.

GENERAL HULL being warned by the fate of Macinaw, thought proper about the last of July, to send an express by way of fort Wayne to captain Heald, who commanded at fort Dearborn near the mouth of Chicago river, at the southwest extremity of lake Michigan, with orders to dismantle the fort, and deliver to the Indians in that neighborhood, all the public property in his possession, which he could not bring away. Captain Wells who lived at fort Wayne, volunteered his services, with the aid of about 50 Miami Indians, to bring away the garrison with the women and children. He set out from fort Wayne about the 3rd, and arrived at Chicago on the 12th of August. For several days a large number of Potawatamies, and Winebagoes had been encamped round the fort, but most of them professed to be friendly. Tecumseh and the British kept up a regular correspondence by runners with those Indians, who were waiting to hear the result of the contest about Malden before they would join either side.

On the 14th captain Heald distributed the public stores among the different tribes, with which they were much pleased. In the evening of the same day, Mr. Griffith who acted as an interpreter and trader at the fort, was informed by a chief whose name was Black Patridge, that "leaden birds had been singing in his ears," and that they ought to be careful on the march they were going to take. From this suggestion, it was evident that the Indians had been holding councils on the subject of commencing hostilities. Their number in the neighborhood of the fort now amounted to five or six hundred.

On the morning of the 15th at sunrise, the troops consisting of about 70 men, with some women and children. marched from the fort, with the pack horses in the centre, and captain Wells with his Indians in the rear. They had proceeded about a mile from the fort, when the front guard was fired on by the savages, who were posted behind a sandbank on the margin of the lake, and in a skirt of woods which the party was approaching, the rest of the country around them being an open prairie. At the same time they saw a body of Indians passing to their rear, to cut off their retreat to the fort. The firing now became general, and the troops seeing nothing but death and massacre before them, formed in line of battle, and returned the fire of the enemy with much bravery and success, as they slowly retreated into the prairie. The Indians made several desperate efforts to rush up and tomahawk them; but every charge was repulsed by the firmness of the troops, who fought with desperation, determined to sell their lives as dear as possible. Captain Wells being killed, his Indians retired from the party and joined the others. Several women and children were also killed; and our ranks were at last so reduced, as scarcely to exceed 20 effective men : yet they continued resolute, and stuck together, resolved to fight while one remained able to fire. But the Indians now withdrew some distance, and sent a small French boy to demand a surrender. The boy was captain Heald's interpreter, who had run off to the Indians at the commencement of the action. He advanced cautiously; and Mr. Griffith, who was afterwards a lieutenant in a company of spies, in colonel Johnson's regiment from Kentucky, advanced to meet him, intending to kill him for his perfidy. But the boy declared, that it was the only way he had to save his life, and appeared sorry that he had been obliged to act in that manner. He then made known his business : the Indians proposed to spare the lives of our men, provided they would surrender. The proposal being made known to the surviving soldiers, they unanimously determined to reject it. The boy returned with this answer to the Indians; but in a short time he came back, and entreated Mr. Griffith to use his influence with captain Heald, to make him surrender, as the Indians were very numerous. The captain, his lady, and Mr. Griffith were all wounded. He at last consented to surrender, and the troops having laid down their arms, the Indians advanced to receive them ; and notwithstanding their promises they now perfidiously tomahawked three or four of the men. One Indian with the fury of a demon in his countenance, advanced to Mrs. Heald with his tomahawk drawn. She had been accustomed to danger; and knowing the temper of the Indians, with great presence of mind, she looked him in the face, and smiling, said "surely you will not kill a squaw." His arm fell nerveless : the conciliating smile of an innocent female, appealing to the magnanimity of a warrior, reached the heart of the savage and subdued the barbarity of his soul. He immediately took the lady under his protection. She was the daughter of general Samuel Wells of Kentucky. The head of captain Wells was cut off; and his heart was cut out and eaten by the savages.

The Indians having divided their prisoners as usual in such cases, it was the fate of captain Heald, his lady and Mr. Griffith, to be taken by the Ottawas on the lake beyond the mouth of the river St. Joseph. Their wounds being severe, they looked upon destruction as inevitable ; but Heaven often smiles when we least expect it. Griffith had observed a canoe, which was large enough to carry them ; and they contrived to escape in it by night.   In this frail bark they traversed the lake 200 miles to Macinaw, where the British commander afforded them the means of returning to the United States.

The attack on the garrison of Chicago, was caused by intelligence received from Tecumseh.   On the night previous to the evacuation of the fort, a runner had arrived with information from Tecumseh, that major Vanhorne had been defeated at Brownstown, that the army under Hull had returned to Detroit, and that there was every prospect of success.   This intelligence decided the Indians in that quarter to join the British side, and they resolved to remain no longer inactive.

After reading the above narrative, which is a plain, unvarnished statement of facts, furnished by an eye witness, what must we think of the British government and its agents, who could thus instigate the sanguinary savage of the forest to deeds of ingratitude, perfidy, and murder?   How low must we estimate the civilization of those, who could court the alliance of these barbarians in war, at the same time knowing, encouraging, and proclaiming to the world, their ruthless mode of warfare, and paying them a graduated price for the scalps of men, women, and children?   I appeal to my countrymen and to the world to say, whether the vengeance of the American people ought not to be hurled alike against these fiends of the forest and their British associates and instigators?   And what kind of an American is he, let me ask, who can defend and justify the conduct of the British government, when all these transactions are known and well authenticated to him?

The various advantages now gained by the allies, including their capture of the whole army at Detroit, completely fixed nearly all the Indians in the British interest.   Very few remained friendly towards the United States; and those who did, were threatened with war and extermination.   Our old friend the Little Turtle had died in the summer, and most of his nation had joined the enemy.   The plans of Tecumseh appeared to be in a successful train of completion ; and the siege of forts Wayne and Harrison at the same moment, as the principal remaining obstacles, in the way of driving the white inhabitants over the Ohio river, were resolved on by his followers.   The Potawatamies and Ottawas were to be assisted in the siege of fort Wayne by the British under major Muir; while the Winebagoes and that part of the Miamies who had determined on hostility, were to take fort Harrison if possible by stratagem.   The first of September was as early as they could be ready for action; and about that time they agreed to make simultaneous attacks on those forts ; which they accordingly carried into execution.   But fortunately Tecumseh and the British were delayed at Malden till the 16th of September, before they could march to join the party at fort Wayne.

In the mean time the most active preparations were making in the states of Ohio and Kentucky to prosecute the war with renewed vigor.   The governor of Ohio, as soon as he had been informed of the dangerous situation of Hull's army, had immediately ordered the remaining portion of the detached militia of his state, amounting to 12 hundred men, to be embodied and marched to Urbanna under the command of brigadier general Tupper.   The secretary of war had also previously called on governor Scott of Kentucky, for 15 hundred men, including the regulars enlisted in that state, to reinforce the northwestern army.   Early in May the governor of Kentucky, in obedience to instructions from the war department, had organized ten regiments, amounting to five thousand five hundred men, as the quota of that state, under the act of congress for detaching one hundred thousand militia for the service of the United States.   All of these regiments had been filled by volunteering, the citizens of Kentucky having eagerly joined the standard of their country as soon as she called for men.

The regiments of volunteers, which had been organized on the north side of Kentucky river, under the command of colonels John M. Scott, Wm. Lewis and John Allen were ordered into service, under the requisition made by the war department. The 17th United States' regiment under colonel Samuel Wells, late general Wells of the militia, who had fought in the battle of Tippecanoe, was to march with this detachment. They were ordered to rendezvous at Georgetown, in Scott county, on the 15th of August, where brigadier general John Payne of Scott, was to receive the command. When the whole assembled, they amounted to more than 2,000 men, there having been a regiment of volunteers ordered to march, above the number required by the government. The patriotic zeal of the citizens of Kentucky was never more conspicuous than on this occasion. The ranks were filled with the most respectable citizens : the most promising young men in the country, the most intelligent, the most wealthy, had eagerly enrolled themselves for service. Many of the officers were men of the highest standing for talents and integrity. Colonel John Allen, who commanded a rifle regiment, was surpassed by none, in his qualifications as an attorney at the bar of Kentucky, and in his estimable qualities and virtues as a private citizen. Major Martin D. Hardin of the same regiment, the intimate friend of the colonel, stood also in the first ranks as a lawyer and a private citizen. He was shortly afterwards appointed secretary of state by governor Shelby, who succeeded governor Scott, in the latter part of this month. Major George Madison was auditor of public accounts, and was held in the highest estimation by his countrymen. He had fought and bled in St. Clair's defeat, and had served his country in many other expeditions against the Indians. Colonels Scott and Lewis were also experienced officers in Indian warfare, and highly esteemed as private citizens. John Simpson esq. a captain in the rifle regiment, had been speaker of the house of representatives in Kentucky, and was now elected a representative in congress. There was indeed no part of this corps of volunteers, in which citizens of the first respectability were not to be found— all ready to meet the hazards and privations of an arduous and perilous campaign, in defence of their country's rights. In noticing individuals in this place, I must not however pass by the reverend Samuel Shannon, who accompanied colonel Scott's regiment as chaplain. This venerable divine, in the early part of the revolution, had left Princeton college, where he was then a student, to enter as a lieutenant into the revolutionary army, in which he served, except when a prisoner, to the termination of the war. At an advanced age, he now stept forward again in defence of his country. He instructed the young soldier in his duties, and animated him by his own zeal, and by placing before him the former indignities of the British, and the many heroic achievements of the revolution. He was a plain old gentleman, but his piety, his patriotism, and his politics, were of the most genuine description.

Early on the 16th of August the troops were paraded and reviewed by governor Scott, whose appearance alone was sufficient to inspire them with sentiments of courage and patriotism. The remembrance of his revolutionary services, and his former campaigns against the Indians, together with the dignity of his appearance and his venerable age, spoke more to the feelings of these intelligent men, than the most eloquent language could have conveyed.

After ten o'clock they were paraded again, and addressed by the reverend James Blythe, Principal of the Transylvania University, in a short and appropriate sermon.   The honorable Henry Clay then addressed them with his usual eloquence, and painted in lively colours, the honor which belongs to the volunteer soldier, fighting to defend the rights of his injured country.   At the very moment, when general Hull was on this day capitulating in the most disgraceful manner in Detroit, Mr. Clay was in this address anticipating the fall of Malden and the conquest of Upper Canada.   How much at variance, the treacherous, dastardly deeds of the general, and the animating, patriotic anticipations of the orator!

On the 17th the troops were inspected by brigade major Garrard, an officer well versed in military tactics and discipline: and on the next day they drew two months pay in advance.   They had been induced to expect 16 dollars more in advance, in lieu of the clothing to which they were entitled; and some of them expressed dissatisfaction at not receiving it. Major Gano of colonel Scott's regiment paraded his battalion, and to try their patriotism proposed to his men, either to go without it, and trust to the justice of the government to furnish the clothing hereafter, or to return home.   Six men *volunteered* to return: they were furnished with an escort to guard them out of camp and through the town with appropriate music. This was a disgrace, which no man of any honor or feeling could have endured.   When arrived at home, some of them were treated with so much contempt by their wives, that they returned to the army and continued to discharge their duty.

While the troops lay at Georgetown, an appropriate address from the general was circulated in camp, and on the 19th they marched for Newport and Cincinnati. The weather was rainy and the roads were deep; but the men were in high spirits, expecting to join general Hull at Malden or Detroit, and acquire laurels in the conquest of Upper Canada.   On the 24th they reached Newport, where the unwelcome news of the sur-

O

render of Detroit and the Michigan territory was received. At first no person could believe the intelligence. It was so wholly unexpected, that the highest
evidence was required to confirm it. Such evidence
was soon afterwards received. The effect on the
minds of the men was very dispiriting : instead of
reaping laurels in Canada, it was now evident, they
would have to contend, with an inferior force, against
the progress of the allies in our own territory. But
their ardor and their spirits soon revived with the idea
and the resolution of acting a conspicuous part in the
front of danger. Having drawn arms and camp
equipage on the 25th and 26th, they crossed the Ohio
on the 27th to Cincinnati.

When the news of the surrender of Detroit, spread
through the states of Ohio and Kentucky, it created
an excitement and indignation as great as the catastro-
phe was unexpected. But one sentiment indeed pervaded the western country. Every citizen seemed animated with a desire to wipe off the disgrace, with
which our arms had been stained; and to avert the
desolation which menaced the frontiers of Ohio and
the western territories. It was well known, that most
of the savage tribes, who had not previously joined
the British standard, but were watching the course of
events, in order to determine what side it would be
best to take, would consider our reverses at Macinaw,
Detroit, and Chicago, as entitling the British arms to
a decided preference, and that they would immediately commence their depredations on the frontiers which
were exposed at every point.

In the mean time the balance of the detached militia in Kentucky had been ordered into service. Governor Harrison who had fought the battle of Tippecanoe, had been authorized to take command of all
the troops of the Indiana and Illinois Territories, and
carry on the war in that quarter against the Indians;
and had also been empowered by the war department,

to call on the governor of Kentucky, for any portion
of the contingent of that state which was not in service. Under this authority he had repaired to Kentucky, and called for the balance of her troops after
the above regiments had been selected for the northwestern army, intending to carry an expedition against
the hostile tribes on the Illinois river. He was at
Frankfort making arrangements for their march, when
the intelligence was received that the army under Hull
was in a critical situation.

A few days before the actual attack on Detroit by
general Brock, an express had been sent by general
Hull, to hasten the reinforcement which had been ordered to join him from Kentucky. By this conveyance several of the principal officers of the army had
written to their friends in Cincinnati, as well as to the
governor of Kentucky, stating their entire want of
confidence in their commander, and their apprehensions of some fatal disaster from his miserable arrangements and apparent imbecility and cowardice. These
letters also declared it to be the common wish of the
army, that governor Harrison should accompany the
expected reinforcements. He was also very popular
in Kentucky, and was anxiously desired as their commander by the troops marching from that state to the
northwestern army. But the authority with which he
had been invested by the President, did not entitle him
to command any corps, which was not intended for
operations in the western territories.

The question of giving Harrison the command of
the detachment on the march from Kentucky for Detroit, presented great difficulties to the mind of governor Scott. The motives to make the appointment
were numerous. He had ample testimony of its being the wish of the army at Detroit. The 4th United
States regiment in particular, which had acquired so
much fame at Tippecanoe under the command of Harrison, he was assured by an officer of that corps, were

eager to see their old commander again placed over
them.   The same desire was felt by the Kentucky militia; and the citizens echoed their sentiments in every
part of the state.   To these may be added his own
ardent attachment to governor Harrison, and entire
confidence in his fitness for the command,   The obstacles in the way of the appointment were, that Harrison was not a citizen of Kentucky, the laws of which
would not sanction the appointment of any other to
an office in the militia, and that a major general had
already been appointed for the detached militia, one
only being required and admissible in that corps.
Had governor Scott been capable of shrinking from
his duty and the responsibility of the occasion, he
might have easily evaded this delicate business, as the
day on which he was deliberating upon it, was the last
but one that he had to remain in office.   That he might
however, neither act unadvisedly, nor appear to assume
too much, in this situation, he determined to ask the
advice of the governor elect, and such members of
congress, and officers of the general and state governments, as could be conveniently collected.   At this
caucus, composed of governor Shelby, the honorable
H. Clay, speaker of the house of representatives in
congress, the honorable Thomas Todd, judge of the
federal circuit court &c. &c. it wa sunanimously resolved to recommend to governor Scott, to give Harrison
a brevet commission of major general in the Kentucky
militia, and authorize him to take command of the detachment now marching to Detroit; and to reinforce it
with another regiment which he had called into service,
and an additional body of mounted volunteer riflemen.
The governor conferred the appointment agreeably to
their advice, which received the general approbation
of the people, and was hailed by the troops at Cincinnati with the most enthusiastic joy.
    The regiment commanded by colonel Barbour, when
ordered into service at the call of governor Harrison,

was directed to rendezvous at the Red Banks, with a view of marching to the aid of governor Edwards at Kaskaskia in the Illinois Territory. The regiments of colonels Wilcox and Miller were ordered to rendezvous at Louisville, and on the Ohio below, for the purpose of marching to Vincennes to protect the Indiana Territory. Colonels Barbee and Jennings were at first ordered to the same place; but in consequence of the perilous situation of the northwestern army, they were now directed by express to rendezvous at Georgetown on the 1st of September, and pursue the other regiments by the way of Newport and Cincinnati for the northwestern frontiers. In the regiment of colonel Jennings the honorable Samuel M'Kee, and Thomas Montgomery, members of congress, were serving as privates in the ranks. They were ready to execute by their personal services in the humblest station, the measures which they advocated in the Legislature of the Union. The regiment of colonel Poague was ordered to rendezvous at Newport, on its way to the northwestern army; and a regiment of dragoons under colonel Simrall was likewise directed to proceed for the same destination.

About this time also, the secretary of war ordered fifteen hundred men from the back parts of the state of Virginia, who were organized and placed by the governor of that state under the command of general Leftwich. Two thousand men were likewise ordered from the back parts of Pennsylvania, who were placed by the choice of their officers under the command of general Crooks. A company of 12 months volunteers, called the Pittsburgh blues, and another of Petersburgh volunteers in Virginia, were also received into service—the whole from those states being destined for the northwestern army.

General Harrison appointed the honorable R. M. Johnson, and John Logan and Wm. S. Hunter esqrs. his aids; and made some other preparatory arrangements before he proceeded to Cincinnati to enter on his command. Information of these proceedings was also transmitted to the war department, with a request that he might be confirmed in the command which he had received from the governor of Kentucky. About the 25th of August, he published an address to the people of that state, accompanied by another from governor Scott, in which they called for a corps of 500 mounted volunteers, to proceed to the northwest without delay. An address was also published on the same subject by the honorable R. M. Johnson, who had previously distinguished himself in congress, by his zeal in the cause of his country. He was directed by general Harrison to remain a few days at George-town, and bring on such mounted troops as might be raised by the 1st of September. Captain John Ar-nold, who had marched a company to Vincennes in May to aid governor Harrison, and who had comman-ded a spy company, and been in the advance guard, in Wayne's battle with the Indians in '94, now raised a company of mounted riflemen 76 strong in five days, and rendezvoused on the 1st of September at George-town. Captain James Johnson raised a similar com-pany in the counties of Scott and Harrison, and went on two days in advance of the troops who rendez-voused on the 1st of Septenber.

In consequence of some of the regiments, which had been intended for Indiana, being ordered to the northwest, general Harrison thought it advisable, to raise an additional force for that Territory. In com-pliance with his request, governor Shelby issued a proclamation early in September, for raising a large corps of mounted volunteers, to repair immediately to Vincennes. The whole of the Kentucky troops des-tined for that quarter were placed under the immedi-ate command of general Samuel Hopkins, a venerable revolutionary officer, who was at this time a member of congress. In obedience to the proclamation of the governor, the citizens crowded again to the standard of their country. To sum up the occurrences of the times in a few words, it may be said, that the whole state of Kentucky, was for several weeks a constant scene of military parade. The most ardent zeal and patriotism prevailed in every breast. Every person seemed willing to march for the defence of the frontiers—the question was not, *who will go?*—it was, *who shall stay?*

Kentucky thus sent upwards of seven thousand of her citizens into the field—while they are marching to their places of destination, to form the armies under Harrison and Hopkins; and before we proceed to detail their operations; it will be proper to notice some other transactions by the executives of Kentucky and the union. The government of the United States, being well apprised of the means taken by the British agents from Canada, to sway the Indians in their favor, made an attempt as soon as war was declared, to allay the rising storm. The various tribes of Indians bordering on our frontiers, were invited to a general council to be held at Piqua on the 15th of August. They were requested to bring their families, and kindle a great council fire; and the most beneficial results were anticipated. Governor Meigs, Thomas Worthington and Jeremiah Morrow esqrs. were appointed commissioners. They repaired to Piqua at the time appointed; but our disasters and the intrigues of the British completely defeated the plans of the government. The Shawanoese brought their families; the Wyandots of Sandusky, the Mingoes, some Delawares and Ottawas, and a few Miamies attended. A large body of Miamies came 5 miles on this side of fort Wayne, where they halted till they received information of the massacre of the garrison of Chicago, and the surrender of Macinaw and Detroit, when they returned and aided the Potawatamies in the siege of fort Wayne. Those who attended professed great friendship; but little reliance however was placed on any of them, except the Shawanoese and Wyandots, who still possessed some integrity. They had been induced to believe, that the Americans by inviting them to bring their women and children, intended to get them all in their power, and then massacre the whole.

A measure of much greater importance and practicability than negotiating with the Indians, was now proposed from another source. Governor Shelby being installed as the executive of Kentucky, hastened to communicate to the war department, his views respecting the military affairs of the western country. Having had much experience in the revolution and in former Indian wars in this quarter, he foresaw the disasters which must result from the plan of having every movement ordered or sanctioned by the war department before its adoption. He therefore recommended the appointment of a BOARD OF WAR, in the western country. His advice was not entirely disregarded on this occasion, and will deserve to be seriously considered by war ministers in future, who may be disposed to think they can direct operations on the frontiers, better than the commanding general, or a Board of War sitting near the scenes of action. In any war in which the United States may engage, if the secretary undertakes to control the general in minor movements and plans, on a distant frontier, defeats, disasters, and disgrace will inevitably ensue. The following is the communication of governor Shelby :

'*Frankfort, Ky. September 5th,* 1812.

'Sir—In a government possessing the same extent of territory as that of the United States, with her inhabitants scattered and detached, and organized as it is, that energy cannot be exercised as in governments more compact.

'Impressed with the truth of the preceding fact, and being called by my fellow citizens to fill the executive department of the goverument of this state, and having entered on the duties of the important station, I feel it a duty incumbent on me, to state to you sir, my ideas on the subject of war measures northwest of the Ohio river.

' When the northwestern army, commanded by general Hull, marched, all western America were flattered with the hope of success; too soon have we experienced a reverse, and that hope which beamed in every countenance a few days since, is now followed by astonishment, by mortification and anxiety, arising from a rapid succession of misfortunes, unknown in the annals of our historical events. The surrender of the fort of Michilimacana and its garrison—Detroit and the army commanded by general Hull—the evacuation of Chicago, and the murder of the garrison, on the way from thence to fort Wayne, by the Indians, are distressing facts.

' The Indians, thus elated with success, encouraged and supported by the British from Canada, will now endeavour to extend their savage and barbarous devastations, along the extensive frontier of the state of Ohio, and the several territories, unless checked by the detachment of militia lately ordered from this state by my predecessor, and the regular troops who have marched under colonel Wells. It is believed from information received from various sources, that the Indians are collecting in force, at several points from Lake Michigan to the Mississippi river, with intent to make vigorous attacks on both the Indiana and Illinois territories; and should they be successful in a direction towards Vincennes, we shall, I fear, for a time have the Ohio river for a barrier, from the mouth of Kentucky to the junction of Ohio and the Mississippi.

' To regain possession of the posts on the waters of the Lakes will require time; but in the mean while, to stop the invasion of the enemy is all important to the welfare of our common country. It is expected that the troops which have marched, and are now marching from this state, the state of Ohio and Indiana territory, will be so arranged by governor Harrison, in whom they have great confidence, as to protect the great extent of frontier, and to act offensively likewise, if properly supplied with provisions and other necessaries.

' It is not to be expected from the success our Indian enemy have met with, and the aid they will receive from the British, that they will be subdued this campaign; they are elated and will act with more vigor, and be more determined than usual. To subdue them is the important question. The time of the present detachment of militia now in service, will expire next February; to keep the enemy in check, it is conjectured their places will be supplied by troops of a similar description, ready to take the field next spring at as early a peri-

P

od, as the nature of the country in which they will have to act, and other circumstances will justify the measure.

' To march an army at a critical moment to act offensively, is an object ever to be desired, and on such movements the success of a campaign often depends. So remote is the scene of war in western America from the seat of the general goverment, and so various are the measures to be pursued, which are to guide an army to honor and success, against a subtle, wary enemy; it appears to me impossible for the President to adopt with certainty, a line of operations to be observed by any officer, appointed to command in this section of the United States: however skilful the commander, and however judicious the arrangements may be at the moment when made, circumstances often occur which render a change necessary. On an emergency of this kind, to be compelled to have recourse to the war department, forward a statement of facts, and receive an answer, will not only greatly retard the movements of an army, but may wholly defeat the desired object.

' From the same *source* other causes may arise, which will often delay the marching of an army, perplex both officers and soldiers, have a tendency to disgust men with the service, and in a long tedious war render it difficult for government to call forth those resources, which the exigency of the case may require.

' The cases here alluded to, will arise from occurrences which it will be impossible for you to correct in due time; and which have come within my own observation in times past. Inattention, or any other misconduct, in quarter masters, contractors, commissaries and paymasters, or either of them, in the western country, so distant from you, may produce irremediable misfortune.

' The circumstances which lead me to these reflections, arise from the delay which took place in marching the first detachment of the militia from this state, under general Payne. Notwithstanding the emergency of the case required the utmost promptitude, being intended to succour general Hull; yet every thing necessary for their equipment, except arms and ammunition, was purchased and prepared after marching orders were issued; and the dispatch at last is greatly to be attributed to the exertion of individuals; nay, even the patriotic spirit of the ladies in making markees and tents. Although it would have been impossible for this army, under any arrangement, to have reached Detroit in time to have relieved general Hull—yet, if it had not been detained at Georgetown and Newport, waiting for the necessary supplies at both places, possibly by forced marches, the garrison at Chicago might have been saved.

I am not disposed to find fault with any arrangement which has been made, nor with any officer of any department of the government; yet, when important facts occur they ought to be made known, and the evil in future prevented. When the orders issued for calling into actual service, three regiments of this state's quota of the 100,000 militia, they were promised two months pay at the place of rendezvous. This I am informed was complied with. In two or three days after these regiments marched from Georgetown, a requisition was made for the residue of this state's quota: Three regiments of infantry and about 300 cavalry have marched to join general Payne; and three other regiments have crossed the Ohio below into the Indiana and Illinois Territories. These troops are certainly entitled to every compensation and equipment, which those first ordered into service received;—yet, I am induced to believe, they have not received the two months pay in advance, nor scarcely any other article of equipment to make them comfortable, and protect them from the inclemency of the weather, nor hospital stores.—Such is the fact as respected two regiments and the cavalry, that passed this place Men who engage for so long a tour as six months, are compelled to expend money for necessary articles of clothing, and the cavalry in considerable addition to that of the infantry. Many thousand dollars of debts have been contracted, under a confidence that two months pay in advance would be made to the whole of the militia, when called into actual service. Both debtors and creditors have been disappointed, except as to the three first regiments; which has occasioned murmurings and discontent— a circumstance to be regretted, not only as it respects the soldiers and their creditors, but as to the effect it may have on a future call of the militia.

'To aid the great objects of the government in arranging and carrying on the necessary war measures, is the duty of every American citizen; but more especially is it the duty of those characters who are selected in the several states, to carry into effect the executive departments thereof. Since coming into my present office, I have seriously reflected on the present situation of our northwestern frontiers, and am induced to believe, that unless some change of measures is adopted, the objects of the President as contemplated at present, will be defeated, however wisely planned—much blood be spilt unnecessarily—immense sums of money improperly spent—and, what I most apprehend and dread, a dissatisfaction among our citizens to the great cause, from some of the reasons heretofore assigned.

'To remedy the mischiefs apprehended, I will take the liberty of suggesting to the President, the propriety of appointing a board of respectable characters, resident in the western country, responsible to him, in any way which it shall be his pleasure to direct, with power to call into service, under the laws of congress, the militia which may be required, from time to time, from the states of Kentucky, Ohio, and the territories of Indiana and Illinois, to direct their operations either of offence or defence—to require from the war department all the munitions of war necessary for the supply of the troops, and all necessary equipments—to have the controul over the subordinate agents of the war department, within the district assigned—and to make it the duty of the board to report to the department of war, from time to time, the measures by them adopted.

'A board thus organized, would not fail of success in all the war measures in this section of the United States : characters properly selected to such an office, would feel a prompt desire to promote our common cause; from their knowledge of the country, they would be able to direct the necessary operations against the enemy, and whenever necessary, being in the vicinity of the army, give their advice to the officer commanding, and order out detachments to his aid, or divert the enemy so as certainly to insure success in the main enterprize, and secure our frontiers from savage cruelty and devastation.

'If such a board was now organized, and had the controul of the present armament, I would pledge myself the Indians would have cause to lament this campaign, and their temerity in joining the British, and deserting the friendship of the United States.   This is not a singular or novel idea—it is one formerly entertained and practised by general Washington, when President of the United States, and still adhered to by all men of experience in this country.

'While I am writing this letter, I have received a dispatch from governor Harrison, dated at Piqua, of the second instant, in which he informs me, that general Winchester is ordered on to take the command of the detachment sent from this state for the relief of general Hull.   This arrangement at once divides the army under governor Harrison, and renders either part unequal to any object of of importance, and ruins the fairest prospects of the expedition.   It shews, however, in the strongest point of view, the utility of the plan that I propose, of forming a board of war measures in the western country, who would have a clear knowledge of the whole ground before them, and could project plans against the enemy, which might with certainty be carried into complete effect.   Notwithstanding our late ill fortune on the lakes, I made great calculations upon the army under governor Harrison—had they proceeded rapidly on, it is more than probable he could, with the force he had, have retaken Detroit with very little loss.   In his army, were many of the most influential and respectable citizens of this state, from whom every thing was to be expected, which possibly could be achieved by any set of men on earth. And I believe had his march not been interrupted, in a very short time, we should have seen the flag of the United States, again waving on the bank of lake Erie.

' Before I had concluded this letter, information was received, that a number of families had been killed by the Indians, on the waters of White river, twelve or fifteen miles from the Ohio, in the Indiana territory; and that the inhabitants thereof, are crossing to this state by hundreds. Should the Indians attack the territories of Indiana and Illinois, in that force which the present situation of our affairs, as relates to the war against Canada, seems almost to invite them to, there is no power here to order men out of this state to their assistance, nor is there the smallest provision made of arms or ammunition for an expedition, should it be expedient to carry one into the Indian towns, to draw them from our frontiers into their own country.

' I have written you a long letter; the happiness and welfare of my country have prompted me to it, and will, I trust, be a sufficient apology.

> ' I have the honor to be,
> Sir, your most obedient servant,
> ' ISAAC SHELBY.'

' *The Hon. Wm. Eustis, Secretary of War.*'

The following is the answer of Mr. Secretary Eustis to the preceding letter. It indicates the extent of the discretionary powers with which general Harrison was entrusted.

> ' *War Department, September 17, 1812.*

' Sir—Your excellency's letter of the 5th inst. has been received and laid before the president. The intelligence and patriotism which have dictated the useful information which you have been pleased to communicate is duly appreciated.

' The embarrassments attending the organization, direction, and supplies of any force, with the difficulty of determining the amount, and time which exigencies may require, at so distant a point from the seat of government, have been sensibly felt. To find an adequate remedy, has engaged much of the attention of the executive.

' From a board of intelligent, influential, and patriotic citizens, much useful information, and other essential advantages might be derived. Whether they could be clothed with the powers suggested, is a question requiring consideration. To meet existing emergencies, after consulting the lawful authority vested in the president—it has been determined to vest the command of all the forces on the western and northwestern frontier in an officer, whose military character and knowledge of the country, appear to be combined with the public confidence. General Harrison has accordingly been appointed to the chief command, with authority to employ officers, and to draw from the public stores, and every other practical source, all the means of effecting the object of his command.

'In the great and unexpected demands created by the late disasters, it will necessarily happen that deficiencies in the supplies will be experienced. Every exertion, however, is making to provide for the troops, the munitions which they require.

'I have the honor to enclose a copy of a requisition made on governor Scott—should requisitions be made beyond the quota assigned to the state of Kentucky, the president is assured of a prompt co-operation on the part of the executive, under the act of February, 1795.

'I have the honor to be,
Very respectfully, Sir,
Your obedient servant,
'WM. EUSTIS.'
'His excellency governor Shelby.'

'P. S. In addition to the supplies ordered from Pittsburgh, ten thousand pair of shoes, five thousand blankets, tents, camp equipage, and quarter master's stores, are on their way from Philadelphia for the northwestern army. A part of them at least are on their way, and will be followed by the remainder without loss of time.'

We will now proceed with the operations of the northwestern army under Harrison. When he arrived at Cincinnati, and took command of the first regiments which had marched from Kentucky, he immediately issued the following general order, which will give an idea of the kind of discipline and tactics, that were practised on this campaign.

'Head Quarters, August 28, 1812.

'The troops will continue their march in the direction of Dayton by way of Lebanon, at an early hour on to-morrow morning.

' The commandants of the several corps will at every convenient opportunity commence drilling their men to the performance of the evolutions, contemplated by the commander in chief for the order of march and battle. The principal feature in all these evolutions, is that of a battalion changing its direction, by swinging round on its centre. This however is not to be done by wheeling, which by a large body in the woods, is impracticable. It is to be performed thus : the battalion being on its march in a single rank, and its centre being ascertained, the front division comes to the right about, excepting the man in the rear of that division, who steps two feet to the right ; at the same time the front man of the second division, takes a position about six feet to the left of the man in the rear of the front division, and dresses with him in a line at right angles to the line of march. These two men acting as markers or guides for the formation of the new alignment, at the word—" form the new alignment—march," the men of the front, file round their guide and form in succession on his right. At the same time the men of the rear division, file up in succession to the left of the guide, and dress in a line with him and the guide of the front division. This manœuvre may be performed by any number of men—by company and platoon as well as by battalion.

' Wм. H. HARRISON,
Maj. Gen. Commanding.'

On the next day the troops marched very early, and on the morning of the 31st, after they had passed Lebanon a few miles, and were about 40 from Cincinnati, the general who had been detained overtook them. To give him an evidence of their esteem and confidence, as he passed from rear to front, they saluted him with three cheers. This reception was gratifying, as it proved that they would cheerfully fight under his command : and such was the ardor of these volunteers, and their confidence in their general, that they would have beaten any equal number of the best British regulars. With the officers of their choice to command them, they would have preferred death on the field of battle to an ignominious retreat or surrender.

On the 1st of September they arrived at Dayton ; and on the next day as they were marching for Piqua, general Harrison was overtaken by an express, with a communication from the war department, which informed him, that he had been appointed a brigadier general in the army of the United States, on the 22nd of August, and assigned to the command of all the forces in the Indiana and Illinois Territories, with instructions to consult and co-operate with general Hull, and with governor Howard of the Missouri Territory. In answer to this communication he declined accepting the appointment, until he could hear the determination of the government, after the surrender of Detroit, and the character in which he was then acting, had been known at the war department. He also wished to know how far his acceptance would make him subordinate to general Winchester, who was to command the northwestern army, in the main design of regaining our lost Territory and taking Malden. He gave it as his opinion, that there was a necessity for having one head in the western country to direct all the military movements; and with regard to the selection of a suitable person, he respectfully suggested the advantages which he possessed over Winchester, in his personal influence in the western states, and in his perfect knowledge of the country, in which he had risen from the youngest ensign in the United States' regiment. The importance of possessing the confidence of the militia troops, and the impossibility of obtaining a correct knowledge of the country from the existing maps, were also briefly noticed in his answer.

On the 3rd the troops arrived at Piqua, 80 miles from Cincinnati, and only three from the outside settlements. Piqua is the Indian name for this place, which is called Washington by the people of Ohio. It is a little village, situate on the west bank of the Great Miami. The general having now ascertained, that fort Wayne was invested by the neighboring Indians, detached from this place, colonel Allen's regiment with two companies from Lewis and one from Scott's regiments, with instructions to make forced marches for its relief. A regiment of 700 mounted men under the command of colonel Adams had also advanced with the same view as far as Shane's crossing of the St. Marys. This corps was composed of the citizens of Ohio, of all ages and conditions, who had, unsolicited by the government, volunteered and organized themselves for the protection of the frontiers, and the relief of fort Wayne. Many gentlemen who held important offices in the state, and not a few of the most wealthy and respectable citizens of Cincinnati, were to be found in this regiment. Such indeed was the ardor of the citizens to serve in this way, that every road to the frontiers was crowded with unsolicited volunteers. Their zeal was highly honorable to themselves, but in the end it proved disadvantageous to the cause: for they consumed much of the provisions, which had been accumulated at the outposts by the orders of general Hull, the want of which was afterwards severely felt.

On the evening of the 4th, general Harrison received further intelligence, that a British and Indian force had left Malden on the 18th of August, to join the Indians already at the siege. Having previously been advised, that general Winchester was ordered by the war department, to take command of the troops destined to reinforce the northwestern army, he had intended to resign them to him at Piqua, for which purpose he had written to Winchester to come on to that place; but on learning the critical situation of fort Wayne, he determined not to wait for Winchester, but to retain the command till he had relieved the fort.

Early next day, the 5th of September, he paraded the remainder of the troops, and delivered them a speech, in which he stated, that fort Wayne was in imminent danger, and that it was absolutely necessary to make forced marches to relieve it. He read several articles of war, prescribing the duty of soldiers, and explained the necessity for such regulations. He then observed, that if there was any person, who would not submit to such regulations, or who was afraid to risk his life in defence of his country, he might return home; as he did not wish to have any person with him who was afraid to fight or unwilling to discharge his duties. One man only said he wished to return; and his friends having obtained leave as usual to escort him on his way, he was hoisted on a rail and carried to the Big Miami, in the waters of which they absolved him from the obligations of courage and patriotism, and then gave him leave of absence.

The troops were detained here till the 6th for want of *flints*, a very small, yet indispensable article. On that day they marched, leaving the greater part of their clothes and heavy baggage at Piqua, and overtook colonel Allen's regiment early on the 8th at St. Marys river, where an express from the general had overtaken him with orders to halt and build some block houses, for the security of provisions and the protection of the sick. This place is commonly known by the name of Girty's town. The men were here put on half rations; but any one who did not like such fare had leave to remain at the block houses. Major R. M. Johnson arrived on the evening of the same day, with a corps of mounted volunteers, consisting of the companies of captains Arnold and Johnson, and a company from Mason county, under the command of captain Ward. The army was now about two thousand two hundred men strong.

While the troops were at Piqua, Mr. Johnson the Indian agent, at the request of general Harrison, had procured some Shawanoe Indians to go down to the mouth of the Auglaize, the site of old fort Defiance, and examine whether any British force had passed up to the siege of fort Wayne. A Shawanoe half blood, by the name of Logan, who had received this name, in consequence of his having been taken prisoner when a boy, by general Logan in an excursion from Kentucky, had also been sent by the agent, to ascertain the situation of the fort. He was an Indian of great merit, and a chief warrior in his tribe. He was about six feet high and robust, with broad shoulders and a prominent forehead. He was much attached to general Harrison and a warm friend to our cause, which he promoted by acting as a guide and a spy for our army. On his trip to fort Wayne, he eluded all the vigilance of the enemy, got into the fort, and returned with the information of its being besieged. He also brought intelligence, that Stephen Johnson, a brother to the Indian agent, had been killed in sight of the fort, while attempting to escape as an express, and that the Indians had tried every stratagem to get possession of the fort. This information was important, as well as the report of the Indians from the Auglaize, that there was no appearance of a British army having gone up the Miami of the Lakes. The hostile Indians were taking similar measures to obtain information of Harrison's movements. On the night of the 8th, while the army lay in tolerable open order, at the St. Marys, the besiegers at fort Wayne sent their spies to examine it. They did not get round the camp before daylight, and returned with a report, that " Kentuc was coming as numerous as the trees."

Early next morning the army marched for fort Wayne, except the mounted volunteers, who remained till 12 o'clock, to rest their horses, and elect a major to command the corps. R. M. Johnson was chosen for this office; and Benjamin S. Chambers was appointed quarter master, and the reverend James Suggette adjutant to his battalion. The army arrived in the evening at the camp of colonel Adams, at Shane's crossing of the St. Marys: and major Johnson came up in the night, and encamped half a mile

above the main army. On the morning of the 10th,
some delay was caused by repairing broken wagons
and making other necessary arrangements. General
Harrison was unremitting in the discharge of his duties. Every department underwent his personal inspection; and the temper and condition of every corps
in the army was known to him. The delay this
morning was not spent idly by the officers and men.
Most of the different corps were paraded and drilled.
Major Johnson's battalion was drilled on horseback,
by captain James Johnson, whose zeal and military
information was surpassed by few men of his age and
opportunities.

In the following general order, which was issued
at this place, the reader will find the system of tactics
pursued by the general in forming his troops for fighting in the woods.

'*H. Q. Second Crossing of St. Marys, Sept.* 10, 1812.

'The signal for a general charge will be beating the roll.
At night the officers and men will lie upon their arms and their
clothes. Two or more guns firing in succession will constitute
an alarm, at which the whole army will parade in the order of
the encampment, which will be a hollow square, unless otherwise directed. When a sentinel discharges his gun in the night,
the officer of the guard to whom he belongs, will immediately
ascertain the cause; and should he have sufficient reason to believe on examination, that an enemy is near, he will cause two
guns to be fired in quick succession. Should the firing proceed
from an insufficient cause to give an alarm, the officer of the
guard will immediately call out "all is well," which will be
repeated through the army. The same shall take place upon
an accidental firing in the day time. The order of battle, for a
rear attack in the day time, while the army are on the march,
will be so far attended to, with respect to the rear line, that the
rear battalions of colonels Lewis and Allen's regiments only
are to turn upon their centres, while the heads of the front battalions are to close up to the front lines, then facing from the
centre, march out until they respectively gain the flanks of the
front line. Should the attack be in front, the senior officer
nearest the flank battalion, will judge of the propriety of bringing up that battalion to form on the flank of the front line.

'The 2nd battalions of colonels Lewis and Allen's regiments, will in all cases close up, as the leading battalions shall advance and make room for them. Captain Garrard's troop forming guard will also close up and act as circumstances may require.

'WM. H. HARRISON,

Maj. Gen. Command'g.'

The army now marched in the following order. The 17th United States' regiment, colonel Wells, and the rifle regiment, colonel Allen, formed the right column, at the distance of two hundred yards from the road : colonels Lewis and Scott's regiment, the left column, at the same distance from the road on the left. The wagons and pack horses were on the road in the centre. The horsemen from Ohio under colonel Adams formed the right flank ; and the mounted riflemen from Kentucky under major Johnson the left. A battalion from the former, commanded by general Lytle, acting as major, constituted the advance ; while captain Garrard's troop of horse from Kentucky, formed the rear guard. Spies were placed from half a mile to a mile in front, and also beyond the right and left flanks.

The progress of the army now was slow, and there was very little water on their route. On the 11th, lieutenant Suggette, adjutant of Johnson's battalion, was sent with 20 men from that battalion to reconnoitre in advance. Logan and two other Shawanoes went with them as guides. They fell in with a party of Indians, who fled immediately, leaving a young Potawatamie chief mortally wounded. In the evening they returned to the army ; and their little encounter, being the first that had occurred, had some effect in raising the spirits of the troops. As soon as the army had encamped this evening, the general, with his aids and the officer of the day, colonel Allen, was careful to ride round to examine the ground and inspect the whole encampment, which without delay was strongly fortified with a breast work of logs, and the under brush was cleared away for thirty paces on the outside. The mounted men encamped within the lines. During the night there were a number of alarms, caused by the Indians attempting to approach and examine the camp. The army was now within 20 miles of fort Wayne, at which it would be able to arrive the next day.

Very early in the morning the whole were in motion, every man being prepared for action, and expecting to meet the Indians at a well known swamp, about 5 miles on this side of the fort. As the army approached it, the horsemen under Johnson and Adams were sent round it to the right and left. It was about a mile long, and three hundred yards wide, except where the road crossed it, at which place it was not more than 100 yards wide. At this season, it was tolerably dry, and no enemy was to be seen, nor any appearance of one, except a recent encampment, immediately beyond the swamp. About a mile farther a single Indian was seen and fired upon, which caused the army to form the line of battle; but no others appearing, the march was resumed, and about two hours before sunset, the troops arrived at the fort. Their arrival was the source of no little joy to the garrison, and the people who had taken refuge in the fort. The Indians had fled, most of them on the evening before, and some only a few minutes before the appearance of the army. These were pursued by the Ohio horsemen, but without success. The fort had been closely invested for ten or twelve days by the Indians, who had made several pieces of wooden cannon, by boring out pieces of timber, and strengthening them with iron hoops. The army encamped round the fort, where a few days previous there had been a handsome little village; but it was now in ruins, having been burnt down by the Indians, together with the United States' factory, which had been erected to furnish the ungrateful wretches with farming utensils.

Until the 1st of September, the savages about the fort had professed friendship, with a view to get possession of it by some stratagem. Captain Rhea who commanded, was addicted to intoxication, for which and his other misconduct he was arrested by general Harrison; but on account of his age he was permitted to resign. The fort was well prepared to resist a siege by Indians, as it had plenty of provisions and water, and about 70 men with four small field pieces. It is delightfully situated on an eminence on the south bank of the Miami of the Lake, immediately below the formation of that river by the junction of the St. Marys from the southwest with the St. Josephs from the north. It is well constructed of block houses and picketting, but could not resist a British force, as there are several eminences on the south side, from which it could be commanded by a six or nine pounder.

This is the place, where the Miami Indians formerly had their principal town; and here many an unfortunate prisoner suffered death by burning at the stake. It was here also, that general Harmer suffered his army to be cut up and defeated in detachments after he had burnt the town in the fall of the year 1790. For more than a century before that time, it had been the principal place of rendezvous between the Indians of the lakes, and those of the Wabash and Illinois, and had been much resorted about the year '56 and previously, by French traders from Canada. The Miami is navigable for boats from this place to the lake, and the portage to the nearest navigable branch of the Wabash, is but seven or eight miles, through a level marshy prairie, from which the water runs both to the Wabash and St. Marys. A canal at some future day will unite these rivers, and thus render a town at fort Wayne, as formerly, the most considerable place in all that country. The corn which had been cultivated in the fields by the villagers, was nearly all destroyed by the Indians: the remains

served as forage for the mounted corps.   Captain
Wells who was massacred at Chicago, had a handsome farm in the forks of the river, with some good
buildings, which were all destroyed in the general devastation.

On the day after the arrival of the army, reconnoitring parties were sent out in every direction; and at
the same time a council of field officers was convened,
in which it was determined, agreeably to plans submitted by general Harrison, to divide the army into
two divisions, and march on the next day in quest of
the Indians and their towns.   The first division was
composed of the regiments of Lewis and Allen, and
captain Garrard's troops of horse, under general Payne
and accompanied by general Harrison.   They were
to destroy the Miami villages at the forks of the Wabash, about thirty miles from the fort.   The other division was to destroy the Potawatamie village on the
Elk Hart river, a branch of the St. Josephs of lake
Michigan : it was to be commanded by colonel Wells,
and to consist of one battalion of his own regiment
under major Davenport, Scott's regiment, the mounted
battalion under Johnson, and the mounted men from
Ohio under Adams.   The greater part of the latter
corps however returned home next morning.   They had
left their homes in the expectation of remaining but a
short period in service, and had already exceeded the
time which they had allowed themselves for the excursion.   When general Harrison was informed of the
intention of the corps to return, he addressed them in
a public speech. in which he requested them to remain
with him, and march on the intended expedition.   General Lytle and Major Dunlap with 150 men determined to stay—all the others adhered to their determination to return.   The main object, which the general
expected to accomplish by the proposed expeditions,
was to destroy the corn of the Indians so that they
could not find the means of subsistence for making
another attack on the fort.

The party under Payne, having traversed a fine region of country, arrived on the 15th at the village in the forks, which was abandoned by the Indians. They encamped in the town; destroyed all its huts and cabins, and cut up the corn and other vegetables in the fields.   Next day the spies discovered several other deserted villages lower down, which were all in like manner destroyed.   The tomb of a chief, built of logs and daubed with clay, was found in one of these villages.   He was laid on his blanket, with his gun and his pipe by his side, a small tin pan on his breast, containing a wooden spoon, and a number of ear rings and broaches—all deemed necessary no doubt on his journey to the other world.   On the 18th they arrived again at the fort, without having lost a man or seen a living Indian.

The party under Wells had to march about sixty miles to the village against which they were sent. Captain Audrain who was son-in-law, and Mr. Wells who was son to the colonel, went with them as guides; and captain Arnold's company marched at the distance of near a mile in front to act as spies.   On the 16th, having crossed the Elk Hart river, above the village about three miles, the line of battle was formed in a plain, thinly timbered.   Major Johnson's mounted battalion was placed in front on the left flank, and major Dunlap's mounted men on the right in front; with orders to advance to the right and left of the town and surround it.   The infantry were formed in line of battle, then broke off by heads of companies, and followed the others in rapid motion.   In a few minutes the mounted men were in the rear of the village; but to the regret of every person it was found destitute of inhabitants, the Indians having fled two days previous.   They had left a considerable quantity of corn, gathered and laid on scaffolds to dry, with abundance of beans, potatoes and other vegetables, which furnished an ample store of provisions for the

S

men and forage for the horses. This village was called Five Medals, from a chief of that name who made
it his residence. On a pole before the door of that
chief, a red flag was hung, with a broom tied above it :
and on another pole at the tomb of an old woman, a
white flag was flying. The body of the old woman
was entire, sitting upright with her face towards the
east, and a basket beside her, containing trinkets, such
as owl and hawk bills and claws, a variety of bones,
and bunches of roots tied together; all of which indicated, that she had been revered as a sorceress, and
probably a doctress.

In one of the huts was found a morning report of
one of Hull's captains—also a *Liberty Hall* newspa-
per, printed at Cincinnati, containing an account of
general Harrison's army. Several coarse bags, which
appeared to have contained shot; and pieces of boxes
with London and Malden printed on them, were also
picked up in the cabins; which proved that these Indians were intimately connected with the British, and
had been furnished with information by some traitor
in our own country. The village with about seventy
acres of corn was totally destroyed; and on the same
evening the army returned as far as the Elk Hart river.
Next morning they marched rapidly towards the fort,
captain Arnold's company being thrown in the rear,
to act as a guard, and to bring up the weak, the sick,
and the lame. This was an arduous task; for the
men having marched very hard, and having been very
scarce of provisions, except the green vegetables taken
in the village, were exceedingly fatigued, and many of
them were taken sick, one of whom died on the return.
When the foot troops gave out through fatigue, they
were aided by the horsemen, who cheerfully dismounted to assist their fellow soldiers. On the 18th the
main body arrived at the fort a few hours after the
party under Payne.

In the mean time colonel Simrall had arrived at the fort on the 17th, with his regiment of dragoons, armed with muskets, 320 strong; and a company of mounted riflemen under colonel Farrow, from Montgomery county, Kentucky.   General Harrison sent them on the evening of the 18th to the town of Little Turtle, about 20 miles to the northwest, with orders to destroy it all, except the buildings erected by the United States for the Little Turtle, whose friendship for the Americans after the treaty of Greenville, had contributed greatly to the preservation of peace.   Colonel Simrall executed his orders with a degree of promptness and dispatch, which indicated the true soldier; and on the 19th he returned in the evening to the fort.   Captain Farrow's company was now placed under major Johnson, whose battalion was thus rendered about 250 strong.

Brigadier general James Winchester now arrived to take command of the first troops, which had marched from Kentucky to reinforce the northwestern army. He too had been a revolutionary officer, and was now advanced in years.   He was a wealthy citizen of Tennessee, where he had lived many years in a degree of elegant luxury and ease, which was not calculated to season him for a northern campaign in the forest.   His arrival produced much uneasiness among the troops; being a regular officer, with whom they were unacquainted, many of the militia seemed disposed not to be commanded by him; and general Harrison with the field officers had to exert all their influence to reconcile the army to the change.   The troops had confidently expected, that general Harrison would be confirmed in the command; and by this time he had completely secured the confidence of every soldier in the army.   He was affable and courteous in his manners, and indefatigable in his attention to every branch of business. His soldiers seemed to anticipate the wishes of their

general : it was only necessary to be known, that he
wished something done, and all were anxious to risk
their lives in its accomplishment. His men would
have fought better and suffered more with him, than
with any other general in America : and whatever
might have been the merits of general Winchester, it
was certainly an unfortunate arrangement, which transferred the command to him at this moment. It is absolutely necessary that militia soldiers should have
great confidence in their general, if they are required,
either to obey with promptness, or to fight with bravery. The men were at last reconciled to march under
Winchester, but with a confident belief, that Harrison
would yet be reinstated in the command ; and which
accordingly was done, as soon as the war department
was informed of his appointment in the Kentucky
troops, and his popularity in the western country.

On the 19th the command of the troops at the fort
was transferred by a general order to Winchester ; and
at the same time he was informed by general Harrison
that any other part of the infantry which he might
deem necessary to the execution of his plans, should
be placed at his disposal. On the same evening general Harrison started back to take command of the forces collecting in the rear ; and to prepare for a mounted expedition against Detroit. He intended to make
a *coup de main* on that place, with a mounted force,
which would march by an unfrequented route from
fort Wayne, up the St. Josephs to the head waters of
the river Raisin. The troops collecting in the rear,
were the three regiments from Kentucky, under Barbee, Poague and Jennings ; and three companies of
mounted riflemen from the same state, under captains
Roper, Bacon, and Clarke ; and also a corps of
mounted men from Ohio, who had rendezvoused at
Dayton on the 15th, in pursuance of a previous call
by Meigs and Harrison, which had been made early
in September, with a view to employ them in an ex-

pedition against some of the Indian towns. This
corps was commanded by colonel Findley, who had
entered the service again, after being surrendered by
Hull. The mounted men and the regiment of Jennings had arrived at St. Marys, where General Harrison met them on the 20th, the rest of the infantry
being still farther in the rear. The general had left
orders at fort Wayne for Johnson's battalion, and colonel Simrall's dragoons, which corps were not included in Winchester's command, to return to St. Marys as soon as possible. Major Johnson had accordingly marched early on the morning of the 20th, and
when he had travelled about 20 miles was met by orders from Harrison to return to the fort, and wait with
the dragoons for further orders ; which was promptly
done, with the exception of ensign *William Holton*,
and about 25 men, of captain Ward's company. They
refused to obey the order to return, and *manfully* proceeded home to Kentucky. The battalion arrived at
the fort in the evening next day, from which in the
mean time general Winchester had removed his camp
into the forks of the river ; and early on the 22nd he
marched down the river on the north side, following
very nearly the route in which Wayne's army returned
after the battle of '94. His object was to go as far as the
old fort Defiance, at the mouth of the Auglaize, and
wait there to form a junction with the infantry in the
rear, who were to come down that river from St. Marys. The following order was issued by the general,
which will serve as a specimen of his tactics and police :

"The front guard in three lines, two deep in the road, and in
Indian files on the flanks at distance of fifty and one hundred
yards, as the ground will admit. A fatigue party to consist
of one captain, one ensign, two sergeants, and two corporals
with 50 men, will follow the front guard for the purpose of
opening the road. The remainder of the infantry to march on
the flanks in the following order: colonels Wells and Allen's
regiments on the right, and Lewis and Scott's on the left. The
general and brigade baggage, commissaries and quarter mas-

ters' stores, immediately in the rear of the fatigue party. The cavalry in the following order : captain Garrard and 20 of his men to precede the guard in front, and equally divided at the head of each line; a lieutenant and 18 men in the rear of the whole army and baggage; the balance of the cavalry equally divided on the flanks or the flank lines.   The regimental baggage wagons will fall according to the respective ranks of their commanding officers.   The officers commanding corps previous to their marching will examine carefully the arms and ammunition of their respective corps, and see that they are in good order.   They will also be particularly careful, that the men do not waste their cartridges.   No loaded muskets are to be put in the wagons.   One half of the fatigue party is to work at a time, and the others will carry their arms.   The wagon master will attend to loading the wagons, and see that the various articles are put in, in good order, and that each wagon and team carry a reasonable load.   The hour of march will be 9 o'clock this morning.   The officer of the day is charged with this order.   The line of battle will be the same as that of general Harrison in his last march to fort Wayne.

'JAMES WINCHESTER, *Brig. Gen.*'

As great caution was observed on the march, and the camp strongly fortified every night, the army advanced very slowly, not exceeding five or six miles a day.   Some Indians were seen, and there was considerable appearance of more being in the country around.   A volunteer company of spies had been organized under captain Ballard, and lieutenant Harrison Munday of the rifle regiment, and ensign Liggett of the 17th United States' infantry.   They generally marched in advance to reconnoitre the country.   On the 25th ensign Liggett obtained permission from his captain, to proceed as far as old fort Defiance, at the mouth of the Auglaize on the south side of the Miami.   Four men of M'Cracken's company from Woodford, Kentucky, went with him.   Late in the evening, while preparing something to eat, they were discovered by a Frenchman and 8 Indians, who crept up and surprised them with a call to surrender.   They were positively assured, that they would not be hurt, and would be permitted to wear their arms till they entered the British camp.   On these conditions they surrendered : but the Indians and Frenchman, as they marched on, concerted in their own language, and executed the following plan, for their destruction.   Five of the Indians, each having marked his victim, walked behind and on one side of the men, and at a given signal fired upon them.   Four of them fell dead—Liggett only escaped the first fire—he sprung to a tree, but was shot also while raising his gun to his face. Next day captain Ballard, with a part of his company, being in advance, discovered the dead bodies, and a party of Indians watching near them.   He formed his men for action, with the Miami on his right; but not liking his position, and perceiving that the Indians were too strong for him, he fell back 200 yards, and formed in a stronger position.   The enemy supposing he had fled, filed off from their right flank, intending to surround him on his left, and cut off his retreat. He heard them pass by on his left without discovering him, and then filed off by the left in their rear, and by a circuitous route arrived safe at the camp.

Lieutenant Munday with another part of the spies presently happened at the same place, and discovering some Indians, who still remained there, formed his men and charged upon them, at the same time saluting them with their own yell.   They fled precipitately, and Munday on discovering their superior numbers, took advantage of their panic to retreat himself. Next morning, the 27th, captain Ballard with the spies and captain Garrard's troop of horse, accompanied by major Woolfork, aid to the general, and some other volunteers, went forward to bury the dead.   The Indians were still in ambush ; but captain Ballard expecting it, approached them in a different direction, so as to disconcert their plans.   He attacked them with a brisk fire, and captain Garrard immediately ordered a charge, on which they fled in every direction, leaving trails of blood from their killed and wounded.

These Indians were the advance of an army destined to attack fort Wayne, and consisting of 200 regulars under major Muir, with four pieces of artillery, and about 1000 Indians commanded by Elliott. They had brought their baggage and artillery by water to the old fort Defiance, at the mouth of the Auglaize, where they had left their boats and were advancing up the south side of the Miami towards fort Wayne. About the time that Liggett's party was massacred, quarter master sergeant M'Coy of Scott's regiment, was taken by the Indians and carried to the British camp. He represented the strength of the army under Winchester much above the truth, and informed them that another army as strong was expected down the Auglaize immediately to join Winchester. Major Muir on receiving this intelligence, which agreed pretty well, as to Winchester's force, with the reports of his spies, considered his situation as critical; and on the defeat of his advance by captain Ballard, on the morning of the 27th, he immediately retreated from his position 12 miles above the Auglaize, to the boats he had left at its mouth, and re-embarked his baggage and artillery the same day. He then determined to give Winchester battle, relying if defeated on effecting a retreat in his boats. He selected an advantageous place for an attack, where Wayne's old trace crosses a creek on the north side of the Miami, about 4 miles above Defiance. But on marching to the ground on the morning of the 28th, he found that about three fourths of the Indians had abandoned the project. The news of another army coming down the Auglaize, and the leaving of the artillery in the boats, had frightened them to this conduct. Major Muir then immediately retreated down the river, to the distance of twenty miles the same day, leaving some mounted Indians to watch the movements of his enemies.

General Winchester had all this time received no certain information of the army thus opposed to him.

On the morning of the 26th, captain Hickman had volunteered to go on horseback with Riddle, an intelligent spy well versed in Indian affairs, and reconnoitre the country down the river. They crossed the Miami to the south side, then crossed the country to the Auglaize, and descended on the east side of that river to the Miami, which they recrossed about 2 miles below the mouth of the former, and returned up the north side to the army. In this route, they had surrounded the enemy without having discovered him. In the first instance they had crossed the Miami above the army of the allies; and where they recrossed it below, the Indians having travelled in a beaten path, and the regulars by water, the traces of a large force were not discoverable. However, the Indian sign which they had seen, combined with the conduct of the skirmishing parties, convinced those experienced in such affairs, that a large body of the enemy was somewhere in the neighbourhood.

The camp was therefore strongly fortified on the night of the 27th, and the march was resumed next day under the expectation of meeting the enemy and having a battle. Presently the spies from each army met and fired at each other; the line of battle was immediately formed; but the enemy having disappeared, the march was again resumed. When the army had arrived within a few miles of the creek, at which Major Muir had prepared that morning to give it battle, a halt was called by general Winchester. He had learnt, that the passage of that creek would be an advantageous place, for the enemy to make an attack, and he determined to cross to the south side of the Miami. A ford being found, the army crossed over, and immediately the trail of the enemy with his artillery was discovered on the south side. An advantageous piece of ground was chosen for a camp, which was well fortified as usual. Spies were sent down to reconnoitre at the mouth of the Auglaize, but they re-

T

turned without much information. They stated, that
the brush was so thick about that place, and the sign
of Indians so abundant, that it was unsafe for spies
on foot to penetrate to the old fort.

A council of war was now held. Some of the officers were for sending a detachment in pursuit of the
enemy; but a large majority were of opinion, that the
enemy must have obtained correct information of the
strength of the army, and have taken a decisive course;
that if he intended to give us battle, he would do it
without our forces being divided; and that if he was
unable to do this, he had no doubt retreated too far
already to be overtaken. The general was of this
opinion; and the council decided, that several mounted parties should be sent out in different directions to
search for the enemy; and that an express at the same
time should be sent to general Harrison to acquaint
him with the situation of the army, and that its provisions were nearly exhausted. These measures were
executed next morning. An express was sent to general Harrison, and four parties of spies were sent to
reconnoitre in different directions. The spies all returned in the course of the day; and from their reports no doubt remained, but that the enemy had retreated. On the next day, the 30th of September,
General Winchester moved his camp down the river, within a mile of Defiance, where he fortified himself again on a high bank of the Miami, and remained there several days, so destitute of provisions, that
the men had to subsist on a very short allowance of
the most indifferent beef. They continued however
to do their duty as soldiers with promptitude and
cheerfulness. On the first of October, colonel Lewis
was detached with 380 men to discover with more certainty, whether the enemy had retreated quite out of
the country. He crossed the Auglaize, and went down
on the south side of the Miami seven or eight miles,
and then crossed to the north side of that river, where

ke saw sufficient appearances of a precipitate retreat, to convince him that the enemy was entirely gone.

We must now recur to the operations of the troops collecting in the rear. We left general Harrison on the 20th September, with the mounted men and Jennings's regiment at St. Marys, the balance of the infantry having not then arrived. The regiments of colonels Barbee, Poague, and Jennings arrived at Newport early in September, with colonel Simrall's dragoons, but they were detained some time before they could draw their arms, ammunition, and two months pay in advance. The dragoons were obliged to arm themselves with muskets, no swords and pistols having arrived. The government had ordered the necessary supplies, but their agents were inattentive and dilatory. Many articles of the first necessity had not yet left Philadelphia, from which place even the tent poles for the army were to be brought, so improvident were some of the arrangements for supplying and conducting the troops on the frontiers. One man only in colonel Simrall's regiment, and he was a substitute, refused to be armed with a musket. His comrades invited him to the water as usual, and having initiated him by baptism into the Legion of dis-Honor, he was permitted to retire from the toils of war. The foot regiments, having at last completed their arrangements, proceeded for their destination, and had all arrived on the frontiers about the 20th of September.

On the 21st colonel Jennings was ordered, to proceed with his regiment across the St. Marys and down the Auglaize towards Defiance, to establish an intermediate post, and escort provisions to general Winchester. Having advanced about 30 miles, he met with considerable sign of Indians, and his spies having advanced to fort Defiance and discovered the enemy there, he halted on the Auglaize, and commenced the building of block houses. Colonel Findley was

sent with his mounted regiment, 350 strong, to destroy
the Ottawa towns on Blanchard's fork of the Auglaize.
About this time general Harrison received a despatch
from the war department, directing him to join general
Winchester with a part of the troops under his command.   This order had been issued on the supposition, that Harrison had accepted the previous appointment, and was still in Kentucky.   In his present situation he could not comply ; but in order to further
the views of the secretary, he immediately determined
to place the regiments of Barbee and Jennings, and
the quota of Ohio troops then in service, at the disposal of general Winchester.

General Harrison now proceeded to Piqua to expedite the supplies for the army, and mature his arrangements for the *coup de main* on Detroit.   But there
on the evening of the 24th, he received another communication from the war department, dated on the 17th
of September which assigned him the command of the
8th military district including the northwestern army.
He was at the same time instructed, to provide for the
security of the western frontiers, to retake Detroit, and
with a view to the conquest of Upper Canada, to penetrate that country as far as the force under his command would justify him to proceed.   He was advised,
that every exertion was making by the government, to
furnish him with a train of artillery from Pittsburgh,
and all other necessary supplies.   The forces now under his command by order of the government, were
estimated at ten thousand strong, including the whole
in the state of Ohio and the different territories.   The
real number was much greater, in consequence of many mounted volunteers having entered the service for
short periods unauthorized by the war department.
But the services which he was required to perform,
were in the opinion of old, experienced, and able officers, the most extensive and arduous, that ever had
been required from any military commander in Ame-

ica. The endless number of posts and scattered settlements, which he was obliged to maintain and protect, against numerous and scattered bands of Indians,
while he was contending with difficulties almost insur-
mountable in the main expedition against the enemy
at Malden, were sufficient to employ all the time, and
talents, and resources, of the greatest military genius
at the head of a well appointed army. His forces
however were raw, undisciplined militia, which nothing but *his* address or Jackson's energy could render
efficient. Chaos and misconduct reigned in every department, and particularly in that of the supplies, in
which the best organization and arrangements were
necessary, to meet the inconceivable difficulties which
were to be surmounted in that line. He had excellent materials for an army in the Kentucky militia,
but he had no time to spend in preparing them for the
field—the season for action was drawing to a close—
not a moment was to be lost in pushing on the campaign.

He immediately digested the following plan for the
march of the army towards Detroit, viz : the right column, to be composed of the Virginia and Pennsylvania troops, to rendezvous at Wooster, and proceed
thence by Upper Sandusky to the rapids of the Miami : the middle column, to consist of 12 hundred Ohio
militia, to march from Urbana where they now were,
by fort M'Arthur on general Hull's route to the Rapids : the left column, to be composed of the regulars
under Wells, and four regiments of Kentucky volunteers, to proceed down the Auglaize and Miami from
St. Marys and Defiance to the Rapids. The mounted
men, under a proper officer selected to command them,
were to proceed on the route, by which he had intended to make the *coup de main* on Detroit. That
intention however was now abandoned ; for if they
should take Detroit, as the infantry could not be ready
to support them in it, they must leave it again to the

aggravated fury of the Indians. The object therefore
at present, was to sweep the western side of the strait
and lake of the Indians, who were scattered from
Brownstown to the Rapids, rioting on the plunder of
the farms which had been abandoned by their owners.

The attention of the general was at the same time
directed to the important subject of the supplies, the
most difficult part of his business in the present campaign. On the 27th he despatched an express to Pittsburgh, to order the artillery and supplies from that
place to proceed to Georgetown on the Ohio, and
thence by New Lisbon and Canton to Wooster.
Such as the state of Ohio could furnish cheap, he pre-
fered to procure in that country, as being the most convenient for a land transportation towards Detroit. The
troops were nearly destitute of winter clothing; and
as the prospect of obtaining an adequate supply from
the government, in due time, was not very flattering,
an appeal had already been made on this subject by
Shelby and Harrison, to the patriotism of the people
of Kentucky, for voluntary contributions of clothing to
the militia of that state.

In the plan of the campaign, the rapids of the Miami were considered as the *first object*, upon which
the forces were to advance from a military *base*, drawn
along the hither edge of the swampy district from Upper Sandusky to St. Marys, by three lines of operations, commencing at St. Marys, fort M'Arthur, and
Upper Sandusky. which places were to be the principal points of concentration and deposit, preparatory to
a general advance and combination at the Rapids.
" This, says colonel Wood of the engineers, was an
excellent plan ; for by sending the corps different
routes, with a view of concentrating somewhere in the
neighbourhood of the enemy, the march of the army
would not only be expedited, but the frontiers much
more effectually protected."

St. Marys was intended to be the principal depot

for provisions, and Sandusky for the artillery and military stores. That portion of the left wing which was now at Defiance, was to serve as a corps of observation; and at that place provisions were also to be accumulated, preparatory to the advance of that corps to occupy the Rapids, which was to take place when the artillery had reached Upper Sandusky, and the other necessary supplies had been accumulated along the military base; and its arrival at the Rapids was to be the signal for a general advance with the supplies on all the lines of operation. A corps of observation was also to be placed at Lower Sandusky, which with Defiance would form the extremities of a second base when the Rapids were occupied. By these arrangements the greater part of the troops would be kept within the bounds of the local contractors, consuming provisions brought forward at their expense, whilst all the energies of the quarter master's department would be employed in accumulating provisions at the principal depots, and providing the means to transport them through the swampy country to the positions taken in advance, and particularly to the Rapids of the Miami.

Having digested these plans, general Harrison returned again to St. Marys and dispatched captain Hite to fort Wayne, with orders for the horsemen under colonel Simrall, and major Johnson, to come to St. Marys as soon as possible. With such promptitude and celerity were these orders obeyed and executed, that the front of Johnson's battalion arrived at the St. Marys, a distance of 63 miles, about 13 hours after the orders were received.

While Simrall and Johnson were lying at fort Wayne, on the 23rd of September, six Miami Indians, headed by the Stone Eater and a nephew of Little Turtle's, and a Frenchman named Langly, came to the fort, pretending that they wished to treat for peace. They said all the Miamies had collected at Mississiniway: that they had searched for general

Harrison towards Vincennes, and that hearing of his march to fort Wayne, they had come there to meet him. Five of them were detained as hostages, and on the 26th the Stone Eater and Langly went to bring in the other chiefs of the tribe, which they promised to do in four days.

The forces now at St. Marys amounted to near 3,000 men. On the morning of the 30th, the companies of captains Roper, Clarke and Bacon, were ordered to elect a major and form a battalion; which associated with Johnson's, would constitute a regiment and elect a colonel. Roper was elected major by the battalion, and R. M. Johnson was elected colonel by the regiment. Captain Arnold was elected major in the place of Johnson, and lieutenant Ellison was elected to command Arnold's company. This new regiment, with colonel Findley's from Ohio, now formed a brigade, which was placed under the command of brigadier general Tupper of Ohio, a gentleman about 50 years of age, of a respectable, soldierly appearance, who had been called into service with the balance of the detached militia of Ohio, which he had left at Urbana. This brigade was intended to march in a few days, on the expedition up the St. Josephs, to scour the the country towards Detroit. But a few hours after it was organized, about 12 o'clock the same day, the express from general Winchester arrived, with intelligence that his march had been much impeded by the Indians; and that on arriving near Defiance he discovered, that they were accompanied by British troops with some pieces of artillery. A few minutes afterwards an express arrived from governor Meigs, with a letter from general Kelso, commanding a detachment of Pennsylvania troops on lake Erie, containing information that on the 16th of September 2,000 Indians with some regulars and militia, and two pieces of artillery, had left Malden on an expedition against fort Wayne.

Orders were immediately issued for a forced march, three days provision were drawn, with ammunition and other necessaries, and in three hours all the forces at St. Marys were in motion to join Winchester, who was supposed to have met all the forces, which the allies could raise in Upper Canada. Early next day, the 1st of October, it began to rain very heavy, which soon made the roads very deep, and rendered the march uncomfortable and fatiguing. The horsemen at first marched on the flanks; but when the foot troops halted for dinner, the horsemen were pushed forward in front, and in the evening passed the camp of colonel Jennings, where he had built a block house. The rain continued very heavy all night, the weather was very cold for that season, and as the troops had no tents, their situation was extremely disagreeable. General Harrison and his staff were similarly situated, and his patience and fortitude served as an example to encourage his men. Beech brush was the substitute for a bed, and answered the purpose of keeping the men out of the mud and water.

The foot troops were halted at fort Jennings; and general Harrison having met another express from Winchester on the evening of the 2nd, with information that the enemy had retreated, sent orders for colonel Barbee to return with his regiment to St. Marys, and colonel Poague to cut a road from fort Jennings to Defiance. The mounted troops had continued their march in five lines. Their number was upwards of one thousand, which made a grand appearance in the woods. The information of the retreat of the enemy, had a very dispiriting effect on the minds of many of the men, who were anxious for a battle before their discharge, which could not be very distant now, as their terms of service would soon expire, and forage could not be procured much longer for so many horses. The general himself was not well pleased, when he discovered, that the intelligence sent to him had been

U

much more alarming, than was authorized by the cir.
cumstances. He arrived in the evening at Winchester's camp; and the troops, having lain all night within three miles of the same place, proceeded early in
the morning past the camp, and went down to the
point at the mouth of the Auglaize, where they en.
camped round the ruins of the old fort.

A few pack horses, loaded with flour, arrived at
Winchester's camp with general Harrison, which with
the intelligence of his confirmation in the command,
was very gratifying to the troops. Their sufferings
however had become so great, as to threaten serious
consequences to the service, if they could not speedily
be relieved. With a view to allay the uneasiness prevailing among them, on the next day after his arrival,
he had all the troops paraded, when colonel Allen and
major Hardin addressed them in very affecting terms,
and portrayed in a lively manner, the confidence and
expectations which this army had excited; and exhorted them to bear their privations with patience and
fortitude. General Harrison then addressed them
himself, as a father would his children. He observed
that his fame and theirs were identified; and then proceeded to flatter their pride as Kentuckians. He af-
fectingly asked them "If you fellow soldiers from
Kentucky, so famed for patriotism, refuse to bear the
hardships incident to war, and to defend the rights of
your insulted country, where shall I look for men who
will go with me?" He then told them, that immense
supplies were lying at St. Marys, to which a direct
road was opening, that rations would be forwarded
with speed, that in the evening he expected a hundred
beeves with more flour, that the government was doing
its best to supply them, and that reinforcements were
coming from Virginia and Pennsylvania, which would
render the army very powerful. General Harrison
was a very eloquent speaker, and on this occasion his
speech had a powerful effect on the troops. When it

was finished, they rent the air with shouts of applause, and harmony with content again prevailed in the camp.

General Harrison now selected a position for a new fort, about 80 yards up the Auglaize, above the ruins of the old one. A fatigue party of 250 men, were detailed and placed under the command of major Joseph Robb, for the purpose of cutting timber for the necessary buildings. General Winchester also moved his camp from the Miami to the Auglaize about a mile from its mouth; and general Harrison accompanied by colonel Johnson, and his original battalion, composed of Johnson's, Ward's, and Ellison's companies, returned to St. Marys, where these troops were honorably discharged on the 7th of October. Poague's regiment was directed, after cutting the road to Defiance, to return to the Ottawa old towns on the Auglaize, about twelve miles from St. Marys, and erect a fort at that place.

The command of the left wing was now confided to general Winchester, who accepted it on the solicitation of general Harrison. His principal employment for the present was to be the transportation of supplies to Defiance for the main expedition. He was also instructed to occupy the Miami Rapids as speedily as possible for the purpose of securing a large quantity of corn, which had been raised at that place by the inhabitants, who had now fled to other settlements for safety. When this instruction was given. general Harrison expected he would be able in two weeks to complete the necessary supplies for advancing against Detroit; and with a view to hasten that result, he soon afterwards recommended to general Winchester, instead of going to the Rapids, to send two of his regiments back within the bounds of the contractors' engagements, to prevent them from consuming the provisions carried in advance.

Before general Harrison left Defiance on the evening of the 4th, he ordered general Tupper to take the whole of the mounted men, who were now about 800 in number, and proceed next morning down the Miami as far as the Rapids, and still farther if he should there find it necessary, to disperse collections of the enemy, who were said to be rioting on the relics of general Hull's provisions, and on the corn of the citizens who had fled to the settlements for safety. He was to return by Defiance or Tawa towns on Blanchard's fork to St. Marys. When this order was issued general Tupper's command was immediately supplied with rations for 8 days, consisting chiefly of beef but including all the flour in camp, which was cheerfully surrendered by the infantry in the hope, that on the intended expedition the mounted men would do something valuable. An application afterwards made by Tupper to general Winchester for more ammunition, could not however be complied with. In the morning the march was not commenced according to orders; and about 12 o'clock a partry of Indians fired on three men immediately on the opposite bank of the Miami, one of whom they killed and scalped and then fled. The camp was considerably alarmed for a moment, and the troops were formed in order of battle. Presently small parties of horsemen began to cross the river to reconnoitre and pursue the enemy. Most of the horses were at grass up the Auglaize, and as fast as the owners could get them, these parties were formed and crossed over to engage in the pursuit. As no general orders were given, some confusion prevailed. every little squad pursuing its own views. Eight or ten different parties had gone, mostly from colonel Simrall's regiment, in one of which was the colonel himself, and major M'Dowell of the same regiment was ready to cross with fifty men, when general Tupper thought proper to order, that no more should leave the camp. He was apprehensive from the boldness of the Indians, that a large body might be lying near in ambush, who would attack the camp from some other quarter. Captain Young with only nine or ten men overtook the Indians, about 50 in number: having fired upon them he retreated, and meeting with no reinforcements returned to camp. It was then too late in the evening to pursue them again with a stronger force. In the morning general Tupper sent Logan with six other Indians down the river to reconnoitre: colonel Simrall in the mean time had prepared a strong party to renew the chase; and not long afterwards general Winchester ordered Tupper to commence his expedition towards the Rapids by pursuing those Indians. General Tupper alleged that he was waiting till his Indian spies should return, with information of the route which the hostile Indians had taken. In the evening those spies arrived, with information that they had seen a party of the enemy, about 50 strong, ten miles down the river. General Winchester now sent for Tupper, and urged him again to proceed in the morning and disperse those Indians in his route. General Tupper replied, that he would prefer to go by the Ottawa towns, which had been destroyed by colonel Findley, and follow the trace from that place to the Rapids. On this day about three hundred of the mounted riflemen, whose terms of service had expired, left the camp and returned home, dissatisfied with the conduct of Tupper, and alleging that their horses were unfit for the expedition. Next morning after an interview with Tupper, general Winchester directed the regiment of colonel Simrall to return to the settlements in Ohio, for the purpose of recruiting their horses; and positive orders were then given to general Tupper to proceed on the expedition. Colonel Simrall being convinced that Tupper would still find some pretext to evade the execution of the order in a proper manner, now willingly returned to the settlements, having first given all his ammunition to the other mounted men, by which their supply was rendered fully adequate to the service.

The dragoons were six months men, and reliance being placed on them for services in a subsequent part
of the campaign, it was thought best to let them retire
and hold themselves in readiness to march, when the
main expedition should be ready to move. The other
mounted men had volunteered for short periods, and
were therefore ordered for the expedition under Tupper, as the only service they would have an opportunity to perform. But discontent and insubordination
now began to be manifest among them. Some of the
Kentuckians were not inclined to march under Tupper, unless accompanied by some field officer from
Winchester's command. Colonel Allen therefore tendered his services to accompany general Tupper in
any capacity he might choose to receive him. The
offer was accepted—but general Winchester having
misunderstood the nature of the arrangement between
them, issued an order directing colonel Allen to take
the command and march towards the Rapids. This
caused a serious misunderstanding between the two
generals. Colonel Allen however having informed
general Winchester correctly on the subject, the order was immediately rescinded. The greater part
of the men having by this time refused to proceed
directly to the Rapids, general Tupper marched them
over the Auglaize, and proceeded to the Ottawa towns,
where he professed to expect reinforcements from
Ohio. The whole of his troops, except about 200,
now refused to march towards the Rapids : he therefore proceeded by the most direct route to Urbana,
and honorably discharged those only, who had been
willing at all times to obey.

Charges were soon afterwards exhibited against
Tupper by general Winchester, for his conduct on
this occasion, in consequence of which an arrest was
ordered by general Harrison. The Ohio brigade under Tupper in the mean time had been advanced to
fort M‘Arthur on Hull's road, and when the officer

went to serve the arrest, the general was gone on an expedition of his own to the Rapids—and as there was no officer in his brigade, who was qualified to succeed him in the command, it was deemed most prudent by the commander in chief to stay the prosecution for the present. A court of enquiry was afterwards demanded by general Tupper at fort Meigs, when no person acquainted with these transactions was there—he was of course honorably acquitted. The failure however appears to have been caused, chiefly by his want of energy and decision, and in some measure by the insubordination of the troops, proceeding from a want of confidence in their general, which will always produce this effect among militia.

As general Harrison was returning from Defiance to St. Marys, he was informed by an express from fort Wayne, that the Indians were collecting again at that place; and when he arrived at St. Marys he found a corps of 500 mounted volunteers, who had come there to join the mounted expedition to Detroit. They were commanded by colonel Allen Trimble, and were despatched to fort Wayne with instructions to proceed again from that post against the White Pigeon's town, a Potawatamie village about 60 miles distant, on the head waters of the St. Josephs of the Lake. When the colonel arrived at fort Wayne, nearly one half of his command refused to advance any farther—he proceeded however with the balance, and destroyed two villages, and would have killed and captured the inhabitants, but for the treachery of one of his guides, who intentionally apprized them of their danger.

The Indian messengers, who had been sent from fort Wayne to bring in the Miami chiefs from Mississiniway to hold a council, were now at St. Marys with a number of those chiefs. They came prepared either to deny or to palliate their hostility, as circumstances might dictate. Finding the general well informed respecting their conduct, they threw themselves on the mercy of the government, and agreed to abide the decision of the president. Five chiefs were named by general Harrison, which they agreed to send in to Piqua as hostages, till the pleasure of the president could be known.

General Harrison now proceeded by Piqua to Urbana, where some of the Ohio troops under general Tupper were stationed, and from that place to Franklinton, making arrangements for expediting the march of the troops, and for hastening the requisite supplies and artillery. The troops under Winchester were now employed for some weeks in completing the new fort, which in honor of their commander was called Fort Winchester, and in making perogues and canoes 5 or 6 miles down the Miami. The regiment under Barbee at St. Marys completed a fort at that place and called it Fort Barbee. Poague's regiment built Fort Amanda on the Auglaize, about 12 miles from the former; and colonel Jennings completed the fort at his encampment. These regiments were at the same time employed in constructing boats and canoes, and in escorting provisions to Defiance. General Harrison kept his head quarters for some time at Franklinton forwarding provisions and military stores towards fort M'Arthur and Upper Sandusky. To the former the Ohio troops at Urbana removed in the latter part of this month. The most diligent exertions were thus making in every quarter to get ready for the main expedition against Malden.

CHAPTER IV.

*Attack on Fort Harrison—massacre of Pigeon Roost—
expeditions of Hopkins—of governor Edwards and
colonel Russell—difficulties of transportation—expedition to the Rapids—to Mississiniway—views
and plans of the general, and prospects of the
campaign.*

WE must leave the northwestern troops for a moment,
making preparations for their advance towards Detroit to regain our lost territory, whilst we take a rapid glance at the military operations in the western
Territories.

On the 3rd. of September, a body of Indians, Kickapoos and Winebagoes, comprising men, women and
children, assembled at Fort Harrison, where captain
Zachary Taylor had the command. They wished to
be admitted into the fort under the pretence of holding
a council—they also pretended to be in great want of
provisions. Captain Taylor gave them something to
eat; but as two young men had been killed on the
preceding evening near the fort, he suspected their
treachery and refused to admit them. They loitered
about the fort, still professing to be friendly, till in the
night of the 4th, when they set fire to one of the block
houses. At the same time a large body of warriors,
who had been lying in ambush, commenced a brisk
fire, which was promptly returned by the garrison.
As the house burned down, the Indians fired over the
ruins into the fort; while captain Taylor with great
presence of mind, pulled down a cabin, and with its
materials constructed a breast work across the opening
produced by the fire. The Indians made several des-

V

perate charges, in which they attempted to fire the
fort in other places, and to enter by the breach; but
they were repulsed and defeated in every attempt.
So critical and alarming however was the situation of
the garrison, that two of the men jumped over the
picketting, preferring the chance of escape through
the ranks of the enemy, to the prospect of being burnt
or massacred in the fort. One of them was killed,
and the other retreated back to the walls of the fort.
after being wounded, and concealed himself behind
some old barrels till morning. At daylight the Indians retreated, but still hovered round the fort for seven
or eight days. Captain Taylor then strengthened the
work where the block house had stood, and prepared
himself for a regular siege. He had lost in this affair
but three killed and three or four wounded—but he
had sustained a serious loss in the burning of the block
house. It contained his provisions, the loss of which
now exposed his men to great sufferance for the want
of food. Some corn which had been cultivated near
the fort, was their only subsistence for several days.
He immediately attempted to send an express to Vincennes with intelligence of the event; but it was several days before any person could escape through the
Indians, and the messenger at last had to pass their
encampment in the night.

Captain Taylor merited and received much applause
for the defence he made. His force did not exceed
50 men, one third of whom were sick; while the number of the enemy was comparatively very great, comprising all the forces they could raise in that quarter
of the country. They had assembled with a determination to take the fort either by stratagem or force;
and captain Taylor for his gallant resistance was immediately brevetted a major.

Exasperated to madness by the failure of their attempt on fort Harrison, a considerable party of Indians now made an irruption into the settlements on the

Pidgeon Roost fork of White river, where they barbarously massacred 21 of the inhabitants, many of them women and children. The children had their brains knocked out against trees; and one woman, who was pregnant, was ripped open, and her unborn infant taken from her, and its brains knocked out. However, this was but a small matter—it amounted to *no essential injury*—it was all for the best, as it was done by the disciples of the *Wabash Prophet*, who was in a close and holy alliance with George the third, *defender* of the faith, and *legitimate* sovereign of the Bible Society nation, which is the bulwark of our most holy religion. Yet it excited the indignation of the uncivilized republican infidels in the neighbouring settlements of Indiana and Kentucky, and several hundred men were collected, and arrived at that place on the second day after the occurrence. The Indians by this time had fled beyond the reach of pursuit. Colonel Keiger of Kentucky, however, with a small party who volunteered to go with him, followed their trail about sixty miles towards the Delaware towns at the head of White river.

The regiments of colonels Wilcox, Miller, and Barbour of the Kentucky militia, were now on their march to Vincennes, but they did not arrive in time to meet the Indians at fort Harrison. Colonel Russell being advised of its critical situation, collected some companies of rangers and Indiana militia, and by forced marches arrived there on the 13th, to the great joy of the garrison, who were in a starving condition. Several wagons with provisions were now ordered up to the fort, under an escort of 13 men commanded by lieutenant Fairbanks of the regulars. After colonel Russel had met and passed this party on his return, they were surprised and literally cut to pieces by the Indians, two or three only escaping. Major M'Gary with a battalion of colonel Barbour's regiment was at the same time on his way with provisions for the garrison ; and being reinforced with some companies of Russell's rangers, they arrived in safety at the fort, having buried the mangled remains of the regulars on their way.

In the Illinois and Missouri Territories, many depredations had also been committed by the Indians. Governor Edwards of the Illinois Territory had been very attentive to these matters. He had sent spies into the Indian country, by whom he had ascertained, that they were greatly elated with their success and the prospect of driving the white people over the Ohio river, and were determined to carry on a desperate war against the frontiers in the month of September. To meet the emergency, he had called, under authority from the war department, on the governor of Kentucky for a regiment of men ; and colonel Barbour's regiment had been ordered by governor Shelby to march to Kaskaskia ; but general Gibson, the acting governor of Indiana, ordered it to Vincennes when fort Harrison was in danger, conceiving that he was authorized to take such a step, as the lieutenant of governor Harrison, who was commander in chief of all the forces in those Territories. Governor Edwards though deprived of this aid, made vigorous exertions to defend his settlements. He embodied a portion of the militia, which he held in readiness to act whenever danger might present. Several companies of rangers were also encamped on the Mississippi above St. Louis, and on the Illinois river. These troops served to keep the savages in check in those regions.

The troops already mentioned, not having been deemed sufficient to prosecute the war in the western Territories, the following address by governor Shelby was published early in this month :

'*Frankfort, September 8, 1812.*

'FELLOW-CITIZENS OF KENTUCKY !

'I have received information from his excellency governor Harrison, commanding the army northwest of the Ohio, dated the 6th inst. at Piqua, that the British and Indians had besieged fort Wayne and perhaps had taken it: that it was the object of the enemy to push on to fort Harrison and Vincennes—and he has required of me to leave nothing undone to relieve those places. In addition to this, information is also received, that the Indians have murdered twenty-one persons not more than twenty miles north of the Ohio! and that a very extensive combination of savages, aided by the British from Canada, are momently expected on the frontier of Indiana and Illinois territories.

'With this information before us—and the requisition of governor Harrison, that a number of mounted volunteers be requested to march to the aid of our suffering fellow-citizens, it is hoped that it will rouse the spirit and indignation of the freemen of Kentucky, and induce a sufficient number of them to give their services to their country for a short period on this interesting occasion.

'It is proposed to accept the service of such a number of mounted volunters as may be adequate to the defence of the said territories: and if necessary, follow the enemy, and carry offensive war into their country, and lay waste their towns.

'The volunteers will rendezvous at Louisville on the 18th day of this month, with at least thirty days provisions. The whole will be commanded by major general Samuel Hopkins; an officer of great merit and experience. Should any company of volunteers not be able to rendezvous on the day appointed, they can follow on and join the army on their march.

'Kentuckians! ever pre-eminent for their patriotism, bravery and good conduct, will I am persuaded, on this occasion give to the world a new evidence of their love for their country, and a determination, at every hazard, to rescue their fellow-men from the murders and devastations of a cruel and barbarous enemy.

'ISAAC SHELBY.'

In compliance with this address, upwards of two thousand mounted volunteers repaired to Louisville, the Red Banks, and other points of the Ohio, on their way to Vincennes. Such indeed was the excess of numbers that the governor turned back several hundreds at Louisville; and two companies from Bath and Montgomery under captains Manifee and Coope, were stopped at Frankfort. At Louisville an old veteran, a volunteer in one of the companies turned back

after fretting a little at his fate, was heard to say by
way of consolation, " Well, well, Kentucky has often
glutted the market with hemp, flour, and tobacco, and
now she has done it with volunteers." These troops
began to arrive at Vincennes about the 31st, and continued daily to arrive until the 2nd of October. Some
difficulty was experienced in organizing them, in consequence of their arriving in this irregular manner.
Four regiments however were formed, to be commanded by colonels Samuel Caldwell, John Thomas, James
Allen and Young Ewing. These regiments constituted two brigades, the first to be commanded by general James Ray of Mercer, an early adventurer in
Kentucky, who was experienced in Indian fighting;
the other to be commanded by general Jonathan Ram-
sey, of Livingston Kentucky. And a few days after
these arrangements were made, another regiment was
added under colonel Samuel South of Madison.
George Walker esq. was appointed judge advocate;
P. Butler, adjutant general; majors William Trigg
and W. A. Lee, aids to general Hopkins; J. C.
Breckinridge, secretary; and William Blair and Joseph Weisiger, acted as volunteer aids. While the
troops were collecting, general Hopkins was too unwell
to attend to business in person, but his aids, and his
quarter master general, colonel R. Taylor of Frankfort Kentucky, were indefatigable in their attention
and exertions.

A corps of 2,000 volunteer mounted riflemen being
thus organized, and every practicable preparation for
their march being made, the general in chief proceeded to lead them early in October against the enemy.
He marched up to fort Harrison, where some delay
took place in perfecting his arrangements, particularly
in relation to the necessary supplies, which were still
very inadequate. Orders were given for drawing ten
days rations, but many of the men did not get more
flour than would last two days, though beef and bacon

were plentiful.   The army then crossed the Wabash
and encamped a few miles from the river, where a
council of all the officers was held, and the general informed them of his intention to march against the prin-
pal Kickapoo village situated on the waters of the Illinois river.   His guides were examined in the council,
and stated the distance to the village to be 85 miles in
a northwest direction.   The plan of the general then
received the unanimous approbation of his officers.
The march was resumed, and after proceeding about
25 miles to the northwest, a trail of Indians was discovered in the prairie, which led to the north.   The
army pursued it, and continued their march in that direction, and even northeast, for several days, frequently crossing trails of Indians which led to the westward.
The want of provisions and forage began to be severely felt by the men and their horses; and a strong suspicion began to prevail among the troops, that the
guides either from ignorance or treachery were leading
them astray.   Some Indian huts and a council house
were at last discovered, from which there were fresh
trails leading to the west.   But the guides still went
to the north, averring that they knew the country well,
and were now near the villages.   Presently one of
them announced, that he had discovered a town with
his spy glass—but on coming nearer, it proved to be
nothing but a fire in the prairie.   This produced chagrin and despondence in the men, and greatly increased their suspicion of the guides.   The general then
turned their march to the west, declaring that he would
act as guide himself.   Next morning a council was
called to consider the condition of the troops and the
policy of further pursuit.   After mature consideration,
the council were unanimous, that in the present starving situation of both men and horses, with a very uncertain prospect of finding the enemy soon, it was most
proper to abandon the pursuit and return.   This decision being made known through the camp, the men

warmly approved it and prepared for its execution.
The general however thought proper to issue an order,
or at least a request, that the army should follow him
one day longer in search of the enemy; but when ready to march the men unanimously took the direction
to Vincennes, notwithstanding the remonstrances of
their general officers. It has since been ascertained
that the village was still 60 or 70 miles further west.
And thus through the lateness of the season, the scarcity of provisions, and the mistakes of the guides, the
expedition entirely failed as to its principal object; but
by exhibiting a formidable force at a greater distance
in the Indian country than any former army had proceeded, a servicable impression was made on the fears
of the enemy. Much crimination and recrimination
having passed between the general, his men and the
citizens, in consequence of this failure, a court of enquiry
was held on the general at his request which reported,
that not one of the charges or their specifications were
supported by evidence; the greater number being ex-
pressly negatived by the evidence adduced on the part of
the prosecution, and the whole of them clearly and fully
refuted. The court therefore acquitted the general, and
gave as their opinion, that his conduct merited the applause rather than the censure of his country.

After the mounted men were discharged, and had
left the frontiers, general Hopkins determined to conduct an expedition of infantry from fort Harrison
against the Indians on the Wabash. A corps of 1250
men were accordingly prepared for this service, consisting of the regiments of Kentucky militia, commanded by colonels Barbour, Miller, and Wilcox; a
small party of regulars under major Z. Taylor, and
about 50 rangers and spies on horseback, under captains Beckers and Washburn. On the 11th of November the march was commenced from fort Harrison,
and conducted with much caution up the east side of
the Wabash. As the enemy had now been long apprised, and well informed, of the intended operations

against them, it was deemed extremely probable that
they would attempt to surprise the detachment, and to
defeat it on its march, and that their arrangements for
this would be chiefly made on the west side of the river, where the ground was the most favorable for such
a scheme; hence the route on the east side was preferred and cautiously pursued. The provisions, forage, and military stores were embarked in seven
boats, which were placed under the command of colonel Barbour with a battalion of his regiment. The
boats and the troops on land, generally encamped together at night, with a view to greater security. A
rise of water in the Wabash from late rains, rendered
the progress of the detachment very slow, so that it
was the 19th before they arrived at the Prophet's town.
Several days were then spent in reconnoitring the
country, and in destroying the neighbouring evacuated
villages, together with the corn and other resources
which had been left about them. The Prophet's town,
containing at this time about 40 cabins; a Winebago
village, four miles lower down, on Ponce Passu creek,
and near the Wabash on the east side, containing
about 40 houses also; and a Kickapoo village on the
west side, containing about 160 cabins; were all completely destroyed. On the 21st a small party of Indians were discovered on Ponce Passu creek, seven
miles east of the Prophet's town, who fired on a reconnoitring party and killed one soldier. On the next
day colonels Miller and Wilcox went out with a party of 60 mounted men, with a view to bury the man
who had been killed, and to obtain more complete information respecting the enemy; but they fell into an
ambuscade and lost 18 of their men in killed, wounded and missing. It was ascertained however, that the
Indians were encamped on the creek in considerable
force. The general now determined to march against
them in the morning; but a violent snow storm with
an extreme degree of cold, which commenced in the

W

night and continued till the evening of the next day, prevented him from moving until the morning of the 24th. On arriving at the creek it was found that the enemy had fled before the fall of snow. The position they had evacuated was as strong as nature could make it. Their camp was secured on the rear and flanks by a deep rapid stream, which run round them in a semicircle; while their front was rendered inaccessible by a bluff, 100 feet high and nearly perpendicular, and which could be ascended at three places only by steep and difficult ravines. As the enemy would not defend themselves in this place, it was evident they had determined not to fight; any further search for them in the wilderness by foot troops at this inclement season, was therefore perfectly nugatory. The general had determined to spend another week at least in endeavoring to find their camps; but this occurrence, together with " the shoeless, shirtless condition of the troops, now clad in the remnants of their summer clothes; a river full of ice; hills covered with snow; a rigid climate, and no certain point to which he could further direct his operations," now induced him with the unanimous advice of his officers, to return immediately to Vincennes. On this expedition the whole detachment behaved with the greatest propriety—performing all their duties with promptitude and alacrity, and enduring many privations and hardships with cheerfulness and fortitude. Not a murmur nor complaint was heard. If the conduct and issue of the mounted expedition was disgraceful in some degree to our militia, their character for exemplary devotion to the common cause was retrieved by the good conduct of the infantry on this occasion. Another and more successful enterprise had also in the mean time been conducted against the Indians by governor Edwards and colonel Russell.

About the time general Hopkins marched from Vincennes with his mounted troops, colonel Russell went

with some rangers, and joined governor Edwards with
a party of regulars and militia, making altogether
about 400 men, with which they penetrated into the
Indian country still further to the northwest, intending
to co-operate with general Hopkins on the Illinois river at Peoria, to which place the latter intended to
conduct his expedition against the Kickapoos.   They
could hear nothing of the general however in that
quarter, and being too weak to continue long by themselves at such a distance in the country of the enemy,
they were obliged to make a stroke and retire.   They
accordingly proceeded against a considerable village
of the enemy, about 20 miles above Peoria, and immediately at the head of the Peoria lake.   They succeeded in surprising its inhabitants, who immediately
fled into a swamp, which lay between the town and
the river.   Our men pursued them with impetuosity
about three miles, frequently up to the waist in mud
and water, nor ceased from the pursuit until they had
driven them over the Illinois river.   Their loss was
very great : upwards of 20 warriors were found dead ;
and many others must have been killed and overlooked in the swamp, beside those who fell in the river and
were carried away by the current.   Our loss was four
wounded—none of them mortal.   The town together
with a large quantity of corn and other plunder was
destroyed, and about 80 horses brought away by the
retiring conquerors.

We must now recur to the movements and transactions of the northwestern army, under the more immediate direction of the commander in chief.   The
troops moving on the line of operations, which passed
from Delaware by Upper to Lower Sandusky, composed of the brigades from Virginia and Pennsylvania, and that of Perkins from Ohio, were now designated in general orders and commonly known as the
right wing of the army : Tupper's brigade moving on
Hull's road formed the centre division : and the Kentuckians under Winchester were styled the left wing.

General Harrison continued his head quarters at Franklinton and Delaware, and was chiefly employed in superintending the supplies. Notwithstanding the failure of the intended expedition to the Rapids under Tupper, he still placed a high degree of confidence in the militia volunteers, of which his army was composed; but fearing that the extreme hardships and difficulties of the campaign might shake their firmness and evaporate their zeal, he thought it important to collect a body of men, on whom he could fully rely in the most desperate circumstances. He therefore ordered, early in October, all the recruits of the regular army in the western states, to be marched to the frontiers. Those in Ohio were to be commanded by lieutenant colonel Campbell; and those of Tennessee, by colonel Anderson, or some field officer of his regiment.

The different corps of the army were now chiefly employed, for several months, in forwarding supplies on the different routes on which they had marched, or were destined to march. The Virginia and Pennsylvania troops were employed in escorting the artillery and military stores towards Upper Sandusky; the Ohio troops conveyed provisions from Manary's block house, near the head of the Big Miami, twenty miles north of Urbana, to forts McArthur and Finley on Hull's road; while the Kentuckians were traversing the swamps of St. Marys and the Auglaise, and descending those rivers in small craft, to carry provisions to fort Winchester and the left wing. The difficulties of this business cannot be adequately exhibited in a cursory statement. The letters of the commander in chief, to the war department, at this period, were constantly filled with details on this subject. On the 22d of October, he thus addressed the government—"I am not able to fix any period for the advance of the troops to Detroit. It is pretty evident, that it cannot be done, on proper principles, until the frost shall become so severe, as to enable us to use the rivers and the margin of the lake, for the transportation of the baggage on the ice.   To get supplies forward, through a swampy wilderness of near two hundred miles, in wagons or on packhorses, which are to carry their own provisions, *is absolutely impossible*." The object however "can be accomplished by using the margin of the lake as above mentioned, if the troops are provided with warm clothing, and the winter is such as it commonly is in this climate."—"No species of supplies are calculated on being found in the Michigan Territory.   The farms upon the river Raisin, which might have afforded a quantity of forage, are nearly all broken up and destroyed.   This article then, as well as the provisions for the men, is to be taken from this state—a circumstance which must at once put to rest, every idea for a land conveyance at this season—since it would require at least two wagons with forage, for each one that is loaded with provisions and other articles."

" My present plan is, to occupy Sandusky and accumulate at that place as much provision and forage as possible, to be taken from thence upon slides to the river Raisin.   At Defiance, fort Jennings and St. Marys, boats and slides are preparing to take advantage of a rise of water or a fall of snow."   He farther stated that he had kept the troops from advancing, with a view to save the expense of supplying them at a greater distance, until the whole should be ready to move on the main expedition ; and that the contractors had as yet done little or nothing towards making the deposits which he had urged them to accomplish.   The principal contractor had let out his contract for the northwestern part of the state at a rate so low, that the subcontractors were unable to furnish the supplies— and some of them too were charactes on whom no reliance could be placed.   The principal contractor it was said would make $100,000 by his contract for that state; yet he was not disposed to make the least sacrifice of his own interests for the public good.

The general proceeds to state in the same letter, that on account of the troops being kept in the interior,— "depredations by small parties of Indians may and will be made, but it is impossible that any considerable body can advance against the settlements, without being in danger of being intercepted on their retreat. I am persuaded that the Indians have done less mischief on the frontiers since the declaration of war, than they did in the same time preceding it. It was suggested to me a few days ago by a member of congress, that the possession of Detroit by the enemy, would probably be the most effectual bar to the attainment of peace. If this was really the case, I would undertake to recover it with a detachment of the army at any time. A few hundred packhorses, with a drove of beeves, without artillery and heavy baggage, would subsist the 1500 or 2000 men, which I would select for the purpose, until the balance of the army could arrive. But having in view offensive operations from Detroit, an advance of this sort would be premature and ultimately disadvantageous."

A few days after the letter was written, from which the above extracts are made, Harrison was informed by generals Perkins and Beall belonging to a detachment of Ohio militia under general Wadsworth, in the northwestern parts of the state, that the opening of a road from a point near Mansfield to Lower Sandusky, in which they had been engaged by the orders of governor Meigs, was forbidden by general Wadsworth; and that a road from Sandusky to the Rapids would be impassable unless causewayed for a distance of 15 miles. This information induced the general to set out immediately to make a personal examination into the state of affairs in that quarter. He found major general Wadsworth commanding 800 men, near the mouth of the river Huron, and 500 more under brigadier general Beall near Mansfield. The two corps were consolidated, and placed under brigadier general Perkins with orders to proceed to lower Sandusky, and open a road thence to the Rapids, making the causeways required by the state of the country. He returned to his head quarters early in November; and about the 15th of that month, the Pennsylvania troops with the artillery passed Mansfield, destined to meet the Virginia troops at Upper Sandusky.

On the 15th of November general Harrison informed the war department, that he did not think it safe to move from the Rapids until one million of rations had been accumulated at that place. Considerable progress had now been made—but he adds "you can scarcely form an idea sir, of the difficulty with which land transportation is effected north of the fortieth degree of latitude in this country. The country beyond that, is almost a continued swamp to the lakes. Where the streams run favorable to your course, a small strip of better ground is generally found, but in crossing from one river to another, the greater part of the way at this season is covered with water. Such is actually the situation of that space between the Sandusky and the Miami Rapids; and from the best information I could acquire, whilst I was at Huron, the road over it must be causewayed at least half the way." He further stated, that in the opinion of the quarter master, it would require two teams, loaded with forage for their own subsistence, for every one employed in carrying other articles from Franklinton to Upper Sandusky, at which place it was necessary to accumulate, not only provisions for the men, but forage to serve at least two thousand horses and oxen, to be employed in advancing on the main expedition. The expenses of such transportation, must of course be enormous. The intention of employing the dragoons on that expedition was for this reason abandoned.

About this time major Hardin had passed between the left wing at fort Winchester and the head quarters of the general—while on the journey he wrote confidentially to governor Shelby, "The late rains have rendered the roads desperate. I learn that this route is considered the best of the three, along which provisions are to be conveyed—if so, I am certain that it is morally impossible to provision the army at Detroit by land. Indeed such is the state of the road, that no wagon can take its own forage from Piqua to the Rapids. As for a water carriage, we could have it to the Rapids; but while the enemy commands the lake, we are there cut short. I therefore deem it impracticable to penetrate Canada from this quarter this season—"

"I know that it will be mortifying to Kentucky for this army to return without doing any thing—but it is better to do that, than to attempt impossibilities. I wish to God the public mind were informed of our difficulties, and gradually prepared for this course..... In my opinion, we should in this quarter disband all, but those sufficient for a strong frontier guard, and for convoys &c. and prepare for the next season."

Having thus exhibited the inglorious labors and difficulties, which this army had to encounter in procuring supplies, we will now with more pleasure recount some of its military movements and exploits. Early in November general Tupper, who had previously marched his command from Urbana to the frontiers on Hull's road, sent his spy company under captain Hinkston to reconnoitre at the Rapids. The captain concealed his men on the southeast side of the river, where he had discovered a British and Indian encampment in the opposite bottom, which was an open prairie. Presently a British officer with a few Indians came over the river, and when they had advanced some distance from their boat, captain Hinkston fired upon them, and took the officer prisoner. He was a captain by the name of Clarke. Having returned with him to general Tupper's camp, he informed the general, that there were three or four hundred Indians and about 75 British at the Rapids, where they had come to carry off the corn, of which a considerable quantity still remained. General Tupper immediately prepared a strong detachment consisting of six hundred and fifty men, who volunteered to go against the enemy. He notified general Winchester of the intended movement, and marched on the 10th from fort M'Arthur, with a light six pounder, and 5 days provisions in the knapsacks of his men. The badness of the road obliged him to leave the six pounder at Hull's packsaddle block house; and when he arrived at Portage river, 20 miles from the Rapids, he sent the spies in advance to reconnoitre. They met him in the evening, five miles on their return, with information that the enemy remained in the same position near the foot of the Rapids. The detachment was now halted till near sunset, to avoid being discovered by the allies, and then marched to a ford about two and a half miles above them. Here spies were again sent to ascertain their precise situation, who returned about nine o'clock, with information that they were encamped in close order, and employed in singing and dancing. Orders were now given to cross the river, with a view to attack them at the dawn of day. Colonel Stafford commanded a battalion on the left flank in single files; colonel Miller's regiment composed the right; and major Galloway commanded a battalion in reserve. In this order they intended to cross the river and surround the enemy's camp. Special instructions were given to each officer; and every soldier, who did not feel willing to cross, had permission to shift for himself. The men were much fatigued, and the weather was very cold. General Tupper pushed into the water and crossed at the head of the first section. The others attempted to cross in double

X

files, with their arms locked together, and when nearly two hundred had got over, the greater part of one
section were washed off their feet, and lost their guns.
The water was waist deep, and ran very swift. The
few horses belonging to the detachment were sent immediately to save the men, and happily succeeded in
getting out the whole. An attempt was next made to
cross on horses, but they being weak were also washed down, and the riders plunged into the current.
Finding it impracticable to get the detachment over at
this place, those who had succeeded recrossed, and the
whole retired to the woods and encamped.

Next morning the 14th, general Tupper despatched
an express to general Winchester, stating his situation,
and suggesting the propriety of a reinforcement, if one
had not already been sent; at the same time remark-
ing, that he could not remain there longer than another
day, unless he could receive a supply of provisions.
He then sent his spies down the river in view of the
enemy, with a design to decoy them over; but the Indians were not to be caught in this way. Only a few
crossed, and they would not venture far on shore,
which was open ground for half a mile. Failing in
this project, the general marched the whole of his
troops down in the woods, and shewed the heads of
his columns in the open ground. This alarmed the
enemy considerably. The squaws ran to the woods—
the British ran to their boats and escaped—the Indians more brave than their allies, paraded and fired
across the river, but without effect. The general then
fell back, in hopes to entice them over; but he could
neither induce them to cross, nor scare them off without a fight like the British. At last he marched back
towards his camp. Some Indians were seen, in the
mean time, to mount their horses and ride up the river; and some of Tupper's men imprudently pursued
a gang of hogs about half a mile from the main body,
while some others went into an adjoining corn field to

gather corn. The mounted Indians, having crossed
the river, came upon the latter party and killed four
of them; and then boldly charged on the left flank,
but were repulsed. A large body at the same time
crossed opposite the head of the column, where they
were met by major Bentley's battalion, and driven
back with some loss. A noted chief by the name of
Split-Log was their commander.

Late in the evening the detachment retreated, leaving *accidentally* in the camp, a sick man who was unable to march, and who fell a prey to the tomahawk
and scalping knife.

On the next morning, the 15th, the express arrived
at Winchester's camp, with Tupper's request for a reinforcement. A detachment of 450 men had already been
organized, and marched that morning under the command
of colonel Lewis, to whom the information in Tupper's
despatch was immediately forwarded. The colonel
proceeded all day in a forced march, down the north
side of the river, and in the night despatched ensign
Todd, quarter master to the advance of the left wing,
accompanied by 5 guides with instructions to proceed
to general Tupper on the other side of the river, and
agree on some point, for a junction of the detachments
on the north side early in the morning, with a view to
attack the Indians in their encampment. At 12 o'clock
in the night, Todd reached Tupper's camp, and found
that it had been abandoned, apparently with much precipitation, as the fires were extinct, and two men were
lying there tomahawked and scalped. He recrossed
the river immediately, and joined colonel Lewis before
day, who then retreated to Winchester's camp, under
the impression that Tupper had been defeated.

This movement to the Rapids by Tupper was sufficiently bold and hazardous for a spirited soldier; but
his conduct after his failure in attempting to cross the
river is not to be commended. He should doubtless
have retreated up the river to a place where he could

cross, and have waited there for the reinforcement under Lewis. After sending for that reinforcement, he
was surely blameable in breaking up his camp and retreating, without communicating to it any intelligence
of such a movement. His men however behaved well,
having acted bravely in every instance, except in retreating, and having performed a severe march, 160
miles in all, on a road which was then a continued
swamp the whole way.

Though but little execution was done on this excursion, it frightened off the British without the corn they
had come for. and alarmed the Indians sufficiently to
induce them to fall back to the river Raisin. It probably had the effect too, of saving the people of that
place from massacre. These Indians had previously
sent them the following message, committed to writing
by a British pen :

'*The Hurons and other tribes of Indians, assembled at the
    Miami Rapids, to the inhabitants of the river Raisin—*

'Friends listen—you have always told us that you would
give us any assistance in your power. We therefore, as the enemy is approaching us within 25 miles, call upon you all to
rise up and come here immediately, bringing your arms along
with you. Should you fail at this time, we will not consider
you in future as friends; and the consequences may be very
unpleasant. We are well convinced, that you have no writing
forbidding you to assist us.
                    'We are your friends at present,
                        'Signed—ROUND HEAD,
                                WALK-IN-THE-WATER.'

The appearance of Tupper's detachment, having
separated them from their British instigators, and
alarmed them for their own safety, may have deterred
them from the hostility threatened in this message.

Shortly after this expedition by general Tupper to
the Miami Rapids, a tragical adventure occurred in
the left wing of the army. which merits to be minutely
recorded. Captain James Logan, the Shawanoe chief,

by the orders of general Harrison, proceeded with a small party of his tribe, to reconnoitre in the direction of the Rapids. "He met with a superior force of the enemy near that place, by which he was so closely pursued, that his men were obliged to disperse for safety in their retreat. Logan with two of his companions, captain John and Bright-Horn, arrived safe at general Winchester's camp, where he faithfully reported the incidents of the excursion. But there were certain persons in the army, who suspected his fidelity, and reproached him with being friendly, and with communicating intelligence, to the enemy. The noble spirit of Logan could not endure the ungenerous charge. With the sensibility of a genuine soldier, he felt that his honor and fidelity should not only be pure and firm, but unsuspected. He did not however demand a court of inquiry—following the natural dictates of a bold and generous spirit, he determined to prove by unequivocal deeds of valour and fidelity, that he was calumniated by his accusers.

On the 22nd of November, he proceeded the second time, accompanied only by the two persons named above, firmly resolved either to bring in a prisoner or a scalp, or to perish himself in the attempt. When he had gone about ten miles down the north side of the Miami, he met with a British officer, the eldest son of colonel Elliott, accompanied by 5 Indians. As the party was too strong for him, and he had no chance to escape, four of them being on horseback, he determined to pass them under the disguise of friendship for the British. He advanced with confident boldness, and a friendly deportment, to the enemy—but unfortunately one of them was Winemac, a celebrated Potawatamie chief, to whom the person and character of captain Logan were perfectly well known. He persisted however in his first determination, and told them he was going to the Rapids to give information to the British. After conversing some time, he proceeded on

his way, and Winemac with all his companions, turned and went with him.   As they travelled on together,
Winemac and his party closely watched the others,
and when they had proceeded about 8 miles, he proposed to the British officer to seize and tie them. The
officer replied, that they were completely in his power; that if they attempted to run, they could be shot;
or failing in that, the horses could easily run them
down.   This consultation was over heard by Logan:
he had previously intended to go on peaceably till
night, and then make his escape : but he now formed
the bold design of extricating himself by a combat
with double his number.

Having signified his resolution to his men, he commenced the attack by shooting down Winemac himself. The action lasted till they had fired three rounds
apiece, during which time, Logan and his brave companions drove the enemy some distance, and separated
them from their horses.   By the first fire, both Winemac and Elliott fell; by the second a young Ottawa
chief lost his life; and another of the enemy was mortally wounded about the conclusion of the combat, at
which time Logan himself as he was stooping down,
received a ball just below the breast bone : it ranged
downwards and lodged under the skin on his back.
In the mean time, Bright Horn was also wounded, by
a ball which passed through his thigh.   As soon as
Logan was shot, he ordered a retreat; himself and
Bright Horn, wounded as they were, jumped on the
horses of the enemy and rode to Winchester's camp,
a distance of 20 miles in 5 hours. Captain John after taking the scalp of the Ottawa chief, also retreated in safety and arrived at the camp next morning.

Logan had now rescued his character, as a brave
and faithful soldier, from the obloquy, which had unjustly been thrown upon him. But he preserved his
honor, at the expense of the next best gift of Heaven—
his life. His wound proved mortal. He lived two

days in agony, which he bore with uncommon fortitude, and died with the utmost composure and resignation. "More firmness and consummate bravery has
seldom appeared on the military theatre," says Winchester, in his letter to the commanding general. "He
was buried with all the honors due to his rank, and
with sorrow as sincerely and generally displayed, as I
ever witnessed," says major Hardin, in a letter to governor Shelby. His physiognomy was formed on the
best model, and exhibited the strongest marks of courage, intelligence, good humour and sincerity. It was
said by the Indians, that the British had offered one
hundred and fifty dollars for his scalp. He had been
very serviceable to our cause by acting as a guide and
a spy. He had gone with general Hull to Detroit,
and with the first Kentucky troops, who marched to
the relief of fort Wayne.

Captain Logan had been taken prisoner by general
Logan of Kentucky in the year 1786, when he was a
youth. The general on parting with him, had given
him his name, which he retained to the end of his life.
Before the treaty of Greenville, he had distinguished
himself as a warrior, though still very young. His
mother was a sister to the celebrated Tecumseh and
the Prophet. He stated, that in the summer, preceding his death, he had talked one whole night with
Tecumseh, and endeavored to persuade him to remain
at peace, while Tecumseh on the contrary endeavored
to engage him in the war on the side of the British.
His wife when she was young, had also been taken
prisoner by colonel Hardin in 1789, and had remained
in the family till the treaty of Greenville. In the army he had formed an attachment for major Hardin,
the son of the colonel, and son-in-law of general Logan, and now requested him, to see that the money
due for his services was faithfully paid to his family.
He also requested, that his family might be removed
immediately to Kentucky, and his children educated

and brought up in the manner of the white people. He observed that he had killed a great chief, that the hostile Indians knew where his family lived, and that when he was gone, a few base fellows might creep up and destroy them.

Major Hardin having promised to do every thing in his power, to have the wishes of his friend fulfilled, immediately obtained permission from the general, to proceed with Logan's little corps of Indians, to the village of Wapoghconata, where his family resided. When they reached near the village, the scalp of the Ottawa chief was tied to a pole, to be carried in triumph to the council house; and captain John, when they came in sight of the town, ordered the guns of the party to be fired in quick succession, on account of the death of Logan. A council of the chiefs was presently held, in which after consulting two or three days, they decided against sending the family of their departed hero to Kentucky. They appeared however to be fully sensible of the loss they had sustained, and were sincerely grieved for his death.

About the time that Tupper's expedition to the Rapids was in execution, general Harrison determined to send an expedition of horsemen against the Miamies, assembled in the towns on the Mississiniway river, a branch of the Wabash. The reader will recollect, that a deputation of chiefs from those Indians, met general Harrison at St. Marys early in October and sued for peace—that they agreed to abide by the decision of the President, and in the mean time to send in five chiefs to be held as hostages. The President replied to the communication of the general on this subject, that as the disposition of the several tribes would be known best by himself, he must treat them as their conduct and the public interest might in his judgment require. The hostages were never sent in, and further information of their intended hostility was obtained. At the time of their peace mission, they were alarmed by the successful movements, which had been made against other tribes from fort Wayne, and by the formidable expedition which was penetrating their country under general Hopkins. But the failure of that expedition was soon afterwards known to them, and they determined to continue hostile. A white man by the name of William Conner, who had resided many years with the Delawares, and had a wife among them, but who was firmly attached to our cause in this war, was sent to the towns to watch the movements of the Miamies. He visited the villages on the Mississiniway river, and was present at several of their councils. The question of war with the United States and union with the British was warmly debated, and there was much division among the chiefs, but the war party at last prevailed. The presence and intrigues of Tecumseh, and afterwards the retreat of general Hopkins, rendered them nearly unanimous for war.

To avert the evils of their hostility was the object of the expedition against Mississiniway. "The situation of this town, as it regards one line of operations, even if the hostility of the inhabitants was less equivocal, would render a measure of this kind highly proper; but from the circumstance of general Hopkins's failure, it becomes indispensable. Relieved from the fears excited by the invasion of their country, the Indians from the upper part of the Illinois river, and to the south of lake Michigan, will direct all their efforts against fort Wayne, and the convoys which are to follow the left wing of the army. Mississiniway will be their rendezvous, where they will receive provisions and every assistance they may require for any hostile enterprise. From that place they can by their runners ascertain the period, at which every convoy may set out from St. Marys, and with certainty intercept it on its way to the Miami Rapids. But that place being broken up, and the provisions destroyed, there will be

Y

nothing to subsist any body of Indians, nearer than
the Potawatamie towns on the waters of the St. Josephs of the Lake." *Harrison.*

The detachment was placed under the command of
lieutenant colonel Campbell of the 19th regiment, and
consisted of colonel Simrall's dragoons, a squadron of
cavalry under major Ball, Elliott's company of United
States' infantry, Alexander's 12 months volunteer riflemen, and Butler's company of Pittsburgh volunteers—all mounted and armed with muskets and rifles,
and forming together a corps of 600 men. They
marched from Franklinton on the 25th of November,
by the way of Dayton, to Greenville; which place
they left on the 14th December for the Indian town,
distant about 80 miles, each man carrying ten days
rations, and as much forage as he could with convenience. The weather was extremely cold, and the
ground hard frozen and covered with snow. On the
evening of the third day, when the party was about
20 miles from their destination, a halt was called to
take some refreshment and hold a council. It was determined in the council to march all night, and to attack the villages very early in the morning. When
they had arrived in the night, within three miles of
the first village, as the guides supposed, they halted
again and waited till daylight, when the march was
again resumed. Their progress was delayed a little
by a difficult swamp, of which the guides were ignorant. Presently the front guard observed four Indians
on horseback, who were pursued; and some person
having imprudently raised the Indian yell, the whole
detachment charged at full speed, and in a few minutes the first village was surrounded. But many of
the Indians had already escaped over the river, on
which the village was built—some who remained made
a little resistance, but the greater part surrendered immediately. Those who had fled were pursued by
captain Johnston, some of them killed, and seven or

eight captured. The result of the whole, was eight
warriors killed, and forty-two prisoners aken, consisting of men, women, and children. Colonel Campbell lost two men killed. In advancing upon the town,
colonel Simrall's regiment formed the left column, major Ball's squadron the right, and the infantry the centre. The prisoners being placed under the infantry as
a guard, and the huts being fired, the dragoons proceeded down the river three miles, to the village of
Silver Heels, and two other small towns; which had
all been abandoned by their inhabitants in confused
precipitation. The towns were burnt, and all the property destroyed or brought away. When the dragoons returned to the first village, as the whole detachment was much fatigued, having been thirty-six
hours on horseback, with little intermission, they determined to encamp till next day. Very little corn
had been obtained, the greater part having been already consumed by the Indians, or hid in the ground.

The encampment for the night was formed on the
bank of the Mississiniway river, about 200 yards
square. The infantry and riflemen were posted on
the bank; colonel Simrall's dragoons formed the left
and half the rear line; major Ball's squadron formed
the right and the rest of the rear. Major Ball being
officer of the day, caused strong guards to be placed
out, with small redoubts at each angle, at the distance
of sixty yards, where a captain's guard with two subalterns were stationed. Beyond these at a similar distance, the sentinels were placed. During the night,
the sentinels reported, that they could perceive Indians round the camp examining it. A fire was also
discovered down the river. From these appearances,
an attack was anticipated, and the men were raised
and directed to have their arms in their hands, two
hours before daylight. Reviellee was beat, and adjutant Payne summoned the field officers and captains
to head quarters to consult about the future operations

against the principal village, which was 12 miles lower down the river. While the officers were in council, about half an hour before day, the Indians made
a violent attack upon the rear right angle. The officers went to their posts, and in a moment the lines
were formed and the fire of the enemy returned with
effect. Captain Pierce who commanded at the re-
doubt where the attack was made, bravely maintained
his post till he was shot and tomahawked. His guard
then retreated to the lines. The angle attacked, was
composed of captain Garrard's right, and the left of
captain Hopkins's company, who resisted the onset
with great firmness. In a few minutes the action became general along the right flank and a part of the
rear. The spies together with the Pittsburgh Blues
promptly reinforced the point assailed, and took their
station on the left of captain Hopkins. The action
continued near an hour, and was gallantly supported
by major Ball's squadron, the reinforcements above
named, and some of captain Elliott's company. At
daylight a gallant charge was made by captain Trotter at the head of his troop, from the left of Ball's
squadron. and by captain Johnston with his company
from the right, with a view to take the Indians in their
flanks and rear. Captain Trotter's command attacked
and dispersed a superior number of Indians, killing
several of them in the encounter. During the attack
the enemy several times advanced close to the lines,
apparently determined to rescue the captives or perish
in the attempt : but when daylight appeared, and they
were charged from the lines, they despaired of success
and fled in every direction. They left about fifteen
dead on the ground, besides what were thrown into
the river and carried away. The loss on the part of
the detachment was eight killed and 48 wounded, several of whom afterwards died. Captain Trotter and
lieutenants Hedges, Basey and Hickman were among
the wounded. Lieutenant Waltz of Markle's com-

pany of volunteers, was killed—like the gallant Spencer in the battle of Tippecanoe, he could not be induced to leave his post after he had received two wounds, one of which threatened the loss of his arm, but was mounting his horse to make a charge, when he was shot through the head. All the officers and soldiers engaged, with very few exceptions, behaved with great firmness and gallantry. Colonel Simrall was afterwards particularly commended in a general order for the excellent discipline of his regiment, which was deemed equal to that of any other in America. Colonel Campbell and majors Ball and M'Dowell were also applauded as excellent officers, besides many others of less rank.

As soon after the battle as the wounded could be dressed and litters made to carry them, the detachment commenced their return. Colonel Campbell had learnt from a prisoner, that Tecumseh with six hundred warriors was but 18 miles below him; of course it was not prudent to remain there any longer, in the condition in which the battle had left him. Many of his men were already very much frostbitten; and in the wilderness through which he had to return, there were many creeks and swamps, which would be rendered impassible by a thaw. His march was very slow on account of the wounded and sick; and provisions soon became very scarce. But captain Hite had been sent express to head quarters on the day after the battle; and a reinforcement of 90 men with provisions was immediately sent to meet the detachment. A strong breastwork was erected every night, and one third of the men were placed on guard. When they arrived at Greenville, about 300 were rendered unfit for duty by frost, sickness, and wounds. They deserve great credit for the firmness with which they endured such extraordinary hardships, as well as for their bravery and good conduct in battle. "But the character of this gallant detachment, exhibiting as it

did, perseverance, fortitude and bravery, would however be incomplete, if in the midst of victory they had
forgotten the feelings of humanity. It is with the
sincerest pleasure, that the general has heard, that the
most punctual obedience was paid to his orders in not
only saving all the women and children, but in spar-
ing all the warriors who ceased to resist; and that,
even when vigorously attacked by the enemy, the
claims of mercy prevailed over every sense of their
own danger, and this heroic band respected the lives
of their prisoners. Let an account of murdered inno-
cence be opened in the records of Heaven, against our
enemies alone. The American soldier will follow the
example of his government, and the sword of the one
will not be raised against the fallen and the helpless,
nor the gold of the other be paid for the scalps of a
massacred enemy." *Harrison*.

The good effects of the expedition were soon felt. It
let us know distinctly who were our friends and who were
our enemies among the Indians. The Delaware tribe from
White river and all others who were determined to remain
at peace, immediately accepted the invitation, which had
previously been given by the government, to come within
the limits of the American frontiers. They were settled by the proper authority, about half way between
Piqua, and the Shawanoe village of Wapoghconata on
the Auglaize. Soon after the return of the detachment to Dayton, so many of colonel Simrall's regiment were found to be unfit for immediate service, and
the intention of employing dragoons on the main expedition was so entirely abandoned, that the general
determined to disband them immediately—they were
accordingly discharged on the 10th of January, and
returned home from a service which had been hard
indeed, but to them not less glorious than severe.

We must now recur again to the toilsome preparations for the main expedition against Malden, and the
inglorious war which our troops were doomed to wage

with the elements, which opposed their progress with all the powers and majesty of mud.

The troops composing the left wing under Winchester, when the season became severe, were exposed to many and great privations. They had left the greater part of their clothing, in the first instance at Piqua, when marching to the relief of fort Wayne, and suffered considerably before they received it again. But as the winter came on, an additional supply of winter clothing became necessary. The government had ordered large supplies of this kind—but there was in this stage of the war an immense difference between the ordering of supplies and delivering them on the frontiers. Harrison and Shelby had also appealed to the patriotism of the people of Kentucky for voluntary contributions : and a considerable quantity of clothing was in this way collected under the superintendence of governor Shelby. The ladies of Kentucky were not wanting in such patriotic services as they had it in their power to render. Of the clothing thus collected however, but very little reached the army before Christmas, and much of it was entirely lost, owing to the misconduct of wagoners and wagonmasters, and the insuperable difficulties of transportation.

Soon after fort Winchester was finished, the left wing moved over the river and encamped on the north bank, for the convenience of firewood. The situation being wet and disagreeable, they presently moved down to a second, and then to a third camp, six miles below the Auglaize. About the first of November they became extremely sickly. The typhus fever raged with violence, so that three or four would sometimes die in one day. Upwards of 300 were daily on the sick list, and so discouraging was the prospect of advancing, that about the first of December they were ordered to build huts for their accommodation. Many were so entirely destitute of shoes and other clothing, that they must have frozen, if they had been obliged

to march any distance.   And sometimes the whole army would be for many days entirely without flour.

All these privations were caused in a great measure
by the difficulties of transportation.   The roads were
bad beyond description : none but those who have actually seen the state of the country, seem ever to have
formed a correct estimate of the difficulties to be encountered.   The road from Loramie's block house to
the St. Marys and thence to Defiance, was one continued swamp, knee deep on the packhorses and up to
the hubs of the wagons.   It was found impossible in
some instances to get even the empty wagons along,
and many were left sticking in the mire and ravines,
the wagoners being glad to get off with the horses
alive.   Sometimes the quarter master taking advantage
of a temporary freeze, would send off a convoy of
provisions, which would be swamped by a thaw before
it reached its destination.   These natural difficulties
were also increased by a great deficiency of funds, and
inadequacy of the other resources which were requisite in the quarter master's department.   The only
persons who could be procured to act as packhorse
drivers, were generally the most worthless creatures
in society, who took care neither of the horses nor the
goods with which they were entrusted.   The horses
of course were soon broke down, and many of the
packs lost.   The teams hired to haul, were also commonly valued so high on coming into service, that the
owners were willing to drive them to debility and
death, with a view to get the price.   In addition to
this, no bills of lading were used, or accounts kept
with the wagoners—of course each one had an opportunity to plunder the public without much risk of de-
tection.   We are hence not to wonder, when such
were the difficulties and the means of surmounting
them, that supplies were not more rapidly accumulated
at the various places of deposit.

The following account will exhibit the difficulties of water transportation. About the first of December, major Bodley an enterprising officer, who was quarter master of the Kentucky troops, made an attempt to send near 200 barrels of flour down the St. Marys in perogues to the left wing below Defiance. Previous to this time the water had rarely been high enough to venture on a voyage in those small streams. The flour was now shipped in 15 or 20 perogues and canoes, and placed under the command of captain Jordan and lieutenant Cardwell, with upwards of 20 men. They descended the river and arrived about a week afterwards at Shane's crossing, upwards of one hundred miles by water, but only twenty by land from the place where they started. The river was so narrow, crooked, full of logs, and trees overhanging the banks, that it was with great difficulty they could make any progress. And now in one freezing night they were completely ice-bound. Lieutenant Cardwell waded back through the ice and swamps to fort Barbee, with intelligence of their situation. Major Bodley returned with him to the flour, and offered the men extra wages to cut through the ice and push forwards; but having gained only one mile by two days labor, the project was abandoned, and a guard left with the flour. A few days before Christmas a temporary thaw took place, which enabled them with much difficulty and suffering to reach within a few miles of fort Wayne, where they were again frozen up. They now abandoned the voyage, and made sleds on which the men hauled the flour to the fort and left it there.

In the mean time general Winchester's wing was suffering the greatest privations. Trusting to this attempt to convey supplies by water, the exertions by land were relaxed. From the 10th to the 22nd of this month, the camp was without flour, and for some time before they had only half rations. Poor beef and hicory roots were their whole subsistence. At the same

Z

time fevers and other diseases raged in almost every tent, in which the sick were exposed, not only to hunger, but to the inclemency of the season. The necessary vigilance of the general induced him to send out reconnoitring parties very frequently, which still farther exposed the men. Yet they disdained to murmur, or to utter a thought derogatory to the honor of their country. About the first of this month general Harrison had thought his supplies in such a state of forwardness, that he could very soon concentrate his fo ces at the Rapids; and had instructed general Winchester to proceed to that place as soon as he had provisions for a few weeks on hand—but in the circumstances above described, his condition was very different from that which would authorize him to advance.

The other divisions of the army had not been pushed out so far as the left wing, and of course had not to encounter such great privations. Their sufferings however were sufficiently great, and the difficulties of transportation with them, may be understood from the details we have given in rela.ion to the left wing. In the following extracts from a letter addressed to the war department by general Harrison, and dated on the 12th of December at Delaware, the reader will find some notice of these difficulties, together with a development of the views and plans of the commanding general at this stage of the campaign.

" Since I had the honor to write on the —— every exertion has been made, and every engine put into operation to procure and forward supplies for the army to the advanced posts. The difficulties which have been, and which are still to be encountered in this business are almost insuperable ; but they are opposed with unabated firmness and zeal. The greatest obstacle to our success is the want of forage, which for this line we are obliged to bring from the neighbourhood of Chillicothe at an immense expense, which can scarcely be conceived."

"I fear that the expenses of this army will greatly exceed the calculations of the government. The prodigious destruction of horses can only be conceived by those, who have been accustomed to military operations in a wilderness during the winter season. The fine teams which arrived on the 10th inst. at Sandusky with the artillery, are entirely worn down; and two trips from M'Arthur's block house, our nearest deposit to the Rapids, will completely destroy a brigade of packhorses."

"If there were not some important political reason, urging the recovery of the Michigan Territory, and the capture of Malden, as soon as those objects can possibly be effected; and that to accomplish them a few weeks sooner, expense was to be disregarded, I should not hesitate to say, that if a small proportion of the sums, which will be expended in the quarter master's department, in the active prosecution of the campaign during the winter, was devoted to obtaining the command of lake Erie, the wishes of the government in their utmost extent, could be accomplished without difficulty in the months of April and May. Malden, Detroit and Macinaw would fall in rapid succession. On the contrary, all that I can certainly promise to accomplish during the winter, unless the strait should afford us a passage on the ice, is to recover Detroit. I must farther observe, that no military man would think of retaining Detroit, Malden being in possession of the enemy, unless his army was at least twice as strong as the disposable force of the enemy. An army advancing to Detroit along a line of operation, passing so near the principal force of the enemy, as to allow them access to it whenever they think proper, must be covered by another army more considerable than the disposable force of the enemy. I mention this circumstance to shew, that the attack ought not to be directed against Detroit, *but against Malden,* and that it depends upon the ice affording a safe passage across the strait, whether I shall be able to proceed in this way or not. Detroit is not tenable. Were I to take it without having it in my power to occupy the opposite shore, I should be under the necessity of hiding the army in the adjacent swamp, to preserve it from the effects of the shot and shells, which the enemy would throw with impunity from the opposite shore. This result is so obvious to every man who has the least military information, that it appears to me as extraordinary as any other part of general Hull's conduct, that he should chuse to defend Detroit rather than attack Malden. There is another circumstance sir, which will claim attention. Admitting that Malden and Detroit are both taken, Macinaw and St. Josephs will both remain in the hands of the enemy, until we can create a force capable of contending with the vessels, which the British have in lake Michigan, and which they will be enabled to maintain there, as long as the canoe route by Grand river and lake Nississin shall remain open, and for six months after.

"I have conceived it proper sir, to lay these statements before you. If it should be asked, why they were not made sooner—I answer, that although I was always sensible, that there were great difficulties to be encountered, in the accomplishment of the wishes of the President, in relation to the recovery of Detroit, and the conquest of the adjacent part of Upper Canada in the manner proposed, I did not make sufficient allowance for the imbecility and inexperience of the public agents, and the villany of the contractors. I am still however very far from believing, that the original plan is impracticable. I believe on the contrary that it can be effected. And as I know that my personal fame is materially interested in its success in the manner first proposed, my feelings are all engaged in opposition to any delay. But I should illy deserve the confidence of the people or the President, if I were capable of being influenced by a private consideration, to withhold from the government any statement, which might throw light upon the operations of an army, the success of which is so important to the character, as well as to the interests of the country. If it should be the determination, to disregard expense, and push on the operations of the army, in the manner that they have been commenced, the President may rely on the exertions of the troops, which I shall employ in the final effort. I shall be much disappointed, if I cannot select three or four thousand men from the army, who will do as much as the same number of men, in a similar state of discipline ever did. If the plan of acquiring the naval superiority upon the lakes, before the attempt is made on Malden or Detroit, should be adopted, I would place fifteen hundred men in cantonments, at the Miami Rapids (Defiance would be better, if the troops had not advanced from thence) retain about one thousand more to be distributed in different garrisons, accumulate provisions at St. Marys, Tawa Town, Upper Sandusky, Cleveland, and Presque Isle, and employ the dragoons and mounted infantry, in desultory expeditions against the Indians. The villages south of lake Michigan might be struck with effect, by making a deposit of corn and provisions at fort Wayne.

"I am much disappointed in the artillery which has been sent me. There are in all twenty-eight pieces, of which ten are sixes, and ten twelve pounders—the former are nearly useless. I had five before, and if I had a hundred, I should only take three or four with me. You will perceive by the return of captain Gratiot, which is enclosed, that all the carriages for the howitzers, and eight out of ten for the twelve pounders, are unfit for use."

Before the above letter was received at the war department, Mr. Monroe had become the acting secretary, after the resignation of Dr. Eustis, and had written a long letter to general Harrison on the military affairs of the northwest. That letter was immediately answered by the general, and the correspondence on these subjects was continued through several others, in which the prospects of the campaign and the proper measures to be pursued, were very comprehensively and ably discussed between the secretary and the general. The result of the whole was, that general Harrison was left to prosecute the campaign in pursuance of his own views; and the government determined to make the most active and vigorous exertions to obtain the command of the lake, which they expected to accomplish early in the spring. Positive instructions were given to the general on two points alone. He was ordered, in the event of entering Canada, to pledge the government to the inhabitants no further, than a promise of protection in their lives, liberty and property. He was also instructed, not to make any transitory acquisitions, or to wrest any of their possessions from the enemy with temporary views only, but to advance prepared to hold all the ground he could gain. He was told that the President was not so anxious to push on the expedition with rapidity, as to be well prepared to render permanent any acquisition that might be made. Some further extracts from this correspondence will be given, after we have detailed some of the movements, which took place about this time, as the different corps were advancing towards a concentration for the main expedition.

Early in December a detachment of Perkins's brigade arrived at Lower Sandusky, and repaired an old stockade which had been erected to protect an Indian store, formerly established at that place by the government. Soon afterwards the whole of the brigade arrived at that post. On the 10th a battalion of Pennsylvanians reached Upper Sandusky with 21 pieces of artillery, which had been brought from Pittsburgh by lieutenant Hukill. A regiment of the same troops, and some companies of the Virginia brigade, were immediately sent after them by general Harrison to strengthen that important depot; and about the 20th he arrived himself and established his head quarters at the same place. Whilst there, he received communications from colonel Campbell, informing him of the result of the expedition to Mississiniway, which induced him to return to Chillicothe, to concert with governor Meigs another expedition to the same place, more effectually to subdue the Indians in that quarter. As he was proceeding again to the frontiers, he received at Franklinton the letter from Mr. secretary Monroe mentioned above, from which the following is an extract.

" At this distance, and with an imperfect knowledge of the actual state of things, it is impossible for the President to decide, satisfactorily to himself, or with advantage to the public, whether it is practicable for you to accomplish the objects of the expedition in their full extent during the present winter. No person can be so competent to that decision as yourself; and the President has great confidence in the solidity of the opinion which you may form. He wishes you to weigh maturely this important subject, and take that part which your judgment may dictate. It is expected that you will forthwith form a clear and distinct plan, as to the objects which you may deem attainable, the time within which they may be attained, and the force necessary for the purpose ; and that you communicate the same with precision to this department. As soon as you have formed this plan, you will proceed to execute it, without waiting for an answer; and as soon as the government is made acquainted with it, measures will be adopted to give to your operations all the aid in its power."

The following are extracts from the answers of general Harrison, which are dated on the 4th and 8th of January at Franklinton.

"When I was directed to take the command in the latter end of September, I thought it possible by great exertions to effect the objects of the campaign before the setting in of winter. I distinctly stated however, to the secretary of war, that there was always a period of rainy weather in this country in the months of November and December, in which the roads within the settlements were almost impassable, and the swamps which extend northwardly from about the 40th degree of north latitude, entirely so; and that this circumstance would render it impossible to advance with the army before that period, without exposing it to inevitable destruction, unless a sufficiency of provisions could be taken on to subsist it until the severe frosts should remove the impediments to transportation.

"The experience of a few days was sufficient to convince me, that the supplies of provisions could not be procured for our autumnal advance; and even if this difficulty was removed, another of equal magnitude existed in the want of artillery. There remained then no alternative but to prepare for a winter campaign. But in order to take advantage of every circumstance in our favor, boats and perogues were prepared in considerable numbers on the Auglaize and St. Marys, in the hope that when the land transportation could not be used, we might by the means of these rivers, take on large supplies to the Rapids of the Miami. An effort was made also, to procure flour from Presque Isle by coasting the lake with small boats. These measures were calculated on, as collateral aids only. The more sure one of providing a large number of packhorses and ox teams was resorted to, and the deputy quarter master general, colonel Morrison, was instructed accordingly. Considering the Miami Rapids as the first point of destination. provisions were ordered to be accumulated along a concave base, extending from St. Marys on the left, to the mouth of the Huron, and afterwards Lower Sandusky on the right. From this base the Rapids could be approached by three routes, or lines of operation, two of which were pretty effectually secured by the posts which were established and the positions taken upon the third. St. Marys, M·Arthur's block house, and Upper Sandusky were selected as principal deposits. The troops, excepting those with general Winchester, were kept within the bounds of the local contractors, that they might not consume the provisions procured by the United States' commissaries, and which were intended to form the grand deposit at the Miami Rapids. It was not until late in October that much effect could be given to these arrangements; and for the six following weeks little or nothing could be done from the uncommonly unfavorable state of the weather, which afforded just rain enough to render the roads almost impassable for wagons, and not a sufficiency to raise the waters to a navigable state. Great exertions however were made to prepare for the change, which might reasonably be expected. The last 20 days of December were entirely favorable to our views, and were so well employed by colonel Morrison as to afford the most flattering prospect of being able to take on to the Rapids early in this month, a sufficiency of provisions and stores to authorize an advance upon Malden from the 25th inst. to the 10th of February. Our hopes were again a little checked by a general thaw, succeeded by a very deep snow whilst the ground was in that soft state. It is however cold again, and we calculate on being able to use with effect the sleds, a considerable number of which I had caused to be prepared.

" The instructions which I received from Dr. Eustis, with regard to the conduct of the war in this department, amounted to a complete *carte blanche.* The principal objects of the campaign were pointed out, and I was left at liberty to proceed to their full execution during the present winter, or to make arrangements for their accomplishment in the spring, by occupying such posts as might facilitate the intended operations. The wishes of the government to recover the ground which had been lost and to conquer Upper Canada, were however expressed in such strong terms, and the funds which were placed at my disposal were declared to be so ample if not unlimited, that I did not consider myself authorized to adopt the alternative of delay from any other motive than that of the safety of the army. My letters have contained frequent allusions to the monstrous expense, which would attend the operations of an army at this season of the year, penetrating to the enemy through an immense forest of one hundred and fifty miles. The silence of the secretary on the subject left me no room to doubt the correctness of the opinion which I had at first formed—that the object in view was considered so important that expense was to be disregarded. I thought it best however to come to a full understanding on the subject, and with this view my letter of the 12th ultimo from Delaware was written.

" My plan of operations has been, and now is, to occupy the Miami Rapids, and to deposit there as much provisions as possible, to move from thence with a choice detachment of the army, and with as much provision, artillery and ammunition as the means of transportation will allow—make a demonstration towards Detroit, and by a sudden passage of the strait upon the ice, an actual investiture of Malden."

"With regard to the amount of force, which such an expedition would require, I have made my calculations, not upon that which the enemy might have at Malden, at the time the enterprise should commence, but upon what they would be able to assemble there time enough to resist us. I know the facility with which troops may be brought at this season, by what is called the back route along the river Thames from the vicinity of Niagara to Detroit and Malden. Had general Smyth's attempts been successful, my plan could have been executed with a much smaller force, than I should deem it prudent to employ under present circumstances. I have indeed no doubt, that we should encounter at Malden the very troops which contended with general Van Ransalear on the heights of Queenstown. It is the same thing with regard to the Indians. The British have wisely dismissed the greater part of them to save their provisions, but a whistle will be almost sufficient to collect them again."

He next states that if our force appeared weak, it would encourage the timid, the cautious and wavering among the Indians and Canadians, to take the field against us; and that if our means of transportation should not be sufficient to carry all the supplies with us at once, very strong detachments would be required to escort the successive trips—for, he continues, "such is the nature of Indian warfare that it is impossible to tell where the storm will fall. It is a rule therefore with me when operating against them, never to make a detachment, neither to the front nor the rear, which is not able to contend with their whole force. From these statements you will perceive sir, how difficult it would be for me at present to ascertain with any degree of correctness, the number of men with which I should advance from the Rapids. It was my intention to have assembled there, from 4500 to 5000 men, and to be governed by circumstances in forming the detachment with which I should advance. This is still my plan, and it was always my intention to dismiss at that period, all that I deemed superfluous."

The nominal amount of the army was ten thousand—but the effective force was much less. "Notwithstanding the large nominal amount of the army under my command, their sufferings for the want of clothing and the rigor of the season reduces the effective number to less than two thirds of the aggregate. You will read with as much pain as I write it, that a fine body of regular troops belonging to the 17th and 19th regiments under colonel Wells, has been nearly destroyed for the want of clothing. The whole of the effective men upon this frontier does not exceed six thousand three hundred infantry.

"Upon the whole sir, my reaching Malden this winter depends upon circumstances which I cannot control—the freezing of the strait in such a manner as to enable me to pass over the troops and artillery."

"General Winchester is I hope now, or will be in a day or two at the Rapids. Provisions in large quantities are progressing thither. I calculate on being there myself by the 20th inst. with the troops which are intended for the march upon Malden. In the event of occurrences which may induce a suspension of operations beyond the Rapids, measures will be taken to make and secure at that place a deposit of provisions equal to the support of the troops in any enterprise that may be undertaken in the spring. Should our offensive operations be suspended until that time, it is my decided opinion that the most effectual and cheapest plan will be to obtain the command of the lake. This being once effected every difficulty will be removed. An army of 4000 men landed on the north side of the lake below Malden, will soon reduce that place, retake Detroit, and with the aid of the fleet proceed down the lake to co-operate with the army from Niagara."

The secretary had written, that "The destruction of the Queen Charlotte, and of the whole of the naval force of the enemy, frozen up as it is presumed to be in the ice, would be an important attainment. It is one which is recommended to your particular attention." To which the general replied—"The enterprise against the Queen Charlotte has been long meditated and shall not escape my attention."

In the letter of the 8th he states—"A suspension of the operations of this army for the winter, without having accomplished the principal object for which it was embodied, is an event which has long been looked for, by most of the well informed men who know the character of the country, and recollect that the army of general Wayne after a whole summer's preparation, was unable to advance more than 70 miles from the Ohio, and that the prudent caution of President Washington had directed it to be placed in winter quarters at the very season that our arrangements were commenced. You do me justice in believing that my exertions have been unremitted, and I am sensible of the commission of one error only, that has injuriously affected our interests; and that is in retaining too large a force at Defiance. The disadvantages attending it were however seen at the period of my committing the management of that wing to general Winchester. Possessing a superior rank in the line of the army to that which was tendered to me, I considered him rather in the light of an associate in command than an inferior. I therefore recommended to him, instead of ordering it, to send back two regiments within the bounds of White's contract. Had this measure been pursued, there would have been at fort Winchester 100,000 rations more than there is at present. The general who possesses the most estimable qualities of the head and heart, was deceived as I was, with regard to the period when the army could advance, and he did not think that the reduction of issues would be so important, as it is now ascertained it would have been."

Instead of sending back any part of his command, general Winchester was constantly anxious, whenever he had a moderate supply of provisions on hand, to advance further and fix his camp at the Rapids. It was to obtain the sanction of general Harrison for such a movement that major Hardin was despatched to head quarters early in November, when he wrote the letter to governor Shelby from which an extract has been given in this chapter. On the 12th of that month general Winchester came to a positive determination to move his camp to the Rapids at every hazard—but his advance was fortunately arrested by the timely arrival of a despatch from general Harrison. In the letter from which we are making these extracts, the general proceeds—"As the greater part of the expenses of the campaign have already been incurred, I beg leave to assure you, sir, that trifling difficulties will not oppose the progress of the army to Malden; but at the same time I also promise you, that no measure shall be adopted but when the prospects of success are as clear as they can be in any military operations."

On the subject of obtaining the command of the lake, he wrote—"I have no means of estimating correctly the cost of a naval armament, capable of effecting this object, but from my knowledge of the expense of transporting supplies through a swampy wilderness, I do believe that the expense which will be incurred in six weeks in the spring, in an attempt to transport the provisions for the army along the road leading from the Rapids to Detroit, would build and equip the vessels for this purpose."

By these copious extracts the reader is made well acquainted, with the causes which have so long retarded the march of the army; with its present situation and resources; and with the ulterior plans and prospects of the general for the present campaign. A few days after writing these letters, he arrived again at Upper Sandusky, together with the whole of the Pennsylvania and Virginia brigades, making his effective force at that place about 1500 strong. On the 12th the balance of the artillery also arrived—"large quantities of every necessary supply were constantly arriving, and the general appearance of the camp announced the near approach of that state of preparation, requisite to the commencement of active operations." *Colonel Wood.* Parties were sent on to open roads, bridge creeks, and pave the way for the army. Artillery had already been sent towards the Miami; and fine supplies of provisions and stores being on hand, it seemed that time, patience, perseverance, and fortitude alone were necessary to enable the army to remove the numerous obstacles and surmount the various difficulties which nature had opposed to its progress and its future glory. But we must in the next place direct our attention to the movements of the left wing under Winchester, for whose arrival at the Rapids the troops at Sandusky were now waiting, as the signal for their advance with all their supplies to the same place.

CHAPTER V.

Advance of the left wing—Success and Disasters at the river Raisin.

GENERAL HARRISON had expected, on his first arrival at Upper Sandusky, about the 18th of December, to be met there by an express from general Winchester, with information of his advance to the Rapids, in conformity with the advice which had previously been given him. As no such information had arrived, he soon afterwards despatched ensign C. S. Todd, division judge advocate of the Kentucky troops, to Winchester's camp on the Miami below Defiance. Todd was accompanied by two gentlemen of the Michigan Territory and three Wyandot Indians. He proceeded directly across the country, and performed the journey with a degree of secrecy and despatch highly honorable to his skill and enterprise, having completely eluded all the scouts of the enemy. He was instructed to communicate to general Winchester the following directions and plans from the commander in chief— "that as soon as he had accumulated provisions for 20 days, he was authorized to advance to the Rapids, where he was to commence the building of huts, to induce the enemy to believe that he was going into winter quarters—that he was to construct sleds for the main expedition against Malden, but to impress it on the minds of his men that they were for transporting provisions from the interior—that the different lines of the army would be concentrated at that place, and a choice detachment from the whole would then be marched rapidly on Malden—that in the mean time he was to occupy the Rapids, for the purpose of securing the provisions and stores forwarded from the other wings of the army."

The left wing, in the mean time, had received a moderate supply of provisions and clothing on the 22d of December, and were now making active preparations to march. The river being frozen up, which rendered their water craft useless, they were obliged to take their baggage on sleds, many of which had to be hauled by the men. Having provided for the sick, and assigned guards to attend and protect them, the march for the Rapids was commenced on the 30th of December—At the same time, Mr. Leslie Combs, a young man of intelligence and enterprise, from Kentucky, who had joined the army, as a volunteer, on its march from fort Wayne to fort Defiance, accompanied by Mr. A. Ruddle as a guide, was sent with despatches to inform the commander in chief of this movement, in order that provisions and reinforcements might be forwarded as soon as possible—general Winchester expected to be met by these at the Rapids by the 12th of January—this however was prevented by an immense fall of snow, which, as Mr. Combs had to traverse, *on foot*, a pathless wilderness of more than one hundred miles in extent, retarded him four or five days longer in reaching even the first point of destination, (fort M'Arthur) than would otherwise have been necessary to perform the whole route. The supplies they had already received, and the prospects now before them, afforded some comfort and encouragement to the troops ; yet their appearance and their real efficiency were still very unpromising. Their progress was slow from the first, and was much retarded after a few days by the snow.

While on this march, general Winchester received another despatch from the commander in chief, recommending him to abandon the movement to the Rapids, and fall back with the greater part of his force to fort Jennings. This advice was given in consequence of the intelligence received from colonel Campbell at Mississiniway, respecting the force of Tecumseh on the Wabash. General Harrison was apprehensive,

2 B

that if the left wing advanced so far as the Rapids, Tecumseh would be able to attack and destroy all the provisions, left on its line of operations in the rear. But as Winchester had already commenced his march, he did not think himself required by this advice to discontinue it and return. Harrison went immediately himself into the settlements of Ohio, to arrange with governor Meigs the means of sending another mounted expedition against the Indians under Tecumseh, at the principal town on the Mississiniway river. Such an expedition however was afterwards deemed unnecessary.

On the 10th of January general Winchester arrived with his army at the Rapids, having previously sent forward a strong detachment of 670 men, under general Payne, to attack a body of Indians, which general Harrison had been informed was lying in an old fortification at Swan creek, a few miles farther down the river. The detachment went several miles below the old British fort at the foot of the Rapids, and having sent their spies to Swan creek, where they could discover no appearance of Indians, the whole returned again to the position which the army was intended to occupy.

On the north bank of the river, above Wayne's battle ground, and directly opposite the point where Hull's road struck the Miami, general Winchester established and fortified his camp, on a handsome eminence of an oval form, covered with timber and surrounded with prairies. On the day of his arrival, a recent Indian camp was discovered about half a mile from this position. Captain Williams was immediately despatched, with 25 men, to pursue the Indians who had left it. He soon overtook and routed them, having exchanged a few shots, by which some were wounded on both sides.

On the 11th of January a despatch was sent to apprise general Harrison of the arrival and situation of the army at the Rapids; but it was sent by the persons who were taking in the starved and worn out packhorses to general Tupper's camp at fort M'Arthur, a place as distant from the Rapids as the head quarters of the general, and from which it must then pass through a swampy and pathless wilderness of 40 miles to Upper Sandusky, where it did not arrive before the general had left that place, and was ultimately received by him at the Rapids where it started.

The time of the Kentucky troops would expire in February, and general Harrison had requested general Winchester to endeavor to raise a regiment among them to serve six months longer; and at the same time had suggested, that it would be imprudent to employ them on any other condition in the expedition against Malden. General Winchester now advised him, by a letter sent on the 12th to Lower Sandusky, that no reliance could be placed on retaining any of them in service after their time had expired. This communication was simply a note respecting the above business, and had only this direction upon it, "His excellency, general William H. Harrison." Of course the writer did not intend that it should have a speedy passage, and inform the general of his arrival at the Rapids; nor did it answer that purpose, as it was delayed several days on its way to head quarters. On the letter sent by the pack horse conveyance of 15 miles a day, was the following endorsement in Winchester's own hand writing: "general Tupper will please to forward this letter by express.—J. Winchester." From all which it is evident, that he relied on the packhorse communication alone, to apprise general Harrison that he had reached the Rapids, although general Harrison had directed him to communicate the intelligence of that event as quick as practicable.

The opinions of the generals respecting the Kentucky troops were afterwards changed. The inactivity and sufferings of the army had dissatisfied them with the service at this time; but it soon became evident, that when actively employed they were not inclined to return home : and general Harrison did not hesitate to include them in his selections for the main expedition, firmly relying that they would not abandon the American standard, in the country of their enemy, when their time of service had expired.

A large store house was now built within the encampment at the Rapids, to secure the provisions and baggage. A considerable quantity of corn was also gathered in the fields, and apparatus for pounding and sifting it being made, it supplied the troops with very wholesome bread.

On the evening of the 13th, two Frenchmen arrived from the river Raisin, with information that the Indians routed by captain Williams had passed that place, and gone on to Malden, with intelligence of the advance of our army. They stated, that the Indians threatened to kill the inhabitants and burn their town, and begged for protection from the American arms. They were charged with a despatch from Mr. Day, a citizen who was friendly to our cause, and who stated that the British were seizing all suspected persons at the river Raisin, and confining them in Malden prison, and that they were preparing to carry off all the provisions of every description. On the 14th another messenger arrived ; and on the evening of the 16th two more came in : they all confirmed the accounts brought by the first express, and solicited protection, as they were afraid that the people would be massacred and the town burnt by the Indians, whenever our army began to advance upon them. They stated the present force of the enemy to be two companies of Canadians, and about 200 Indians, but that more Indians might be expected to assemble.

The greatest ardor and anxiety now prevailed in the army, to advance in force sufficient to defeat the enemy at that place. A council of officers was called by the general, a majority of whom were decidedly in favor of sending on a strong detachment. Colonel Allen supported that side of the question with much ardor.

General Winchester agreed to the opinion of the majority, and on the morning of the 17th detached colonel Lewis with 550 men to the river Raisin. A few hours afterwards, he was followed by colonel Allen with 110 more, who came up with Lewis late in the evening, where he had encamped at Presque Isle. Early in the morning of the same day, general Winchester prepared a despatch to inform Harrison of this movement. He stated that his principal object was to prevent the flour and grain from being carried off by the enemy; that if he got possession of Frenchtown he intended to hold it; and that, of course, a co-operating reinforcement from the right wing might be necessary. Before the express had started with this letter, information was received from colonel Lewis at Presque Isle, a distance of 20 miles in advance, that there were 400 Indians at the river Raisin, and that colonel Elliott was expected from Malden, with a detachment destined to attack the camp at the Rapids. This intelligence was also inserted in the letter to Harrison, which was then despatched by the way of Lower Sandusky.

Colonel Lewis remained all night at Presque Isle, and in consequence of the information noticed above, which he received by express from the river Raisin, he set out very early in the morning, intending if possible to anticipate colonel Elliott at Frenchtown. That village is in the middle between Presque Isle and Malden, the distance from each being 18 miles. The greater part of his march was on the ice of the Miami bay and the border of Lake Erie. When he had arrived within 6 miles of the town, he was discovered by some Indians, who hastened to give the alarm to the main body of the enemy. Before the detachment left the border of the lake, a halt was called to take some refreshment. Having resumed the march, a piece of timbered land was passed, and as the troops proceeded in the open plain they were formed in three lines, each corps being in its proper place for action. The right was commanded by colonel Allen, and was composed of the companies of captains McCracken, Bledsoe and Matson.   The left was commanded by major Graves, and was composed of the companies of captains Hamilton, Williams and Kelly.   The centre consisted of the companies of captains Hightower, Collier and Sebree, and was commanded by major Madison.   The advanced guard consisted of the companies of captains Hickman, Glaves and James, under the command of captain Ballard, acting as major.

When they arrived within a quarter of a mile of the village, and discovered the enemy in motion, the line of battle was formed, in the expectation of receiving an attack ; but it was soon evident that the enemy did not intend fighting in the open field.   The detachment then broke off by the right of companies, and marched under the fire of the enemy's cannon, till they arrived at the river, where the small arms began to play upon them.   The line of battle was then formed again, on the bank of the river, and the long roll beat as the signal for a general charge, which was immediately executed with much firmness and intrepidity.

The enemy were posted among the houses, and the picketting of the gardens, on the north side of the river. Majors Graves and Madison were ordered to dislodge them, which they effected with great gallantry, advancing at the heads of their battalions under a heavy shower of balls.   The enemy routed and retreating from this place, were next met by colonel Allen at some distance on the right, who pursued them about half a mile to the woods.   Here they made a stand again, with their howitzer and small arms, covered by some houses and a chain of fences, with a brushy wood full of fallen timber in their rear.   Majors Graves and Madison were now ordered with their battalions to possess themselves of the wood on the left, and move rapidly on the main body of the enemy, where they were contending with colonel Allen.   These orders were promptly executed; and as soon as they had commenced their fire, colonel Allen also advanced on the enemy; who were soon compelled to retire into the woods, into which they were closely pursued. The contest with Allen's command now became very warm, as the enemy concentrated all their forces on the right, with the intention of forcing his line. They were however kept constantly on the retreat, though slowly, as our men were too much exhausted to rush upon them with rapidity. In this manner they were driven to the distance of two miles, every foot of the way under a continual charge. The action commenced at 3 o'clock, and the pursuit was continued till dark, when the detachment returned in good order, and encamped in the town.

In this warmly contested action every officer and soldier did his duty. There was not a solitary instance of delinquency. The troops amply supported "the double character of Americans and Kentuckians." It is of course unnecessary to notice the particular merits of individuals, where every man completely filled his sphere of action. Our loss was 12 killed and 55 wounded. Among the latter were captains Hickman, Matson and Ballard. The loss of the enemy could not be ascertained. They left 15 dead on the ground where the action commenced: but the principal slaughter took place in the woods, from which in the night they carried off all their dead. From the obstinacy with which they contended so long against a force somewhat superior, from the appearances next day in the woods, and from the reports of persons who saw them after the battle, it is believed that their loss was extremely severe. They were commanded by major Reynolds of the British army, who had about 100 British troops in the battle, and about 400 Indians.

The detachment was now in a place where it could be amply accommodated with all the necessaries of life, and where the wounded could be well lodged and supplied with every thing required by their situation.

On the night after the battle, an express was sent to carry intelligence of the success to general Winchester, at whose camp he arrived before daylight; and another was then immediately sent from that place to general Harrison, by the way of Lower Sandusky, to apprise him of the event. On the morning after the battle, colonel Lewis determined, with the advice of his officers, to hold the place and await a reinforcement. His first orders from Winchester had been, " to attack the enemy, beat them, and take possession of Frenchtown and hold it." He was authorized, in a despatch sent after him however to exercise some discretion with respect to holding the position.

As soon as the intelligence of this success was known at the Rapids, it produced a complete ferment in camp. All were anxious to proceed to Frenchtown in support of the advanced corps. It was evident that corps was in a critical situation. They were but 18 miles from Malden, where the British had their whole force; and it was not to be doubted but that an effort would be made by them, to regain the ground they had lost, or to defeat this advance of our army, which at first was inconsiderable, and was now much reduced by the killed and wounded. Preparations were therefore made to reinforce colonel Lewis, and on the evening of the 19th, general Winchester marched himself with 250 men, which was all that could be spared from the post at the Rapids. He arrived at the river Raisin in the night on the 20th, and encamped in an open lot of ground on the right of the former detachment. Colonel Lewis had encamped in a place where he was defended by garden pickets, which were sufficiently close and strong to protect his men against an attack of small arms. Colonel Wells commanded the reinforcement, and to him the general named, but did not positively order, a breast-work for the protection of his camp. The general himself established his quarters in a house on the south side of the river, about 300 yards from the lines! On the 21st, a place was selected for the whole detachment to encamp in good order, with a determination to fortify it on the next day—About sunset colonel Wells solicited and obtained leave to return to the Rapids. Certain information had been received that the British were preparing to make an attack, and that they would make it with the utmost despatch in their power was a matter of course. Colonel Wells reached the Rapids that night, at which place general Harrison had arrived on the 20th, and had made every exertion in his power to hasten the reinforcements.

Before we proceed to the tragedy of the 22nd, we must take a review of the arrangements and exertions which in the mean time had been made in the rear. When general Winchester marched from his camp below Defiance for the Rapids, on the 30th of December, he sent an express to advise general Harrison of that movement; but, in consequence of a snow storm, which delayed the bearer, the general did not receive the intelligence at Upper Sandusky before the 11th of January. He then immediately ordered on some droves of hogs, and held the artillery in readiness to march as soon as he should be advised of Winchester's arrival at the Rapids. But no farther intelligence was received, until the evening of the 16th, when a letter from general Perkins at Lower Sandusky, enclosing one he had received from general Winchester of the 15th, at last informed general Harrison, that Winchester had arrived at the Rapids, that he meditated some movement against the enemy, and that he wanted Perkins to send him a battalion from Lower Sandusky. This intelligence alarmed general Harrison, and he immediately gave orders for the artillery to advance by the way of Portage river, accompanied by a guard of 300 men commanded by major Orr. Escorts of provisions were also ordered to follow, on the same route; but, owing to the extreme badness of the road, very little progress could be made. Even the lighter pieces of

2 C

artillery could not be got forward with any degree of expedition. At the same time an express was despatched to the Rapids by general Harrison for information, with orders to return and meet him at Lower Sandusky, for which place he set out the next morning himself, and arrived there on the following night. He found that general Perkins had prepared a battalion, with a piece of artillery, to be commanded by major Cotgrove; which was ordered to march on the 18th; and the general now determined to follow it himself, and have a personal consultation with general Winchester. At 4 o'clock on the morning of the 19th, he received the letter in which Winchester informed him of the advance of colonel Lewis to the river Raisin, together with the objects and prospects of the expedition. He immediately ordered the remaining regiment of Perkins's brigade to march to the Rapids, and proceeded there himself. On his way he met an express from Winchester, with intelligence of the success of Lewis in the battle of the 18th. On the morning of the 20th he arrived at the Rapids, and found that general Winchester had proceeded the evening before to the river Raisin, having left general Payne in his camp with 300 men. Major Cotgrove, with the piece of artillery in his train, was so retarded by a swamp on the road, and other obstacles to his progress, that he had reached no farther than the Miami bay on the night of the 21st. By marching early next morning he arrived within 15 miles of the river Raisin, before he was met by the fugitives from the massacre.

When Harrison arrived at the Rapids on the 20th, he despatched captain Hart, the inspector general, to Winchester at Frenchtown, with intelligence of the movements in the rear, and with instructions to the general, "to maintain the position at the river Raisin at any rate." On the next day, the 21st, a despatch was received from general Winchester, in which he stated, that if his force were increased to the amount of 1000 or 1200, it would be sufficient to maintain the ground he had gained. On the evening of the same day the regiment of Perkins's brigade arrived at the Rapids, and the remaining Kentuckians under Payne were then ordered to march to general Winchester, which they did the next morning. The corps thus advancing under Cotgrove and Payne would make the force under Winchester considerably stronger than the amount deemed by him sufficient. But they were one day too late.

On the 22nd, about 10 o'clock, the news of the attack on general Winchester's camp was received at the Rapids. General Harrison immediately ordered the regiment of general Perkins's brigade to march with all possible expedition, and proceeded himself after the reinforcement under Payne, which he soon overtook. Some men were presently met, who had escaped from the battle, and who stated that Winchester's forces were totally defeated, and that the British and Indians were pursuing them towards the Rapids. This report only induced the general to urge on his men with more rapidity; but several other fugitives were soon afterwards met, from whom it was ascertained beyond a doubt, that the defeat was total and irretrievable, and that all resistance had ceased early in the day on the part of the Americans. A council of the general and field officers was then held, by whom it was decided to be imprudent and unnecessary to proceed any farther. Some parties of the most active and enterprising men were now sent forward, to assist and bring in those who might escape, and the rest of the reinforcements then returned to the Rapids.

BATTLE AND MASSACRE OF RAISIN. We must now relate the tragical events which occurred on the 22nd and 23rd to the advanced detachment at Frenchtown. Late in the evening, after colonel Wells had left the camp, a Frenchman came to general Winchester from the neighborhood of Malden, with information that a large force of British and Indians, which he supposed to be near 3,000, were about to march from that place shortly after he left it. This intelligence however must have been discredited alike by the officers and men, for no preparations were made by the one, nor apprehensions exhibited by the other. The most fatal security prevailed—many of the troops even wandered about the town till late in the night. Colonel Lewis and major Madison alone seemed to be on the alert— they cautioned their men to be prepared at all times for an attack.

Guards were placed out this night as usual; but as it was extremely cold, no pickett guard was placed on the road, on which the enemy was to be expected. The night passed away without any alarm, and the reveillee began to beat at day-break on the morning of the 22d. A few minutes afterwards, three guns were fired in quick succession by the sentinels. The troops were instantly formed, and the British opened a heavy fire on the camp from several pieces of artillery, loaded with bombs, balls, and grape shot, at the distance of 300 yards. This was quickly followed by a charge, made by the British regulars, and by a general fire of small arms and the Indian yell on the right and left. The British had approached in the night with the most profound silence, and stationed their cannon behind a small ravine, which ran across the open fields on the right. As soon as the regulars approached within the reach of small arms, a well directed fire from the picketts round Lewis's camp soon repulsed them on the left and centre: but on the right, the reinforcement which had arrived with Winchester, and which was unprotected by any breast-work, after maintaining the contest a short time, was overpowered and fell back. About this time general Winchester arrived, and ordered the retreating troops to rally behind a fence and second bank of the river, and to incline towards the centre and take refuge behind the picketts. These orders were either not heard or properly understood, and the British continuing to press on the retiring line, whilst a large body of Indians had gained their right flank, the troops were completely thrown into confusion, and retreated in disorder over the river. A detachment, in the mean time, had been sent from the picketts, to reinforce the right wing, which was carried with it in the retreat; and colonels Lewis and Allen both followed it, with a view to assist in rallying the men. Attempts were made to rally them on the south side of the river, behind the houses and picketts of the gardens; but all the efforts of general Winchester, aided by the two colonels, were in vain. The Indians had gained their left flank, and had also taken possession of the woods in their rear. In their confusion and dismay they attempted to pass a long narrow lane, through which the road passes from the village. The Indians were on both sides, and shot them down in every direction. A large party, which had gained the wood on the right, were surrounded and massacred without distinction, nearly one hundred men being tomahawked within the distance of one hundred yards. The most horrible destruction overwhelmed the fugitives in every direction.

Captain Simpson was shot and tomahawked at the edge of the woods near the mouth of the lane. Colonel Allen, though wounded in his thigh, attempted to rally his men several times, entreating them to halt and sell their lives as dear as possible. He had escaped about two miles, when at length, wearied and exhausted, and disdaining perhaps to survive the defeat, he sat down on a log, determined to meet his fate. An Indian chief, observing him to be an officer of distinction, was anxious to take him prisoner. As soon as he came near the colonel, he threw his gun across his lap, and told him in the Indian language to surrender, and he should be safe. Another savage, having at the same time advanced with a hostile appearance, colonel Allen by one stroke with his sword laid him dead at his feet.

A third Indian, who was near him, had then the honor of shooting one of the first and greatest citizens of Kentucky. Captain Mead, of the regular army, who had fought by the side of colonel Daveiss when he fell in the battle of Tippecanoe, was killed where the action commenced. Finding that the situation of the corps was rendered desperate by the approach of the enemy, he gave orders to his men, "my brave fellows, charge upon them," and a moment afterwards he was no more.

A party with lieutenant Garrett, consisting of 15 or 20 men, after retreating about a mile and a half, were compelled to surrender, and were then all massacred but the lieutenant himself. Another of about 30 men had escaped near three miles, when they were overtaken by the savages, and having surrendered, about one half of them were shot and tomahawked. In short, the greater part of those who were in the retreat fell a sacrifice to the fury of the Indians. The snow was so deep, and the cold so intense, that they were soon exhausted, and unable to elude their pursuers. General Winchester and colonel Lewis, with a few more, were captured at a bridge about three quarters of a mile from the village. Their coats being taken from them, they were carried back to the British lines, where colonel Procter commanded.

The troops within the picketting, under majors Graves and Madison, had with Spartan valor maintained their position, though powerfully assailed by Procter and his savage allies. The British had posted a six-pounder behind a small house, about 200 yards down the river, which considerably annoyed the camp, till its supplies of ammunition, which were brought in a sleigh, were arrested by killing the horse and his driver. Major Graves, in passing round the lines, was wounded in the knee—he sat down and bound it up himself, observing to his men, "never mind me, but fight on." About 10 o'clock colonel Procter, finding it useless to sacrifice his men in vain attempts to dislodge this little band of heroes, withdrew his forces to the woods, intending either to abandon the contest, or to wait the return of the Indians, who had pursued the retreating party. The loss sustained by our men was inconsiderable; and when Procter withdrew, they employed the leisure it afforded them to take breakfast at their posts.

As soon as Procter was informed that general Winchester was taken, he basely determined to take advantage of his situation to procure the surrender of the party in the picketting. He represented to the general, that nothing but an immediate surrender would save the Americans from an indiscriminate massacre by the Indians. A flag was then seen advancing from the British lines, carried by major Overton, one of the general's aids, and accompanied by colonel Procter himself and several other officers. Having halted at a respectful distance, major Madison, with brigade major Garrard, proceeded to meet them, expecting that the object of the flag was to obtain a cessation of hostilities, for the British to bear off their dead. They were much mortified to find, that major Overton was the bearer of an order from general Winchester, directing the officer commanding the American forces to surrender them prisoners of war. This was the first intimation they had that their general had been taken. Colonel Procter, with great haughtiness, demanded an immediate surrender, or he would set the town on fire, and the Indians would not be restrained in committing an indiscriminate massacre. Major Madison observed, "that it had been customary for the Indians to massacre the wounded and prisoners after a surrender, and that he would not agree to any capitulation, which general Winchester might direct, unless the safety and protection of his men were stipulated." Colonel Procter then said " Sir do you mean to dictate to me?" " No," replied Madison, " I mean to dictate for myself, and we prefer selling our lives as dear as possible, rather than be massacred in cold blood." Procter then agreed to receive a surrender on the following terms, that all private property should be respected, that sleds should be sent next morning to remove the sick and wounded to Amherstburg, on the island opposite Malden, that in the mean time they should be protected by a guard, and that the side arms of the officers should be restored to them at Malden.

Major Madison, after consulting with Garrard, thought it most prudent to capitulate on these terms. Half the original force was already lost; the balance would have to contend with more than three times their number; there was no possible chance of a retreat, nor any hope of a reinforcement to save them; and worst of all, their ammunition was nearly exhausted, not more than one third of a small keg of cartridges being left.

Before the men had given up their arms, the Indians came among them and began to plunder them. Information being given to major Madison of this conduct, he ordered his men not to suffer an Indian to come into the lines, and that if they persisted in doing it, or in plundering, to fire upon them and bayonet them. This decided conduct restrained the savages, and none of his men, who were marched with him to Malden, were robbed or injured by the Indians. The inhabitants of the town, being much alarmed for the safety of their persons and property, united with general Winchester in soliciting safety and protection from the British.

Colonel Procter informed the American officers that his own wounded must be taken to Malden in the first instance; but that early in the morning, their wounded should also be removed, and in the mean time that a guard should be left with them. About 12 o'clock the prisoners were marched off; doctors Todd and Bowers of the Kentucky volunteers, were left with the wounded; and major Reynolds with two or three interpreters was all the guard left to protect them.

Captain Hart, the inspector general, being among the number of the wounded, expressed much anxiety to be taken with the prisoners; but captain Elliott of the British army, who had been intimately acquainted with him in Kentucky, assured him that he need not be under the least apprehension for his safety, that the Indians would not hurt those who were left, and that upon the honor of a soldier, he would send his own cariole for him next morning and have him taken to Malden.

Soon after the British forces were withdrawn, major Reynolds began to exhibit symptoms of uneasiness, often walking about and looking towards the road leading to the Rapids, and no doubt expecting the approach of general Harrison with reinforcements, which would have been a most auspicious event for the wounded. The greater part of the Indians went with the British to Stoney creek, six miles on the road towards Malden, where they were promised a frolic by their employers. A few stragglers remained, who went from house to house in search of plunder. Some of them remained in town till late in the night; and before day, the interpreters who had been left with them, abandoned the houses in which they lay. Their anticipations were now very gloomy; the whole night indeed was spent with feelings vibrating between hope and despair. Daylight at last appeared, and their hopes began to brighten; but in a very short time they experienced a sad reversal. About sunrise, instead of sleds arriving to convey them to Malden, a large body of Indians, perhaps two hundred in number, came into the town painted black and red. Their chiefs held a council in which they soon determined to kill all the wounded who were unable to march, in revenge for the warriors they had lost in battle. Soon afterwards they began to yell, and to exhibit in their frantic conduct, the most diabolical dispositions. They began first to plunder the houses of the inhabitants, and then broke into those where the wounded prisoners were lying, some of whom

2 D

they abused, and stript of their clothes and blankets, and then tomahawked them without mercy. Captain Hickman was dragged to the door, where he was tomahawked and then thrown back into the house. This appeared to be the signal for consummating their destruction. The houses of Jean B. Jerome and Gabriel Godfrey, which contained most of the prisoners, were immediately set on fire, and the greater part of the wounded consumed in the conflagration. Many of them who were able to crawl about, endeavored to get out at the windows; but as fast as they appeared they were tomahawked and pushed back. Some who were not in those houses, were killed and thrown into the flames; while others were tomahawked, inhumanly mangled, and left in the streets and highways.

The few who were judged able to march, were saved and taken off towards Malden; but as often as any of them gave out on the way, they were tomahawked and left lying in the road. Major Woolfolk, secretary to general Winchester, had found an asylum in the house of a French citizen; but he was discovered by the Indians, who placed him on a horse and were carrying him away. They took him by the house of Laselle, a fellow who had been suspected for giving intelligence to the British before the battle, to whom he promised a large sum of money, if he would purchase him from the Indians. Laselle replied that it was out of his power, but that probably his brother would, who lived in the next house. The Indian who had taken him, being willing to sell him, had turned to go there, when another savage shot him through the head. He was then tomahawked and scalped, and left to the hogs for two days, by which he was partly devoured before the inhabitants removed him. The fate of major Graves has never been correctly ascertained. It is believed that he was put into a cariole at the river Raisin, and taken towards Detroit; but whether he was murdered on the way to that place, or reserved for greater sufferings, is not distinctly known.

The circumstances respecting the fate of captain Hart have been fully ascertained. When the Indians first entered the house, where he lay with captain Hickman, major Graves and others, and before the massacre had commenced, he was carried by doctor Todd into an adjoining house, which had been plundered of its contents. An Indian then met them, who knowing the profession of the doctor, enquired why the surgeons were left with the wounded. He was told that it was by the directions of colonel Procter; and that captain Elliott was a friend to captain Hart, and had promised to send for him that morning. The Indian shook his head and observed, that Procter and Elliott "were damned rascals, or they would have taken care of them last evening." He then said, " you will all be killed —but keep still—the chiefs are in council, and maybe the wounded only will be killed." Captain Hart offered him 100 dollars to carry him to Malden; but he replied, you are too badly wounded. The savages now began to tomahawk the prisoners; and doctor Todd was tied and carried to Stoney creek, where there was a camp of the wounded British. He informed captain Elliott and the surgeon, of what was going on at French-town, and requested them to send back, and endeavor to save some of the wounded. Captain Elliott replied, that it was too late; that those who had been badly wounded were killed before that time; and that all who were still preserved by the Indians were now safe. Doctor Todd spoke of captain Hart in particular, and stated that many, who would be saved in the first instance, being unable to march far, must ultimately be sacrificed, unless means were taken to preserve them. To which Elliott replied, that charity began at home; that his own wounded must first be conveyed, and that if any sleds then remained, he would send them back. Doctor Todd was so anxious to get some person of in-

fluence sent back, that he tried to excite the avarice of
the surgeon, by informing him that the surgical instru-
ments, which were very valuable, were in the house
with the wounded. He soon found that he had now
touched the master passion of the British soul. An
interpreter was immediately sent back for the instru-
ments; but the conflagration had consumed every thing
before he arrived. The conversation of captain Elliott clearly proved, that the British officers had deliberately resolved to abandon the wounded prisoners to
an indiscriminate massacre, in direct violation of their
solemn engagements at the surrender. If they did not
instigate, they at least permitted the horrible scene
without regret.

After Doctor Todd had been taken from captain Hart,
one of the Indians agreed to carry him to Malden for
100 dollars. The fellow placed him on a horse, and
was going through the commons of the town, when he
met with another, who claimed the captain as his prisoner. To settle the dispute, they agreed to kill him
and divide the remainder of his money and clothes between them. They accordingly dragged him off his
horse and despatched him with a war club. When
he found that his destruction was inevitable, he submitted with fortitude and composure to his fate.

Many other instances of the massacre of individuals and small parties might be mentioned. Some who
were exhausted by marching, were killed at Brownstown, and several others at the river Rouche. Doctor Bowers was saved by an Ottawa chief, and was a
witness to the massacre of four or five at Sandy creek.
For several days after the battle, fresh scalps were
brought into Malden by the savages. Some of the
prisoners however, who had been carried off by the
Indians, were fortunate enough to make their escape:
whilst others were doomed to suffer death in the flames,
to gratify the revenge of the brutal barbarians. Such
indeed were the monstrous acts of barbarity, commit-

ted on the maimed and defenceless prisoners, that no language can depict them in colours sufficiently dark. And all this was done by the allies of his Britannic Majesty, the sovereign of a nation pretending to rank high in the civilized world! a nation professing to be christians! a nation that is venerated by the federalists of America, and which claims preeminence in every thing that is great, and good, and honorable in human nature! but against which, the volumes of history, and the records of Heaven, contain the longest, blackest catalogue, of crimes and barbarities, that ever have been perpetrated on this globe.

Procter was no doubt peculiarly qualified by nature and education, for the perpetration of such deeds as these—but the principles on which the patronage of the British government is administered, will always produce an abundant supply of such characters, without the aid of uncommon individual depravity. Under that government there is no road to preferment so sure, as that which leads through oppression, perfidy, and blood! For the massacre at the river Raisin, for which any other civilized government would have dismissed, and perhaps have gibbetted the commander, colonel Procter received the rank of major general in the British army!

The American army in this affair lost upwards of 290 in killed, massacred, and missing. Only 33 escaped to the Rapids. The British took 547 prisoners, and the Indians about 45. The loss of the enemy, as the Americans had no chance to ascertain it, was of course never correctly known by the public. From the best information that could be obtained, it is believed to have been in killed and wounded, between three and four hundred. The Indians suffered greatly, and the 41st regiment was very much cut up. Their whole force in the battle was about 2,000, one half regulars and Canadians, commanded by colonels Procter and St. George; the other, composed of Indians,

commanded by Round-Head and Walk-in-the-Water,
Tecumseh was not there—he was still on the Wabash,
collecting the warriors in that quarter.

Colonel Procter arrived at Amherstburg with his
prisoners on the 23rd, and crowded them into a small
muddy woodyard, where they were exposed all night
in a heavy rain, without tents or blankets, and with
scarcely fire enough to keep them from freezing, many
of them being very indifferently clothed. Such treatment was very severe on men, who at home enjoyed
all the comforts and luxuries of life, and whose humanity would have disdained to treat any conquered
foe in this manner. Procter after he had left the battle ground, never named the guard nor sleds, which
he had promised for the wounded Americans; nor
would he pay any attention to the subject, when repeatedly reminded of it by general Winchester and
major Madison. Captain Elliott once replied to their
solicitations, that " the Indians were very excellent
surgeons." From the whole tenor of Procter's conduct, it is evident that he was determined from the first,
to abandon the wounded to their fate. It is true, that
he had not the means of transportation for his own and
the American wounded at the same time ; but it is equally true, that he had it in his power to comply with his
promise, made before the surrender, to place a guard
over them, which would be able to protect them from
the fury of the savages. What a contrast, between
this base perfidy of the British *officers*, in exposing
their prisoners to massacre, after *stipulating* to protect
them ; and the noble humanity of the American *tars*,
in sacrificing their own lives, to save their foes who had
surrendered *unconditionally !*

The prisoners were detained at Amherstburg till
the 26th, when they were divided into two parties, the
first of which was marched on that day, and the other
on the day following. Some who were badly wounded, were left behind with surgeons to attend them.

They proceeded up the rivers Detroit and Thames, through the interior of Upper Canada, to Fort George on the Niagara strait. On this journey they suffered many hardships and indignities from the severity of the weather; the want of provisions, and from the inhumanity of their guards. At Fort George they were paroled, and returned home by the way of Erie and Pittsburgh, and thence down the Ohio river. The condition of the parole was, not to bear arms against his majesty or *his allies*, during the present war, until regularly exchanged. When some of the Kentuckians inquired, who were his majesty's allies—they were answered, that "his majesty's allies were known;" from which it appears, that some of these tools of British baseness, were ashamed of the association which their sovereign had formed. General Winchester, colonel Lewis, and major Madison were detained, and sent by Montreal to Quebec, at which place, and at Beaufort in its vicinity, they were confined till the spring of 1814, when a general exchange of prisoners took place, and they returned home.

Ensign I. L. Baker, who had been taken by the Indians on the 22nd, and had witnessed many of their subsequent barbarities, was brought to Detroit and ransomed by an American gentleman at that place, before the march of the prisoners. General Winchester directed him to take charge of the wounded, who were left at Sandwich. He continued there till the 15th of February, discharging in a very able and assiduous manner, the duties required in that situation. During his stay, he obtained a variety of information, concerning the conduct of the allies, which he afterwards reported to general Winchester. He ascertained that about sixty prisoners had been massacred by the Indians after the day of battle; and that they had probably between 30 and 40 prisoners still alive. The prospect of their release however was now very gloomy, as Procter had issued an order, *forbidding indi-*

viduals to purchase any more of them! while a stipu-
*lated price was still paid for all the scalps brought in
by the savages!* The dead of the American army were
still unburied—left to be devoured by hogs and dogs.
When ensign Baker mentioned this subject to the British officers, they still replied that the Indians would
not suffer them to be buried. The citizens of Detroit
used great exertions, to procure provisions for the accommodation of the wounded, and to ransom the prisoners from the Indians. Many young ladies, with
the characteristic benevolence of their sex, were very
instrumental in this business. The names of many
persons were reported on this account by ensign Baker;
but among them Augustus B. Woodward esq. was
most preeminently distinguished by his zealous and
unwearied exertions for the benefit of the unfortunate
Americans. On the part of the British, colonel James
Baubee acted with generosity and friendship; and colonel Elliott with major Muir were likewise found on
the side of humanity in many serviceable acts.

Colonel Procter some time after the defeat, issued a
proclamation, by which he required the citizens of
Michigan either to take the oath of allegiance to his
Majesty, or to leave the Territory. This measure, together with his violations of the capitulation of general Hull, induced judge Woodward to address him in
a letter, in which he complained of the infractions of
that capitulation, by the Indians in the British employ;
reminded him, that he had pledged his honor, before
the late battle, to protect the inhabitants; and then informed him of the scandalous scenes of barbarity and
devastation, which had occurred since the capitulation
of the 22nd; and concluded with proposing a conven-
tion between him and the citizens, which would tend
to secure them for the future, in the rights stipulated
by general Brock. In reply, colonel Procter, who
had already acted with so much perfidious barbarity,
now exhibited another trait in his accomplished cha-

racter. He had the *meanness* to deny, that any capitulation had taken place at the river Raisin, and to assert that the Americans had surrendered at discretion! At the same time he called for proofs of the barbarities which had been committed! On the next day, the judge sent him the affidavits of such persons as happened to be then in Detroit, who had witnessed the conduct of the Indians, and remonstrated against his purpose of forcing the citizens to swear allegiance to the British government, reminding him that it was contrary to the law of nations, and that "in a state of open and declared war, a subject or citizen of one party, cannot transfer his allegiance to the other, without incurring the penalties of treason, and while nothing can excuse his guilt, so neither are those innocent who lay temptations before him." A passport was soon afterwards obtained by the judge, who repaired by the way of Niagara to the City of Washington. Many other citizens also abandoned all their property and fled from the sway of the red and white savages.

The following are extracts from the general order, issued by the commander in chief of the British forces, concerning the battle of the 22nd—while it avows the employment of the Indians, and sanctions the savage mode of warfare, it will serve as a specimen of the veracity of British official accounts.

"His excellency, the commander of the forces, has the highest satisfaction in announcing to the troops under his command, another brilliant action achieved by the gallant division of the army at Detroit under colonel Procter. Information having been received, that an advanced corps of the American army under brigadier general Winchester, amounting to upwards of 1000 (900) strong, had entered and occupied Frenchtown, about thirty-six miles south of Detroit, colonel Procter did not hesitate a moment in anticipating the enemy, by attacking this advanced corps, before it could receive support from the forces on their march under general Harrison. At day break, on the 22nd January, colonel Proctor, by a spirited and vigorous attack, completely defeated general Winchester's division, with the loss of between four and five hundred slain (less than 300) for all who attempted to save themselves by flight, were cut off by the *Indian warriors.* About 400 of the enemy took *refuge in the houses* of the town, and kept up a galling fire from the windows; but finding farther resistance unavailing, they *surrendered themselves at discretion!* On this occasion the gallantry of colonel Procter was most nobly displayed in his *humane* and unwearied exertions! *which succeeded in rescuing the vanquished from the revenge of the Indian warriors!!!"*

"Colonel Procter reports in strong terms the gallantry displayed by *all descriptions* of troops and the able support received from colonel St. George, and from all the officers and men under his command, whose spirited valor and steady discipline is above all praise. The Indian chief Round-Head, with his band of warriors rendered essential service by their bravery and good conduct. It is with regret that colonel Proctor reports 24 killed and 158 wounded!!!"

"The commander of the forces is pleased to appoint, till farther orders, or until the pleasure of his royal Highness the Prince Regent is known, colonel Vincent of the 49th regiment, and colonel Procter of the 41st regiment, to have the rank of brigadier generals in Upper Canada."

The disgrace of this mass of falshoods however, is not to be imputed to the commander in chief—he merely repeated the story told him by Procter.

In this defeat, though the detachment cut off was not large, the American cause sustained a great injury; and on the state of Kentucky the stroke was peculiarly severe. Colonel Wells immediately returned to that state, with all the information that had been collected respecting the battle and massacre.   The effect on the feelings of the community was truly deplorable.   Almost every family in the state had some friend or intimate acquaintance in the army, for whose fate the most anxious and distresssing apprehensions were excited.   The accounts given by the fugitives, on which alone the public had to depend, were altogether indefinite, and extremely exaggerated.   It was weeks and even months before much information was received, on which a perfect reliance could be placed.   The return of the prisoners at last relieved the anxious uncertainty of the greater part of the people; but some were still left in doubt, and for ever must remain in doubt, respecting the fate of their best friends and most intimate connexions.   Some idea of the public anxiety and distress may be formed from the facts, that the army thus barbarously destroyed, was composed of the most interesting and respectable citizens of the state; and that from the previous intelligence from it, the highest expectations were formed of its success and glory.

A disaster so calamitous would necessarily excite much discussion with respect to its causes; and as much blame was thrown upon those, who committed no error, and who were not instrumental in causing the defeat of Winchester, which proved to be the defeat of the campaign, it may not be amiss to vindicate in a cursory manner, the conduct of those, on whom public opinion, or the censure of their enemies, was unjustly severe.   General Harrison was blamed by his enemies, for the advance of the detachment to the river Raisin; for not reinforcing it in time; or finding that impracticable, for not ordering a retreat; besides many other matters of less importance.

It is evident from the statement of facts already made, that general Harrison is not answerable for the advance of the detachment.   It was sent by general

Winchester, without the knowledge and consent of Harrison; and contrary to his views and plans for the future conduct of the campaign, and to the instructions, communicated with his plans through ensign Todd, before the left wing had marched for the Rapids. If the advance was improper, the blame does not lie upon Harrison; if it was proper, general Winchester is entitled to the credit of having ordered it. The following extract from the journal of colonel Wood, shews the impression made at head quarters by the first intelligence of the advance received at that place.

"This news for a moment paralyzed the army, or at least the thinking part of it, for no one could imagine that it was possible for him to be guilty of such a hazardous step. General Harrison was astonished at the imprudence and inconsistency of such a measure, which if carried into execution could be viewed in no other light than as attended with certain and inevitable destruction to the left wing. Nor was it a difficult matter for any one to foresee and predict the terrible consequences, which were sure to mark the result of a scheme no less rash in its conception than hazardous in its execution."

With respect to reinforcing the detachment, a recurrence to facts equally proves that Harrison is not blamable, as he made every exertion in his power to support it. It was not until the night of the 16th, that he received the information, indirectly through general Perkins, that Winchester had arrived at the Rapids. By the same express he was advised, that Winchester *meditated* some unknown movement against the enemy. Alarmed at this information, he immediately made every exertion which the situation of his affairs required. He was then at Upper Sandusdy, his principal deposit of provisions and munitions of war, which is sixty miles from the Rapids by the way of Portage river, and seventy-six by the way of Lower

Sandusky; and about 38 more from the river Raisin. He immediately sent an express direct to the Rapids for information; gave orders for a corps of 300 men to advance with the artillery, and escorts to proceed with provisions; and in the morning he proceeded himself to Lower Sandusky, at which place he arrived in the night following, a distance of forty miles, which he travelled in seven hours and a half over roads requiring such exertion, that the horse of his aid, major Hukill, fell dead on their arrival at the fort. He found there, that general Perkins had prepared to send a battalion to the Rapids, in conformity with a request from general Winchester. That battalion was despatched the next morning, the 18th, with a piece of artillery; but the roads were so bad, that it was unable, by its utmost exertions, to reach the river Raisin, a distance of 75 miles, before the fatal disaster.

General Harrison then determined to proceed to the Rapids himself, to learn personally from general Winchester, what were his situation and views. At four o'clock on the morning of the 19th, while he still remained at Lower Sandusky, he received the information, that colonel Lewis had been sent with a detachment to secure the provisions on the river Raisin, and to occupy with the intention of holding the village of Frenchtown. There was then but one regiment and a battalion at Lower Sandusky, and the regiment was immediately put in motion, with orders to make forced marches for the Rapids; and general Harrison himself immediately proceeded for the same place. On his way, he met an express with intelligence of the successful battle, which had been fought on the preceding day. The anxiety of general Harrison to push forward and either prevent or remedy any misfortune which might occur, as soon as he was apprised of the advance to the river Raisin, was manifested by the great personal exertions which he made in this instance. He started in a sleigh with general Perkins, to overtake the battalion under Cotgrove, attended by a single ser, vant. As the sleigh went very slow from the roughness of the road, he took the horse of his servant and pushed on alone. Night came upon him in the midst of the swamp, which was so imperfectly frozen that the horse sunk to his belly at every step. He had no resource but to dismount and lead his horse, jumping himself from one sod to another which was solid enough to support him. When almost exhausted, he met one of Cotgrove's men coming back to look for his bayonet, which he said he had left at a place where he had stopped, and for which he would have a dollar stopped from his pay unless he recovered it. The general told him, he would not only pardon him for the loss, but supply him with another, if he would assist him to get his horse through the swamp. By his aid, the general was enabled to reach the camp of the battalion.

Very early on the morning of the 20th he arrived at the Rapids, from which place general Winchester had gone, on the preceding evening, with all his disposable force to the river Raisin. Nothing more could now be done, but wait the arrival of the reinforcements from Lower Sandusky.

The original force of general Winchester at the Rapids had been about 1300, and all but 300 were now gone in advance. The battalion from Lower Sandusky was hurried on as fast as possible ; and as soon as the regiment arrived, 350 strong, on the evening of the 21st, the balance of Winchester's army was ordered to proceed, which they did the next morning under general Payne. The force now advancing exceeded by 300, the force deemed sufficient by general Winchester to maintain his position. But whether sufficient or not, it is evident from the preceding statement of facts, that no more could be sent, and that greater exertions could not be made to send it in time. Instead of censure being due to general Harrison, he merits praise for his prudent exertions, from the moment he was apprised of Winchester's arrival at the Rapids.

" What human means," says colonel Wood, " within the control of general Harrison, could prevent the anticipated disaster, and save that corps which was already looked upon as lost, as doomed to inevitable destruction? Certainly none—because neither orders to halt, nor troops to succour him, could be received in time, or at least that was the expectation. He was already in motion and general Harrison still at Upper Sandusky, 70 miles in his rear. The weather was inclement, the snow was deep, and a large portion of the black swamp was yet open. What could a Turenne or an Eugene have done under such a pressure of embarrassing circumstances, more than Harrison did?"

If it should be asked why detachments from the centre and right wing, were not sent sooner to the Rapids, to form a junction with and to strengthen the advance under Winchester, the answer is obvious—The object of the advance to that place was to guard the provisions, artillery, and military stores, to be accumulated there for the main expedition, for which purpose Winchester's command, as it would daily be strengthened by the arrival of escorts, was amply sufficient; and it was important, that a force unnecessarily large should not be sent there, to consume the accumulating provisions, before the main expedition was ready to move.

After the success of the detachment on the 18th, there were powerful reasons, why the position it occupied should not be abandoned. The protection of the French inhabitants was now an imperative duty. The advance to their town had been made at their solicitation; and when the battle had commenced, many of them joined the American forces and fought with great gallantry; and afterwards they attacked and killed the straggling Indians, wherever they met them. Their houses were opened to our men, and they offered to give up the whole of the provisions, which yet remained to them, upon condition that they should not again be abandoned to the fury of the savages, or subjected for what they

had done to be immured in the prisons of Malden.
The amount of provisions to be secured was believed
to be very considerable. The duty of protecting the
faithful inhabitants however, had been so strongly impressed by their conduct, on the minds of general Winchester and his men, that an order to retreat would perhaps not have been very promptly obeyed. They
proved their fidelity again, by engaging in the battle of
the 22nd. Whatever firing was done from the windows
on that day according to Procter, must have been done
by the inhabitants. On the other hand, the forwardness of the supplies, and of the other corps in the rear,
was such that in a few days the most ample reinforcements would have arrived, and the main expedition
could have moved very early in February.

From the whole of the facts, which are now before
the reader, he will be able to judge for himself, with
respect to the causes of the disaster. The advance to
the river Raisin was a very important movement; it
was made from the best and most urgent motives; but
it is questionable whether it was not too hazardous and
premature. It was a rule with general Harrison, and
undoubtedly a very good one, never in Indian warfare
to send out a detachment, unless indispensably necessary, and then to make it sufficiently strong to contend
with the whole force of the enemy. The rule was peculiarly applicable in this instance. Frenchtown was
within 18 miles of Malden, the head quarters of the
enemy, while it was more than double that distance
from the Rapids, and about 100 miles on an average
from the other corps of the American army. The idea
of reinforcing an advanced corps at that place, to support it against any speedy movement of the enemy, was
hence altogether chimerical. It should have been strong
enough in the first instance, or with the reinforcements
to be immediately sent after it from the Rapids, to maintain its ground, against the whole disposable force of
the enemy, for a week at least. And this was probably

the case. The greatest error, judging from the information we possess after the affair is over, does not appear to have been so much the advance of the detachment, as the neglect to fortify the camp. The force actually on the ground, if well posted and well defended by fortifications, and amply supplied with ammunition, could certainly have resisted such an attack as was made, until reinforcements had arrived. On the 21st general Winchester thus addressed general Harrison: "All accounts from Brownstown and Malden agree in stating, that the enemy is preparing to retake this place; if he effects his purpose, he will pay dear for it. A few pieces of artillery however, would add to our strength, and give confidence to our friends in this place." Though possessed of this information, and lying so near the enemy, that they could march at any time in the evening, and attack him before day next morning, yet he suffered his men to go to rest that night in an open camp, in which they had lain a whole day since his arrival at that place.

"Unsuspicious and elated with this flash of success," says colonel Wood, "the troops were permitted to select, each for himself, such quarters on the west side of the river, as might please him best; whilst the general, not liking to be amongst a parcel of noisy, dirty freemen, took his quarters on the east side! not the least regard being paid to defence, order, regularity, or system in the posting of the different corps." After speaking of the battle and massacre, he proceeds "Thus was there a corps of 1000 men, the elite of the army, totally sacrificed in the most wanton manner possible; and that too, without the slightest benefit to their country or posterity. With only one third or one fourth of the force destined for that service; destitute of artillery; of engineers; of men who had ever seen or heard the least of an enemy; and with but a very inadequate supply of ammunition; how he ever could have entertained the most distant hope of success, or what right

2 F

he had to presume to claim it, is to me one of the
strangest things in the world. An adept in the art of
war, is alone authorized to deviate from the ordinary and
established rules, by which that art for a great length
of time has been usefully and successfully applied.

" Winchester was destitute of every means of sup-
porting his corps long at the river Raisin, was in the
very jaws of the enemy, and beyond the reach of suc-
cor. He who fights with such flimsy pretensions to
victory, will always be beaten, and eternally ought
to be."

If Harrison committed an error, it appears to me,
that it consisted in allowing too great a latitude of discretion to general Winchester. His responsibility for
the conduct of the army, his accurate knowledge of the
country, his experience in Indian warfare and knowledge of the caution it required, all entitled him to control, in the most positive manner, the movements of
general Winchester's command. On the contrary he
had always " considered him rather in the light of an
associate in command, than an inferior." In all the
correspondence of Harrison with Winchester, he had
treated him with the most respectful confidence, and
had recommended, instead of ordering, the measures
which he wished him to pursue ; and in his letters to
the war department, the same decorous and sensitive
respect for the character, and confidence in the opinions
of Winchester were constantly preserved and expressed. Had Winchester not inferred from this treatment,
that he was at liberty to take the most important steps
without obtaining the approbation of general Harrison,
the advance to the river Raisin could not have been
made prematurely. It has been alleged in justification
of Winchester, and in derogation of Harrison, that the
communications of the latter had induced the former to
believe, that he would be supported in this movement.
Some of Harrison's letters might have raised an expectation, that the supplies and troops of the right wing

would have been sufficiently advanced for this purpose. But the last letter from Harrison, received on the evening before the detachment marched for the river Raisin, combined with the instructions communicated through ensign Todd, must have left but little room for such an expectation. The letter was dated on the 3rd of January, at Franklinton. The following is an extract.

"The hogs are progressing so fast towards the Rapids, that it is necessary the force destined to occupy it should march as soon as possible. If any thing happens to prevent your going on immediately, send an express through the woods to Upper Sandusky, that I may send on two regiments from thence."

From this it must have been evident to Winchester, that no troops were approaching from Sandusky; and from his suggestion that " a cooperating force from the right wing might be acceptable" it is evident, that his calculations on being supported by Harrison, had but little influence in his determinations.

CHAPTER VI.

*Termination of the first campaign under Harrison—
preparations for the second—first siege of fort
Meigs.*

ON the night of the 22nd, after all the information
had been collected that was attainable, respecting the
disasters of that day, a council of the general and field
officers was called at the Rapids by general Harrison,
who submitted to their consideration the following ques-
tions : whether it was probable that the enemy would
attack the camp at that place? and if he did make an
attack, whether the force then in camp, consisting of
900 men and a single piece of artillery, would be able
to make an effectual resistance? Major M'Clanahan
of the Kentucky volunteers who had escaped from the
action, assisted at this council. He was of opinion,
that the force of the enemy in the battle had been from
1600 to 2000 British and Indians, with six pieces of
artillery principally howitzers. After mature deliberation it was the unanimous opinion of the council, that
it would be proper to retire a short distance on the road
upon which the artillery and reinforcements were approaching. For should the position at the Rapids be
maintained, yet by getting in its rear the enemy would
be able to defeat the reinforcements in detail, and to
capture the all important convoys of artillery, military
stores and provisions coming from Sandusky. Although the enemy might not advance with his whole
force against the camp at the Rapids, yet it was deemed highly probable that the Indians at least would
cross the river on the ice below that place, and endeavor to intercept the convoys, of the approach of which
they must have received information.

The position which had been selected, and the camp which had been formed by general Winchester at the Rapids, were also very injudicious, and untenable against any formidable force. The position was on the wrong side of the river; for it frequently happens in the winter, that heavy rains suddenly swell the current and break up the ice, so as to render the stream wholly impassable for many days together. This would prevent the convoys from reaching the camp, whilst the enemy might cross on the ice at the mouth of the bay, and destroy them without opposition.

The attempt to fortify the position had also destroyed all its natural advantages. The camp was a parallelogram with its longest side on the river, corresponding to the form of the hill on which it was placed, the abrupt declivity of which afforded the enemy a better fortification, at point blank shot in the rear, than the breast work of logs by which the lines were protected. The flanks were also at a convenient distance from the ends of the hill to be annoyed from them by the enemy. By reversing the order and making the flank lines the longest, so as to extend quite across the hill, the rear would have been rendered secure, and the flanks would have been at too great a distance to be annoyed from the extremities of the hill.

On the next morning therefore the army abandoned the Rapids, having first set fire to the block house, in which there was a quantity of provisions that would be useful to the enemy if they advanced to that place. Having retired as far as Portage river about 18 miles distant, the general there established and strongly fortified his camp, to wait for the artillery and a detachment of troops under Leftwich, expecting that he would be enabled by their arrival to return in a few days to the banks of the Miami.

This retrograde movement was altogether unnecessary in the actual state of things; but we are not to judge the commander of an army by the information respecting the enemy which may be found in the page of the subsequent historian, but by that which at the time was in-his possession; and in the present case we may remark, that immediately after experiencing a defeat for the want of a cautious and strict conformity to military principles, it would have been excusable in the officers of the army to have carried that virtue to excess.

General Harrison was disappointed in his expectation of returning in a few days to the Rapids, by an unfortunate rain, which arrested the progress of the artillery and troops under Leftwich, at the distance of 25 miles from his camp at Portage. The rain commenced on the 24th and continued several days, so that the road was rendered wholly impassable for the artillery, although it was fixed upon sleds. In the mean time spies were sent towards the river Raisin, to discover the situation of affairs in that quarter: and on the 31st of January, doctor M'Keehan of the Ohio militia, volunteered at the request of the general to carry a flag to Malden, to ascertain the condition of the wounded, and to carry them a sum of money in gold to procure accommodations. His fate deserves to be recorded, as it still farther illustrates the character of the enemy. He was accompanied by two men, and furnished with an open letter to general Winchester, and another addressed to any British officer, describing the character in which he went, and also with written instructions for his own conduct; all of which he was directed to shew to the first British officer he met. He stopped to lie the first night, in a cabin at the Rapids, where he fixed his flag in his cariole at the door. In the night he was discovered, and attacked by some Indians, who killed one of his men; and having robbed himself and the other of all they had, took them prisoners to captain Elliott, who was stationed with some other Indians about 20 miles farther on. Elliott treated him politely, and sent him forward to Procter. When he came into the presence of that magnanimous Briton, he immediately began to abuse general Harrison, found fault with M'Keehan's instructions, and declared that the flag was only a pretext to cover some bad design. These insinuations were indignantly repelled by the doctor, who was told that he should be sent back, by a different route from that which he came. After some days he was recognised in his official character, and directed to attend the wounded. On the 2nd of March he was arrested by colonel Procter, and accused of carrying on a secret correspondence. Without giving him even the form of a trial, he was then sent off to fort George, and thence to Kingston, and finally to Montreal, where he was imprisoned in a dungeon, and all the time, from the period of his arrest, was misused in the true British style. After lying in the dungeon thirty days, he was liberated at the intercession of lieutenant Dudley of the American navy; and by way of reparation was informed by adjutant general Baynes, that the outrages he had suffered were contrary to his orders.

On the 30th of January, general Leftwich arrived at Portage river with his brigade, a regiment of Pennsylvania troops, and the greater part of the artillery; and on the first of February general Harrison marched with his whole force, amounting now to 1700 men, to the foot of the Rapids, and encamped on the south east side of the river, at a place which he deemed much stronger and more suitable in other respects than that which had been occupied by Winchester. He still entertained a belief that he would be able to execute in the present season, the long intended expedition against Malden, and continued to exert himself in preparation. All the troops in the rear were ordered to join him immediately, except some companies which were left in the forts on the Auglaize and St. Marys. He expected he would be able by the 11th or 12th of February to advance towards Malden, if not with hea-

vy artillery sufficient to reduce that place, at least with
a force that could scour the whole country, disperse
the Indians, destroy all the shipping of the enemy, the
greater part of their provisions, and establish a post
near Brownstown, till the season would permit the advance of the artillery. The Ohio and some of the
Kentucky troops soon arrived at the Rapids, which
rendered his advance 2000 strong. The accession of
all the others, would scarcely however, raise his effective force to four thousand men, so greatly were the
different corps now reduced from their nominal and
original amount.

The present was the season, in common years, when
the most intense frosts prevailed in this country, by
which its lakes and swamps were rendered perfectly
firm, and secure for any kind of conveyance: yet the
weather now continued so warm and rainy, that the
roads were entirely broken up, and travelling on the
ice rendered altogether unsafe. A trial of its strength
on the border of the lake, was effectually made on the
evening of the 9th. Intelligence being received that a
party of Indians were driving off the cattle from a small
French village, about 14 miles from the Rapids, general Harrison prepared a strong detachment, and pursued them that night 26 miles on the ice, with a six-
pounder in his train. He found the ice so weak in
many places, that the horses of several officers who
were mounted, broke through it; and in one place the
six-pounder broke through and was nearly lost. The
Indians were not overtaken; and in the morning, the
detachment returned to camp.

The 11th of February at last arrived, and still the
balance of the troops with the necessary supplies had
not been able to reach the Rapids: the roads by this
time had also become absolutely impassable for any
kind of carriage, it being scarcely possible to traverse
them with a single horse. Under these circumstances
general Harrison was at length constrained, with much

reluctance and mortification, to abandon all thoughts of advancing this season against Malden.   And thus terminated, without gaining any decisive advantage over the enemy, a campaign which was prosecuted with incalculable expense to the government, and immense labors and hardships on the part of the general and his men.   The great difficulties to be encountered in the prosecution of a winter campaign through the swampy wilderness in the northwestern parts of Ohio, were doubtless sufficient to defeat all the exertions and perseverance which could reasonably be expected from human nature: yet the indefatigable industry of the general, and the unshaken firmness of his brave compatriots, would probably have surmounted every obstacle, had it not been for the mismanagement and misfortunes of general Winchester in conducting the advance of the left wing.   The apparently unimportant error of sending the intelligence of his arrival at the Rapids, by the driver of the old packhorses, would seem to have been the determining cause of the failure. The roads were then so well frozen, that the artillery and convoys of provisions might have been pushed forward with considerable despatch; but for want of that intelligence at head quarters, some delay was produced by which the critical moment for advancing was lost.

It was certainly unfortunate that a winter campaign was ever attempted.   When general Harrison was first appointed to the command of the northwestern army, the precise season of the year had arrived, which had arrested the progress of the army under general Wayne in the year '93.   Although 18 months had then been employed in preparation, and in disciplining the troops, the prudent caution of general Washington preferred a postponement of the meditated chastisement of the Indians till another year, to the risk of attempting it at a season, which so greatly multiplies the difficulties at all times presented by the nature of the country and the peculiar activity of the enemy to be opposed.

2 G

It was in compliance with *his* instructions, that the American army was cantoned at Greenville in September '93, and the auxiliary volunteer force from Kentucky dismissed. The latter had been in part drawn from the most remote counties of Kentucky, and a considerable portion of the whole expense which would have attended their employment had already been incurred. To tread in the footsteps of Washington and Wayne could have been dishonorable to no administration and their commander. Why then was a winter campaign attempted? The orders of the government to general Harrison were indeed not positive on this head : but it is impossible that he could hesitate to believe that their wishes and expectations were decidedly in favor of recovering Detroit and taking Malden during the winter. Their letters afford ample evidence that such were their views; and their having ordered 10,000 men to the field, many of whom were from the Alleghany mountains, whose terms of service would all expire by the end of winter, was an unquestionable evidence of their intentions. The force was much greater than was necessary merely for the defence of the frontiers. After the most mature reflection the general determined to endeavor to surmount all the difficulties which would oppose the winter campaign. He was fully apprised of their extent, and had even given a decided opinion to the government before his appointment, that in the event of the capture of Hull's army, it would be impracticable to reestablish our affairs in that quarter until the following year. After being invested with the command, he had altered his opinion so far only as to believe, that a season favorable to his operations, combined with some address, and with much labor and expense, might possibly enable him to advance, either before the swamps became impassable in the fall, or in the middle of winter when they were hard frozen; and he believed that the uncommon solicitude of the government and the people made it necessary to attempt it. The preparations for the advance of the army however, could not be completed in time for advancing in the fall; and the openness of the winter, with other unfavorable occurrences, defeated him in that season.

Many persons were impatient at the delay of the northwestern army, who did not know, that before it could arrive at Detroit, it had to pass a wilderness of 180 miles, and many who knew that circumstance did not know, that the greater part of that desert was a frightful swamp, and that the best of it would be considered impassable for carriages of any kind, by the people of the Atlantic states. With the knowledge which the general possessed of the country, he could not for a moment have thought of passing, in the latter part of the fall or beginning of winter, the swampy district which crosses every approach to the lake, even if his preparations for the march had been complete. But this was far from being the case. At a time when it was supposed by many, that he might have been in full march upon Malden, some of the pieces of artillery, which were intended to reduce that fortress, had just been forwarded from Washington City, and a part of the timber for the carriages of the latter was still standing in the woods near Pittsburgh. The very unexpected surrender of Hull had thrown all the western arrangements of the government into confusion. Reinforcements had been ordered for *his* army, and during the excitement produced by his surrender, additional reinforcements were ordered into the field, before any arrangements had been made to furnish them with provisions and clothing, and to supply the place of the artillery which was lost in Detroit.

After the termination of the campaign, the attention of general Harrison was directed to the fortifying of his position at the foot of the Rapids; to the distribution of the troops, which would remain after the discharge of the Kentucky and Ohio corps; and to the

accumulation of provisions at his present post for the
next campaign. In the latter business, very little could
be effected at present. It was necessary, to wait for
the opening of the rivers in the spring, to bring down
the immense stores accumulated on the St. Marys and
Auglaize by water conveyance. From Lower Sandusky there was some progress made in transportation, by
going round on the ice of the Sandusky and Miami
bays and border of the lake. A battalion of Ohio
troops, recently called into service, together with a company of regulars, were distributed in the forts on the
Auglaize and St. Marys; in each post on Hull's road,
a subaltern's command was stationed; at Upper Sandusky a company was placed, and another at Lower
Sandusky. The balance of all the troops were collected at the foot of the Rapids, where they amounted
to 15 or 1800 men, which was deemed by general Harrison to be too small a force for that important post.
The direction of its fortification was entrusted to colonel Wood, who was then captain in the corps of engineers. "So soon as the lines of the camp were designated, large portions of the labor were assigned to each
corps in the army, by which means a very laudable
emulation was easily excited. Each brigade or regiment commenced the particular portion of work allot-
ted to it with great spirit and vigor. The camp was
about 2500 yards in circumference, the whole of which,
with the exception of several small intervals left for
batteries and block houses, was to be picketted with
timber 15 feet long, from 10 to 12 inches in diameter,
and set 3 feet in the ground. Such were the instructions of the engineer. To complete this picketting, to
put up 8 block houses of double timbers, to elevate 4
large batteries, to build all the store houses and magazines required to contain the supplies of the army, together with the ordinary fatigues of the camp, was an
undertaking of no small magnitude. Besides an immense deal of labor was likewise required in excavat-

ing ditches, making abatis, and clearing away the wood about the camp; and all this was to be done too at a time when the weather was inclement, and the ground so hard frozen that it could scarcely be opened with the mattock and pick-axe. But in the use of the axe, mattock and spade consisted the chief military knowledge of our army; and even that knowledge however trifling it may be supposed by some, is of the utmost importance in many situations, and in ours was the salvation of the army. So we fell to work, heard nothing of the enemy, and endeavored to bury ourselves as soon as possible." *Colonel Wood.* The position thus fortified and denominated camp Meigs, was deemed the most eligible that could be selected, for the protection of the frontiers and the small posts in the rear of it. As a depot for the artillery, military stores and provisions, it was also indispensably necessary to maintain it, for it was now impossible to bring them away.

It will be proper in this place, to notice some transactions, which occurred after the defeat at the river Raisin, in the states which had troops in the northwestern army. When general Harrison at Lower Sandusky, received the information from general Winchester, that the Kentucky troops were not disposed to remain in service after their six months had expired, he immediately addressed a letter to governor Shelby, in which he appealed to the patriotism of that chief and the people of his state for reinforcements. He requested that a corps of 1500 men might be raised and marched to the army with all possible despatch, to supply the place of the Kentuckians then in the field. The legislature of Kentucky was in session, and the governor in a confidential message, communicated the information and request, which he had received from general Harrison. A law was immediately passed, offering the additional pay of 7 dollars per month, to any 1500 of the Kentucky troops, who would remain in service, till a corps could be sent to relieve them.

This law with an address from the legislature to the troops, was immediately despatched to them by colonel Anthony Crocket, who arrived at the northwestern army about the 8th of February. The men had suffered so much, by the unparalleled privations, which they had to encounter in a winter campaign, in that rigorous climate and unfavorable country—and they were now so anxious to return to their friends at home—that they partially resisted the strong appeal to their patriotism in the address of the Legislature, supported by the offer of additional pay. They would not engage for any specified length of time—but if their general was ready to advance against the enemy, they would not hesitate to accompany him without any pecuniary inducement. A similar offer was made about the same time by the state of Ohio, and afterwards by Pennsylvania, to their respective troops, which was attended with similar success.

In the mean time the legislature of Kentucky was engaged in passing an act, to authorize the governor to detach a corps of 3000 men from the militia, of which 1500 were intended to march immediately to general Harrison. On the 2nd of February, they received intelligence of the victory obtained at Frenchtown by colonel Lewis, which produced the liveliest joy at the capitol—but a sad reverse was at hand. In the evening the Theatre was unusually crowded, and the hearts of the people teemed with gratulation at the victory obtained by their fellow citizens in arms—when colonel Wells arrived about 8 o'clock in the night, with information of the defeat and massacre at the river Raisin! what a shock to the feelings of the people! The flower of the Kentucky troops, and of the citizens of that state, were totally defeated and barbarously cut to pieces! The sad reality filled every mind with horror—the fictitious scene of public amusement, was quickly abandoned for the private firesides, to mourn the loss of friends and the misfortunes of the country.

But the public spirit did not sink under the pressure
of this calamity. Though many widows and orphans
were left to mourn the loss of husbands and fathers;
yet the monstrous outrage of the 22nd only roused the
indignation of the yeomanry, and one universal call
for vengeance on the unprincipled foe, was heard from
one extreme of the state to the other.

On the next day the governor put his approving sig-
nature to the law for calling out 3000 militiamen; and
the legislature, placing the utmost confidence in the patriotism, energy, and military talents of that veteran,
passed a resolve, in conformity with the constitution,
" advising him to command personally in the field" at
any time when he could best promote the public interests by such personal service. At the Rapids on the
13th, the fragments of the regiments, originally commanded by colonels Allen, Scott, and Lewis, were honorably discharged; and about the same time the original troops from Ohio were also permitted to retire.
The Kentucky regiments under Barbee, Poague, and
Jennings terminated their period of service on the 1st
of March and returned home. The Virginia and Pennsylvania troops still formed a competent force at the
fort, but their time was also drawing to a close.

The commanding general, considering the destruction of the enemy's vessels at Malden, as an object of
the greatest importance, and as one which might be
accomplished by an expedition on the ice of the lake,
prepared in the latter part of February for an enterprise of that kind, which he entrusted to the command
of captain Langham, a young officer of great promise.
The detachment with which he was to execute it, consisted of 170 volunteers, from the different corps at
the Rapids, who were capable of any enterprise that
valour and perseverance could effect. They were provided with all the combustible materials and instru-
ments necessary for such an undertaking; and the particular party charged with setting fire to the vessels,

was placed under the immediate direction of Mr. Ma-
dis, conductor of artillery, a young French gentleman
who had been an officer of the navy in his native country, and who was distinguished for his great zeal in
our cause, and for his knowledge of all the duties of
the artillery service. Sleighs were provided for the
whole detachment, and they were directed to go down
the lake to the Bass Islands, and proceed from one
Island to another in the chain running towards Malden, managing their movements so as to set out from
the Middle Sister about dark, that they might reach
the destined scene of action some hours before day.
When they came near to Malden, the sleighs were to
be left and the party to proceed on foot, being all provided with mockersins or cloth socks to prevent their
feet from making a noise on the ice. Having completely fired the vessels they were to return to their
sleighs, which it was supposed would convey them so
rapidly away, as to render pursuit perfectly nugatory.
On the second day after their departure, general Harrison advanced with a considerable detachment for the
purpose of meeting any party which might pursue
them. But at the mouth of the Miami bay, he had
the infinite mortification to meet captain Langham returning. He had proceeded but a short distance from
the Bass Islands, when he found the whole lake open,
which of course put a stop to his progress. In most
winters the passage of the lake on the ice is practicable at this period. Had it been so at this time, there
is good reason to believe that the scheme would have
succeeded, and have illuminated the setting darkness
of the campaign with a blaze of glory. The subsequent conduct of captain Langham has proved, that a
better choice for the leader of such an enterprise could
not have been made ; nor could a more proper person
have been selected for firing the vessels than Mr. Ma-
dis, from his intimate acquaintance with every thing

relating to them, and his acknowledged bravery which he had displayed in the campaign of general Hull.

As soon as the despatch of general Harrison, dated on the 11th of February, in which he informed the government, of the termination of the campaign, and of his consequent arrangements, was received at the war department, the present secretary, general Armstrong, sent him instructions in several successive letters, for the future conduct of the war on the northwestern frontiers. He was instructed to continue his demonstrations against Malden, as a diversion in favor of the attempts to be made on Canada below : but no real movement against Malden was to be made, until the government had obtained the command of lake Erie, which it expected to accomplish by the middle of May. The vessels of war for this purpose were now building at Presque Isle in Pennsylvania. Cleveland was fixed upon, as the depot for the troops to be employed in the expedition. Those troops were to consist of the 17th and 19th regiments now in the northwestern army, and but very partially filled—the 24th regiment now at Massac, and three new regiments of regulars, two of which were to be raised in Ohio, and the other in Kentucky. If these regiments were not filled in time, the deficiency was to be made up from the militia. To curtail the enormous expense of militia service, some general rules were adopted in relation to their employment—No requisition was to be made, but by some officer regularly authorized—and was then to be for a definite number, in which the officers and privates should bear the same proportion, as in the regular army—and until so organized, they were not to be received into service. The general was instructed to maintain the post at the Rapids, unless by possibility he should be unable to subsist a sufficient force there for that purpose : and to ensure him the possession of a sufficient force, he was authorized to employ the two regiments *to be* raised in Ohio, or so

2 H

many of them as would answer his purpose.   He was
also instructed to promote the recruiting service, in order to have the regiments filled in time for the expedition.   Such were the plans of the new secretary for
the approaching campaign; and with these nominal
forces was the general required to maintain the northwestern posts, with the provisions and military stores
now accumulated in them; and to protect the frontiers
against the Indians, and make demonstrations against
Malden.   Fortunately general Harrison, before he received these instructions, had called for reinforcements
of militia from both Kentucky and Ohio; but the whole
number expected would not be sufficient to garrison the
different posts completely.

In answer to these instructions, the general remonstrated against abandoning the use of militia, and leaving the frontiers in such a defenceless situation.   He
represented the numerous Indian tribes, residing contiguous to our out posts, who were either hostile, or
would soon become so, when not overawed by an American army.   As soon as the lake became navigable,
the enemy from Malden could also make a descent
with the utmost facility on fort Meigs, the important
deposit of the artillery and military stores, from which
they could not be removed through the swamps, and to
which it was necessary to carry, on the high waters in
the spring, the immense supplies deposited on the Auglaize and St. Marys.   The works at the Rapids had
been constructed for a force of 2000 men; for the general had thought it necessary to maintain a force at
that place, which would be able to contend in the field
with all the disposable force of the enemy, in order to
prevent him from getting into its rear, and destroying
the weaker posts which more immediately protected
the frontiers.   The government was assured, that the
regular force on which they relied, could not be raised
in time, even for the intended expedition; and that as
large supplies were not prepared, at points where they

could be transported by water, the surest plan would be to march a large militia force, which not being delayed and dispirited for the want of supplies, would behave well and effectually accomplish the objects of the campaign. The probability that the force on which the government relied, would be too small to effect its object, was represented as a great obstacle in the way of the recruiting service, which at best was found to be very tedious.

In the following extract from a letter of general Harrison to governor Shelby, the general expressed himself more explicitly on this subject. "My sentiments upon the subject of the force necessary for the prosecution of the war, are precisely similar to yours. It will increase your surprise and regret, when I inform you, that last night's mail brought me a letter from the secretary of war, in which I am restricted to the employment of the regular troops raised in this state to reinforce the post at the Rapids. There are scattered through this state, about 140 recruits of the 19th regiment, and with these I am to supply the place of the two brigades from Pennsylvania and Virginia, whose terms of service will now be daily expiring. By a letter from governor Meigs I am informed, that the secretary of war disapproved the call for militia, which I had made on this state and Kentucky, and was on the point of countermanding the orders. I will just mention one fact, which will shew the consequences of such a countermand. There are upon the Auglaize and St. Marys rivers, eight forts which contain within their walls property to the amount of half a million of dollars from actual cost, and worth now to the United States four times that sum. The whole force which would have had charge of all these forts and property, would have amounted to less than twenty invalid soldiers."

The determination of the government to rely on raising regulars, was caused in part by the inefficiency

of the militia.   This species of troops on the northern
frontier had in many instances refused to pass the limits of the United States, under the pretence that it
was unconstitutional : and in the western country,
where they had in general behaved well, the campaign
had been enormously expensive, and had accomplished
no important object.   On the other hand, it was hoped
that the recruiting service would now be more produc-
tive, under a law which had recently passed in congress.   This law authorized 20 regiments to be raised
to serve only twelve months; and at the same time the
pay and bounty were greatly enhanced.   The plan
however was not well suited to the western country.
The recruiting of regulars will always be slow, where
a superabundant population has not rendered the army
a place of refuge from hard labor, low wages and star-
vation.   Hence by the time a regiment of 12 months
men can be filled, one half the number on an average
will have served half their time ; so that neither in
respect of economy nor discipline, can such troops be
much preferable to militia : and such proved to be the
case in the present attempt.   Colonels M'Arthur and
Cass were appointed brigadier generals, to command
the troops destined to form the northwestern army ;
and governor Howard was appointed a brigadier, and
assigned to the command of the Indiana, Illinois, and
Missouri Territories.

In the mean time general Harrison had left the frontiers, and repaired to Cincinnati where his family resided, having entrusted the command of fort Meigs to
general Leftwich.   Upon the failure of the expedition
under captain Langham, he saw that it was now impossible to annoy the enemy in any manner, and that
until the lake became navigable, it would be equally
impossible for the enemy to make any formidable attack on his posts.   He was equally confident, that as
soon as the lake became completely open in the spring,
an attack would be made on some of his advanced po-

sitions, and most probably on fort Meigs, on the safety of which depended the success of our operations in
the next campaign : at the conclusion of the last, that
place had become from inevitable necessity as well as
from choice, the grand depot of nearly all the artillery,
military stores, and provisions belonging to the northwestern army ; for unless the provisions in the posts
on the waters of the Miami were taken to fort Meigs,
while the waters were navigable in the spring, they
would be rendered useless for any operations in advance of those places, until midsummer, when the
roads would become sufficiently dry and firm for their
land transportation.   Before the period when the attack on that place was to be expected, its garrison
would be reduced to insignificance by the discharge of
the militia ; the general hence deemed it his duty to
repair to the interior, and hasten out with reinforcements to take their place ; and this was particularly
necessary, as it was probable that they would be too
late, unless their march were hastened, by those extraordinary and expensive measures, to which a commander in chief can with propriety resort, but of which
few subordinate officers will take the responsibility.
The general had also a powerful motive for visiting
Cincinnati in the state of his family—they had suffered and were still suffering the most unexampled afflic-
tions of disease.

   Governor Meigs had ordered 2 regiments to be organized, which rendezvoused at Dayton and several
other points in Ohio, in the early part of March, and
were placed under the command of brigadier general
John Wingate, who proceeded with one of the regiments under colonel Mills to St. Marys, to garrison
the posts in that quarter.   The number of men in his
brigade however, proved greatly deficient.   From one
division of militia, from which 250 men were to be
detached, only forty appeared in the field : and the

whole amount obtained was insufficient to garrison the small posts only.

The governor of Kentucky acting under the law recently passed in that state, had on the 16th of February, ordered 3000 men to be drafted and organized into four regiments under colonels Boswell, Dudley, Cox and Caldwell, to be commanded by brigadier general Green Clay. The two former rendezvoused at Newport about the 1st of April, at which place general Harrison had waited till the first three companies arrived, which he furnished with a packhorse for every two men, and sent them on by forced marches. He had received letters from the Rapids informing him, that the Virginia and Pennsylvania brigades would leave that place the moment their time was out, which would be on the 2nd of April—and as the openness of the season would soon render the lake navigable, and the enemy had learnt, from a prisoner they had taken, the situation of our affairs, an immediate attack upon fort Meigs was anticipated. This state of affairs was communicated to the war department, and the propriety of calling out the balance of the Kentucky draft, to be placed at fort Wayne to keep the Indians in check, was pressed on the attention of the government. The general immediately set out for the Rapids, leaving the Kentucky regiments to follow him with the utmost expedition in their power. In the mean time the Virginia and Pennsylvania troops returned home, except about 230 of the latter, who had volunteered under the influence of patriotic sentiments and the eloquence of their chaplain, doctor Hersey, to remain till the reinforcements had arrived. When the general afterwards arrived, these patriotic men informed him through their officers, that upon their reaching home in the course of a few weeks, depended their raising crops in the ensuing season, but that they were determined never to abandon him, until he thought their services could be spared without danger to the

fort. The general dismissed them on the arrival of
the advanced companies of the Kentucky militia.

While general Harrison was in the interior, he addressed several letters to the commanders of the Pennsylvania and Virginia brigades, which were read to
those troops, setting forth the exposed situation of the
camp, the probability of an attack, and the awful consequences of leaving the camp, almost to the mercy of
the enemy. "Those letters did honor to general Harrison, but they proved of no avail as respects the Virginia troops. They were calculated to rouse the feelings, and excite the energies of him, who had the smallest regard for his country's welfare; but Leftwich had
determined on leaving the camp as soon as possible,
and cared not what became of those who remained.
Nor did he do or say any thing to get a part of his
men to remain a few days. His conduct during the absence of general Harrison was highly reprehensible
indeed; for instead of completing the unfinished works,
he pretended that the men could not be made to work,
said they were sickly, that the weather was bad, and
what was most vexatious indeed, permitted them to
burn the picketting timber for fuel, instead of getting
it from the woods. After general Harrison left camp,
not a single thing towards finishing the works was done,
until captain Wood returned on the 20th from Sandusky, to which place he had been sent to give directions for its fortification. He had the extreme mortification to find nothing at all done in his absence, except
the destruction of the unfinished lines. This was most
perplexing to him indeed, as the ultimate responsibility in case of an attack, would in a great measure at-
tach to him, the fortifying of the camp having been
solely committed to his charge. Many young officers,
Croghan, Bradford and Langham, were extremely cha-
grined and vexed at this old phlegmatic Dutchman,
who was not even fit for a packhorse master, much
less to be entrusted with such an important command."
Colonel Wood.

After the departure of Leftwich, the command devolved on major Stoddard, who had only the remaining Pennsylvanians, a battalion of 12 months volunteers under major Alexander, a company of artillerists, and small fragments of the 17th and 19th regiments of infantry, amounting in all to 500 men—with which to maintain an unfinished fortress, calculated for an army of 2000. But Stoddard was an excellent officer, and made every exertion in his power to complete the fortifications.

Little skirmishes now frequently took place in the vicinity of the camp with reconnoitring parties of Indians : and about the last of March a party of citizens arrived from Detroit with information that Procter had issued orders for assembling the militia at Sandwich on the 7th of April, to assist in an expedition against camp Meigs. One of them, a respectable inhabitant of Detroit, stated that he had frequently heard major Muir, with whom he was intimate, speak of the plan of attack, on which Procter had already determined—It was, to erect strong batteries on the north side of the river to be manned and played upon the camp by the regulars, while the Indians completely invested the camp on the south side—and in the opinion of major Muir, it would require but a few hours of cannonading and bombarding, *to smoke out* our troops into the hands of the Indians. Various other persons soon afterwards arrived from the same place, and confirmed this information. They frequently stated, that Procter had said he would march the northwestern army to Montreal by the first of June. The utmost exertions were now made, and every possible means were taken to render the camp as impregnable as the situation of things would admit. "On the 8th of April, lieutenant colonel Ball arrived with 200 dragoons, as fine fellows as ever drew a sword—they were cordially received, and their presence seemed to give new life to some of the old veterans, who were almost broken down with colds and hard work." *Wood.*

On the 12th general Harrison arrived at the camp, having brought with him all the troops, being about 300 men, which could possibly be spared from the posts on the Auglaize and St. Marys. He descended by water from fort Amanda, expecting from the information he had received, that fort Meigs was already invested. Had that been the case, he intended to storm the British batteries in the manner, in which he afterwards ordered colonel Dudley to do it. On his way from the interior, he wrote back to governor Shelby for the balance of the Kentucky draft. This was in direct violation of his instructions from the secretary of war; but the critical situation of affairs in his opinion authorized the measure; and if the secretary disapproved it, he would still have time to countermand the march of the troops. The most vigorous exertions were now made in the fort to prepare for a siege; and scouts were constantly sent out to watch for the approach of the enemy. A vigilant eye was directed down the river, and reconnoitring parties were frequently sent in boats to the mouth of the bay to survey the lake. On the 19th a scouting party brought in three Frenchmen from the river Raisin, who stated that the British were still making active preparations for an attack, and were assembling an immense Indian force. The Prophet and Tecumseh had arrived with 600 warriors from the country between lake Michigan and the Wabash. This intelligence convinced the general that no attack by the Indians was to be expected on the posts in his rear, or on the settlements of the Big Miami and Wabash. He therefore sent an express to governor Shelby to countermand the march of the troops which he had recently requested.

General Clay had still not arrived with the detachment under his command. His progress was very much impeded by the deepness of the roads, and the fulness of every little stream he had to cross. The companies which Harrison had despatched in advance, by the way of fort M·Arthur and Portage, unencumbered with heavy baggage, constituted a battalion of Boswell's regiment, under the command of major Johnson. They were so fortunate as to reach the camp at the Rapids before the arrival of the enemy. When the rest of the detachment arrived on the waters of the Miami, the regiment of colonel Dudley was ordered to descend the Auglaize with boats containing provisions and baggage, and to wait at Defiance for the general, who embarked on the St. Marys with the balance of Boswell's regiment, in boats also freighted with baggage and provisions. They had all arrived at Defiance on the 3rd of May, where the general was met by an express from camp Meigs, with intelligence that it was already invested by the allies.

Towards the latter part of April, the enemy was frequently discovered in small parties about the fort, by the scouts sent out by the general; on the 26th his advance was discovered at the mouth of the bay; and on the 28th as captain Hamilton was going down the river with a small reconnoitring party, he discovered the whole force of the British and Indians approaching within a few miles of the fort. An express was now sent to general Clay, with letters also for the governors of Ohio and Kentucky. This perilous journey was undertaken by captain Oliver, the commissary to the fort, a brave and intelligent officer, who possessed every necessary qualification for such an enterprise. He was accompanied by a single white man, and an Indian, and was escorted some distance from the camp by captain Garrard with 80 of his dragoons. The troops in the fort were paraded, and the general addressed them in animated terms on the approaching crisis. His popular eloquence reached the hearts of his brave companions, and was answered with shouts of applause and devotion. Presently the gunboats of the enemy came in view down the river, and approached to the site of the old fort Miami, on the opposite side from camp Meigs. There the British began to land and mount their guns; and as soon as their ordnance was on shore, their boats were employed to carry the Indians to the southeast side of the river, where they soon completely invested our camp; and nothing but their hideous yells and the firing of musketry was now to be heard.

The general was indefatigable in his attention to all the operations required by the situation in which he was placed. On the next morning after the arrival of the enemy he issued a general order from which the following is an extract.

"Can the citizens of a free country who have taken arms to defend its rights, think of submitting to an army composed of mercenary soldiers, reluctant Canadians goaded to the field by the bayonet, and of wretched, naked savages? Can the breast of an American soldier, when he casts his eyes to the opposite shore, the scene of his country's triumphs over the same foe, be influenced by any other feelings than the hope of glory? Is not this army composed of the same materials with that which fought and conquered under the immortal Wayne? Yes fellow soldiers, your general sees your countenances beam with the same fire, that he witnessed on that glorious occasion; and although it would be the height of presumption to compare himself of that hero, he boasts of being that hero's pupil. To your posts then fellow citizens, and remember that the eyes of your country are upon you."

The British had established their main camp about two miles down the river at the place of their landing; and in the night they had commenced three batteries opposite the fort, on a high bank about 300 yards from the river, the intervening low ground being open and partly covered with water. Two of them were gun batteries with 4 embrasures, and were situated higher up the river than the fort; the other was a bomb battery situated rather below the fort. They had progressed so far in the night, that they were now able to work at them in daylight. A fire however was opened upon them from the fort, which considerably impeded their progress. It was under the directions of captain Wood, the senior officer of the engineers, captain Gratiott, being unwell, but able occasionally to take charge of a battery.

"The enemy's mode of attack being now thoroughly understood, a plan previously arranged and suggested to the general, to counteract such an attack as the one already commenced by the enemy, was adopted and directed to be carried into execution as soon as possible. The whole army was turned out subject to the orders of the engineer, and the general seemed impatient for the new works to be in a state of progression. Scarcely time was allowed the engineer to lay out his works—however he had matured and digested his plan well, and nothing of consequence need occasion much delay."

"The works went on extremely well; never did men behave better on any similar occasion, though some thought the immense trenches commenced entirely unnecessary. .... Orders had been given for them all to be kept in the trenches through the night, but it was so extremely dark, and the rain poured down in such torrents, that it was thought best to let them retire to their tents. .... Next day one third only of the army was on duty at a time, and was relieved every three hours. The Indians were getting to be very impudent, and it became necessary for us to keep an eye to them, and occasionally give them a few shells and grape." *Colonel Wood.*

The ground had been covered by a very heavy forest of oak and beech trees; which had been cleared away by immense labor to the distance of 2 or 300 yards from the lines. Some scattering trees still remained and the trunks of others were lying on the ground. Behind these and the stumps, the Indians would creep up within shooting distance, and in several instances were able to do some execution; but in general they suffered most themselves. On the left the trees had not been felled to so great a distance, and there the savages mounted into their tops with the utmost agility, and from those elevated stations were able to send forth tremendous vollies of musketry. The distance however was so great that but few of their balls took effect. "Their ethereal annoyance however proved a great stimulus to the militia; for although they did their duty with alacrity and promptitude, yet their motions were much accelerated by it—and let who will make the experiment, it will be invariably found, that the movements of militia will be quickened by a brisk fire of musketry about their ears."

The enemy continued diligently to labor on their batteries. On the morning of the 30th, they were ready to fix their cannon, which they accomplished under a warm fire from the fort, by which they lost several lives. A number of boats loaded with British as well as Indians were then seen crossing to the southeast side, which led the general to suspect that they intended to amuse him with their batteries, while they would attempt to storm his works in the opposite direction. Orders were given for the troops who were not on duty, to rest with their muskets in their arms, so as to be ready at a moment's warning to take their posts.

On the morning of the first of May, it was discovered that the British batteries were completed; and about 10 o'clock they appeared to be loading, and adjusting their guns on certain objects in the camp. By this time our troops had completed a grand traverse, about 12 feet high, upon a base of 20 feet, 300 yards long, on the most elevated ground through the middle of the camp, calculated to ward off the shot of the enemy's batteries. Orders were given for all the tents in front to be instantly removed into its rear, which

was effected in a few minutes,—and that beautiful prospect of cannonading and bombarding our lines, which
but a moment before had excited the skill and energy
of the British engineer, was now entirely fled, and in
its place nothing was to be seen but an immense shield
of earth, which entirely obscured the whole army.
Not a tent nor a single person was to be seen. Those
canvass houses, which had concealed the growth of the
traverse from the view of the enemy, were now protected and hid in their turn. The prospect of *smoking
us out*, was now at best but very faint. But as neither
general Procter nor his officers were yet convinced of
the folly and futility of their laborious preparations,
their batteries were opened and five days were spent
in arduous cannonading and bombarding to bring them
to this salutary conviction. A tremendous cannonade
was kept up all the rest of the day, and shells were
thrown till eleven o'clock at night. Very little damage however was done in the camp; one or two were
killed and three or four wounded—among the latter,
was major Amos Stoddard of the 1st regiment of artillery—a revolutionary character, and an officer of
much merit. He was wounded slightly with a piece
of shell, and about ten days afterwards died with the
locked jaw.

The fire of the enemy was returned from the fort
with our 18 pounders with some effect, though but
sparingly—for the stock of 18 pound shot was but
small, there being but 360 of that size in the fort when
the siege commenced, and about the same number for
the 12 pounders. A proper supply of this article had
not been sent with the artillery from Pittsburgh. The
battery of the enemy supplied us with 12 pound shot;
but they had no eighteens, all their large guns being
twenty fours. On the second day they opened their
fire again with great fury, and continued it all day, but
without any better effect.

It had been apprehended in camp, that the enemy, finding he could not effect his object by his first plan of attack, would transfer his guns to the other side of the river, and establish batteries upon the centre or flanks of the camp. Works calculated to resist him in such an event had therefore been undertaken, and were already in a state of forwardness. On the 3rd about 11 o'clock our expectations were verified. Three pieces and a howitzer were suddenly opened on the camp from the bushes on the left. But they were soon silenced, and compelled to change their position by a few 18 pound shot from our batteries. They resumed their fire again on the same side, but with no important advantages. On this day however they did rather more execution from their fire on every side than they had done before. On the 4th their fire was again renewed, but with less vehemence and vivacity. Those who were serving their guns appeared to move as if they were executing orders which they disapproved, and making exertions which they knew would fail—and to depress them still more, the troops in camp, when their fire was not very brisk, would shew themselves above the intrenchments and give them three cheers, swinging their hats in the air.

On the first three days the fire of the enemy was incessant and tremendous; five and eight inch shells and 24 pound shot had fallen in showers in the camp. Our batteries at different times had been served with great effect, as was afterwards acknowledged by some of the principal officers of the enemy. But the scarcity of ammunition, and not knowing how long the siege might continue, had compelled us to economise our fire. "With a plenty of ammunition, we should have been able to have blown John Bull almost from the Miami .... It was extremely diverting to see with what pleasure and delight the Indians would yell, whenever in their opinion considerable damage was done in camp by the bursting of a shell. Their

hanging about the camp, and occasionally coming pretty near, kept our lines almost constantly in a blaze of fire; for nothing can please a Kentuckian better than to get a shot at an Indian—and he must be indulged."
Colonel Wood.

The approach of general Clay at this crisis, with a reinforcement of 12 hundred Kentuckians, requires our attention. Captain Oliver, the express sent from camp, found him at fort Winchester, at which place the cannonading at the siege was distinctly heard. On the 4th the general was ready to descend in 18 flats, the sides of which were raised high enough to cover his men from the fire of Indians on the banks— Major David Trimble who had accompanied him from Kentucky, voluntarily tendered his services to precede the detachment in a barge with 15 men, accompanied by captain Oliver, to apprise general Harrison of their approach. To penetrate to the camp, thus exposed in an open boat, was deemed extremely hazardous. Such an attempt had already been made by captain Leslie Combs, who was sent down in a canoe with five or six men, by colonel Dudley on his arrival at Defiance. The captain had reached within a mile of the fort, when he was attacked by the Indians, and compelled to retreat, after bravely contending with superior numbers till he had lost nearly all his men.

It was the intention of general Clay to leave Defiance about 12 o'clock, and to reach camp Meigs in the night, or at least by day light in the morning; but it was late in the evening before he got in motion, and when he arrived at the head of the Rapids, 18 miles above the camp, the moon had gone down, and it was so dark and rainy, that his pilot refused to conduct him through them before day—he was therefore compelled to encamp till morning.

Major Trimble reached the fort about midnight, and informed general Harrison that the detachment eleven hundred strong, would probably arrive about daylight.

Harrison immediately determined to make a general sally against the enemy on general Clay's arrival, for which he made preparations at camp, and despatched captain Hamilton and a subaltern, with the necessary orders to general Clay. Captain Hamilton proceeded up the river in a canoe, and met the detachment five miles above the fort after daylight, in consequence of their pilot having detained them till morning instead of descending in the night as at first was intended. The captain immediately delivered the following orders to general Clay—"You must detach about 800 men from your brigade, and land them at a point I will shew you, about a mile, or a mile and a half above camp Meigs. I will then conduct the detachment to the British batteries on the left bank of the river. The batteries must be taken, the cannon spiked, and carriages cut down; and the troops must then return to their boats and cross over to the fort. The balance of your men must land on the fort side of the river, opposite the first landing, and fight their way into the fort through the Indians. The route they must take will be pointed out by a subaltern officer now with me, who will land the canoe on the right bank of the river, to point out the landing for the boats." The general was also informed, that the British force at their batteries was inconsiderable, the main body being at their camp a mile and a half further down—and that the Indians were chiefly on the same side with the fort. General Clay's order of descending the river was the same as in the line of march in solid column, each officer taking position according to his rank. Colonel Dudley being the oldest colonel led the van. As soon as captain Hamilton had delivered the orders, general Clay who was in the 13th boat from the front, directed him to go to colonel Dudley, with orders to take the 12 front boats and execute the plans of general Harrison on the left bank, and to post the subaltern

with the canoe on the right bank, as a beacon for his
landing.

General Harrison intended, while the detachment
under Dudley was destroying the batteries on the north
side, and general Clay was fighting the Indians above
the fort, to send out a party to destroy the batteries on
the south side; but his plans were marred in the execution.

General Clay ordered the five boats remaining with
the one he occupied, to fall into a line after his; and
in attempting to do it, they were driven on shore and
thus thrown half a mile in the rear. The general kept
close to the right bank, intending to land opposite to
the detachment under Dudley, but finding no guide
there, and the Indians having commenced a brisk fire
on his boat, he attempted to cross to the detachment.
The current however was so swift, that it soon carried
him too far down for that project; he therefore turned
back, and landed on the right bank further down. Captain Peter Dudley with a part of his company was in
this boat, making in the whole upwards of 50 men,
who now marched into camp without loss amidst a
shower of grape from the British batteries and the fire
of some Indians. The boat with their baggage and 4
sick soldiers, was left as the general supposed, in the
care of two men who met him at his landing, and by
whom he expected she would be brought down under
the guns of the fort. In a few minutes however she
fell into the hands of the Indians. The attempt which
he had made to cross the river induced colonel Boswell
with the rear boats to land on the opposite side; but
as soon as captain Hamilton discovered the error under
which he acted, he instructed him to cross over and
fight his way into camp. When he arrived at the south
side his landing was annoyed by the Indians; and as
soon as his men were on shore he formed them and returned the fire of the enemy: at the same time he was
directed by captain Shaw from the commanding gene-

ral, to march in open order through the plain to the
fort.   As there was now a large body of Indians on
his flank, general Harrison determined to send out a
reinforcement from the garrison to enable him to beat
them.

Major Alexander's battalion, composed of the Pittsburgh blues, the Petersburgh volunteers &c.; major
Johnson with a part of his battalion; and the companies of captains Nearing and Dudley were ordered to
prepare for this service.   They were ready to join the
Kentuckians as they arrived at the gates of the fort.
Colonel Boswell then formed his men on the right;
major Alexander on the left; and Johnson in the centre.   In this order they marched against the Indians
and drove them at the point of the bayonet, though
much superior in numbers, to the distance of half a
mile into the woods.   The greatest ardor was displayed by the troops, and when it became necessary to return, it was with the utmost difficulty that the officers
of the Kentucky detachment could restrain their men
from the pursuit.   General Harrison had taken his
position upon a battery to watch with a glass the various operations which at this moment claimed his attention.   He discovered a body of British and Indians
filing along the edge of the woods to fall on the rear
and left of the corps under Boswell.   He immediately
despatched John T. Johnson esq. his volunteer aid,
to recall them from the pursuit.   His horse was killed
under him before he could reach the detachment.   The
order was then repeated by major Graham, and the reluctant though necessary retreat was at last commenced;
the Indians then rallied and pursued them some distance, doing more execution while our men were retreating, than they had done in all the rest of the contest.

The detachment under colonel Dudley in the mean
time had made their appearance at the batteries on the
other side of the river, and were performing their share
in the operations of this eventful day—but before we

direct our attention to them, we will go through the occurrences on the south side. General Harrison now ordered a sortie from the fort, under the command of colonel John Miller of the regulars, against the batteries which had been erected on that side. This detachment was composed of the companies and parts of companies commanded by captains Langham, Croghan, Bradford, Nearing, Elliott, and lieutenants Gwynne and Campbell, of the regulars; the volunteers of Alexander's battalion; and captain Sebree's company of Kentucky militia. The whole amounted only to 350 men. Colonel Miller accompanied by major Todd, led on his command with the most determined bravery; charged upon the British and drove them from their batteries; spiked their cannon, and took 41 prisoners including an officer, having completely beaten and driven back the whole force of the enemy. That force consisted of 200 British regulars, 150 Canadians, and 500 Indians, being considerably more than double the force of the brave detachment which attacked them; but our troops charged with such irresistible impetuosity that nothing could withstand them.

In this sortie, in which all the troops engaged were distinguished for their good order and their intrepid, impetuous bravery, the militia company of captain Sebree was particularly noticed by the general for its uncommon merit. With the characteristic ardor of the Kentuckians, they rushed into the thickest ranks of the enemy, and were for some time entirely surrounded by the Indians—they still bravely maintained their ground against more than 4 times their number—but they must ultimately have been cut to pieces, had not lieutenant Gwynne of the 19th regiment boldly charged upon the Indians with a part of captain Elliott's company, and released them from their desperate situation. The British and Indians suffered severely, and were routed in great confusion—and a few more men would have enabled the general to disperse and capture the whole force of the enemy remaining on the south side of the river. Colonel Miller now returned to the fort with his prisoners, having lost many brave men on the field, and had several of his officers wounded. As he retired the enemy rallied and pressed hard on his rear, till he arrived near the breastwork.

The operations on the north side of the river will now claim our attention. The detachment under Dudley effected a landing in tolerably good order, considering the roughness of the Rapids and the swiftness of the current, and were immediately marched off through the open plain to the hill, which was covered with timber. No specific orders were given by the colonel: even his majors were left to conjecture the object of the enterprise. After marching some distance, the troops were formed into 3 columns: colonel Dudley commanded at the head of the right; major Shelby on the left, and captain Morrison, acting as major, in the centre. The right column kept the edge of the woods on the brow of the hill, which was in some places half a mile from the river, across the open bottom. The centre column marched parallel to the first, at the distance of 150 yards in the woods; and the left, a similar distance still further out. The distance to the batteries of the enemy was two miles; but they were in full view from the ridge on which Winchester had encamped, and above which the colonel marched unperceived by the enemy into the woods. When the detachment arrived within half a mile of the batteries, which were cannonading the camp, major Shelby was ordered on the suggestion of captain Hamilton, to march the left forward as expeditiously as possible, till its rear passed the head of the other two columns, and then to wheel to the right and march towards the river. The batteries were thus to be surrounded, and the whole of the British force captured and destroyed: but while the other columns were still several hundred yards from the batteries, they raised the Indian yell, charged upon

them at full speed, and carried them without the loss
of a man, having frightened off the few artillerists who
were serving them, almost without knowing by whom
they were assailed.

The most complete success was thus achieved as
respected the great object of the enterprise. The British flag was cut down, and the shouts of the garrison
announced their joy at this consummation of their
wishes. General Harrison was standing on the grand
battery next the river, and now called to the men, and
made signs to them, to retreat to their boats—but all in
vain—they remained at the batteries for some time,
viewing the curiosities of the place, and without destroying the carriages, magazines, or even spiking the
whole of the cannon. The general at last offered a
reward to any person, who would cross the river and
order them to retreat. Lieutenant Campbell undertook
to perform this service, but before he could get over,
the fate of the detachment was decided. About the
time the batteries were taken, a body of Indians lying
in ambush had fired on a party of spies under captain
Combs, who had marched down on the left of major
Shelby. Presently colonel Dudley gave orders to reinforce the spies, and the greater part of the right and
centre columns rushed into the woods in confusion, with
their colonel among them, to fight the Indians—whom
they routed and pursued near two miles from the batteries. The left column remained in possession of the
ground, till the fugitive artillerists returned with a reinforcement from the main British camp and attacked
them. Some of them were then made prisoners at the
battery, others fled to their boats, and a part who were
rallied by the exertions of their major, were marched
by him to the aid of colonel Dudley. The Indians
had also been reinforced, and the confusion in which
major Shelby found the men under Dudley, was so
great as to amount to a cessation of resistance, while
the savages skulking around them, continued the work

of destruction in safety.—At last a retreat commenced in disorder, but the greater part of the men were either captured by the Indians, or surrendered to the British at the batteries. Colonel Dudley after being wounded was overtaken and despatched by the tomahawk. The number of all those who escaped and got into the fort from the whole detachment, was considerably below 200. Had the orders which colonel Dudley received been regarded, or a proper judgment exercised on that occasion, the day would certainly have been an important one for the country, and a glorious one for the army. Every thing might have been accomplished agreeably to the wishes and instructions of the general, without the loss of but few men.

When the approach of the detachment under Dudley was reported to Procter, he supposed it to be the main force of the American army; from which he was apprehensive that he might sustain a total defeat: he therefore recalled a large portion of his troops from the opposite shore. They did not arrive in time however to partake in the contest on the north side. Tecumseh was among them.

The prisoners were taken down to head quarters, put into fort Miami, and the Indians permitted to garnish the surrounding rampart, and to amuse themselves by loading and firing at the crowd, or at any particular individual. Those who preferred to inflict a still more cruel and savage death, selected their victims, led them to the gateway, and there *under the eye of general Procter, and in the presence of the whole British army, tomahawked and scalped them!"* Colonel Wood. This work of destruction continued near two hours, during which time upwards of 20 prisoners, defenceless and confined, were massacred in the presence of the magnanimous Britons to whom they had surrendered, and by the allies too with whom those Britons had voluntarily associated themselves, knowing and encouraging their mode of warfare. The chiefs at the same time

were holding a council on the fate of the prisoners, in
which the Potawatamies who were painted black were
for killing the whole, and by their warriors the murders
were perpetrated. The Miamies and Wyandots were
on the side of humanity and opposed the wishes of the
others. The dispute between them had become serious when colonel Elliott and Tecumseh came down
from the batteries to the scene of carnage. As soon as
Tecumseh beheld it, he flourished his sword and in a
loud voice ordered them "for shame to desist. It is a
disgrace to kill a defenceless prisoner." His orders
were obeyed, to the great joy of the prisoners, who had
by this time lost all hopes of being preserved. In this
single act, Tecumseh displayed more humanity, magnanimity, and civilization, than Procter with all his
British associates in command, displayed through the
whole war on the northwestern frontiers.

The prisoners were kept in the same place till dark,
during which time the wounded experienced the most
excruciating torments. They were then taken into the
British boats and carried down the river to the brig
Hunter and a schooner, where several hundred of them
were stowed away in the hold of the brig, and kept
there for 2 days and nights. Their sufferings in this
situation are not to be described by me : I leave them
to be imagined by those who can feel for the wrongs of
their country. They were finally liberated on parole
and landed at the mouth of Huron river below the Sandusky bay. General Procter made a proposition to
exchange the Kentucky militia for the friendly Indians
residing within our frontiers—men who were not prisoners to us, but our friends who had taken no part in
the war. Whether he made this proposal by way of
insult, or for the purpose of recruiting his allies, is
known only to himself. General Harrison through
courtesy told him he would refer the subject to the consideration of the president.

After the termination of the fighting on the 5th, no more occurred worthy of notice while the enemy continued the siege. Immediately after the firing had ceased on on that day, general Procter sent major Chambers over to demand the surrender of the fort. Harrison replied to the proposition, that he considered it an insult, and requested that it might not be repeated. The demand was made as a finesse, to prevent us from molesting him in the retreat which he meditated. Intelligence of the capture of fort George by the American forces under general Dearborn, was now received at the British camp, which considerably alarmed general Procter. His situation appeared to be hazardous—for the wind now blew constantly up the river—Harrison's forces he expected would soon be reinforced—and the Indians began to desert his standard in great numbers. He had flattered them with the hopes of splendid success and rich rewards. The Prophet and his followers were to have the Michigan territory for their services in capturing the fort; and general Harrison was to be delivered into the hands of Tecumseh. But their prospects were now completely reversed; and it is a rule with them to follow the fortunate and adhere to the strong. Procter now saw, that if he was delayed much longer he would probably be captured, and leave Upper Canada unprotected, as reinforcements were not to be expected there, while the American arms were successful below. He therefore made his arrangements to retreat as soon as possible. Nearly all the Indians had left him very much dissatisfied; and during the night of the 8th a considerable stir was apparent in his camp—early next morning his troops were seen to be moving off. A sloop and several gunboats were near the camp receiving the artillery and baggage, and on them our batteries were opened as long as they remained in that situation. Major Chambers had promised on the part of general Procter to furnish us with a list of the prisoners in his possession; but he retreat-

2 L

ed with too much precipitation to comply. He left a
quantity of cannon ball, with a fine sling carriage, and
several other valuable articles. He had however shared
with the Indians in the plunder of the boats, in which
the Kentucky militia had descended, after a few of them
had been brought over to the fort by those who escaped
from the defeat.

The whole force of the enemy at the siege was about
600 regulars, 800 Canadian militia, and 1800 Indians.
The force in the fort did not much exceed 1200, and perhaps not more than 1000 effectives, who had to defend
a fortification large enough for three times that number.

On the day after the enemy had retreated, a detachment was sent over the river to collect and bury the
dead. After a diligent search, 45 bodies were found
on the battle ground and buried; among them was colonel Dudley, who was very much cut to pieces. Beside these, there were a few found in other places,
which with those massacred at the old fort, would make
the number of killed upwards of 70. The Indians had
also kept between 30 and 40 prisoners, having concealed them on the evening after the battle, and hurried them off next day to prevent them from being delivered up. In the two sorties from the fort, and in the
fort during the siege, our loss was 81 killed, and 189
wounded—among the latter were major Stoddard, who
afterwards died of a locked jaw, and the gallant captain Bradford, shot through both thighs, of which he
recovered; and also major Hukil, slightly. An unusual number of the wounded were carried off, in consequence of exposure during the siege; and from the
same cause, a considerable degree of sickness began to
prevail among the troops.

The loss of the British and Indians could not be ascertained; but it was undoubtedly very severe. In
the romance, which governor Prevost styled a general
order, he stated the loss of regulars and militia at 15
killed, and 46 wounded!!! In the same Gulliverian
production, he says—"The commanding general has

great satisfaction in announcing to the troops, the *brilliant* result of an action, which took place on the banks of the Miami river, on the 5th inst. with part of the northwestern army of the United States under major general Harrison, and which terminated in the *complete defeat* of the enemy, and capture, dispersion, or destruction of *thirteen hundred men*, by the gallant division of the army under general Procter. Five hundred prisoners were taken, exclusive of those who fell into the hands of the Indians.—"

The defeat of colonel Dudley very naturally became the subject of much speculation in Kentucky; and a considerable diversity of opinion existed, respecting the causes of the disaster and the actors concerned in it. The subject however appears very plain. Those who were in the defeat, commonly attribute it, very justly, to their own imprudence and zeal, which were not properly controlled and directed by the orders and example of their leader. There was nothing difficult or hazardous in the enterprise—the whole misfortune resulted from the imprudent manner of its execution. The batteries were easily taken, and the retreat was perfectly secure; but the detachment wanted a head to direct and restrain its Kentucky impetuosity to its proper object. " It rarely occurs that a general has to complain of the excessive ardor of his men—yet such appears always to be the case when the Kentucky militia are engaged. It is indeed the source of all their misfortunes; they appear to think that valor alone can accomplish every thing—" says general Harrison in his orders after this battle had been fought.

The following letter from general Harrison, dated at Franklinton on the 18th of May, to governor Shelby of Kentucky, to whom he was accustomed to communicate his sentiments without reserve, will throw much additional light on the plan of this battle and the manner of its execution.

" In the extra Gazette of this place you will find general Clay's report to me, of his proceedings on the morning of the 5th inst. by which you will perceive that my orders were clearly delivered to him, and I have no doubt were well understood by colonel Dudley; and nothing could be more easy of execution. I had no less than four 18 pounders, a 12, and a 6, so placed as to cover their retreat effectually for two thirds of their way to their boats. But it appears that no disposition was made for a retreat; and some of those who got off assert, that neither of the majors knew the object, or the manner it was to be executed. Nothing can prove more clearly the ease with which the whole party might have retired to the boats, than the circumstance of upwards of 180 having effected it with the encumbrance of some wounded. They were pursued by some Indians who dared not enter the open plain which skirted the river, and did our men little or no injury. Never was there an opportunity more favorable to strike a brilliant stroke, than was presented on this occasion, if the plan had been properly pursued. The enemy were completely surprised and distracted. When colonel Dudley made the attack on the north side of the river, ten boats loaded with troops were crossed a mile and a half below, but did not get to the scene of action till it was over. Had colonel Dudley retreated after having taken the batteries, or had he made a disposition to retreat in case of defeat, all would have been well. He could have crossed the river, and even if he had lost one or two hundred men, he would have brought me a reinforcement of 600, which would have enabled me to take the whole British force on this side of the river. The Indians would then have abandoned general Procter; and as the wind blew up the river, so that he could not get off, the whole of his regulars and militia must have been captured. If I could have spared a reinforcement of 200 men only to colonel Miller, the British regulars and militia would have all been taken, before they could have crossed the river. But I had not a single company to spare, as at the suggestion of general Clay I had sent off under his command, all that part of his brigade, which had reached the fort, and all the dragoons I could mount, to assist colonel Dudley in recrossing the river, and was thus deprived of their services at a most critical moment. That the Indians would have abandoned the British that very night, in case they had not succeeded against colonel Dudley, is evident from numbers having left them with that circumstance in their favor.

"I can say with confidence, that the plan of the attack was approbated by every officer that witnessed the scene. Even the British officers acknowledge, that they were completely surprised, and that they had not the least idea of our intention, until it burst upon them, by the commencement of the firing on this side, after they had weakened themselves by making detachments to the other, that were of no use as they did not arrive in time. I believe every candid man in both armies will admit, that an unlucky blunder saved that of the enemy from destruction."

All the troops engaged in the defence of fort Meigs distinguished themselves by their unexampled good conduct. The intrepid bravery and skill with which the sortie was executed by the regulars commanded by colonel Miller, were not surpassed on any other occasion in the whole war. The battalion of volunteers under major Alexander were equally distingushed in the same sally. That battalion consisted of a small company of riflemen, raised in the neighborhood of Greensburg in Pennsylvania, and originally commanded by Alexander as captain—a company of light infantry from Pittsburgh, under the command of captain James Butler, a worthy son of general Butler who fell in St. Clair's defeat—and a company of light infantry from Petersburg in Virginia commanded by captain M'Rea, who had requested the government to send them to the northwestern army, that they might serve under their countryman general Harrison. The privates in this battalion were mostly young gentlemen of affluence, or at least in easy circumstances, and of the most respectable families—who had volunteered their services from motives of patriotism. Having been tenderly raised, they were not well qualified to sustain the hardships of a northwestern campaign in the winter season; but on all occasions they distinguished themselves by their gallantry and good conduct. The Pittsburgh company in the opinion of the general was equal in discipline, particularly in the precision with which it performed its evolutions, to any regulars he had ever seen. He was also entirely satisfied with the conduct of the Ohio regiment under colonel Mills.

General Harrison having ascertained, that the enemy had abandoned his hopes of reducing fort Meigs for the present, and had retreated from the American territory, deemed it unnecessary for him to confine himself to that place any longer, as his attention to the recruiting service and other matters would be more important. He therefore left general Clay in the command of the garrison, having much confidence in his abilities; and proceeded with an escort of major Ball's squadron, whose horses had been preserved in the fort during the siege, to Lower Sandusky where he arrived on the evening of the 12th. His business there was to provide for the better protection of that place and Cleveland; and for the security of the prisoners, who were to march from Huron through the wilderness to Mansfield. He sent them arms and ammunition, to protect themselves against the Indians, and had the country reconnoitred between Lower Sandusky and the lake, through which the Indians must pass to attack them. "He thought these steps proper, although he had the *solemn promise* of general Procter, that the Indians should not be suffered to go in that direction." The prisoners were landed at Huron agreeably to the stipulation with general Harrison, from which place some of them proceeded by the most direct route to Chillicothe, while others went by the way of Cleveland for the sake of keeping in the settlements for the convenience of subsistence. General Harrison also went into the interior from Lower Sandusky.

The reader will recollect, that general Harrison on his way to fort Meigs, had called on the governor of Kentucky for the other two regiments, which had been organized in that state; and that he afterwards directed them not to be sent. Before the second depatch was received, they had rendezvoused at Frankfort, and were waiting for further orders. Governor Shelby then disbanded them; and as they had already been put to considerable inconvenience, in arranging their private affairs and equipping themselves for a tour of six months, it was deemed too burthensome still to hold them in readiness to march, and they were therefore exonerated from further service under the law in pursuance of which they had been organized. These measures produced a considerable ferment in the public mind, as it was known a few days afterwards that the British had invested fort Meigs. The people were very anxious to overwhelm Upper Canada in the approaching summer, and were impatient at any thing which looked like delay and imbecility. They did not well understand the policy of the government, in merely acting on the defensive, till the command of the lake should be obtained ; and they did not perceive that any efficient preparations were making for another campaign.

In the state of Ohio the most active exertions had been made to raise reinforcements for the relief of fort Meigs. When apprehensions of an attack on that place had first been excited, the governor of Ohio had taken precautionary measures, having on the 19th of April detached two companies of militia to Lower Sandusky, four to Upper Sandusky, and two to Franklinton, to relieve the garrisons at the former places, and be ready to perform such other services as the occasion might require. And when the despatch from general Harrison was received, in which he informed the governor, that " the heads of the enemy's columns were in sight, and the Indians in view on both sides of the river," he commenced the most active exertions to call out a mounted force, to repair immediately to the scene of operations. He issued a proclamation, calling on the patriotism of the citizens, for the defence of this country. In a few days a number of companies and detachments rendezvoused at Franklinton, drew arms and other necessaries, and marched towards Upper Sandusky. Scouting parties were sent on, to ascertain if possible the situation of the fort. The governor on the 3rd of May addressed a letter to general M'Arthur, requesting him to use his influence to raise volunteers, and suggesting the propriety of employing to the best advantage, the 12 months regulars under him and general Cass. He stated that his object was, to force his way to fort Meigs if necessary, and in any event to protect the stores at Upper Sandusky, and relieve the frontier inhabitants from the panic which had seized them. Great alarm indeed prevailed throughout the whole state, and great exertions were made in every place by men of patriotism and influence. A mounted force, upwards of three thousand strong, was thus raised within 5 days from the time these exertions commenced. By the 8th of May some of the infantry companies, detached in April, arrived at Lower Sandusky; and at the same time 500 mounted men reached Upper Sandusky—on the next day they were one thousand strong—governor Meigs was in the front, and marched with them towards Lower Sandusky, where they arrived on the 11th, and would have proceeded next day to the Rapids. But information now reached them, that the enemy had retreated; and on the next day general Harrison arrived at Lower Sandusky himself. Measures were immediately taken to stop those who were advancing in the rear: and on the 14th, those who had arrived at the head quarters of the governor, were disbanded by a general order, in which they received the thanks of the commander in chief, and were justly applauded for the patriotic ardor and alacrity, with which they had repaired to the standard of their country.

It was fortunate for the American cause, that the enterprise of general Procter against fort Meigs was delayed so long. Had he been ready to sail as soon as the lake became navigable, and so timed his movements as to arrive at the fort during the first week in April, immediately after the last militia of the winter campaign were discharged, and before general Harrison arrived with reinforcements, he must have succeeded against that post. The garrison was then left very weak, being considerably less than 500 effectives. The works too, were then very incomplete, and entire-

ly too large for that number, as the fortified camp included 7 or 8 acres of ground. The place was still
with propriety denominated *camp Meigs*, more frequently than it was styled a fort. Its capture would
have been a most serious loss, as it contained nearly
all the artillery and military stores of the northwestern army, beside a large amount of provisions. General Harrison repeatedly in the winter had pressed on
the attention of the government, the necessity of preparing a force to take the place of the militia then in
service; but instead of doing this, we have seen, that
the new secretary, at the critical moment when the last
of those troops were disbanded, restricted general
Harrison to the use of regulars, which were still to be
levied in a country, where it is almost impossible to
raise a regiment of regulars through the whole year.
Without the aid of the Ohio and Kentucky militia,
which the general called into service without the authority, and contrary to the views, of the war department, it is highly probable, that the important post at
the Rapids would have been lost.

When general Procter returned to Malden, his militia were disbanded, and his Indians were distributed
in different cantonments. The Chippeways returned
home; the Potawatamies were stationed about 6 miles
up the river Rouge, where old Five-Medal and
Knoxas lived; the Miamies were encamped round
Brownstown with the Wyandots, and also up the river Detroit as far as Magauga. They were employed by the British as scouts, a party being sent regularly once a week into the vicinity of camp Meigs. Some
of them hunted a little, but none of them pretended to
plant corn, as they were regularly supplied with rations
from Malden and Detroit.

The naval preparations to obtain the ascendency on
the lake, were in the mean time progressing with rapidity, though still far from being complete at the middle of May, the period fixed for their completion by

2 M

the war department. Captain Perry of the navy, who had for some time commanded at Newport, Rhode-Island, was designated in March for the command of the naval forces on lake Erie, by commodore Chauncey who was commander in chief on the lakes. He came on to the town of Erie soon afterwards, having assisted on his way in the capture of fort George by general Dearborn; and took upon himself to superintend the erection of the navy which he was destined to command. The harbor of Erie is an excellent place for the business he had to accomplish. The bay is nearly surrounded by land, and its narrow entrance is so shallow, that heavy armed vessels cannot pass it. Hence the enemy could derive no advantage from his naval superiority in an attempt to destroy our vessels on the stocks. A regiment of Pennsylvania militia was stationed there for their protection. Captain Jessup was also directed by the war department, early in March, to repair to Cleveland, and superintend the construction of boats, to aid in the transportation of the northwestern army; and 200 of the Ohio militia were stationed there to protect the work.

CHAPTER VII.

Colonel Richard M. Johnson's mounted regiment;
with various other incidents.

IN the early part of the campaign of 1812, colonel
R. M. Johnson had personally witnessed the great efficiency and usefulness of mounted riflemen, employed
against the Indians—and was hence induced, when he
returned to congress, to lay before the war department,
a plan for a mounted expedition against the Indians
during the ensuing winter. The object of the expedition, was to destroy the subsistence of the Indians and
otherwise disable them, so as to prevent their committing depredations in the spring to revenge the destruction of their villages on the Wabash and Elk Hart
rivers. The good effect to be expected from its execution were more distinctly stated to be—security to
the northwestern frontiers from fort Wayne to the
Mississippi—safety to the convoys of provisions for
the northwestern army, when its force was diminished
in the spring—and the neutrality of the savages in future, from the powerful impression that would be made
on their fears. It was believed, that the winter season would favor the enterprise, by enabling the horsemen, while snow was on the ground and the leaves
off the bushes, to hunt up and destroy the sculking
Indians.

The force to be employed and its organization, were
proposed to be two regiments, including in each eight
companies of eighty privates, and making altogether
1280 men. This was deemed amply sufficient to traverse the whole Indian country, from fort Wayne past
the lower end of lake Michigan, round by the Illinois

river, and back to the Ohio near Louisville; and to disperse and destroy all the tribes of Indians and their resources to be found within that compass. The proposition was also communicated by colonel Johnson to the governor of Kentucky, and was submitted by the secretary of war to general Harrison, in a letter dated 26th December, 1812, from which the following is an extract. "The President has it in contemplation, to set on foot an expedition from Kentucky of about 1000 mounted men, to pass by fort Wayne, the lower end of lake Michigan, and round by the Illinois back to the Ohio near Louisville, for the purpose of scouring that country, destroying the provisions collected in the Indian villages, scourging the Indians themselves, and disabling them from interfering with your operations. It is expected that this expedition will commence in February; and it will terminate in a few weeks. I give you the information, that you may take it into consideration in the estimate of those arrangements, you may find it necessary to make, for carrying into effect the objects of the government. I send you a copy of the proposed plan, on which I wish to hear from you without delay. You will particularly state, whether you can effect these objects in the manner which is suggested, by adequate portions of the force now in the field; and in that case, whether it will be better to suspend the movement of this force until the spring." *Monroe.*

General Harrison had already anticipated in part, the objects of the proposed expedition, by sending colonel Campbell to Mississiniway; and was dissuaded by that experiment from attempting any thing more extensive during the winter. It was also already so late in the season, that the hard freezing would be over, before the proposed force could be raised and marched through the Indian country; and its progress would therefore be arrested by impassable swamps during the wet weather in the spring. The general intended however to follow up the blow on the Mississiniway, by striking at the main village farther down that river, and had visited Chillicothe to engage governor Meigs to organize a new corps of mounted men, to act with the dragoons then in service. The governor promptly cooperated in the measure; but on ascertaining the situation of the dragoons, they were found to be so frost bitten, and their horses so reduced, that they were wholly unfit for farther service during the winter; and the intended stroke was afterwards abandoned. The following are the views of general Harrison, respecting the proposition of colonel Johnson, which are extracted from letters to the war department of the 4th and 8th January. "I am sorry not to be able to agree with my friend, colonel Johnson, upon the propriety of the contemplated mounted expedition. An expedition of this kind directed against a particular town will probably succeed. The Indian towns cannot be surprised in succession, as they give the alarm from one to the other with more rapidity than our troops can move. In the months of February, March, and April, the towns are all abandoned. The men are hunting, and the women and children, particularly to the north of the Wabash, are scattered about making sugar. The corn is in that season universally hid in small parcels in the earth, and could not be found. There are no considerable villages in that direction. Those that are there, are composed of bark huts, which the Indians do not care for, and which during the winter are entirely empty. The detachment might pass through the whole extent of country to be scoured, without seeing an Indian, except at the first town they struck, and it is more than probable, that they would find *it* empty. But the expedition is impracticable to the extent proposed. The horses, if not the men, would perish. The horses that are now to be found, are not like those of the early settlers, and such as the Indians and traders now have. They

have been accustomed to corn, and must have it. Colonel Campbell went but 70 or 80 miles from the frontiers, and the greater part of his horses could scarcely
be brought in. Such an expedition in the summer and
fall would be highly advantageous, because the Indians are then at their towns, and their corn can be destroyed. An attack upon a particular town in the winter, when the inhabitants are at it, as we know they
are at Mississiniway, and which is so near as to enable the detachment to reach it without killing their
horses, is not only practicable, but if there is snow on
the ground is perhaps the most favorable."

January 8th—" The expedition contemplated from
Kentucky may supercede the necessity of that which I
was proposing. But I am still of the opinion given
in my last, that no attempt on the enemy beyond Mississiniway would be attended with any advantage, if
it did not end in the destruction of the detachment
employed to execute it. I repeat that the Indians are
not at this season to be found in their towns, that they
invariably take their families with them upon their
hunting excursions, and that their provisions are always buried in small parcels, each family hiding its
own."

In consequence of these suggestions, the winter expedition was abandoned, and the attention of the government was directed to the organization of a mounted corps for the spring. Accordingly general Armstrong who was now secretary of war, gave the following authority to colonel Johnson on the 26th of
February, 1813. "Sir, you are hereby authorized to
organize and hold in readiness, a regiment of mounted
volunteers—the organization as to the number of officers and men, to be conformable to the military establishment of the United States. The governor of the
state of Kentucky will be required to commission the
officers when selected, to serve four months after being
called into actual service; and six months if required

by the United States—the pay of officers and men to commence from the actual service and march of the corps, under the direction of the war department. After marching orders, the contractors and commissaries' agents in the different districts through which it passes, will supply the regiment with forage for the horses, and provision for the men, if required so to do. The keepers of military stores, will also furnish said corps with ammunition on regular returns of the effective force of the regiment. If any difficulty arises as to rank, the commanding general will settle the same, after the corps shall have reached its place of destination." *Armstrong*.

As soon as congress adjourned, colonel Johnson hastened to Kentucky with feelings of indignation at the cruelties inflicted on his fellow citizens at the river Raisin ; and on the 22nd of March published the above authority, accompanied by an address on the subject of raising the men, in which he appealed to the patriotism of the citizens, and detailed the terms, equipments, and prospects of the service. He immediately selected individuals to raise companies in different parts of the state—the platoon and other officers to be chosen by the men who enroled themselves, as this mode was deemed most consistent with the principle of volunteering. The service was exactly of that kind, which suited the habits and views of the Kentuckians ; and as much zeal to avenge the wrongs they had endured, was now prevalent among the people, the regiment was soon filled, and in a few weeks was ready to take the field, although the personal enemies of colonel Johnson, and the opposers of the administration, made considerable opposition to the measure, which they represented as an irregular and unconstitutional exercise of authority. The organization was submitted to governor Shelby, who aided in procuring the necessary funds to enable the colonel to accommodate his men. Captain James Johnson, his

brother, a man of sterling merit and undaunted bravery, received the appointment of lieutenant colonel of
the regiment—the honorable Samuel M'Kee, a representative in congress, and colonel Duval Payne, were
selected as majors.   Mr. M'Kee declined the appointment, and colonel D. Thompson accepted it.   They
were all men of high standing and genuine patriots.

After the discharge of the regiment under Cox and
Caldwell, the public attention was fixed on the mounted
regiment, as the only efficient corps in Kentucky, by
which fort Meigs could be relieved and the frontiers
protected; and colonel Johnson, young, ardent and
enterprising, anxiously wished for a theatre, on which
he might distinguish himself in the cause of his country; and was much pleased, soon after the intelligence
of the siege had arrived, to receive a letter from governor Shelby from which the following are extracts.
" The information received from various sources, of an
attack on fort Meigs, by a large body of the British
and Indians, justifies a belief, that a reinforcement
ought to be sent to the aid of general Harrison.   The
enemy can be met only by horsemen; and as you have
a regiment of mounted infantry nearly organised, the
crisis will in my opinion justify its immediate march
to the scene of operations.   You have my entire approbation and sanction to do so.   I will in conformity
with the wishes of the secretary of war, expressed in
his order of the 26th February, under which the regiment was raised, issue commissions to the officers; and
as far as depends on the executive of this state, the
men who march under you shall be allowed tours of
duty, according to the time they may be in service.
Captains Whitaker, Coleman, and Payne, have each
raised a company of cavalry, and reported themselves
for service this season.   As I do not expect a call for
cavalry, they have my approbation to join your regiment, and in case they do so, will be commissioned
accordingly."

"The officers and men must look to the general government alone for a compensation for their services." *Shelby.*

Upon the authority of the above letter, colonel Johnson immediately issued an order for his regiment to assemble. "The regiment of mounted volunteers was organised under the authority of the war department, to await its call, or to meet any crisis which might involve the honor, the rights and the safety of the country. That crisis has arrived. Fort Meigs is attacked. The northwestern army is surrounded by the enemy, and under the command of general Harrison is nobly defending the cause of the country against a combined enemy, the British and Indians. They will maintain their ground till relieved. The intermediate garrisons are also in imminent danger, and may fall a bleeding sacrifice to savage cruelty, unless timely reinforced. The frontiers may be deluged in blood. The mounted regiment will present a shield to the defenceless; and united with the forces now marching, and the Ohio volunteers for the same purpose, will drive the enemy from our soil. Therefore on Thursday the 20th of May, the regiment will rendezvous at the Great Crossings in Scott county, except the companies &c. which will rendezvous on the 22d at Newport;—at which place, the whole corps will draw arms, ammunition &c." *R. M. Johnson.*

In pursuance of this order, the companies of captains Stucker, M'Afee, Davidson, Ellison, and Combs, and several small fractions, rendezvoused in Scott on the 20th; and captains Matson, Coleman, Payne, Warfield and Craig met at Newport on the 22d. As the former companies were marching on the 21st towards Newport, they met John T. Johnson esq. volunteer aid to general Harrison, with the following general order. "Head Quarters, Franklinton, May 16th, 1813. The commanding general has observed with the warmest gratitude, the astonishing exertions, which

2 N

have been made by his excellency governor Meigs, and
the generals and other militia officers of this state, in
collecting and equipping a body of troops for the relief
of camp Meigs.   But the efforts of these men would
have been unavailing, had they not been seconded by
the patriotic ardor of every description of citizens,
which has induced them to leave their homes, at a most
critical season of the year, regardless of every consideration, but that of rendering service to their country.
The general found the road from Lower Sandusky to
this place literally covered with men, and amongst them
many who had shared in the toils and dangers of the
revolutionary war, and on whom of course there existed no legal claims for military services.   The general
has every reason to believe, that similar efforts have
been made in Kentucky.   He offers to all these brave
men from both states, his sincere acknowledgments;
and is happy to inform them, that there is at present
no necessity for their longer continuance in the field.
The enemy has fled with precipitation from camp
Meigs, and that is in a much better situation to resist
an attack, than when the last siege was commenced.
                      " By order of the general,
                            "R. GRAHAM, *Aid.*"
    This order excited considerable murmurs in the state
of Ohio.   The volunteers had marched under the expectation of being led immediately against the enemy;
and they reflected on general Harrison and the government for being too tardy in their movements.   Those
who understood the situation of the country, and the
difficulty of supplying a large army through a swampy
wilderness of 140 miles in extent, were however satisfied that nothing better could be done.   There being a
necessity in the first instance for obtaining the command
of the lake, for which the greatest exertions were making, it would have been extravagant folly to retain so
large a mounted force in service at fort Meigs, or to
have led them through the wilderness against the enemy.

When the order met the front companies in Johnson's regiment, it was understood as disbanding that regiment also, and produced much depression and chagrin among the men. Some of the companies turned back a few miles, and at length a halt was called till colonel Johnson should arrive, who had been detained a few hours in the rear. When he came up, he did not consider the order as even discharging the regiment from present service, and determined to march on at least, till he received the positive orders of general Harrison on that subject. This determination restored harmony and cheerfulness to the ranks, and the march was resumed with new devotion to their leader.

Colonel Johnson went on before them to Newport, to organize the balance of the regiment, and receive orders from general Harrison, who had returned to Cincinnati on a visit to his family : and on the next day, these companies were ordered by the lieutenant colonel to proceed by way of the north bend of Ohio river, above the mouth of the Big Miami, where they arrived on the 24th, and received information, that the regiment was received into the service of the United States by general Harrison. Their colonel was ordered by general Harrison to take command of fort Wayne and the posts on the Auglaize, to scour the northwestern frontiers, to make incursions into the country of the Indians, and if possible to cut off small parties, who might infest the forts, or be marching from the Illinois and Wabash towards Malden and Detroit ; and never to remain at one place more than three days. As the regiment would be employed in this manner for some time, before the expedition against Malden could be put in motion, colonel Johnson now gave his captains permission to send back an officer from each company, to raise more men. They were to meet the regiment at fort Winchester on the 18th of June, at which time it was believed the fleet would certainly have command of the lake. Three lieutenants returned on this recruiting service, and the balance then crossed the river and marched up the Big Miami on the 26th. They arrived and formed a junction with the other part of the regiment, on the 28th at Dayton.

The organization of the regiment was here finally completed as follows :

R. M. Johnson, colonel. James Johnson, lieutenant colonel.

1st battalion. Duval Payne major. R. B. M'Afee, Richard Matson, Jacob Elliston, Benjamin Warfield, John Payne, (cavalry) Elijah Craig, captains.

2nd battalion. David Thompson, major. Jacob Stucker, James Davidson, S. R. Combs, W. M. Price, James Coleman, captains.

Staff. Jeremiah Kertly, adjutant. B. S. Chambers, quarter master. Samuel Theobalds, judge advocate. L. Dickinson, sergeant major.

James Suggett, chaplain, and major of the spies. L. Sandford, quarter master sergeant. Afterwards was added, doctor Ewing, surgeon—doctors Coburn and Richardson, surgeon's mates.

From this place the regiment proceeded in a few days towards St. Marys, and arrived there on the 1st of June. This march was very much incommoded by high waters and bad roads. At this season of the year there are marshes and quagmires in every quarter of the country, which are extremely difficult to pass. As soon as the troops had all arrived, the colonel issued a general order, establishing the police of the camp, requiring the companies to be regularly mustered and drilled, and appointing a day for their inspection.

From St. Marys colonel Johnson went to the village of Wopoghconata on the Auglaize, to procure some Shawanoe Indians to act as guides and spies. During his absence, the regiment was employed in training under the superintendence of the lieutenant colonel, and in making other necessary arrangements for their future service. In a few days the colonel returned with 12 or 13 Indians, among whom was the celebrated Anthony Shane, a half blood whose father was a Frenchman. In his integrity, and fidelity to our cause, the utmost confidence was placed. He had been an active partizan in the war against general Wayne; but since the treaty of Greenville he had become unalterably attached to the Americans.

An order of march and battle was now issued, and it was enjoined on the officers to understand it as soon as possible, and be able to execute it correctly. It is certainly the duty of every general, or commandant of an independent corps, to give his men an order of battle as early as possible after taking the field, which may afterwards be varied as circumstances may require. The officers and men of every army, ought to be well acquainted with the manner of forming and with the duty of each corps, previous to their being led into action. It will tend to preserve them from confusion and consequent disaster. Hence the general who fails entirely to give an order of battle, or who defers it until a few minutes before a battle, is guilty of the most criminal neglect. This is particularly the case in militia, and other raw troops, where the state of discipline does not enable the commander with facility and certitude, to throw his army on any emergency into the necessary form. Colonel Johnson seemed to be well apprised of its importance, and faithfully discharged his duty in this respect.

On the 5th the regiment marched towards fort Wayne, with a view to protect some boats loaded with flour and bacon, which had been sent down the St. Marys by general Wingate of the Ohio militia, who was stationed with a small guard at St. Marys. When the troops arrived at a handsome prairie about half way to Shane's crossing, they were halted and practised in forming the line of battle, till every man was well acquainted with his place and his particular duties. The men were also abundantly supplied with ammunition, and well prepared for action.

A very heavy rain having fallen to-day, the St. Marys was found impassable when the regiment arrived at Shane's crossing in the evening. On the next day by felling trees into it from both banks, a rude bridge was constructed, over which the men passed with their baggage, while their horses were crossed by swimming. The rest of the way to fort Wayne was found very difficult, all the flats and marshes being covered with water, and the roads very miry. They arrived on the evening of the 7th, and found that all the boats had reached the fort in safety but one, which had struck on a bar in sight of the fort. While the boatmen were endeavoring to get her off, a party of Indians fired on and killed two of them, and the other in attempting to swim over the river was drowned. Colonel Johnson with his staff and a few men had just arrived at the fort and stript their horses. As soon as they could make ready they mounted and crossed to the boat. The Indians fired upon the advance and then retreated. The spies being of opinion, that the party of Indians was much stronger, than that with the colonel, he deferred the pursuit till the regiment all arrived. He then took a strong detachment and pursued them about ten miles, when a rainy night coming on, he returned to the fort. Next morning the 8th, a council of officers was held, which determined, after collecting all the information they could from the spies, to make an excursion towards the southeast end of lake Michigan, and visit the Indian villages in that direction. In the evening the regiment deposited their heavy baggage in the fort, drew ten days provision, and crossed the St. Marys to encamp in the forks. This stream was now just beginning to rise at the fort, though on the evening of the 5th it had been at the top of its banks at Shane's crossing, but 40 miles from its mouth by land. Hence if we suppose the current to run three miles an hour, which is near the truth, the distance by water would be upwards of 200 miles, so extremely crooked is the course of the river.

On the next day, the regiment marched early on the trail of the Indians, which led towards the village of Five Medals, that had been destroyed last year, but which it was believed had been rebuilt. They had marched forty miles before night, and the colonel intended after grazing and resting a while, to resume the march and attack that village at daylight in the morning. But a heavy rain came on, and prevented him from executing this plan. In the morning they proceeded, and after encountering many obstacles in crossing high waters and marshes, they arrived at the Elkhart river, before it had risen so as to be impassable, and in half an hour afterwards the village of Five Medals was again surrounded. But it was not occupied at present. Colonel Johnson now determined to visit a town called Paravash on the other side of the St. Josephs of the lake; and in the morning of the 11th, the line of march was resumed in that direction; but on arriving at the St. Josephs it was found to be impassable, and the intention of reaching that place was abandoned. The colonel then determined to advance with rapidity to the White Pigeon's town, at which place he arrived in the afternoon, having seen a few Indians on his route, who made their escape in a canoe over a stream which the horsemen could not pass. The village which had been the most considerable in that region of the country, was also unoccupied at present. The main trace of the Indians, from Chicago and the Illinois country to Detroit, passes through this town. It appeared to have been but little travelled this spring. The regiment remained encamped near it till next day; and as colonel Johnson had now fulfilled his instructions to visit this trace, and intercept the enemy if now making use of it; and as the provisions of the troops had been much damaged by the rain, he determined to return to fort Wayne. There is an Indian path leading directly to that place from the village, on which the regiment returned, and reached the fort on the 14th, having performed a march of near 200 miles, with heavy rains every day, and in a region never before traversed by so large a force of Americans. By this excursion, our knowledge of the country was enlarged, and it was ascertained that all the Indians in the British service, who had been at the siege of fort Meigs, were still kept in the vicinity of Malden, as no considerable body of them had returned to their country.

In the mean time the savages were committing many depredations on the Illinois and Missouri territories, where a skirmishing warfare was carried on, very much to the annoyance of the frontier settlers. It would be too tedious to enter on a detail of all the little transactions of this kind in that quarter: we shall only mention a few of the most prominent incidents. Much apprehension was entertained, that all the Indians on the Missouri and Mississippi rivers would be induced by the intrigues of the British and Tecumseh to join in the general confederacy against us. In April the Mississippi Indians invested fort Madison, though many of the tribes professed to be friendly. They did but little execution there, and soon afterwards formally besieged fort Mason, a post which had been established on the Mississippi by governor Howard, about 80 miles above St. Louis. Captain Boone who commanded a company of rangers succeeded in getting into the fort, by which it was rendered completely secure against their forces. They remained before it for 8 or 10 days, and succeeded once in setting fire to some of the cabins, which were burnt down, and at the same time a violent assault was made on the fort, which was gallantly repulsed by the garrison without much loss.

A war with the powerful Osage nation was now apprehended. During the winter governor Howard had been absent at the City of Washington, and before his

return authority had been given to raise three companies of rangers in his territory. This being known
to the Osage Indians, they applied to Mr. secretary
Bates for permission to furnish one of the companies,
which was granted; and on their appearance at St.
Louis, they were supplied with arms and ammunition
for the service. But when the governor returned he
disapproved of employing the Indians in any way, and
sent them home. Anxious to engage in the war, they
shewed evident symptoms of displeasure at this treatment, and said they would have satisfaction of the
Americans for it. It was hence supposed, that they
also would be induced to attack the frontiers. Fort
Madison had already been evacuated, as too remote
from the settlements to be maintained; and under the
apprehension of an attack from the Osages, the officers
at fort Mason held a council, and determined to abandon that place also, and retire to fort Howard, within
40 miles of St. Louis; which they effected about the
1st of May. A chain of posts was then established
from fort Howard across the country to the Missouri;
and about the same time the governor received the appointment of brigadier general in the army of the United
States, and was succeeded in the former office by William Clarke esq. who had explored the country westward to the Pacific ocean with captain Lewis.

Early in the spring, the celebrated Robert Dickson,
a British trader and emissary, had been sent among the
Indians on the frontiers of those territories, to excite
them to war, and raise recruits for the service under
Procter and Tecumseh. He visited all the tribes on
the Illinois and Mississippi rivers from Prairie de
Chien to Green bay, and in the neighborhood of Chicago, at which place a general rendezvous was to be
held, professedly for the purpose of descending the Illinois river, and attacking that territory. By making
great promises of presents and plunder, he succeeded
in collecting nearly one thousand warriors at Chicago

2 O

early in June; and after exciting considerable alarm
in the mind of governor Edwards of the Illinois territory, he led them in separate detachments towards Detroit, along the main trace which passes by the White
Pigeon's town.   They passed that village but a few
days after the regiment of colonel Johnson had left it;
by which the latter missed a glorious opportunity to
meet the enemy and distinguish themselves.

The followers of Dickson were a horde of as wild
and cruel savages as ever disgraced human nature.
They were the most worthless and abandoned despe-
radoes from all the tribes he had visited; and were
worthy to be the accomplices of the humane and honorable Procter, by whom Dickson had been sent to
collect them.   Among the chiefs who commanded them,
was the great Potawatamie, *Mai-Pock*, a monster who
was distinguished by a girdle, sewed full of human
scalps, which he wore round his waist, and strings of
bear's claws and the bills of owls and hawks, round
his ancles—as the trophies of his prowess in arms,
and as a terror to his enemies.   It is remarkable that
after these savages joined the British standard, to combat for the "defender of the faith," victory never
again declared for the allies in the northwest.   For
the cruelties they had already committed, and those
which were threatened by this inhuman association, a
just God frowned indignant on all their subsequent
operations.

It is a fact, that in July and August, the British by
their unparalleled exertions had collected nearly all
the warriors of the north and northwest into the neighborhood of Malden, where they were regularly supplied with rations by their employers.   Their camps
extended from Brownstown to Detroit, besides a number on the east side of the straight.   As they neither
hunted nor labored for their subsistence, their support
was a heavy burthen on the British contractors and
commissaries.   The number of warriors was about

2,500—but including the subsistence of the women and children they had brought with them, the amount of rations issued exceeded seven thousand. As the British expected an attack from the American army, and as this assemblage of savages constituted their main force, it was necessary to keep them well supplied with the means of subsistence and the munitions of war. Dickson who had been so instrumental in collecting this horde of barbarians was a Scotchman by birth, and certainly proved his loyalty, and deserved well of his employers, by his great zeal, industry and address in this service.

After the return of the mounted regiment to fort Wayne, they remained there a few days and then proceeded down the river with an escort of provisions to fort Winchester. A sufficient number of men were put in the boats containing the provisions to man them well, and the balance of the men proceeded down the road opened by Winchester on the north side of the Miami, encamping every night with the boats. After they had arrived at fort Winchester, colonel Johnson received a dispatch from general Harrison, recommending him to make an attack on the enemy at Raisin and Brownstown. Although the general only recommended this movement, yet it was done in such a way, that colonel Johnson as a gallant soldier felt himself bound to execute it. General Harrison had just heard of the success of our arms against the enemy below, and that general Procter was ordered in that direction to assist in repelling the invaders. Believing that Procter had left Malden with a considerable portion of his force, the general supposed that an excellent opportunity had offered, to attack his savage allies in the Michigan Territory, by a coup de main with the mounted regiment. Colonel Johnson however was unable to execute this plan immediately. His horses were so exhausted by their late expedition, that some rest was necessary before they could perform another march so difficult as that to Brownstown. A considerable de. tachment of his men were also engaged in escorting provisions from St. Marys, and could not be collected for this service immediately. A strong reinforcement was also daily expected from Kentucky, the expedition was therefore deferred for a few days.

The service recommended by the general was considered extremely hazardous. For a mounted regiment about 700 strong, with worndown horses destitute of forage, to march at least 100 miles through swamps and marshes, and over difficult rivers, with guides not very well acquainted with the country, to attack a body of Indians who could in a few hours raise more than double the force of the regiment, would have been a bold and perilous enterprise, and might have ended in their total discomfiture. For had they succeeded in battle, it is very doubtful whether they could have made good their retreat encumbered with wounded and obstructed by swamps, while a strong force of the enemy could have pursued and been ready at every advantageous place to attack them. Colonel Johnson however resolved to attempt it, as soon as his troops could be put into a condition, which promised vigorous exertions.

But fortunately for the regiment, on the next day an express arrived from general Clay commanding at fort Meigs, with information that the British and Indians threatened to invest that place again, and with a request that colonel Johnson would march his regiment there immediately for its relief. Orders to march were given without delay; and such was the zeal and promptitude of both officers and men, that in half an hour they were all ready to march, and commenced crossing the Miami opposite the fort. The provision boats were manned, and those who were unfit for duty, or had horses unfit to travel, were left with the garrison. That night they proceeded no farther after crossing the river, than Winchester's old camps; but in the morning they advanced in order and celerity, and arrived at the head of the Rapids at five in the evening, where colonel Johnson was met by another express from general Clay, advising him to be very cautious in his advance to the fort. The heads of the columns were then drawn up in close order, and the colonel in a short and impressive address, instructed them in their duties. If an enemy were discovered, the order of march was to be in two lines, one parallel to the river, and the other in front, stretching across from the head of the former to the river on the right. He concluded with saying "We must fight our way thro' any opposing force, let what will be the consequences, as no retreat could be justifiable. It is no time to flinch—we must reach the fort or die in the attempt." Every countenance responsive to the sentiments of the speaker, indicated the same desperate determination. The ground on which the enemy had gained their barbarous triumph over Dudley, was again to be traversed; and the allies would doubtless hope to realise another 5th of May, in another contest with Kentucky militia. The march was again resumed, and the regiment arrived at ten o'clock in the night opposite fort Meigs without molestation, and encamped in the open plain between the river and the hill on which the British batteries had been erected. The boats were left at the head of the Rapids, as it was deemed hazardous in the present state of the water to bring them down in the night.

At day light, when the morning gun fired, the horses of the regiment were frightened, and ran through the camp, running over several of the men and hurting them badly. They proceeded down the river a considerable distance, and with much trouble and risk to the men were caught and brought back. About 10 o'clock the regiment crossed to the fort, and encamped above it in a handsome plain clothed with blue grass. General Clay who commanded in the fort, was very

cautious and vigilant, and daily sent spies down the
river to reconnoitre and watch for the enemy.

Since he had been in command, he had repaired all
the injuries, which the fort had sustained during the
siege, and had cleared off the timber to a greater distance from it, burning that which was lying down, and
erasing the works where the British batteries had
stood.   He had also assisted in bringing down a considerable portion of the provisions from the posts on
the Auglaize and St. Marys.   His troops at the same
time had suffered excessively by sickness.   During
the month of June and a part of July, a most fatal
epidemic prevailed in the camp, which carried off from
three to five, and sometimes as many as ten in a day.
It was computed that near 200 fell a sacrifice to it,
within the space of six weeks, which was a dreadful
mortality for the number of men in the garrison.   The
disease had been caused in the commencement, most
probably by the exposure of the men during the siege;
but the bad water which they had to use, and the flat,
marshy, putrescent condition of all that region of country, was well calculated to destroy an army of men,
who were alike unused to such a climate, and to the
life of a soldier.

The apprehension of an attack at this time, was
caused by information which general Clay had received from a Frenchman and a private of colonel Dudley's regiment, who came to fort Meigs on the 20th of
June from Detroit.   The latter had been a prisoner
with the Indians.   They stated that the allies had determined to renew the attack on the fort, and were to
march about the time they had arrived.   From the
circumstantial information which they possessed, no
doubt was left on the minds of the officers in the garrison, but that an attack was in preparation.   The
force of the Indians was estimated at near four thousand—and reinforcements of regulars from the Niagara were expected to the amount of one thousand.   The

Canadian militia had been disbanded as unfit for the service. When this information was received, it was immediately communicated by an express to general Harrison, and duplicates of the despatch were sent to the governors of Ohio and Kentucky.

General Harrison was at Franklinton when the intelligence reached him. He determined to set out the next morning for Lower Sandusky, and immediately addressed a letter to the war department and another to governor Meigs on this subject, in which he stated that he did not believe fort Meigs to be the object of the attack, but that it would be Lower Sandusky, Cleveland, or Erie. The 24th regiment, United States' infantry, under the command of colonel Anderson, was now at Upper Sandusky, and was ordered to proceed immediately to Lower Sandusky. Major Croghan with a part of the 17th was ordered to the same place, and also colonel Ball with his squadron of cavalry, who had been stationed at Franklinton.

Immediately before general Harrison was called to the outposts by the impending attack, he held a council at Franklinton, with the chiefs of the friendly Indians, consisting of the Delaware, Shawanoe, Wyandot, and Seneca tribes. He informed them that circumstances had come to his knowledge, which induced him to suspect the fidelity of some of the tribes, who seemed disposed to join the enemy in case they succeeded in capturing fort Meigs—that a crisis had arrived, which required all the tribes who remained neutral, and who were willing to engage in the war, to take a decided stand either for us or against us—that the President wanted no false friends—that the proposal of general Procter to exchange the Kentucky militia for the tribes in our friendship, indicated that he had received some hint of their willingness to take up the tomahawk against us—and that to give the United States a proof of their good disposition, they must

either remove with their families into the interior, or
the warriors must accompany him in the ensuing campaign and fight for the United States. To the latter
condition, the chiefs and warriors unanimously agreed;
and said they had long been anxious for an invitation
to fight for the Americans. TAHE, the oldest Indian
in the western country, who represented all the tribes,
professed in their name the most indissoluble friendship for the United States. General Harrison then
told them he would let them know, when they would
be wanted in the service—"but you must conform to
our mode of warfare. You are not to kill defenceless
prisoners, old men, women, or children." He added
that by their conduct he would be able to tell, whether
the British could restrain their Indians from such horrible cruelty. For if the Indians fighting with him
would forbear such conduct, it would prove, that the
British could also restrain theirs if they wished to do
it. He humorously told them he had been informed,
that general Procter had promised to deliver him into
the hands of Tecumseh, if he succeeded against fort
Meigs, to be treated as that warrior might think proper. "Now if I can succeed in taking Procter, you
shall have him for your prisoner, provided you will
agree to treat him *as a squaw*, and only put petticoats
upon him; for he must be a coward who would kill a
defenceless prisoner."

The government of the United States at last reluc-
tantly agreed to employ Indians in their army, against
the savages employed by the British. The thing was
perfectly justifiable, as a measure of self defence: yet
there is only one reason which reconciles me to it. We
thus demonstrated, that the north American savage is
not such a cruel and ferocious being, that he cannot be
restrained by civilized man within the bounds of civilized warfare. In several instances, subsequent to the
present period, strong corps of Indians fought under
the American standard, and were uniformly distin-

guished by their orderly and humane conduct. Had the Indians been employed by the British on the condition that they must conform to the rules of civilized warfare, no instance of savage cruelty in this war, would now be recorded against them, in the page of history, and in the celestial register of human crimes; but they employed the savages on a different principle—and I repeat that if the British officers in Upper Canada did not directly instigate, they at least very willingly permitted, the savages to massacre the prisoners, who had surrendered, not to the savages, but to themselves after receiving a solemn promise of protection.

On the evening of the 26th, general Harrison overtook the 24th regiment on its way to Lower Sandusky; and immediately selected all the men who were able to make a forced march. They amounted to 300, and were pushed forward for fort Meigs under the command of colonel Anderson. The general arrived at the fort on the evening of the 28th, and in a few hours afterwards the detachment under Anderson also made its appearance. As no farther information had been received, respecting the designs of the enemy, general Harrison ordered a detachment of Johnson's regiment to proceed the next day to the river Raisin to procure intelligence. Colonel Johnson took command of the detachment himself, and was accompanied also by the lieutenant colonel, the whole being 150 strong. They left the fort about 11 o'clock, and although the high water obliged them to go considerably out of their way to get over some of the creeks, they reached Frenchtown that night after 12 o'clock, and searched the whole town in hopes of taking a prisoner; but none of the enemy could be found. All the inhabited houses were visited by the colonel, and enquiry made respecting the enemy. The intelligent part of the citizens all agreed in stating, that they had heard of no reinforcements of regulars arriving at Malden, nor any consi-

2 P

derable number of Indians, since the siege of fort Meigs—that the Indians had pressed general Procter to make another attack, and were much dissatisfied at his putting it off—that the success of our arms below had been kept from their knowledge some time, but was at last divulged to them by a trader, for which he was seized by Procter, but afterwards released at the demand of the Indians—that they held councils, the proceedings of which were kept secret from the British—and that 100 warriors of the Ottawa tribe had passed the river Raisin in boats to take scalps in the vicinity of Lower Sandusky.

Colonel Johnson on the next day returned to fort Meigs, taking with him two Frenchmen, one of them a citizen of Michigan, and the other a British subject. He had learnt that about 20 Indians had proceeded towards fort Meigs with a view to steal the hors s of the army; and on his return he struck their trail, and pursued them. But in a few miles he found, that they had altered their minds and changed their course, having probably got intelligence of his excursion. On his arrival at the fort his regiment was reinforced by 100 men, brought by lieutenants Cardwell, White, Branham, and Lapsley from Kentucky.

General Harrison now deemed it unnecessary for him to remain any longer at fort Meigs, and on the 1st of July proceeded to Lower Sandusky with an escort of 70 mounted men commanded by captain M'Afee, at which place they arrived by dark, although the road was a continued and deep swamp. General Harrison expected with this escort and colonel Ball's squadron, to be ready to oppose the party of Indians, of whose expedition colonel Johnson had brought intelligence; but on the morning of that day they had been in the vicinity of the fort, and had killed at a farm house 3 men, a woman, and two children, and then made their escape in view of the garrison. Colonel Ball had not yet arrived, and there was of course no troops at the place, who could move with sufficient speed to intercept them, nor was the whole number there sufficient to make the attempt. Colonel Wells commanded, and the garrison consisted of 140 Ohio volunteers, whose term of service having expired, they were anxious to go home. General Harrison however prevailed upon them to remain some time longer.

On the evening of the 2nd colonel Ball's squadron arrived at Lower Sandusky, and on the next day proceeded with general Harrison to Cleveland. The object of the general in going to that place, was to make arrangements for the better security of the provisions, and of the boats which were constructing at that post. They were now guarded by a few regulars, and a small but excellent company of militia called the Chillicothe guards. General Harrison caused a small fort to be erected on the bank of the lake, drew a company of artillery, and another of 12 months' infantry from the interior, directed the boats to be sunk in a deep part of the Cayago river, as fast as they were finished, and had the magazine of provisions, which was at some distance from the town, prepared for conflagration, should the enemy land with a force, which our troops could not meet in the field. When the general afterwards left the place, colonel Ball remained there in command.

The mounted regiment had been ordered to proceed by Lower Sandusky to the river Huron, where it was intended, that they should remain a while to recruit their horses. They marched on the 2nd from fort Meigs, but did not arrive at Sandusky until the evening of the 3rd. THE FOURTH OF JULY, the anniversary of independence, was celebrated by the garrison and mounted men together, in great harmony and enthusi- asm. Colonel Johnson delivered an appropriate ad- dress; and a number of toasts, breathing sentiments of the republican soldier were then drank, and cheered by the shouts of the men, the firing of small arms, and the discharge of a six pounder from the fort. The militia soldier whose patriotism was satisfied with going to the boundary line and looking at the enemy, while he refused to cross and fight them, was strongly reprobated in one of their toasts,

Considerable exertions were now making to finish the works of fort Stephenson, which had been planned and commenced in April by major Wood. They were soon afterwards completed, so as to contain a larger garrison and make a more formidable resistance. On the 6th colonel Johnson's regiment proceeded in detachments to Huron, and encamped on the shore of the lake, where they were supplied with forage by boats from Cleveland on the next day; and on the 8th lieutenant colonel J. Johnson returned in the boats with a party of 50 men to procure more forage. On the morning of the 9th a despatch was received from general Harrison which the colonel immediately answered, sending captain Payne for that purpose in a barge with a few men, though the lake was at that time extremely rough. The object of these expresses not being explained at the time, considerable curiosity and uneasiness were excited among the men, by the haste and secrecy observed.

General Harrison had just received the following letter from the war department, which he enclosed to colonel Johnson with orders to act accordingly. The letter had been delayed by being sent to Cincinnati and from thence following the movements of the general.

' *War Department, June 9th,* 1813.

' Sir, General Howard and governor Edwards urge the necessity of more troops in that quarter; and there being no other disposable force for that purpose at this time, the president directs that you order colonel Johnson with his regiment of mounted volunteers directly to Kaskaskias, to report to general Howard.

' I have the honor, &c.
' JOHN ARMSTRONG.

' General Harrison.'

In reply colonel Johnson remonstrated against the order—he did not insist on the wishes of his men, which however to be indulged among friends in social life, were not to be mentioned against a military command; but represented his inability to comply, with any advantage to the country, or honor to the corps. He stated that his horses were in such a situation, that it would require ten days to put them in a condition for a journey of 400 miles to Kaskaskias—that it would require 30 days to perform it through the swamps they must traverse—that allowing 20 days more, to recruit the horses after their arrival, and to reach the frontiers, they would then have but 20 days left for service till their time would expire—that so many of his men were already dismounted, he could not expect after leaving captain Payne's cavalry as directed, to reach that place with more than 400—that he would hence arrive there with a reduced corps too late for the service—that governor Edwards was unnecessarily alarmed, his territory not being in danger, as the greater part of the Indians were collected at Malden—that the present position and circumstances of the regiment could not be known to the president at the time the order was given—that they would have an opportunity of rendering important services and acquiring laurels by remaining in the northwestern army, and would be rendered wholly useless by going to the west. On these grounds he entreated the general to detain him, or to leave to him the responsibility under existing circumstances of disobeying the order. In addition to these, many other considerations were pressed by lieutenant colonel Johnson, who was at head quarters. But the general replied that the order from the war department was so peremptory, that he could not authorize the suspension of the march even for a day; although he regretted extremely that the regiment would be separated from him in his contemplated movements against Upper Canada.

The following letter from colonel Johnson to general Harrison, which was written on the fourth of July, will exhibit the condition, the sentiments, and views of the regiment, from which the reader may imagine their feelings on this occasion, recollecting that the colonel was a distinguished partizan of the administration in congress, and that his regiment included a number of prominent characters in Kentucky.

                ‘ *Camp at Lower Sandusky, July 4th,* 1813.

   ‘ DEAR SIR—I arrived at this place last evening with a part of the mounted regiment, after two days march from camp Meigs, leaving two companies four miles in the rear, who were unable to reach this place ; besides about twenty horses left on the way, which I am in hopes will be able to get back to camp Meigs or come to this place in a few days, where we can keep them together and recruit them. Having been in the most active service for upwards of forty days, and having travelled upwards of 700 miles, much of it forced marching, it is natural to conclude, that most of the horses are weak ; and we feel great pleasure, and obligations to you, in finding your arrangements such as to enable us to recruit the horses of the regiment. To be ready to move with you, to Detroit and Canada, against the enemies of our country, is the first wish of our hearts. Two great objects induced us to come—first, to be at the regaining of our own territory and Detroit, and at the taking of Malden— and secondly, to serve under an officer in whom we have confidence. We could not have engaged in the service without such a prospect, when we recollected what disasters have attended us for the want of good generals. We did not want to serve under cowards, drunkards, old grannies, nor traitors, but under one who had proved himself to be wise, prudent and brave. The officers of the mounted regiment had some idea of addressing you on their anxiety to be a part of your army in the campaign against Canada, and of giving you a statement of the importance of having an opportunity to make the regiment efficient for such a campaign by recruiting their horses. As to the men, they are active, healthy and fond of service. This morning I have sent out 100 on foot to scour the surrounding country ; and wherever we are we wish continual service. Our regiment is about 900 strong when all together. I have left 100 at Defiance to regain some lost horses, and to guard that frontier.

   ‘ You have not witnessed the opposition I encountered in raising the regiment. Every personal enemy, every traitor and tory, and your enemies, all combined—but in vain. Nothing but

the hurry which attended our march prevented me from having
1500 men.   Nothing but the importance of the service, which I
thought we could render, would have justified my absence from
the present catch penny congress.   (The great object of the session was to raise a revenue.)   My enemies, your enemies, the
enemies of our cause, would exult if the mounted regiment should
from any cause, be unable to carry a strong arm against the
savages and British, when you strike the grand blow.

'It is with much diffidence I write you any thing touching
military matters; but the desires of my soul and the situation
of the regiment, have induced me thus freely and confidentially
to express myself.   In the morning we shall leave this place for
Huron, ready to receive your orders, which will always be
cheerfully executed at every hazard.

> 'Your obedient servant,
> 'RH: M. JOHNSON.'

Little did the colonel expect, when winding up this
letter, that he was going to Huron to receive an order
of banishment to the wilds of the west.   When he did
receive it finally however, by the return of his express,
it was "cheerfully executed at every hazard," and
without a murmur.   His men would "not disgrace
him and themselves by any unsoldierly opposition to
the orders of the president," however contrary to their
views and wishes.   The only service they were expected to render by this counterplot movement, was to
aid governor Edwards who was continually represent-
ing to the government, that Dickson would certainly
invade his territory with several thousand Indians;
when in fact Dickson had been recruiting only for general Procter, and was now at Malden with all the Indians he could raise, intending to fight general Harrison as soon as Procter could make his arrangements.
Both the secretary of war and general Harrison had
constantly been of the opinion, that while the enemy had
Malden to protect and the northwestern army to destroy, they would attempt no considerable movement
against the western territories; and their opinion proved
to be correct.   General Harrison immediately informed
the war department of the situation of colonel Johnson's

regiment, and of the great anxiety which they had shewn to remain in the northwestern service.

After receiving the final orders of the general on the 13th, and having selected the route by Upper Sandusky, fort M'Arthur, St. Marys, Greenville, Delaware towns on White river, fort Harrison and Vincennes, as the most eligible of those recommended by the general, the troops marched by detachments and arrived at Upper Sandusky on the 16th. Some of the companies passed by Lower Sandusky, at which place major Croghan had arrived with part of the 17th regiment and taken command of the fort. At Upper Sandusky colonel Johnson ascertained that it was indispensably necessary to change his route so as to pass Urbana, for the purpose of procuring grain and other necessaries for the regiment. They proceeded again in detachments and arrived at that place in a very unfavorable condition on the 19th and 20th. A considerable number of horses had been lost already, and many of the men were sick with the measles and other fevers. The prospect of marching through the wilderness to Vincennes became every day more gloomy; and it was now evident, that if that route was pursued, but a small portion of the regiment could be expected to reach their destination, on account of sickness and the loss of horses. A meeting of the officers was therefore held, and an address drawn up and presented to the colonel, in which they solicited him to change their route and allow them to pass through Kentucky. They represented the cheerfulness and promptitude, with which the regiment had to this moment, executed the orders of the government and their commandant; and had performed a march of near 800 miles in the whole, over roads of the worst description, swimming the numerous streams they had to cross, and generally proceeding by forced marches from 30 to 50 miles a day—that the regiment was very much reduced and scattered by the loss of horses; and by the time it reached Kaskaskias would be rendered wholly inefficient, and perhaps entirely useless—and that by going through Kentucky they would be able to raise more men, and remount those who had lost their horses, or had rendered them unfit for the expedition, and would ultimately reach their destination as soon as by the more direct route through the wilderness, and be in a condition to render efficient service. In reply the colonel remarked, that "It was not until the arrival of the regiment at this place, that the entire impracticability of carrying to Kaskaskias one half the horses was certainly known, without re-cruiting many days, or changing the route to Kentucky. Under the whole view of the subject, no hesitation exists as to the propriety and evident necessity of granting the request of the officers." The regiment was therefore ordered to march through Kentucky for the above purposes, and to rendezvous at Vincennes on the 20th of August. To justify this step in violation of his positive orders, the colonel relied on its evident propriety; and it proved in fact to be the salvation of the regiment.

While the regiment was at Urbana, intelligence was received that colonel William Russell was preparing an expedition against the Indians from the Indiana territory; and he was at this time marching through their country with a strong mounted corps of rangers and volunteer militia. An excursion had also been previously made by colonel Bartholomew, which it will be proper in this place to notice. In the spring the Indians had committed many depredations on the frontiers of Indiana, in the way of murdering the inhabitants and stealing their horses and cattle. The Delawares were strongly suspected of either secretly aiding in the mischief, or of committing it themselves. Colonel Bartholomew of that territory hence determined to visit their towns on White river with a military force, and if any proofs of their hostility could be discovered, to retaliate and chastise them effectually for it. He

2 R

accordingly assembled three companies of mounted men at Valonia, commanded by captains Peyton, Biggers and Dunn, and amounting to 140 men. Having selected majors Tipton and Owen for his aids, he proceeded up the country till he had reached the upper Delaware towns, which he found uninhabited; and returning by the lower towns he found them in the same condition. Some Indian sign was discovered, but only one Indian was seen during the whole excursion. Those who had not gone to reside in the interior of the state of Ohio, had left the villages where they formerly resided for some other region.

Soon after this excursion, colonel Russell of the United States army, who commanded the rangers of Indiana, which had been raised under the act of congress, authorizing ten additional companies for the protection of the western territories, projected another expedition to penetrate as far as the Mississiniway villages. He requested Joseph Allen esq. of Kentucky to raise a company and join him at Valonia early in July; and also invited major general Thomas, and brigadier general Cox of the Kentucky militia, to join in the expedition. They repaired accordingly to that place, which is about 50 miles from Louisville near White river, and carried about 100 volunteers to the standard of colonel Russell, whose whole force then amounted to 500 men. The colonel determined to march this force in five lines with an officer having the rank of major at the head of each line. Generals Thomas and Cox, colonels Evans and Wilson, and major Zach. Taylor, were assigned to these posts; and the corps then proceeded directly to the Delaware towns which were found still unoccupied. He then marched towards the Mississiniway, intending if possible to surprise any Indians who might be found in the villages on that river. In five days he reached the main village at the mouth of that river, which he found vacant; and from every appearance, it was supposed the Indians had been gone about two months. There were nearly two hundred houses in this village, which extended about a mile in length; and two miles further up the river, there were the remains of a large encampment, and a block house with several port holes large enough for a six pounder. This had been erected by Tecumseh in the preceding autumn with a view to resist the progress of general Hopkins, and had been a place of general rendezvous for the concentration of his forces. The encampment had apparently been large enough to contain one thousand Indians. It was now abundantly evident, that all the Indians of the Wabash were gone to Malden to serve under the banners of general Procter. Colonel Russell therefore proceeded down the Wabash by Tippecanoe to fort Harrison, having taken a circuit of more than 400 miles through the Indian country, without having seen an Indian or lost a man.

CHAPTER VIII.

The second siege of fort Meigs—repulse of the British at Lower Sandusky by major Croghan—and Perry's victory on lake Erie.

VERY early in July the Indians had begun again to infest the vicinity of fort Meigs. A small party of fourteen footmen were permitted by captain Craig to return home from that place by the way of fort Winchester. They had proceeded but a few miles up the river, before they were attacked by a party of Indians, and totally defeated, but two of them being able to make their escape. A party of eighteen horsemen commanded by lieutenant Craig, were going up the river to guard down some flour which had been left in the Rapids, and were but two or three hundred yards from the former party when the attack was made upon them. Advancing towards the place of attack, they met one of the footmen who had escaped, and at the same time were fired on by three Indians, who were ambuscading the road to intercept the retreat of the footmen. Lieutenant Craig immediately ordered a retreat, and was obeyed by all but three of his men, who pursued the little party of Indians—one of whom, Mr. Wiant, having wounded an Indian, dismounted, pursued him 200 yards, killed him, and returned in safety with his scalp and his gun. On their return to the fort, colonel Gaines was detached with a party of regulars to reconnoitre the ground. Before his arrival the Indians had dispersed, and made their escape in different directions, and only one of our men was found dead at the place of the encounter. Lieutenant Craig was arrested for his conduct in this affair, and was sentenced

by a court martial to be cashiered. Wiant was promoted by general Clay to the rank of ensign, and was
presented with the best sword in the depot of that place.

This occurrence inspired the garrison with more caution in their excursions; but it was now generally believed that the enemy had abandoned their intention of
attacking the fort. The storm however had not passed
by : it was only restrained with a view to accumulate
more force, and burst upon us with more suddenness
and effect. The Indians of the northwest, who had
been urging general Procter to renew the siege, became
still more importunate on the arrival of Dickson with
his wild savages from the west; and the expedition
was now delayed only in consequence of the prisoner
and Frenchman having escaped with the intelligence of
their intention to execute it immediately.

General Clay however was very vigilant, and daily
sent scouts down the river to watch for the enemy.
This service fell chiefly on the company of captain
Craig of Johnson's regiment, who had been left at the
fort by the orders of general Harrison, with 140 men
and about 90 horses. The captain being of opinion,
that this service was too much to be performed by his
men alone, remonstrated against it, but without effect,
and finally determined to leave the fort and follow his
regiment. This caused the general to arrest him, and
ultimately he resigned.

On the 20th of July, a party was sent down towards
the lake by land, and another in boats which proceeded
out a few miles on the lake, but all returned without
making any discovery, except hearing the firing of cannon towards Malden. On the same evening however
lieutenant Peters, conductor of artillery, who was returning with a few men from Lower Sandusky, was
pursued by a party of Indians; and late in the evening
the boats of the British army could be distinctly seen
down the river. Early next morning a picket guard,
consisting of a corporal and ten men, was sent to a point

about 300 yards below the fort, where it was soon surprised by the Indians, and seven of the men killed and captured. A large army of British and Indians were now seen encamped below the old British fort Miami on the north side of the river; and soon afterwards the Indians had possessed themselves of the wood in the rear of the fort. They carried off some horses and oxen, and through the day occasionally fired into the fort, but entirely without effect, as they were frequently warned by our grape and cannister to keep at a respectful distance.

In the night captain M'Cune was sent express to general Harrison to apprize him of the siege; and the men in the fort were diligently employed in making the necessary arrangements. As it was expected, that the British would erect batteries during the night, and commence a cannonade next day, great exertions were made to throw up new traverses, to deepen the trenches, and to cover the magazines. The men who were permitted to rest, were required to sleep on their arms. General Clay and his staff were incessant in their attention to every part of the lines, and to all the operations going on in the camp. After midnight lieutenant Montjoy came into the fort from Portage blockhouse, with a party of 20 regulars, having made an extraordinary escape in penetrating through a large body of Indians with the loss of but one man.

On the 23rd a large body of mounted Indians, supposed to be 800 strong, were seen passing up the river under the command of Tecumseh, with the intention it was supposed of attacking fort Winchester. On the evening of the next day, as every thing still remained quiet round the fort, colonel Gaines went out as far as the edge of the woods with 200 men, and made the circuit of the fort, with a view to ascertain whether any batteries had yet been commenced by the enemy. A stronger detachment was sent over from the British camp to attack him, but it did not arrive in time to intercept his return to the fort. On the 25th the enemy removed their camp over the river to the south side, and encamped behind a point of woods, which partly concealed them from the garrison. This movement connected with their other conduct, induced a belief in the fort, that they would make an attempt to carry it by storm; but the project they had in view was not of such a desperate character. Care was still taken by general Clay to keep the commander in chief well informed of occurrences at the fort.

General Harrison had returned from Cleveland to Lower Sandusky several days before the arrival of the enemy, and received at that place from the express, the information that camp Meigs was again invested. He then immediately removed his head quarters to Seneca town, about nine miles up the Sandusky river, where he constructed a fortified camp, having left major Croghan with 160 regulars in fort Stephenson, and taken with him to Seneca about 140 more, under the immediate command of colonel Wells. A few days afterwards he was reinforced by the arrival of 300 regulars under colonel Paul, and colonel Ball's corps of 150 dragoons, which made his whole force at that place upwards of 600 strong. He was soon joined also by generals M'Arthur and Cass; and colonel Owings with a regiment of 500 regulars from Kentucky, was also advancing to the frontiers; but he did not arrive at head quarters before the siege of fort Meigs had been abandoned by the enemy. From the position at Seneca, the general would be able to fall back for the protection of his principal depot at Upper Sandusky, should the enemy endeavor to turn his left flank and attack that place; or he would be able, should the safety of fort Meigs require it, to proceed there undiscovered on a secret route, and cut his way into the fort with a reinforcement; or as soon as his force should be competent to cope with that of the enemy in the field, he would be favorably situated to make a descent upon

them and raise the siege. Fort Meigs and Upper
Sandusky were the objects to be defended—Lower
Sandusky was comparatively nothing.

It was the opinion of general Harrison, that the
movement of the Indians towards fort Winchester, was
intended as a feint to draw his attention in that direction, while an attack would be made on Lower Sandusky or Cleveland. The former had been pronounced untenable, and as it contained nothing valuable
except 200 barrels of flour, and was in no respect an
important post, arrangements had been made to evacuate and destroy the fort, in case the British should approach it in force from the lake. Much industry was
used to reconnoitre the route to Upper Sandusky, as
well as to watch the lake for the approach of the enemy to Lower Sandusky or Cleveland. The express
from fort Meigs was sent back with information, that
the general had not a sufficient force with him to justify his advancing immediately to that place; that he
would collect his troops at Seneca, and be ready as
soon as possible to relieve the garrison; that the governor of Ohio would be advised of the situation of our
affairs, and if the enemy persevered in his attempt, a
sufficient force would be collected in a short time, to
overpower and destroy him at once. The express arrived at the fort with this intelligence on the morning
of the 26th; and on the evening of that day, a heavy
fire commenced on the Sandusky road, about the distance of a mile from the fort. The discharge of rifles
and musketry, accompanied by the Indian yell, could
be clearly distinguished; and by degrees the apparent
contest approached towards the fort, though sometimes
it appeared to recede. It lasted about an hour, and
came in the end near the edge of the woods. The
general pronounced it a sham battle, intended to draw
out the garrison to relieve a supposed reinforcement.
A few discharges of cannon at the fort, and a heavy
shower of rain, at length put an end to the scheme, no

doubt to the great mortification of its projectors. The express from general Harrison had providentially arrived in time, to preserve the garrison from the possibility of being deluded by this artifice of the enemy. On the next day the British moved over to their old encampment, and on the 28th embarked in their vessels and abandoned the siege. The force which Procter and Tecumseh brought against us in this instance, has since been ascertained to have been about 5000 strong. A greater number of Indians were collected by them, for this expedition, than ever were assembled in one body on any other occasion during the whole war.

Having raised the siege of camp Meigs, the British sailed round into Sandusky bay, whilst a competent number of their savage allies marched across through the swamps of Portage river, to co-operate in a combined attack on Lower Sandusky, expecting no doubt that general Harrison's attention would be chiefly directed to forts Winchester and Meigs. The general however had calculated on their taking this course, and had been careful to keep patroles down the bay, opposite the mouth of Portage, where he supposed their forces would debark.

Several days before the British had invested fort Meigs, general Harrison with major Croghan and some other officers, had examined the heights which surround fort Stephenson; and as the hill on the opposite, or southeast side of the river, was found to be the most commanding eminence, the general had some thoughts of removing the fort to that place, and major Croghan declared his readiness to undertake the work. But the general did not authorize him to do it, as he believed that if the enemy intended to invade our territory again, they would do it before the removal could be completed. It was then finally concluded, that the fort which was calculated for a garrison of only two hundred men, could not be defended against the heavy artillery of the enemy; and that if the British should

approach it by water, which would cause a presumption that they had brought their heavy artillery, the
fort must be abandoned and burnt, provided a retreat
could be effected with safety. In the orders left with
major Croghan it was stated—"Should the British
troops approach you in force with cannon, and you can
discover them in time to effect a retreat, you will do so
immediately, destroying all the public stores."

"You must be aware, that the attempt to retreat in
the face of an Indian force would be vain. Against
such an enemy your garrison would be safe, however
great the number."

On the evening of the 29th general Harrison received
intelligence by express from general Clay, that the
enemy had abandoned the siege of fort Meigs ; and as
the Indians on that day had swarmed in the woods
round his camp, he entertained no doubt but that an
immediate attack was intended either on Sandusky or
Seneca. He therefore immediately called a council of
war, consisting of M'Arthur, Cass, Ball, Paul, *Wood,*
Hukill, Holmes, and Graham, who were unanimously of
the opinion—that fort Stephenson was untenable against
heavy artillery—and that, as the enemy could bring
with facility any quantity of battering cannon against
it, by which it must inevitably fall and as it was an
unimportant post, containing nothing the loss of which
would be felt by us, that the garrison should therefore
not be reinforced but withdrawn and the place destroyed. In pursuance of this decision the general immediately despatched the following order to major Croghan.

'Sir. Immediately on receiving this letter, you will abandon
fort Stephenson, set fire to it, and repair with your command
this night to head quarters. Cross the river and come up on
the opposite side. If you should deem and find it impracticable
to make good your march to this place, take the road to Huron
and pursue it with the utmost circumspection and despatch.'

This order was sent by Mr. Conner and two Indians, who lost their way in the dark, and did not ar-

rive at fort Stephenson before 11 o'clock the next day.
When major Croghan received it, he was of opinion
that he could not then retreat with safety, as the Indians
were hovering round the fort in considerable force.
He called a council of his officers, a majority of whom
coincided with him in opinion, that a retreat would be
unsafe, and that the post could be maintained against
the enemy, at least till further instructions could be
received from head quarters. The major therefore
immediately returned the following answer.

'Sir, I have just received yours of yesterday, 10 o'clock
P. M. ordering me to destroy this place and make good my retreat, which was received too late to be carried into execution.
We have determined to maintain this place, and by heavens
we can.'

In writing this note, major Croghan had a view to
the probability of its falling into the hands of the enemy, and on that account made use of stronger language
than would otherwise have been consistent with propriety. It reached the general on the same day, who
did not fully understand the circumstances and motives
under which it had been dictated. The following order was therefore immediately prepared, and sent with
colonel Wells in the morning, escorted by colonel Ball
with his corps of dragoons.

'July 30th, 1813.

'Sir, The general has just received your letter of this date,
informing him that you had thought proper to disobey the order
issued from this office, and delivered to you this morning. It
appears that the information which dictated the order was in-
correct; and as you did not receive it in the night as was expected, it might have been proper that you should have reported
the circumstance and your situation, before you proceeded to its
execution. This might have been passed over, but I am directed
to say to you, that an officer who presumes to aver, that he has
made his resolution, and that he will act in direct opposition to
the orders of his general, can no longer be entrusted with a se
parate command. Colonel Wells is sent to relieve you. You
will deliver the command to him, and repair with colonel Ball's
squadron to this place. By command, &c.

'A. H. HOLMES, Asst. Adjutant General.'

The squadron of dragoons on this trip met with a party of Indians near Lower Sandusky, and killed 11 out of 12. The Indians had formed an ambush and fired on the advanced guard consisting of a sergeant and five privates. Upon seeing the squadron approach they fled, but were pursued and soon overtaken by the front squad of captain Hopkins's troop. The greater part of them were cut down by colonel Ball and captain Hopkins with his subalterns, whose horses being the fleetest overtook them first. The loss on our part was two privates wounded and two horses killed.

Colonel Wells being left in the command of fort Stephenson, major Croghan returned with the squadron to head quarters. He there explained his motives for writing such a note, which were deemed satisfactory; and having remained all night with the general who treated him politely, he was permitted to return to his command in the morning, with written orders similar to those he had received before.

A reconnoitring party which had been sent from head quarters to the shore of the lake, about 20 miles distant from fort Stephenson, discovered the approach of the enemy by water on the evening of the 31st of July. They returned by the fort, after 12 o'clock the next day, and had passed it but a few hours, when the enemy made their appearance before it. The Indians shewed themselves first on the hill over the river, and were saluted by a 6 pounder, the only piece of artillery in the fort, which soon caused them to retire. In half an hour the British gun boats came in sight; and the Indian forces displayed themselves in every direction, with a view to intercept the garrison should a retreat be attempted. The 6 pounder was fired a few times at the gun boats, which was returned by the artillery of the enemy. A landing of their troops with a 5 1-2 inch howitzer was effected about a mile below the fort; and major Chambers accompanied by Dickson was despatched towards the fort with a flag, and was met

on the part of major Croghan by ensign Shipp of the
17th regiment. After the usual ceremonies major Chambers observed to ensign Shipp, that he was instructed
by general Procter, to demand the surrender of the fort,
as he was anxious to spare the effusion of human blood,
which he could not do, should he be under the necessity of reducing it, by the powerful force of artillery,
regulars, and Indians under his command. Shipp replied that the commandant of the fort and its garrison
were determined to defend it to the last extremity;
that no force however great could induce them to surrender, as they were resolved to maintain their post, or
to bury themselves in its ruins. Dickson then said, that
their immense body of Indians could not be restrained from massacreing the whole garrison in case of success—of which we have no doubt, rejoined Chambers,
as we are amply prepared. Dickson then proceeded to
remark, that it was a great pity so fine a young man
should fall into the hands of the savages—sir, for God's
sake surrender, and prevent the dreadful massacre that
will be caused by your resistance. Mr. Shipp replied,
that when the fort was taken there would be none
to massacre. It will not be given up, while a man is
able to resist. An Indian at this moment came out of
an adjoining ravine, and advancing to the ensign, took
hold of his sword and attempted to wrest it from him.
Dickson interfered, and having restrained the Indian,
affected great anxiety to get him safe into the fort.

The enemy now opened their fire from their 6 pounders in the gun boats and the howitzer on shore, which
they continued through the night with but little intermission, and with very little effect. The forces of the
enemy consisted of 500 regulars, and about 800 Indians commanded by Dickson, the whole being commanded by general Procter in person. Tecumseh was
stationed on the road to fort Meigs with a body of
2000 Indians, expecting to intercept a reinforcement on
that route.

Major Croghan through the evening occasionally
fired his 6 pounder, at the same time changing its place
occasionally to induce a belief that he had more than
one piece. As it produced very little execution on the
enemy, and he was desirous of saving his ammunition,
he soon discontinued his fire. The enemy had directed
their fire against the northwestern angle of the fort,
which induced the commandant to believe that an attempt to storm his works would be made at that point.
In the night captain Hunter was directed to remove the
6 pounder to a blockhouse from which it would rake
that angle. By great industry and personal exertion
captain Hunter soon accomplished this object in secrecy. · The embrasure was masked, and the piece
loaded with a half charge of powder, and double charge
of slugs and grape shot.

Early in the morning of the 2nd, the enemy opened
their fire from their howitzer, and three 6 pounders,
which they had landed in the night, and planted in a
point of woods about 250 yards from the fort. In the
evening, about 4 o'clock, they concentrated the fire of
all their guns on the northwest angle, which convinced
major Croghan that they would endeavor to make a
breach and storm the works at that point ; he therefore
immediately had that place strengthened as much as
possible with bags of flour and sand, which were so
effectual, that the picketting in that place sustained no
material injury. Sergeant Weaver with five or six
gentlemen of the Petersburg volunteers and Pittsburgh
blues, who happened to be in the fort, was entrusted
with the management of the 6 pounder.

Late in the evening when the smoke of the firing had
completely enveloped the fort, the enemy proceeded to
make the assault. Two feints were made towards
the southern angle, where captain Hunter's lines were
formed ; and at the same time a column of 350 men
were discovered advancing through the smoke, within
20 paces of the northwestern angle. A heavy galling

fire of musketry was now opened upon them from the fort, which threw them into some confusion. Colonel Short who headed the principal column soon rallied his men, and led them with great bravery to the brink of the ditch. After a momentary pause he leaped into the ditch, calling to his men to follow him, and in a few minutes it was full. The masked port hole was now opened, and the 6 pounder, at the distance of 30 feet, poured such destruction among them, that but few who had entered the ditch were fortunate enough to escape. A precipitate and confused retreat was the immediate consequence, although some of the officers attempted to rally their men. The other column, which was led by colonel Warburton and major Chambers, was also routed in confusion by a destructive fire from the line commanded by captain Hunter. The whole of them fled into the adjoining wood, beyond the reach of our small arms. During the assault, which lasted half an hour, the enemy kept up an incessant fire from their howitzer and five 6 pounders. They left colonel Short, a lieutenant, and 25 privates dead in the ditch; and the total number of prisoners taken was 26, most of them badly wounded. Major Muir was knocked down in the ditch, and lay among the dead, till the darkness of the night enabled him to escape in safety. The loss of the garrison was 1 killed and 7 slightly wounded. The total loss of the enemy could not be less than 150 killed and wounded.

When night came on, which was soon after the assault, the wounded in the ditch were in a desperate situation. Complete relief could not be brought to them by either side with any degree of safety. Major Croghan however relieved them as much as possible— he contrived to convey them water over the picketting in buckets, and a ditch was opened under the pickets, through which those who were able and willing, were encouraged to crawl into the fort. All who were able preferred of course to follow their defeated comrades.

and many others were carried from the vicinity of the fort by the Indians, particularly their own killed and wounded; and in the night about 3 o'clock, the whole British and Indian force commenced a disorderly retreat. So great was their precipitation, that they left a sail boat containing some clothing and a considerable quantity of military stores; and on the next day 70 stand of arms, and some braces of pistols were picked up round the fort. Their hurry and confusion was caused by the apprehension of an attack from general Harrison, of whose position and force they had probably received an exaggerated account.

It was the intention of general Harrison, should the enemy succeed against fort Stephenson, or should they endeavor to turn his left and fall on Upper Sandusky, to leave his camp at Seneca and fall back for the protection of that place. But he discovered by the firing on the evening of the 1st, that the enemy had nothing but light artillery, which could make no impression on the fort; and he knew that an attempt to storm it without making a breach could be successfully repelled by the garrison; he therefore determined to wait for the arrival of 250 mounted volunteers under colonel Rennick, being the advance of 700 who were approaching by the way of Upper Sandusky, and then to march against the enemy and raise the siege, if their force was not still too great for his. On the 2nd he sent several scouts to ascertain their situation and force; but the woods were so infested with Indians, that none of them could proceed sufficiently near the fort to make the necessary discoveries. In the night a messenger arrived at head quarters with intelligence, that the enemy were preparing to retreat. About 9 o'clock major Croghan had ascertained from their collecting about their boats, that they were preparing to embark, and had immediately sent an express to the commander in chief with this information. The general now determined to wait no longer for the reinforcements, and immediately set out with the dragoons, with which he reached the fort early in the morning, having ordered generals M'Arthur and Cass, who had arrived at Seneca several days before, to follow him with all the disposable infantry at that place, and which at this time was about 700 men, after the numerous sick, and the force necessary to maintain the position, were left behind.   Finding that the enemy had fled entirely from the fort so as not to be reached by him, and learning that Tecumseh was some where in the direction of fort Meigs with 2000 warriors, he immediately ordered the infantry to fall back to Seneca, lest Tecumseh should make an attack on that place, or intercept the small reinforcements advancing from Ohio.

In his official report of this affair, general Harrison observes that, " It will not be among the least of general Procter's mortifications, to find that he has been baffled by a youth, who has just passed his twenty-first year.   He is however a hero worthy of his gallant uncle, general George R. Clarke."

"Captain Hunter of the 17th regiment, the second in command, conducted himself with great propriety; and never was there a set of finer young fellows than the subalterns, viz. lieutenants Johnson and Baylor of the 17th, Anthony of the 24th, Meeks of the 7th, and ensigns Shipp and Duncan of the 17th."

Lieutenant Anderson of the 24th was also noticed for his good conduct.   Being without a command, he solicited major Croghan for a musket and a post to fight at. which he did with the greatest bravery.

"Too much praise," says major Croghan, " cannot be bestowed on the officers, noncommissioned officers, and privates under my command for their gallantry and good conduct during the siege."

The brevet rank of lieutenant colonel was immediately conferred on major Croghan by the president of the United States, for his gallant conduct on this occasion. The ladies of Chillicothe also presented him an elegant sword, accompanied by a suitable address.

Among the scouts sent down the bay, after the enemy had retreated, was a little party of Wyandot Indians, who surprised and captured a few British soldiers, who had been left behind in the retreat. The Indians brought them to camp, without doing them any injury; and conscious that they had done their duty, they were frequently seen telling the story to their brother warriors, and laughing at the terror which had been manifested by the soldiers, who no doubt expected to be massacred or carried off and destroyed by torture. But the Indians who followed the American standard had not, like those in the British service, been encouraged to commit the most horrible barbarities.

This second invasion of Ohio like the former, brought the patriotism of that state into action. As soon as governor Meigs received certain information, that the enemy had entered his territories, he issued his orders in which he called on the militia to rise en masse and repel the invaders. The division lately commanded by general M'Arthur literally obeyed the call. Every man prepared himself to march against the enemy; and through the state generally the greatest military ardor and activity prevailed. It was supposed that at least ten thousand men were under arms and marching to the frontiers. The enemy however did not wait for their arrival. The foremost corps of mounted volunteers was not able to reach head quarters, before general Procter had rendered their services unnecessary by his precipitate flight from Lower Sandusky. It then became necessary, as in the former case, to disband them again, without their having an opportunity to fight; which again produced much discontent and chagrin among them. Many of them were even highly exasperated against the general, for not retaining and employing them efficiently against the enemy.

They had volunteered not only with the expectation of being opposed to the invaders of their state, but also of being employed in the main expedition against Upper Canada, which it was now evident would soon be carried into execution. When a considerable number of them had arrived at Upper Sandusky, and the retreat of the enemy was known, governor Meigs addressed a letter to general Harrison, respecting the course to be pursued with them. The general immediately repaired to that place for the purpose of explaining his situation and views to the governor, and reconciling the volunteers to the measures he would be obliged to adopt. After a personal interview with the governor, he committed his explanations to writing, on the 6th of August, which he addressed to that officer, as follows :

'Your excellency's letter of the 4th inst. was handed to me yesterday morning by colonel Brush. The exertions which you have made, and the promptitude with which your orders have been obeyed, to assemble the militia to repel the late invasion, is truly astonishing and reflects the highest honor on the state. Believing that in a personal interview, I could best explain to you the intentions of the government and my own views, I determined to come to this place to see you. I now have the honor to repeat to you in this way, the result of my determination on the employment of the militia, and most of the facts on which my determination is founded. It has been the intention of government, to form the army destined for operations on lake Erie, exclusively of regular troops, if they could be raised. The number was limited to 7000. The deficiency of regulars was to be made up from the militia. From all the information I at present possess, I am convinced there will be a great deficiency in the contemplated number of troops, even after the militia now in service, and whose time of service will not expire immediately, have been added to the regulars. I have therefore called on the governor of Kentucky for two thousand effective men. With those there will still be a deficiency of about 1200. Your excellency has stated to me, that the men who have turned out on this occasion, have done it with the expectation of being effectually employed, and that should they be sent home, there is no prospect of getting them to turn out hereafter should it be necessary. To employ them all is impossible. With my utmost exertions, the embarkation cannot be effected in less than 15 or

18 days, should I even determine to substitute them for the regular troops which are expected. To keep so large a force in the field, even for a short period, would consume the means which are provided for the support of the campaign, and which are only provided for the number above stated. Under these circumstances, I would recommend a middle course to your excellency, viz. to dismiss all the militia but two regiments of ten companies, each of 100 men, and the usual proportion of field, platoon, and noncommissioned officers &c. that the corps be encamped at or near this place, until it is ascertained whether their services will be wanted. A short time will determine the question. Permit me to request your excellency to give your countenance and support to the exertions which general M'Arthur will make to fill the 26th regiment of 12 months troops. It appears that the venerable governor of Kentucky is about to take command of the troops of that state. Could your excellency think proper to follow his example, I need not tell you how highly grateful it would be, dear sir, to your friend,

'W. H. HARRISON.'

Governor Meigs soon afterwards proceeded to disband the volunteers from his state, very much to their displeasure and mortification. They believed that their services were slighted, and that general Harrison intended to stigmatize them as unfit to be led against the enemy. His explanations were deemed unsatisfactory; and persons inimical to him, were ready to encourage the popular discontent, by misrepresenting his motives in this case, and his conduct in relation to the affair at Lower Sandusky. A considerable number of the disbanded officers met together and entered into sundry resolutions, in which they depreciated his military talents, and declared that they never would repair to his standard again. The publication of these resolves, produced an explanatory letter from major Croghan, in which he contradicted the misrepresentations which had been made, and declared his high respect for the general and confidence in his military talents. A meeting of the general and field officers of the regular troops at Seneca was also held, and a public address prepared by them, in which they declared their confidence in the general, and their entire approbation of his conduct;

and that his late plans and movements had been taken
with the advice of all the general and field officers under his command. The public confidence in the general, so necessary to the commander of militia troops,
was thus preserved at a critical moment, against the
attacks of those who were discontented and inimical to
his fame. The retained regiments of the Ohio volunteers were encamped at Upper Sandusky, but governor
Meigs did not think proper under all the circumstances
of the case to continue to command them in person.

General Harrison returned again to Seneca, to superintend the arrangements for the expedition against
Upper Canada. On the 9th of August at Lower Sandusky, a British boat was discovered coming up the
river with a flag. When it landed below the fort, captain Hunter was sent to meet the commander, who
proved to be lieutenant Le Breton, accompanied by
doctor Banner, with a letter from general Procter to
the commandant at Lower Sandusky, their object being
to ascertain the situation of the British wounded and
afford them surgical aid. Captain Hunter invited them
to the fort. Le Breton seemed to hesitate as if he expected first to be blindfolded, as usual in such cases;
but captain Hunter told him to come on, that there was
nothing in the fort which there was any occasion to
conceal; and when he introduced him to major Croghan
as the commandant of the fort, he appeared to be astonished at the youthful appearance of the hero, who had
defeated the combined forces of his master.

As the letter of general Procter also contained a
proposition for the paroling of those prisoners, who
might be in a condition to be removed, the flag was sent
by major Croghan to head quarters at Seneca. General Harrison replied to the letter of Procter, that "major Croghan conformably to those principles which are
held sacred in the American army, had caused all possible care to be taken of the wounded prisoners, that
his situation would admit—that every aid which sur-

gical skill could give was afforded," and that he had
already referred the disposal of the prisoners to his
government and must wait for their determination.
Doctor Banner in the mean time had examined the
situation of the wounded, and was highly gratified with
the humane treatment they had received. He informed
major Croghan that the Indians were highly incensed
at the failure of the late expedition, and were kept
together with the utmost difficulty.

The principal object of our attention will now be
the preparations for the expedition against Malden.
The progress of the naval preparations had been very
slow—the building of the fleet was not completed, till
a much later period than that originally fixed by the
war department; and after its completion, still farther
delay was caused by the want of seamen. Yet after
all this delay on the part of the fleet, the regular forces
enlisted for the expedition, were very far short of the
calculations made at the war office. The whole regular force of the northwestern army in July, did not
much exceed two thousand men; and it was not until
the 20th of that month, that general Harrison was
authorized by the government, to make his call on the
adjoining states, for the militia necessary to complete
the intended army. On that day at Lower Sandusky,
he received a letter from the secretary of war, informing him that commodore Perry was instructed to communicate with him, respecting naval movements and co-
operation, and that he was authorized to take of the
militia, what in his judgment would be necessary. He
then immediately addressed the following letter to the
governor of Kentucky.

'My dear Sir—I have this moment received a letter from
the secretary of war, in which he authorizes me to call from the
neighboring states, such number of militia as I may deem requisite for the ensuing operations against Upper Canada. It
was originally intended that the army should consist of regular
troops only; but it is now ascertained that the contemplated

number cannot be raised. It is indeed late—very late—to call out militia; but still it will be better to do this, than to enter upon operations on which so much depends with inadequate forces. I am not uninformed, as to the difficulties your excellency may have to encounter to organize another detachment of militia. I believe however it will not be impossible for you to reanimate your patriotic fellow citizens, and once more to bring a portion of them into the field. What that portion will be, your own judgment must determine. I have sent major Trimble my aid de camp, to inform you of many circumstances which I have not time, nor indeed would I like to commit to paper. Send me as many good men as you can conveniently collect, or as you may deem proper to call out—not less than 400 nor more than 2000. The period has arrived, when with a little exertion, the task assigned to this section of the Union may be finished and complete tranquillity restored to our frontiers.

' To make this last effort, why not my dear sir, come in person ? You would not object to a command, that would be nominal only. I have such confidence in your wisdom, that you in fact should " be the guiding head, and I the hand." The situation you would be placed in, would not be without its parallel. Scipio the conqueror of Carthage, did not disdain to act as the lieutenant of his younger and less experienced brother Lucius. I refer you to major Trimble who is instructed to communicate many particulars to you.'

This letter was delivered to governor Shelby on the 30th of July by major Trimble, who farther detailed the plans of general Harrison to the governor; and stated that the general would expect 1500 men from Kentucky at least, if that number could be furnished conveniently by the state. Governor Shelby proceeded without delay to make arrangements for raising the men; and being confident that the delays necessarily attendant on a draft, and on the marching of foot troops so great a distance, would prevent a drafted corps of that description from reaching head quarters in time, he determined on his own responsibility to rely on raising the necessary number of mounted volunteers. Neither the government nor the general had intended to employ this kind of troops; but the experienced governor of Kentucky well knew, that no other species of force could be raised and marched from his state with sufficient promptitude to answer the purpose; and he knew that a great many of his fellow citizens were anxious for an opportunity to proceed in this manner against their inveterate and merciless enemies. With a degree of energy and decision characteristic of his whole life, he therefore immediately appealed to the patriotism of his fellow citizens to join him in an expedition of this kind. The following circulars, addressed to individuals of military pretensions and popularity, and to the militia of the state, were published on the next day :

' Frankfort, July 31st, 1813.

' DEAR SIR—The following address to the militia of Kentucky will inform you of the call that has been made upon the governor of Kentucky for a reinforcement to the northwestern army; and of my views as to the mode of complying with it. I forward one to you particularly, sir, under the hope that you will exert your influence to bring into the field all the men in your power. Be so good as to acknowledge the receipt of this letter, and apprize me of the calculations which I may make of the number of men that can be raised in your county—and whether it will suit your convenience to go with us. I shall at all times take a pleasure in acknowledging the public spirit by which you will be actuated—and the obligations you will lay me under.

' I have the honor to be, very respectfully, sir,
' Your obt. servant,
' ISAAC SHELBY.

' COLONEL A.— Z.—'

' TO THE MILITIA OF KENTUCKY.

' FELLOW SOLDIERS—Your government has taken measures to act effectually against the enemy in Upper Canada. General Harrison, under the authority of the president of the United States, has called upon me for a strong body of troops to assist in effecting the grand objects of the campaign. The enemy in hopes to find us unprepared, has again invested fort Meigs; but he will again be mistaken; and before you can take the field he will be driven from that post.

' To comply with the requisition of general Harrison, a draft might be enforced; but believing as I do, that the ardor and patriotism of my countrymen has not abated, and that they have waited with impatience a fair opportunity of avenging the blood of their butchered friends, I have appointed the 31st day of August next, at Newport, for a general rendezvous of KEN-

TUCKY VOLUNTEERS. I will meet you there in person. I will lead you to the field of battle, and share with you the dangers and honors of the campaign. Our services will not be required more than sixty days after we reach head quarters.

'I invite all officers, and others possessing influence, to come forward with what mounted men they can raise: each shall command the men he may bring into the field. The superior officers will be appointed by myself at the place of general rendezvous, or on our arrival at head quarters: and I shall take pleasure in acknowledging to my country the merits and public spirit of those who may be useful in collecting a force for the present emergency.

'Those who have good rifles, and know how to use them, will bring them along. Those who have not, will be furnished with muskets at Newport.

'*Fellow Citizens!* Now is the time to act; and by one decisive blow, put an end to the contest in that quarter.

'ISAAC SHELBY.

'*Frankfort, July 31st, 1813.*'

The reader will observe, that the governor cautiously avoids calling for any specific number of men, or even hinting what force was required by general Harrison. He was well convinced that the number wanted would rally at his call, and he did not wish to let the enemy have a chance to know what force he was about to bring into the field against them.

Colonel Johnson's regiment was also ordered to return to the northwestern service. He had scarcely reached Kentucky, before general Harrison had been authorized to recall him, by a letter from the war department; in which the secretary expressed his regret, that the order for his march had ever reached general Harrison; and that the latter, knowing the impropriety of the order, had not on that ground delayed its execution. An express was immediately sent after the regiment, but was unable to overtake it, before the men had dispersed and proceeded to their respective homes. Colonel Johnson then ordered his regiment to rendezvous again at the Great Crossings on the 15th, and at Newport on the 17th of August. The officers were particularly requested to make every exertion to march

2 U

complete companies, by recruiting volunteers to serve
sixty days after the 20th of August, or ninety days if
required.   Their exertions were attended with the
most complete success—the companies were not only
filled, even beyond the limit of the law, but in many
instances more offered their services than the officers
deemed it prudent to accept.   The zeal and abilities
of colonel Johnson, together with his unremitting attention to the interests of his men, inspired his fellow
citizens with confidence in him as a military leader,
and securing the universal esteem of his troops, united
them as a band of brothers in the common cause.

But such was now the ardor of the Kentuckians, at
the flattering prospect of finishing the war in the northwest, that the filling of one regiment was but a very
small part of the forces they were ready to furnish.
The address of the governor, like an electric spark, set
fire to all the combustible spirits of the state, and with
one consent they were heard to say—come, let us rally
round the eagle of our country, for *old King's mountain*
will certainly lead us to victory and conquest.   Men
of influenc in every part of the state came forward,
and were generally followed by most of their neighbors
who could make it convenient to leave their homes.

With a view to apprize the government of the measures he had taken, and to secure their approbation of
his course, the governor on the 1st of August, addressed
a letter to the war department, from which the following is an extract.   " Much delay would have been the
inevitable consequence of ordering out the militia in the
ordinary mode of draft.   As mounted volunteers, a
competent force can, I feel confident, be easily raised.
I have therefore appointed the 31st of this month, at
Newport in this state, for a general rendezvous of
mounted volunteers.   I have the honor of enclosing for
the information of the president, a copy of my address
to the militia of this state on the occasion.   The prospect of acting effectually against Upper Canada will,

I have no doubt, call forth a large force to our stand-ard, and they will be immediately marched to the head quarters of the northwestern army, in such bodies as will most facilitate their movements.   When there they can act as footmen, or mounted, as circumstances may require.   I shall take great pleasure to hear from the president on this subject, previous to my departure from this place, and I request the favor of you to lay this letter immediately before him for his consideration, and that you will be pleased to apprize me of the result by the earliest conveyance."

The following are extracts of letters from the gov-ernor to general Harrison. On the 2nd of August, after stating the measures he had taken, he proceeds " I need not observe to you, how important it will be to have rations and forage provided on the way. It will be impossible to move on without the latter. In-deed a supply must be laid in, at Georgetown in this state. Men who travel from the southern parts of it, will require both rations and forage at that place to en-able them to proceed. I beg you may attend to this subject, and let me know what is to be expected. Seeing that you cannot be reinforced in any other way, the government must not stickle at the trifling expense of a little forage, to obtain an efficient force for the main objects of the campaign.—No apology was neces-sary to invite me to your standard. Had I more age and much greater experience, I would not hesitate to fight under your banner, for the honor and interest of my beloved country."

August 8.—"I have received information from various parts of the state, that the volunteer scheme will suc-ceed ; but it is impossible to speak with any kind of cer-tainty at so early a stage of the business. I flatter myself, that I shall be able to bring into the field from two to three thousand or upwards. My present view is, that all these men will ride to the margin of the lake, and if they cross over, leave about one tenth to bring the

horses back some distance, and herd them in parcels
in the best range, until the campaign expires. Many
of the volunteers, that will compose this corps, will be
gentlemen: who care less about emoluments than their
own ease and convenience, and must have their horses
taken care of, to ride home again. A great proportion
of the volunteers will come from the southwestern part
of the state, who will have to travel from two to three
hundred miles, before they arrive at the point of rendezvous. Many of them too, will be poor men, who
will not be able to proceed, unless forage and rations
are both supplied. Indeed I shall expect, that forage
will be directed to be furnished at Georgetown in this
state. Horses will otherwise become so weak, that it
will be impossible for them to proceed farther.

"Your aid de camp, major Trimble, has stated that
you would not guarantee the pay of more than 2000
men, but would accept the services of a much larger
number. Were I to make this public, I am confident
it would damp the ardor of the volunteers. Even gentlemen of fortune, of whom there are many that will go
in the ranks, could not with any confidence encourage
their poorer neighbors, to hazard their lives and lose
their time for nothing. It is at any rate a great sacrifice, for a citizen of Kentucky to make for the mere pay
of a common soldier for the service of himself and horse.
I hope you will reflect on this subject and authorize
payment for all that go, at least for 4000 men, should
that many turn out: for I shall otherwise not be able
to draw the distinction between those that will be entitled to receive pay and those that will not."

These extracts exhibit the solicitude of governor
Shelby to raise a force sufficient to give a decisive
blow, and to take care that such a force should be received into service, and should not be disappointed and
defeated by the want of accommodations on their way.

To these letters general Harrison replied on the 18th
of August at Seneca, that "every arrangement has

been made for the proper accommodation of the volunteers agreeably to your suggestion. I am so well persuaded that the government will approbate the measure of receiving the men, whom you may bring with you above the contemplated 2000, that I will not hesitate to say that I will accept them. Every thing is in a fair train for the commencement of operations on your arrival. Our fleet is now off Sandusky bay. I shall go down to it to morrow morning, and take with me 70 men to act as marines. I wish the commodore to go immediately to Malden, and endeavor to bring the enemy to action. Colonel Bartlett says, that you shall have forage.—

"I have been much disappointed in the number of regular troops. However we are daily adding a little to them. The Pennsylvania regiment of militia, which were stationed at Erie, and which were to have joined me, have refused to march. This circumstance has determined me to accept your surplusage. I am determined not to have it believed again, that I am at the head of an army, when I have only the amount of a regiment, as was the case lately."

When the war department authorized general Harrison to proceed in completing his army from the militia, he was informed that the regiment stationed at Erie was placed under his command; but when he called upon them, they declined the service. Some of them volunteered to go in the fleet, and "The rest," says the general in a letter to the war department, "have resolved that they will come on to join this army as ordered, provided they get two months pay before hand." However, like the disobedient son, in the parable, they afterwards repented and came, bringing with them the boats from Cleveland to Sandusky bay for the embarkation of the other troops.

Major Trimble having arrived at head quarters from Kentucky, addressed a letter to governor Shelby on the 18th, in which he says—"Every thing here looks like invasion, and you may rely on seeing the Canada shore soon after you arrive. Should Kentucky fail to do her duty at this time, she will be damned for ever. She will have to hide her head, and pray for the mountains to fall upon her and cover her." The major was a Kentuckian, and the sentiment here expressed was common to his patriotic fellow citizens. They were determined in this last effort, to sustain the reputation of their state, and to inflict a signal punishment on the enemy, by whose barbarities they had suffered so much.

We must now turn our attention to the naval affairs on the lake, which at an early period this year claimed the attention of both governments. The British however had already the command of the lake, being in possession of a considerable fleet on its bosom; whilst the Americans had not a single armed vessel above the falls of Niagara. Great industry and exertion were hence necessary on our part, to enable us to meet the enemy on equal terms in the present campaign. With this view, workmen were employed and the keels of two brigs and several schooners were laid early in March at Erie, to which place commodore Perry as we have noticed already, was sent to superintend their construction and equipment. There was abundance of timber convenient; but every other article had to be transported from other places, mostly from Pittsburgh and Philadelphia; and such were the difficulties which had to be encountered, that the progress in fitting out the fleet, did not keep pace with the expectations formed by the government. One regiment of militia and a few regulars were employed for the protection of the workmen and the vessels they were building. No attempt however was made to molest them, till the 20th of July, when the undertaking was nearly completed. The enemy had this season built a 20 gun brig at Malden, and with this addition to their force, they probably deemed their naval superiority so decided, as to be

careless about the progress of our labors; or perhaps
it was their policy to let us spend our time and labor
in the completion of our vessels, before they paid them
a destroying visit. The manner in which they conducted the campaign however, appears to us reprehensible. Had general Procter proceeded with his regulars, militia, and Indians, supported by a train of heavy
artillery, against our preparations at Erie, instead of
wasting his time and strength in vain attempts on fort
Meigs, he might have done us much greater injury,
and perhaps have defeated us in the present campaign,
by preventing the erection of a navy competent to the
command of the lake. If he had only destroyed the
boats prepared at Cleveland, he would have caused us
more serious difficulties than any we experienced from
his formidable invasions. But it has been stated,
that his Indians were not disposed to leave *terra
firma*, and hazard themselves in a cruise so far down
the lake.

However about the 20th of July, while the land forces were sent on a *demonstration* against fort Meigs,
the larger vessels of their fleet proceeded down the lake
to *reconnoitre* at Erie; in sight of which they remained
two or three days, apparently threatening, and perhaps
really intending, to attack the place; but without having made an attempt, they at last stretched over the
lake towards Long Point. Their menace excited a
considerable bustle and alarm at Erie, lest the vessels
in their present advanced state should be destroyed,
and the flattering prospects of the campaign be thus
blasted. Major general Meade who commanded the
militia of the adjacent country, immediately issued an
order to the contiguous brigade of his division, to repair
en masse to Erie for the protection of the fleet. The
order was promptly obeyed, and in a few days upwards
of fifteen hundred men were assembled at the place
appointed. Captain Perry in the mean time, in order
to amuse the enemy, had sent out two of his gun boats,

which gave them a few shot; but they kept at so great a distance that no damage was done.

Commodore Perry now redoubled his exertions to finish his equipments, which he at last completed about the 2nd of August, and on the two following days succeeded in getting his heaviest vessels over the bar at the mouth of the harbor. The water being but 6 or 7 feet deep, it was necessary to buoy them up with his light vessels and scows; all of which was accomplished in the face of the enemy, who had returned in his fleet on the evening of the 3rd, and remained in sight all the next day, but without offering any molestation to the progress of this work. As soon as our fleet was completely over the bar, the enemy again left us and sailed towards Long Point. A sufficient number of sailors not having yet arrived to man our vessels, the commodore now proposed to receive volunteers for 48 hours from the Pennsylvania militia, and a sufficient number accepted his invitation to enable him to sail next morning in pursuit of the enemy. He crossed the lake to Long Point, and then proceeded up the British shore some distance without discovering their fleet, which had in fact returned to Malden, for their new brig and other reinforcements, on discovering the force which Perry was able to bring against them. Our fleet then returned to Erie, to discharge the militia volunteers, that were on board, and supply their place with sailors. In the mean time general Meade had discharged all the militia, who had come forward at his call, to meet the menaced descent of the British. The fleet being equipped for action, and able to give the enemy chase, their services were no longer required in the field of Mars, but were much needed in their harvest fields at home.

Lieutenant Elliott was bringing about ninety sailors, from the fleet under commodore Chauncey on lake Ontario, to man the fleet on Erie. Boats were sent down the lake to meet them, which brought them up in safety, and enabled our commodore to spread his canvass again, and proceed up the lake. He arrived off Sandusky bay on the 5th, and captain Richardson, who had been sent by the general to Erie, and had now returned in the fleet, came out immediately to head quarters to announce its arrival and request a company of soldiers to act as marines. General Harrison accompanied by several other officers went down to the fleet, taking with him a company, commanded by captain Stockton, of the 28th regiment of 12 months regulars under colonel Owings from Kentucky, including all the seamen that could be found in the army; and also about 20 volunteers under lieutenant Coburn from Payne's company of Johnson's regiment. The Kentuckians, some of whom had probably never seen a ship before, relying on their skill to shoot, were thus ready to meet the enemy on any element, however novel the intended enterprise might be to them. In the consultation between the land and naval commanders, it was agreed that the commodore should proceed immediately off Malden, to brave the enemy's fleet, and if possible bring them to action, before he should take our troops on board to transport them over the lake. It was apprehended however that the enemy would be prudent enough to decline the contest, until our fleet was encumbered with our land forces.

As soon as our commodore had displayed his canvass before Malden, a considerable bustle took place on board the British fleet, but no attempt was made to come out and engage him, although he did not fail to challenge them to the combat. Finding that they did not intend to fight, he sent the Ariel as near them as she could proceed with safety, to examine them more narrowly. Their new brig, which they called the Detroit, was launched; and the two fleets were apparently of equal force. The British however had the superiority—their vessels were larger than ours, were better manned, and carried a greater number of guns,

The following were the vessels, and number of guns in each fleet.

American.	guns.		British.	guns.		
Brig Lawrence	20		Ship Detroit	19,	& 2 hwt's.	
Niagara	20		Q. Charlotte	17,	& 1 do.	
Caledonia	3		Scr. Lady Prevost	13,	& 1 do.	
Schr. Ariel	4	(1 burst.)	Brig Hunter	10		
Scorpion	2		Sloop Little Belt	3		
Somers	2 & 2 swvls.		Schr. Chippeway	1	& 2 swvls.	
Tigress	1					
Porcupine	1		Total	63	4 hs.	2 s.
Sloop Trippe	1		American	54	0	2
Total	54 2 swivels		Superiority	9	4	0

The commodore did not remain long off Malden, but finding the enemy not inclined to meet him, returned to Put-in Bay in Bass island, where we shall leave him a few days, to watch the sailing of the British fleet under commodore Barclay, whilst we notice some other occurrences.

General Harrison having learnt that much dissatisfaction prevailed among the British Indians, since the repulse of the allies at Lower Sandusky, determined to make use of means to detach them completely if possible from the British cause. He sent some friendly Wyandot chiefs, in whom he had confidence, to confer with the warriors of their tribe, who had joined the British under Walk-in-the-water, and also with the other hostile tribes in general, with a view to negociate a peace and reconcile them to a neutral course in the approaching contest. When these commissioners arrived at Brownstown, information of their business was immediately communicated to Elliott, and they were obliged to deliver their talk, which should have been addressed to the Wyandots alone, to a general council of all the hostile chiefs, at which Elliott and M'Kee were present. They were answered by Round Head, who was entirely in the British interest, and who spoke what Elliott pleased to dictate. A private message

however was sent by Walk-in-the-water, that he would
use his best exertions to detach the Indians from the
British, and that he had determined not to fight us, but
on the advance of our army to seize the Huron church
at Sandwich, with all the warriors he could engage to
assist him, and defend himself there against the British
and their adherents.   The general was thus convinced,
that no material defection was to be expected among
the allies of the British.

General M'Arthur was sent about this time, to take
the command at fort Meigs, with instructions to draw
in the pickets and construct a fortification on a smaller
scale, and to make arrangements for embarking the
heavy artillery with such military stores as might be
found necessary.

The mounted regiment under colonel Johnson, assembled in pursuance of his orders at the places appointed for their rendezvous, bringing with them a great
accession of strength in new recruits.   Every company
in the regiment had more than its legal complement of
men.   Captain M'Afee had 152, including officers and
privates; captains Combs and Davidson had each upwards of 130.   The colonel received orders from general Harrison, to march immediately to the frontiers, for
the purpose of escorting provisions from the posts on
the St. Marys and Auglaize to fort Meigs, preparatory
to the embarkation of the troops for the main expedition.   The regiment marched by companies, and on the
20th arrived at Dayton, where the colonel received
information, that the Indians had recently killed two
men and a woman, some distance within the frontiers
near Piqua, and that the citizens much alarmed and
enraged, had assembled in considerable number, with
a determination to take revenge on the friendly Shawanese and Delawares, residing near that place, whom
they accused of committing the murders.   Colonel
Johnson immediately pushed forward in advance of the
regiment with captain Coleman's company, and on

arriving at Piqua was informed by John Johnson esq.
the Indian agent, that he had called on the chiefs for
an explanation, and had been assured by them with
much candor and promptitude, that the British were
attempting to embroil them with their white brethren,
by sending hostile Indians to commit depredations in
their vicinity, in the expectation that the whites would
charge it to them. Two murders had also been committed near Manary's blockhouse, and the Shawanese
at Wopoghconata had informed the agent, that a hostile
party had previously passed that place, by whom it
was evident the murders must have been committed.
It was with great difficulty however that the citizens
could be pacified. The circumstances being made
known to general Harrison, he published an address
to the frontier inhabitants, assuring them that he had
received satisfactory evidence that the murders were
committed by the hostile Indians, and entreating the
people not to take redress into their own hands, but to
rely on the government which would certainly inflict
exemplary punishment for any aggressions committed
by the friendly Indians. This address with the arrival
of the mounted regiment quieted the minds of the people, and reconciled them to trust for safety and satisfaction to the army and the government.

As the means for transportation were not yet in readiness, the regiment was separated into several detachments, and stationed at different posts, where the companies were all diligently drilled under the superintendence of the field officers. Much credit is due to
lieutenant colonel James Johnson for the ability and
diligence with which he attended on all occasions to
the training of his men. To him they were greatly
indebted for that proficiency in the knowledge of their
duties, which rendered them terrible to the enemy in
the day of battle. The good conduct and ardor of the
troops were also much promoted, by the practice of
addressing them publicly on their duties, which was

pursued by the colonel and some other officers, who were possessed of talents for extemporary speaking. Colonel Johnson had taken particular care at all times, to have his men completely familiarized with an appropriate order of battle. In his orders of this description, he provided for two very important matters in Indian fighting—for outflanking the enemy, and for charging through their lines and forming in their rear. The following are extracts on these points. "The balance of the two columns, *(in the order of march)* viz. captains Matson and Ellison, shall join and extend the line of battle, on the right and in line with captain M'Afee; and the right flank *(in the order of march)* on the same principle shall extend the line of battle by filing to the right, with positive orders on each flank to outflank the enemy, captain Craig's company remaining on horseback until he turns his flank and gets in his rear: and so of the left column and left flank, captain Combs extending the line of battle on the left, and captain Rice uniting with him, but being on the extreme left, he shall not dismount until he outflanks and gains the rear of the enemy." In an order of the 3rd of September, he directs, that "captain Warfield will march on the right of captain Ellison, and form with him a column of double files. Captain Rice will march on the left of captain Combs, and captain Hamilton on the right of captain Coleman, each forming a line of double files. These double lines are to form the charging column, and are to charge through the line of the enemy, and form in their rear, by wheeling to the right and left, at a moment when a general and exhausted fire of the enemy may render it practicable. But should a general retreat of the enemy render this impossible, each column will display to the right and left, and fall upon the flanks of the enemy. Major Payne will lead the right column; major Thompson the left; and the colonels the centre. The charging columns are to act principally on horseback."

These orders were much approved in the regiment, as
being well adapted for Indian fighting: for in contending with savages, the only chance to save the men,
is to make a bold dash at the enemy in the beginning,
and never turn your back upon them afterwards.   To
stand and fight them in regular order, only exposes the
men and hazards the victory; for in such a case, they
will kill two to one of the best marksmen that can be
opposed to them.   The best method, is to outflank
them, rush upon them, drive them from their lurking
places, and pursue them closely.

About the 1st of September, the troops were enabled
to proceed in the business of transportation, about 30
wagons, and a brigade of packhorses, having arrived
for that purpose.   The greater part of the regiment
had arrived at fort Winchester on the 9th of September, a day which had been appointed by the president
at the request of congress, as a day of fasting, humilia-
tion, and prayer.   Those who chose to observe it in
that manner, were encouraged to do so; and although
there is in general but little religion to be found in an
army, yet on the evening of this day, a number of little
parties were seen in different parts of the lines, paying
their devotions to the God of armies, and chanting his
praises with plainness, sincerity, and zeal; whilst their
less pious, but moral and orderly compatriots, preserved around them, the strictest order and decorum.   A
pleasing tranquillity pervaded the ranks, and the patriot soldier seemed to feel a cheering confidence, that
the God of battles would shield him in the hour of
danger.   The author of this history could not but feel
a kind of pious zeal, approaching a complete reliance,
that the special protection of heaven would be enjoyed
by the American army, while nobly fighting in the
cause of justice and humanity.   Such were the harmony
and good order constantly prevailing in this regiment,
and such the mutual confidence and good will between
the officers and men, that there is scarcely an individual

among them, who does not look back to those days as
the happiest of his life, and who did not love and respect his commandant as an elder brother.

The next day, the 10th of September—an important
and memorable day in the present campaign—was
spent by the regiment in training, and in fighting sham
battles, the exact miniature of that, which they were
soon to fight in reality. A line of infantry was formed,
and the horses were practised to charge through it at
full speed; and such was the tractability and the force
of custom in this noble animal, that in a little time
there was scarcely a horse in the regiment, that would
flinch at a line of infantry enveloped in a blaze of fire
and smoke. Those who are unacquainted with the
docility of this animal, would scarcely believe, that he
could be brought to have so much contempt for danger,
to understand so well the different sounds of the trumpet, and seemingly to participate in the sentiments and
views of his rider. The beautiful description of the
horse, which is given in holy writ, was fully verified
in our trainings. " He paweth in the valley, and re-
joiceth in his strength : he goeth on to meet the armed
men. He mocketh at fear, and is not affrighted ; neither turneth he back from the sword. The quiver rat-
tleth against him, and the glittering spear, and the
shield. He swalloweth the ground with fierceness
and rage ; neither believeth he that it is the sound of
the trumpet."

A few days afterwards the regiment proceeded towards the Rapids, using the precaution to march in a
body, as several straggling parties of Indians had lately
been discovered, and it was known that Tecumseh had
a considerable mounted force, with which it was probable he might attempt some enterprise in that quarter
of the country.

Governor Shelby was also now advancing towards
the frontiers with a strong corps of mounted volunteers.
Early in August he had selected general John Adair

of Mercer, for his first aid—a gentleman whose mili
tary talents were universally acknowledged and respected. In the latter part of the month instructions
were issued for all officers commanding volunteer corps,
to draw arms and ammunition on their arrival at Newport, and then proceed towards the head quarters of
the northwestern army by slow marches; and major
George Walker was despatched in the capacity of brigade major and quarter master to superintend the business at Newport. On the 1st of September, about
three thousand five hundred men, all sturdy Kentuckians, had crossed the Ohio, with their venerable governor at their head, like an ancient oak, still green,
strong, and majestic; for although he had now reached
the 63rd year of his age, yet the vigor of his person,
and the decisive energy of his mind, were such as are
rarely found in those, who have numbered half his
years.

The arsenal at Newport was drained of all the arms
fit for use, and still there was a deficiency of 7 or 800.
The governor immediately wrote to general Harrison
advising him of this circumstance. "I have ordered
(he continues) all my forces to concentrate at Springfield, where I shall halt a day or two for some ammunition and hospital stores, and endeavor to organize the
army, after which not a moment shall be lost till we
join you. We are about 3500 strong, as near as I can
at present judge, and all mounted. In a letter I had
the honor to address you before I left Frankfort, I
took the liberty to recommend the calling on governor
Meigs for an additional force of his militia, to enable
you to make a sure stroke on the enemy. I am still of
the same opinion; for although you may be restricted
to a particular number, to make the descent into Canada,
you ought to put nothing to hazard. Should you even
transcend your powers, if we are fortunate your country will approve the measure, and if otherwise, she
cannot complain. I shall be sorry to see any attempt
made to invade the enemy's country, until we are pre-

pared to hold every inch of ground that we may conquer. I shall be highly gratified to hear from you on my march, and to be apprized of so much of your views, as it may be proper and safe to communicate."— *Shelby.*

The organization was not entirely completed at Springfield; forage being scarce, it became necessary to move on towards Urbana, to which place major Walker, and colonel Joseph M'Dowell, were sent in advance to make preparations, the former being appointed quarter master general, with the rank of colonel, and the latter adjutant general with the same rank. At Urbana the organization was completed. The troops were formed into 11 regiments, to be commanded by colonels Trotter, Donaldson, Poague, Montjoy, Rennick, Davenport, Taul, Calloway, Simrall, Barbour, and Williams. Out of these regiments five brigades were formed, to be commanded by brigadier generals Calmes, Chiles, King, Allen, and Caldwell. three of these brigades formed a division under major general William Henry; the other two formed a division under major general Joseph Desha. John Crittenden esq. was appointed 2nd aid to the governor; W. T. Barry esq. secretary; and Thomas T. Barr esq. judge advocate general. Each commandant of a regiment appointed his own staff and surgeons, and the office of hospital surgeon was given by the governor to doctor A. J. Mitchell.

About the 9th of September the volunteers marched from Urbana, and on the 12th arrived at Upper Sandusky, where Tahe, the ancient Wyandot chief, was introduced to governor Shelby: he had expressed a great desire to see the governor of Kentucky. The following letter from general Harrison was received at this place.

' *Head Quarters, Seneca, 12th September,* 1813.

' You will find arms at Upper Sandusky; also a considerable quantity at Lower Sandusky. I set out from this place in an

2 W

hour. Our fleet has beyond all doubt met that of the enemy. The day before yesterday an incessant and tremendous cannonading was heard in the direction of Malden by a detachment of troops coming from fort Meigs. It lasted two hours. I am all anxiety for the event. There will be no occasion for your halting here. Lower Sandusky affords fine grazing. With respect to a station for your horses, there is the best in the world immediately at the place of embarkation. The Sandusky bay, lake Erie, and Portage river form between them a peninsula, the isthmus of which is only one mile and a half across. A fence of that length, and a sufficient guard left there, would make all the horses of the army safe. It would enclose fifty or sixty thousand acres, in which are many cultivated fields, which having been abandoned, are now grown up with the finest grass. Your sick had better be left at Upper Sandusky or here.

'HARRISON.'

Within half an hour after the above letter was written, the general received the following laconic note from the commodore, by express from Lower Sandusky.

'*U. S. Brig Niagara, off the Western Sister &c.*
'*September 10th, 1813. 4 P. M.*

'DEAR GENERAL—We have met the enemy and they are ours—two ships, two brigs, one schooner and a sloop.

'Yours with great respect and esteem,
'OLIVER HAZARD PERRY.'

This exhilarating news set Lower Sandusky and camp Seneca in an uproar of tumultuous joy. The general immediately proceeded to the former place, and issued his orders for the movement of the troops, and transportation of the provisions, military stores &c. to the margin of the lake, preparatory to their embarkation. An encampment had already been formed there, which was now enlarged and some blockhouses commenced. Governor Shelby on the receipt of the letter from Harrison at Upper Sandusky, had proceeded with his suite in advance of his troops, and met the news of the naval victory at fort Ball; from which place he addressed a hasty note to major general William Henry,

who had been left in command at Upper Sandusky,
informing him of the glorious result on the lake, that
the army would consequently pass into Canada without loss of time, and that he must use his best exertions to reach the point of embarkation as soon as
possible.   General Henry, a veteran of the revolution,
well knew the importance of despatch, and pressed
forward on bad roads, through deep swamps, at the
rate of thirty miles a day, with all the forces until they
arrived at head quarters on the margin of the lake, on
the 15th and 16th of September; at which place the
governor had previously arrived on the 14th, a few
minutes before the fleet had made its appearance, returning from its victorious battle.   On the 15th upwards
of 300 British prisoners were landed from the fleet,
and placed under the care of the infantry.   A few days
afterwards they were escorted by a guard of Kentucky
militia under quarter master Payne to Franklinton and
Chillicothe.

VICTORY ON THE LAKE.   We must now turn our
attention to the particulars of the naval battle.   After
remaining a few days in Put-in-Bay, commodore Perry
had returned in full view of Malden, and offered battle
again to the British fleet, which they again declined;
but they now appeared to be making great exertions to
get ready for a contest.   The commodore then withdrew, and came down the lake off Sandusky bay, in
hopes that the enemy would follow him, or at least
come out on the lake.   While at this station, three
American citizens, who had made their escape from
Detroit, arrived at the fleet in an open boat, from whom
it was ascertained that the enemy had been greatly
straitened for provisions, since our fleet had been on
the lake.   They had previously brought up a considerable portion of their supplies on the lake from Long
Point.   By the same persons the force of the enemy
was stated to be, 800 regulars, 1000 militia, and near
2000 Indians.   On the 5th of September, the commo-

dore informed general Harrison in a letter from Sandusky bay, that his men were suffering very much by
sickness, and that his fleet could not transport more
than 3000 men, with which number he would be so
crowded, as to be unable to use any of his guns. A
few days afterwards he returned to Put-in-Bay to wait
for the sailing of the British fleet.

At sunrise on Friday morning, the 10th of September, the enemy were discovered standing out from
Malden. The American squadron immediately weigh-
ed anchor, and proceeded to meet them. It was the
intention of commodore Barclay, to engage his opponent before he could clear the islands near the head of
the lake; and the wind, being in the southwest, was
favorable to his plan; but before 10 o'clock the American fleet had gained the open lake, between the islands and the mouth of the river Detroit. About the
same time the wind changed to the southeast, and thus
brought the American squadron to the windward. Our
commodore then formed his line of battle, and bore up
against the enemy. An hour of awful suspense ensued.
All hands stood ready, as soon as the winds could
bring the hostile fleets together, to commence the desperate conflict, which was to decide the command of
the upper lakes, and sink or save a British province.
The fleets were new, and traversed a new theatre of
war. The British commodore however, was old in
experience and well advanced in years. He had bled
in the battle of Trafalgar, and had imbibed the naval
tactics of Nelson. The American was young, and had
never heard the thunder of a hostile ship; but skilled
in the theory of naval war, and teeming with the courage and enterprise of an American freeman, he was
ready for the contest with a foe superior in force and
experience.

At 15 minutes before 12, the enemy opened his fire;
but it was not returned for 10 minutes by the American
fleet, which was much inferior in long guns. The bat-

tle then commenced on both sides; but owing to the superiority of the British in long guns, their fire was found to be the most destructive, and being chiefly directed against the Lawrence, the foremost ship, in which the commodore sailed, he was induced to make every exertion to close with the enemy, directing the other vessels to follow his example. In a short time every brace and bowline of the Lawrence was shot away, and she became unmanageable, notwithstanding the great exertions of her sailing master. In this situation she sustained the conflict with the Detroit and Queen Charlotte, upwards of two hours within cannister distance, until every gun was rendered useless, and the greater part of her crew either killed or wounded. The commodore now finding, that she could no longer annoy the enemy, conceived the bold design of leaving her, and passing in an open boat to the Niagara, which the lowness of the wind had long prevented, with the lighter vessels, from coming into close action. At half past 2 the wind increased, and enabled captain Elliott to bring up the Niagara in gallant style. The commodore then consigned the Lawrence to the command of lieutenant Yarnall, whose bravery already displayed was a sure pledge, that he would do every thing in his power for the honor of the flag; and proceeded towards the Niagara, standing erect in an open boat, a fair mark for the musketry of the enemy, within the range of which he had to pass, bearing his flag with the motto " Don't give up the Ship." His men, more careful of his life, pulled him down by force from the dangers of an incessant fire, directed at him by the enemy. When safe on board the Niagara, the remnant of his crew in the Lawrence gave three cheers for joy at his success. He then expressed his fears to captain Elliott, that the victory was lost, by the lighter vessels remaining at so great a distance in the rear. The captain replied, that he hoped not, and immediately tendered his services to bring them up to a position, where they could render more

effectual service.   The Niagara was now at the head
of the lines, and captain Elliott had to proceed on this
service, down the whole line of the enemy, in a small
boat exposed to their incessant fire; yet he accomplished the perilous enterprise uninjured, though completely soaked with the water thrown upon him, by the
balls which struck around him.   He brought up the
remotest gun boats, and placed them under the sterns
of the heaviest vessels of the enemy, where they were
enabled to do much execution.   In the mean time the
commodore in the Niagara, which had been but little
injured, made the signal for close action, and determined to pass through the enemy's line.   He bore up
and run ahead of their two ships and a brig, giving a
raking fire to them from his starboard guns, and to their
large schooner and sloop on the larboard side, at half
pistol shot distance.   By this bold project of breaking
through the line of the enemy, all the guns of the Niagara were brought, at the same moment, to bear on
his vessels in the most effectual manner; and at the
same time the gun boats were brought by captain Elliott,
to pour destruction into the sterns of his large ships,
and the other small vessels to play upon them within
grape and cannister distance.   Such a galling, destructive fire, could not be long sustained by the British—
their two ships, a brig, and a schooner, quickly surrendered.   The sloop and the other schooner attempted
to escape by flight; but the American schooners soon
compelled them to strike.   The whole squadron was
thus captured, not a vessel having escaped to carry the
dismal news to Malden.

Soon after commodore Perry had left the Lawrence,
he had the extreme mortification to see her flag come
down.   But he was perfectly satisfied, that she had
been defended to the last extremity, and that a shew
of farther resistance, would have been a wanton sacrifice of the remains of her brave crew.   The enemy
however were so shattered at that time, that they were

unable to take possession of her, and her brave commander soon hoisted her flag again. Though several times wounded, he refused to quit the deck, and had the satisfaction to see the whole fleet of the enemy surrender, while his flag was flying over the shattered hulk of the Lawrence. Many other instances of individual heroism were displayed—too numerous indeed to be noticed in a general history.

On the evening after the battle, the commodore announced his victory to the secretary of the navy, by the following modest and much admired letter.

'Sir—It has pleased the Almighty to give the arms of the U. States, a signal victory over their enemies on this lake. The British squadron, consisting of two brigs, two ships, one schooner, and one sloop have this moment surrendered to the force under my command, after a sharp conflict.

'PERRY.'

It was indeed a sharp conflict, and even late in the battle the victory was extremely doubtful. During the first two and a half hours, the American squadron fought to a great disadvantage, the action being chiefly sustained all that time by the Lawrence. The fresh breeze which sprung up, about the time that vessel was entirely disabled, turned the fortune of the day in our favor, by enabling all our vessels to press on the enemy, break through his line, and rake him effectually in every direction.

The loss on board the Lawrence was 22 killed and 61 wounded; and the vessel was so completely cut up, that it was absolutely necessary to send her immediately into a safe harbor. The loss in the whole fleet was 27 killed and 96 wounded. The Niagara had only 2 killed—the Caledonia, Somers and Trippe had none. The loss of the enemy was 72 killed, about double that number wounded, and upwards of 300 prisoners. Commodore Perry in his first accounts of the battle, in the above letters to general Harrison and the secretary of the navy, committed a trifling error in styling the Lady Prevost a brig—he afterwards reported her a schooner. Her commander, captain Barclay, the senior officer in the British fleet, was severely wounded. The captain of the Queen Charlotte was killed, and also the 1st lieutenant of the Detroit.

After the battle with fire arms was over "another engagement took place—it was a war of politeness and humanity. The British officers refuse to retain their swords, and the magnanimous Perry declines receiving them. They pass repeatedly back and forward between the two commodores. American generosity finally triumphs. The British officers are forced, by his overwhelming kindness and humanity, to retain those very swords, which his superior skill and bravery had compelled them to surrender. And as an additional mark of his liberality, the commodore advanced them $1000 on his own account, to defray their expenses in travelling to such places as might be assigned them." Every exertion was also made to render the prisoners and wounded of the enemy, as comfortable in their captivity as our own troops. Such generous conduct made a lasting impression on the gratitude of the brave and gallant captain Barclay.

On the day after the battle the funeral obsequies of the British and American officers, who had fallen in the action, were performed in an appropriate and affecting manner. An opening on the margin of Put-in-Bay was selected for the interment of their remains. The crews of both fleets attended. The day was fine and pleasant. Nature seemed hushed in silence, and a dead calm prevailed on the lake. The solemn looks of the officers and men, the procession boats keeping time with their oars to the solemn dirge that was playing, the mournful waving of the flags, the deep toned peals of minute guns—all together gave the scene a melancholy grandeur which may be felt, but cannot be described—How different from the scene of yesterday!

Now all united as brothers, to perform the last honors due to the departed brave of both nations. Three Britons had fallen, captain Finnis and lieutenants Garland and Stockoe—and two Americans, lieutenant Brooks and midshipman Lamb. They lie on a lonely beach, where the future traveller will scarcely find their humble graves.

The American people who delight to honor their brave and magnanimous defenders, bestowed many marks of their gratitude and admiration, on commodore Perry and his brave associates. The following resolves were passed in congress and carried into execution.

'*Resolved* by the senate and house of representatives of the United States of America, in congress assembled, That the thanks of congress be, and the same are hereby presented to captain Oliver Hazard Perry, and through him to the officers, petty officers, seamen, marines, and infantry, serving as such, attached to the squadron under his command, for the decisive and glorious victory gained on lake Erie, on the 10th of September, in the year 1813, over a British squadron of superior force.

'*Resolved,* That the president of the United States be requested to cause gold medals to be struck, emblematic of the action between the two squadrons, and to be presented to captain Perry and to captain Jesse D. Elliott, in such manner as will be most agreeable to them; and that the president be farther requested to present a silver medal, with suitable emblems and devices, to each of the commissioned officers, either of the navy or army, and a sword to each of the midshipmen and sailing masters, who so nobly distinguished themselves on that day.'

This brilliant victory at once immortalized the heroes who achieved it, and opened Upper Canada to the American arms. The captured vessels were safely towed into Put-in-Bay, the Lawrence was sent to Erie to be dismantled, and commodore Perry was ready, after he had landed his prisoners at the mouth of Portage, to transport the northwestern army to Malden.

CHAPTER IX.

Invasion of Upper Canada, and capture of the army under general Procter.

ON the evening of the 16th of September, general M'Arthur received orders at fort Meigs to embark the artillery, military stores and provisions at that place, in vessels which were sent from head quarters to receive them; and to march the regulars of the garrison across the country to the rendezvous at the mouth of Portage, preparatory to their embarkation with the rest of the army. He had already reduced fort Meigs to a small post, in the upper corner of the old works, and quickly executed the orders for his removal. The remaining Kentuckians at that place under general Clay, had determined to accompany general Harrison, though their term of service had nearly expired; and the general himself had particularly solicited the governor for leave to accompany him, in case his men were not permitted to go. He now embarked with his suite, and a number of his men, in the transport vessels which had come for the stores.

The mounted regiment under colonel Johnson, which was now also at fort Meigs, received orders from general Harrison to encamp under the guns of the fort and wait for further orders. The company of captain Warfield had gone from Piqua with the governor's troops to Portage, and the captain had obtained permission from general Harrison for his company to cross with him into Canada. This circumstance connected with some others, and with the orders received from the general, produced much uneasiness in the balance of the regiment, lest it might have been determined at head quarters, to leave them on this side of the lake.

In concentrating his forces for the invasion of Canada, general Harrison had notified the Wyandot, Shawanee, and Seneca Indians near Upper Sandusky, that they would be received into his service; and about 260 had in consequence joined him at Seneca and accompanied him to the point of embarkation, under their chiefs, Lewis, Blackhoof, and Snake. The two regiments of Ohio militia which had been left at Upper Sandusky were subsequently discharged.

In bringing down the military stores and provisions, from the posts on the Sandusky river, to the vessels in the lake, a short land carriage became necessary to expedite the embarkation. The peninsula formed by the Sandusky bay on the right, and by Portage river and lake Erie on the left, extended between fifteen and twenty miles from the anchorage of the shipping in the mouth of Portage; at which place the isthmus on which the army was encamped, was less than two miles across from one river to the other. The boats in going round the peninsula to the shipping, would have to travel upwards of forty miles, and to be exposed to the dangers of the lake navigation. It was therefore deemed the most safe and expeditious to transport the stores and drag the boats across the isthmus, which was accomplished between the 15th and 20th of the month, whilst the army was detained in making other necessary arrangements.

The Kentucky troops were encamped across the narrowest part of the isthmus, above the place of embarkation; and each regiment was ordered to construct a strong fence of brush and fallen timber in front of its encampment, which extended when finished, from Portage to Sandusky river. Within this enclosure, their horses were turned loose to graze on ample pastures of excellent grass. The preparations for the expedition being nearly completed, it became necessary to detail a guard to be left for the protection of the horses. The commandants of regiments were ordered by the governor to detach one twentieth part of their commands for this service; and colonel Christopher Rife was designated as their commander. In furnishing the men, many of the colonels had to resort to a draft, as volunteers to stay on this side of the lake could not be obtained. The Kentuckians had no constitutional scruples, about crossing the boundary line of the United States; and no greater insult could be offered to one of Shelby's volunteers, than to insinuate that he did not desire to cross into Canada.

This however was not exactly the case with all the militia assembled at the mouth of Portage. When the order for embarking was issued, the gentlemen of the Pennsylvania regiment from Erie, were unfortunately seized with *constitutional scruples.* General Harrison personally addressed them, and requested the officers for the honor of their state, to endeavor to prevail on their men to embark. After making an attempt to persuade them, one of the captains returned to general Harrison, and observed in a pusillanimous tone—" I believe the boys are not willing to go, general." Harrison eyed him with contempt and replied "The *boys,* eh! I believe some of the officers *too,* are not willing to go. Thank God, I have Kentuckians enough to go without you." However about 150 of them were prevailed on to embark, under the lieutenant colonel and major, the commandant of the regiment being sick.

On the 20th general Harrison embarked with the regular troops under generals McArthur and Cass, and arrived the same day at Put-in bay in Bass Island, about 10 miles distant from the point of embarkation. Next morning the governor sailed with a part of his troops, having ordered major general Desha to remain at Portage and bring up the rear, which he performed with great alacrity and vigilance. On that and the succeeding day all the militia arrived at Bass Island. Colonel Rife was left in command at

Portage, with doctor Maguffin as his surgeon, and with instructions to pay particular attention to the bashful Pennsylvanians, who ought for their backwardness to be disowned by their state. The whole army remained on Bass Island on the 24th, waiting for the arrival of all the necessary stores and provisions at that place. The winds and the weather were as favorable for this movement, as Heaven could make them. It seemed as if all the elements had conspired to favor the expedition. The felicity of the troops in this respect was the subject of general remark ; and indeed the finest season had been enjoyed for all the preliminary movements and preparations.

During the stay of the army at this place, the Kentuckians left by general Clay at fort Meigs arrived at head quarters to join the expedition. Their services not being wanted they were here discharged, and returned home ; except the general, major Dudley and a few others, who proceeded with the army as far as Sandwich. Some of the Pennsylvanians, who had ventured as far as this Island, were now permitted to indulge their *scruples* and retire also from the service : the others continued as far as Sandwich.

On the 25th, the whole army moved to the Middle Sister, a small island containing about five or six acres of ground, which was now crowded with men, having about four thousand five hundred upon it. Whilst the transport vessels were bringing up the military stores and provisions on the 26th, general Harrison sailed with commodore Perry in the Ariel, to reconnoitre off Malden, and ascertain a suitable point on the lake shore for the debarkation of his troops. They came in view of Amherstburg, but could not examine the fort, the position of which was on the river above the town, by which it was concealed from their sight. The block house on Bare point, three miles below Malden, had been destroyed. A dead silence and tranquillity prevailed along the coast, and the inhabitants appeared to view the reconnoitring vessels with extreme indifference. These circumstances induced the general to suspect, that the enemy had made arrangements to surprise him in the act of landing his forces; or possibly that he might have destroyed his works and retreated. The army however approached the shore on a subsequent day in full expectation that the enemy would meet them on their landing.

Late in the evening the general returned to the army on the Middle Sister. The following general order was now issued, prescribing the order of debarkation, of march, and of battle.

'As it is the intention of the general to land the army on the enemy's coast, the following will be the order of debarkation, of march, and of battle. The right wing of the army will be composed of the Kentucky volunteers under command of his excellency, governor Shelby, acting as major general—the left wing, of the light corps of lieutenant colonel Ball, and the brigades of generals M'Arthur and Cass. This arrangement is made with a view to the localities of the ground, on which the troops will have to act, and the composition of the enemy's force, and is calculated in marching up the lake or strait, to place the regular troops in the open ground on the lake, where it is probable they will be opposed by British regulars, and the Kentucky volunteers in the woods, which probably will be occupied by the enemy's militia and Indians. When the signal is given for putting to shore the corps of lieutenant colonel Ball will precede the left wing, and the regiment of volunteer riflemen under colonel Simrall the right wing. These corps will land with the utmost celerity consistent with the preservation of good order, and as soon as landed will seize the most favorable position for annoying the enemy, and covering the debarkation of the troops of the line. General Cass's brigade will follow lieutenant colonel Ball's corps, and general Calmes' the regiment of colonel Simrall. The other regiments will follow and form in succession after those which precede them, the right wing with its left in front, displaying to the right, and the left wing with its right in front displaying to the left. The brigades of generals King, Allen, and Caldwell, will form successively to the right of general Calmes. The brigades of generals M'Arthur and Chiles will form the reserve, under the immediate command of general M'Arthur. The general will command in person the brigades of Cass and Calmes, assisted

by major general Henry. His excellency governor Shelby will
have the immediate command of the three brigades on the right,
assisted by major general Desha. As soon as the troops dis-
embark, the boats are to be immediately sent back to the fleet.
It will be observed, that the order of landing here prescribed, is
somewhat that of direct *echellon*, displayed into line upon the
advanced corps of the right and left wings. It is the intention
of the general however that all the troops which are provided
with boats, should land in as quick succession as possible; and
the general officers commanding towards the extremities of the
line are authorised to deviate from this arrangement, to counteract any movement of the enemy, by landing any parts of
their commands previous to the forming of the corps which are
herein directed to precede them. The corps of lieutenant colonel Ball, and the volunteer regiment of colonel Simrall will
maintain the position they occupy on landing, until the troops
of the line are formed to support them; they will then retire
through the intervals of the line, or to the flanks and form in
the rear of the line. A detachment of artillery with a six
pounder, four pounder and howitzer, will land with the advanced light corps. The rest of the artillery will be held in
reserve and landed at such points as major Wood may direct.
The point of landing for the reserve under brigadier general
M'Arthur cannot now be designated. It will be made to support any part of the line which may require aid, or be formed
on the flanks as circumstances may require. The arrangements for landing the troops will be made entirely under the
direction of an officer of the navy, whom commodore Perry has
been so obliging as to furnish for that purpose. The debarkation of the troops will be covered by the cannon of the vessels.
The troops being landed and the enemy driven off, or not opposing the landing, the army will change its front to the left,
and form in order of battle in the following manner. The two
brigades of regular troops, and two of the volunteers, to be formed in two lines at right angles to the shore of the lake. The
brigades of generals M'Arthur and Calmes to form the front
line, and those of Cass and Chiles the second line, the regular
troops still on the left, and that flank resting on the lake shore.
The distance between the two lines will be three hundred yards.
The remaining three volunteer brigades will be drawn up in a
single line of two ranks, at right angles to the lines in front,
its head on the right of the front line, forming a crotchet *en po-
tence* with that line, and extending beyond the second line. The
corps of lieutenant colonel Ball will form the advance of the
left wing at the same distance of 300 yards, and colonel Simrall's regiment that of the right wing at the same distance.
Some light pieces of artillery will be placed in the road lead-

ing up the lake, and at such other points as major Wood may
direct. When the order is given for marching, the first and
second line will advance by files from the heads of companies, or in other words those two lines will form two columns
marching by their flanks by companies at entire distances. The
three brigades on the right flank, will be faced to the left and
marched forwards, the head of this column still forming *en po-
tence* with the front line. It is probable that the two brigades
of the front line will extend from the lake some distance into
the woods on the right flank, and it is desirable that it should
be so; but should it be otherwise, and the crotchet or angle be
at any time in the open ground, governor Shelby will immediately extend the front line to the right by adding to it as many
companies of the leading brigade of the flank column, as will
bring the angle, and consequently the left column itself completely within the woods. It is to be presumed that the enemy
will make their attack upon the army on its march, that their
regular troops will form their right upon the lake, their militia
occupy the ground between their regulars and the woods, and
that the Indians will make a flank attack from the woods. The
formation herein prescribed is intended to resist an arrangement of this kind. Should the general's conjecture on this subject prove correct, as it must be evident that the right of the
enemy cannot be turned, as on that wing the best of his troops
will be placed, it will be proper to refuse him our left, and direct our principal effort to uncover the left flank of his regulars,
by driving off the militia. In the event here supposed, it will
therefore be proper to bring up a part, or the whole, of general
Cass's brigade, to assist the charge to be made by general Calmes, or that the former should change positions with the brigade of volunteers in the second line. Should the general
think it safe to order the whole of Cass's brigade to assist the
charge made by general Calmes, or that the former should
change positions with the volunteers in the second line, or should
the general think it safe to order the whole of Cass's brigade
to the right, without replacing it with another, general Cass
will march it to the right, formed in oblique *echellons* of companies. It will be the business of general M'Arthur, in the
event of his wing being refused, to watch the motions of the
enemy, and with the assistance of the artillery, prevent his
front line at least from intercepting the progress of our right.
Should the enemy's militia be defeated, the brigade of ours in
advance, will immediately wheel upon the flank of the British
regulars, and general M'Arthur will then advance and attack
them in front. In the mean time his excellency governor Shelby can use the brigade in reserve of the second line, to extend
the flank line from its front or left, or to reinforce any weak

part of the line. In all cases where troops in advance are obliged to retire through those which are advancing to support them, it will be done by companies in files, which will retire through the intervals of the advancing line, and immediately form in the rear. The light troops will be particularly governed by this direction. The disposition of the troops in the right flank, is such as the commanding general thinks best calculated to resist an attack from the Indians, which is only to be expected from that quarter. His excellency governor Shelby, will however use his discretion in making any alteration which his experience and judgment may dictate.

'Lieutenant colonel Ball, colonel Simrall, and the officers commanding on the flank line, are to send out small detachments in advance of the two former corps, and to the flank of the latter. Should they discover the enemy in force, immediate notice will be sent to the lines. The general commanding on the spot, will immediately order the signal for forming in order of battle, which is the beat, *to arms.* All signals will be immediately repeated by all the drums of the line. The signal for the whole to halt is, *the retreat.* Drums will be distributed along the line at the heads of companies, and taps occasionally be given to regulate their march. Lieutenant colonels Ball and Simrall are to keep the general constantly informed of the discoveries made by the advanced parties, and when it shall become necessary for their corps to retire, they will form on the flank, or in the rear of generals M'Arthur and Calmes' brigades, and receive the orders of their brigadiers respectively.'

'WILLIAM HENRY HARRISON.'

Such were the directions given for the debarkation, the marching, and fighting of the troops; in which we find all that lucid minuteness, so necessary in the orders given to an army composed *emphatically* of raw troops, and whose officers in general were but little superior in the knowledge of tactics to the men they commanded. After this perspicuous developement however, of the operations to be performed, the debarkation was subsequently effected with surprising celerity and good order, not indeed under the opposition of a hostile force, but in the momentary expectation of an attack.

On Monday the 27th, the whole army was embarked early in the day, and set sail from the Middle Sister for the Canada shore, general Harrison having

2 Y

previously circulated a general order among the troops, in which he exhorted them to remember the fame of their ancestors, and the justice of the cause in which they were engaged. To the Kentuckians he said "remember the river Raisin; but remember it only, whilst victory is suspended. The revenge of a soldier cannot be gratified on a fallen enemy."

The winds were propitious, and the whole army approached the shore, in an oblique direction, and in good order, aiming to land in an open field about four miles below Malden. The signal to land was given, and the whole flotilla in succession pulled to shore in elegant style. Not an enemy was to be seen. Some Indians had made their appearance on the coast a few minutes before, but the fire of the fleet had driven them off. It was about three o'clock in the evening when the army landed: the line of march was soon formed, and in less than two hours the advanced corps under Ball and Simrall arrived at the *Ruins of Malden*. The whole army came up, the American flag was hoisted, and possession was taken of the town of Amherstburg. General Procter had burnt the fort and navy yard and retreated up to Sandwich, under the impression that there were at least ten thousand Kentuckians coming against him.

Immediately after the capture of the fleet, general Procter had sent spies to reconnoitre the forces of general Harrison. They had viewed the Kentuckians, while encamped on the plains of Sandusky, and had reported their numbers to general Procter, as being from ten to fifteen thousand men. This information at once determined him to burn Malden and make his escape by retreating up the rivers Detroit and Thames, and pursuing the *back route* to the lower parts of the province. No doubt his guilty fears, lest he should fall into the hands of men, whose friends he had suffered to be massacred by the savages, had also much influence on his mind in bringing it to this determination. It is only from such fears, and from his misconception of our force, that we can account for his conduct; for the army of regulars, militia, and Indians, which it was in his power to have concentrated against us, was nearly equal to all the forces of general Harrison; and the country above Malden abounded with provisions for their support. The inhabitants were probably not very willing, to contribute their substance for the sustenance of the Indians; but general Procter had the power, and it was his duty, to collect adequate supplies, as long as the country could furnish them; and on the 13th he had proclaimed martial law, to "take effect as far as supplying the wants of the troops under his command, or the sending away or apprehending all traitorous or disaffected persons might render it expedient." To supply the great assemblage of Indians at that place however, consisting of warriors, squaws, and children, was by no means an easy task. Before the retreat 15,000 rations were issued daily—a fact which proves that Procter had a very powerful auxiliary force of Indians.

As soon as he had ascertained the loss of the fleet, he had commenced his preparations for retreating. About the time martial law was proclaimed, he had embarked a considerable quantity of military stores in boats, and sent them up to Sandwich. On the 17th, he had given orders to collect and bring away all the cattle and provisions on the coast below Malden. He now kept his head quarters at Sandwich, having left colonel Warburton in the command of Malden; to whom he gave orders on the 20th to destroy the public property and buildings, and retreat to Sandwich; but in the indecisive confusion of a guilty mind, the execution of this order was again suspended, till the morning of the 26th, when the place being finally evacuated was at length destroyed.

General Tecumseh whose conscience could not accuse him of so many crimes, and whose Indian heroism knew how to endure their consequences, was entirely opposed to the retreating measures of general Procter. On the 18th of September, in the name of all the Indian chiefs, and warriors, he addressed the following speech to general Procter, as the representative of their great father, the king.

'FATHER, listen to your children! You have them now all before you.

'The war before this, our British father gave the hatchet to his red children, when our old chiefs were alive. They are now dead. In the war, our father was thrown on his back by the Americans, and our father took them by the hand without our knowledge; and we are afraid that our father will do so again at this time.

'Summer before last, when I came forward with my red brethren, and was ready to take up the hatchet in favor of our British father, we were told not to be in a hurry, that he had not yet determined to fight the Americans.

'Listen! When war was declared, our father stood up and gave us the tomahawk and told us that he was then ready to strike the Americans; that he wanted our assistance; and that he would certainly get us our lands back, which the Americans had taken from us.

'Listen! You told us, at that time, to bring forward our families to this place; and we did so; and you promised to take care of them, and they should want for nothing, while the men would go and fight the enemy; that we need not trouble ourselves about the enemy's garrisons; that we knew nothing about them, and that our father would attend to that part of the business. You also told your red children that you would take good care of your garrison here, which made our hearts glad.

'Listen! When we were last at the Rapids it is true we gave you little assistance. It is hard to fight people who live like groundhogs.

'Father, listen! Our fleet has gone out; we know they have fought; we have heard the great guns; but we know nothing of what has happened to our father with that arm. Our ships have gone one way, and we are much astonished to see our father tying up every thing and preparing to run away the other, without letting his red children know what his intentions are. You always told us to remain here and take care of our lands; it made our hearts glad to hear, that was your wish. Our great father, the king, is the head, and you represent him. You always told us that you would never draw your foot off British ground; but now father, we see you are drawing back, and we are sorry to see our father doing so without seeing the enemy. We must compare our father's conduct to a fat dog, that carries its tail upon its back, but when affrighted, it drops it between its legs and runs off.

' *Father, listen!* The Americans have not yet defeated us by land; neither are we sure that they have done so by water : *we therefore wish to remain here and fight our enemy, should they make their appearance.* If they defeat us, we will *then* retreat with our father.

' At the battle of the Rapids, last war, the Americans certainly defeated us ; and when we retreated to our father's fort at that place the gates were shut against us. We were afraid that it would now be the case ; but instead of that, we now see our British father preparing to march out of his garrison.

' *Father!* You have got the arms and ammunition which our great father sent for his red children. If you have an idea of going away, give them to us, and you may go and welcome for us. Our lives are in the hands of the Great Spirit. We are determined to defend our lands, and if it be his will, we wish to leave our bones upon them.'

Had Procter followed the advice of Tecumseh, and fought the American forces before he retreated, the result must have been more glorious at least, if not entirely favorable, to the British arms.

On the night of the 27th, the American forces encamped round the ruins of Malden, their general having determined to pursue the enemy in the morning. In a letter to the war department, written on the evening of the 27th, he says "I will pursue the enemy tomorrow, although there is no probability of overtaking him, as he has upwards of 1000 horses, and we have not one in the army. I shall think myself fortunate to collect a sufficiency to mount the general officers. It is supposed here, that general Procter will establish himself upon the river Trench, or Thames, 40 miles from Malden." Procter had pressed into his service all the horses of the inhabitants, which they had not effectually concealed. One only, and that a very indifferent one, could now be procured. On it the venerable governor of Kentucky was mounted, and proceeded with the army towards Sandwich, where they arrived on the 29th, without meeting any obstruction from the enemy; except that the bridge over the Aux Canards river had been torn up, but was soon repaired again. There had been considerable expectation among the commanding officers, that a formidable resistance would be made at this bridge, but no enemy was to be seen; and on arriving at Sandwich it was ascertained, that general Procter had retreated from that place early on the preceding day. The Indians however were in considerable force in the suburbs of Detroit, the inhabitants of which, who had already been very much plundered, were in great apprehension of an immediate massacre; but a few discharges of grape shot from the fleet, which had come up the river, soon compelled them to fly to the woods for safety. General M'Arthur went over with his brigade and took possession of the town; and on the same evening general Harrison issued his proclamation for re-establishing the civil government of the territory. All persons who had been in office at the time of the capitulation, were directed to resume their functions, and administer the laws which had then been in force.

On the 30th, which was a very wet day, the troops continued in Sandwich. The few inhabitants who remained in the town, were requested to drive in beef cattle for the subsistence of the army; and being informed, that if this was not done, foraging parties must be sent into the country, who would probably commit depredations on the people, which it was the wish of the general to prevent, they complied and brought in a plentiful supply. Complaints however were made to governor Shelby, by some of the citizens, that his soldiers had in some instances violated their property; upon which the following general order was issued, which effectually checked such misconduct. It is preserved in this place as a precedent for the benefit of British commanders.

'The commander in chief of the Kentucky volunteers has heard with extreme regret, that depredations have been committed upon the property of the inhabitants of this town, by some of the troops under his command. He did not expect, that it would ever be necessary for him to admonish citizens, who are proud in the enjoyment of property at home, of the impropriety of wantonly injuring that of others. Violations of this kind, whilst they disgrace the individuals who are guilty of them, will tend to injure the character of the army, and detract from the merit which the success of the present campaign would entitle them to claim. While the army remains in this country, it is expected that the inhabitants will be treated with justice and humanity, and their property secured from unnecessary and wanton injury. The commander in chief of the Kentucky volunteers enjoins it upon the officers of every grade, to use their exertions to prevent injury from being done to the private property of the inhabitants. He is determined to punish, with the utmost rigor of martial law, any one who shall be guilty of such violation.'

The inhabitants of Canada had fled from their houses and hid their property, on the approach of the American army, fully expecting that the Kentuckians, *like the British*, would plunder and massacre all before them : but they found themselves very happily disappointed in these expectations.

We have now arrived at a point, where it becomes necessary to advert to the advance of the mounted regiment under colonel Johnson, which now became an important corps in the operations of the army.

We left the mounted regiment encamped at fort Meigs about the middle of September, very uneasy lest they should not have an opportunity of participating in the perils and glories of the campaign. On the 20th lieutenant Griffith, who had been sent with a scouting party to the river Raisin, returned to camp with an Indian prisoner called Misselemetaw, who was a chief counsellor to Tecumseh, and uncle to the celebrated Logan, but a man of very different principles and con duct. He had been the leader of the Indians at the massacre of the Pigeon Roost in the Indiana territory. Griffith had caught him asleep in a house at the river Raisin. He told colonel Johnson, that the Indians had been watching the movements of his *army*, had examined his encampments, and seen him arrive at fort Meigs; and that they estimated his forces to be at least 2400. He farther stated that the Indians about Browns-town, amounting to 1750 warriors, had determined to give him battle at the river Huron—and that they were still ignorant of the fate of the British fleet. He was an Indian of excellent information, and had been the constant companion and friend of Tecumseh. Being under an impression that he would now certainly have to die, he gave colonel Johnson a long and apparently very candid account of past transactions, since the treaty of Greenville to the present day. He said the British had supplied the Prophet's party with arms and am-munition before the battle of Tippecanoe; that Tecum-seh's plan for a common property in their lands had been strongly recommended and praised by colonel Elliott; and that the British had used every means in their power, since the year 1809, to secure the friend-ship and aid of the Indians, in the event of a war with the United States—having often invited them to Mal-den and made them presents for that purpose; and having also represented to them, that they should re-ceive British aid to drive the Americans over the Ohio river, after which they should live in the houses of the inhabitants and have their daughters for wives. He said he was now convinced that the British had again deceived them, and that the Great Spirit had forsaken him in his old age for his cruelty and wickedness.

Captain Coleman who had been sent to head quar-ters to ascertain the destination of the regiment, now returned to camp, having left the army on its way from Bass island to the Middle Sister. He brought infor-mation from the general, that the regiment would certainly be called upon in a few days to cooperate with the army in the direction of Detroit. This news, together with the probability of having a brush with the Indians at least, once more raised the hopes and animated the spirits of the men.

On the evening of the 25th orders were received by express from general Harrison, for the regiment to march immediately to the river Raisin, as it was probable the army would land the next day on the Canada shore. Early next morning the regiment marched, fully expecting that they would have to encounter a strong Indian force in the neighborhood of Brownstown. The colonel took with him from fort Meigs, four light pieces of artillery, which he placed under the command of captains E. Craig, Turner, Gist, and Sandford, each with a command of 10 men. On the second day they reached the river Raisin. Frenchtown was generally abandoned, only a few French families remaining in it. The fine orchards of peach and apple trees were loaded with excellent fruit.

The bones of the massacred Kentuckians were scattered over the plains for three miles on this side of the river. The detachment which had visited that place under colonel Johnson in June, had collected and buried a great many of them; but they were now torn up, and scattered over the fields again. The sight had a powerful effect on the feelings of the men. The wounds inflicted by that barbarous transaction, were again torn open. The bleaching bones still appealed to heaven, and called on Kentucky to avenge this outrage on humanity. We had heard the scene described before—we now witnessed it, in these impressive memorials. The feelings they excited cannot be described by me—but they will never be forgotten—nor while there is a recording angel in heaven, or a historian upon earth, will the tragedy of the river Raisin be suffered to sink into oblivion. Future generations will often ponder on this fatal field of blood; and the future inhabitants of Frenchtown will long point out to the curious traveller, the garden where the intrepid Madison for several hours maintained the unequal contest of four to one, and repulsed the bloody Procter in every charge. Yonder is the wood, where the gallant Allen fell! Here the accomplished Hart and Woolfolk were butchered! There the brave Hickman was tomahawked and thrown into the flames! That is the spot where the lofty Simpson breathed his last! And a little farther doctors Montgomery, Davis and M'Ilvain, amiable in their manners and profound in science, fell in youth and left the sick to mourn their loss! The gallant Meade fell on the bank in battle, but his magnanimous lieutenant Graves, was reserved for massacre! for a massacre perpetrated by savages under the *influence of Britain*— a nation impiously styled "the bulwark of our religion."

At this place an express arrived from the main army, which he had left on the Middle Sister on the morning of the 26th. He was sent while Harrison was reconnoitring off Malden, by the attentive and prudent governor of Kentucky, to apprize colonel Johnson of the progress and prospects of the army, that he might regulate his march accordingly. Next morning before the regiment marched, their faithful guide, Anthony Shane of the Shawanee tribe, observed that he knew the spot where captain Simpson had been killed. The colonels, with captain M'Afee and doctor Ewing, went with him to the place, and found the bones, which they buried. The frame of captain Simpson was easily known from the others by its length, the captain having been upwards of six feet and a half high. A detachment of 100 men was now sent in advance to the river Huron, to throw a bridge over that stream for the passage of the troops; who arrived, and partly crossed it in the evening; and the balance, with the baggage wagons and artillery, crossed in the morning, on the floating bridge which had been prepared for them. Soon after the passage of this river, an express arrived from general Harrison, with information that the enemy had burnt Malden and fled up the river Detroit, and that the army had reached the Petit Cote settlement in full pursuit. This news put the regiment at half speed, which was continued all day. They passed through Brownstown, now evacuated, and the Magauga village, from both of which the Indians had fled, and had likewise deserted all their huts on the Detroit river. Arriving at the river De Corce, they found there a part of the company of captain Warfield, which had been sent over by the general to repair the bridge. The Indians had formed an ambuscade at this place, behind a long row of pickets on the opposite side of the river, where they had waited for the regiment all the preceding night, in the expectation that colonel Johnson would march by night into Detroit. Disappointed in this, they had retired. Captain Warfield had brought boats to take up the artillery by water, with a view to expedite the march; but on consultation the colonel determined to keep them with him, as they were not much encumbrance. At the river Rouge the regiment encamped, and after dark received intelligence, that 500 Potawatamies were lying about 6 miles up that river. While the officers were consulting on the propriety of attacking them, major Trigg arrived with a reinforcement of four companies of regulars and one of militia, from head quarters at Sandwich, where some uneasiness had been felt for the safety of the regiment. In consequence of the information brought by major Trigg, the project of attacking the Indians was dropped, and some apprehension was felt, that an attack would be made by them in the night. This however did not happen; but while the troops were crossing the river in the morning, a Frenchman came down and stated, that a party of Indians were crossing above, for the purpose of giving them battle. The battalion of major Trigg, and the volunteers who had crossed, were immediately formed in front to cover the passage of the balance. No attack however was made, and the whole detachment arrived in Detroit, before 12 o'clock on that day, which was the last of September.

When general Harrison saw the regiment passing up to Detroit, he sent over major Charles S. Todd with orders for them to cross as soon as possible to Sandwich. As the men had not dismounted when he arrived, they marched down to the river immediately, but no boats could be procured to carry them over. They returned and encamped, while lieutenant colonel Johnson went over to procure boats. Late in the evening he returned with a few, having made arrangements for procuring others in the morning.

On the 1st of October, governor Shelby went, a little after daylight, to the quarters of general Harrison, in pursuance of an appointment to consult with him respecting the further pursuit of the enemy. He found the general alone, and directly mentioned the appointed subject of consultation. The general, as if his mind was entirely occupied with it, immediately replied— we must not be heard; and led the governor into a private room, into which he had directed his aids to conduct him, in case he had arrived before the general was ready to receive him. Here they soon came to the conclusion, that Procter might be overtaken in three or four days of hard marching; and it was determined not to lose a moment in preparing for the pursuit. The governor was requested to collect his general officers at head quarters in the course of an hour, that their opinions might be taken on the occasion. They were convened accordingly at the room of the general; and he there stated his design of pursuing the enemy, observing that there were but two ways of doing it—one of which was, to follow him up the strait by land—the other, to embark and sail down lake Erie to Long Point, then march hastily across by land 12 miles to the road and intercept him. "But the governor thinks, and so do I, that the best way will be, to pursue the enemy up the strait by land." The general officers unanimously concurred in the same opinion, together with general Adair, first aid to the governor, who had been invited to the council. I have been thus particular in stating the facts, relative to the determination to pursue the enemy, because it has been reported and believed, that general Harrison never would have pursued farther than Sandwich, had it not been for governor Shelby, and that he differed with the governor, respecting the route to be taken; but the fact is, there never was a difference of opinion between them, neither on the propriety of the pursuit nor the manner of performing it. The determination and preparations of the general to pursue, had never been suspended; and the chief object of the councils was to obtain the approbation of the governor and general officers for the route he preferred.

Colonel Johnson having been ordered to bring over his regiment with the greatest despatch, governor Shelby went over himself immediately after the council, to communicate the result to the colonel, and apprize him of general Harrison's determination to pursue the enemy next day. Every possible exertion was made by colonel Johnson and his officers to get over the river, but they were so obstructed by the wind and waves, that the whole of their men and horses were not got over till late in the evening. The marching of the army however, had been unavoidably delayed till next day by other causes.

It was necessary that a considerable detachment should be left at Detroit, to protect the citizens of Michigan from the depredations of the Indians, with which general Procter had threatened them before his retreat. It was ascertained that Five-medal, Maipock, and other chiefs, had remained on the west side of Detroit river, with the Miamies, and a large portion of the Potawatamies, and of some other tribes. General M'Arthur's brigade was therefore left at Detroit to keep

them in check; and its place in the line was supplied
by that of general Calmes, now commanded by colonel
Trotter, in consequence of the indisposition of the general.   The brigade of general King took the place
vacated by that under Trotter.   The corps of colonel
Ball was attached to the command of general Cass.
The mounted regiment formed the front guard, with
instructions to cover the whole front of the army, with
small parties one mile in advance, and at least half that
distance on the right flank.   Colonel Simrall's regiment constituted the rear guard.   Such were the arrangements made for an early march on the morning of
the 2nd of October, the baggage, provisions and ammunition wagons in the mean time being sent up the river
in several vessels of the fleet.

At sunrise on the 2nd, the foot troops were in motion, except the brigade of general Cass, who had to
wait for their knapsacks and blankets, which had been
left at the Middle Sister, with a view to disencumber
these troops for the expected contest at the point of
debarkation.   A vessel had been sent back for them,
but she had not yet arrived.   The mounted regiment
was also detained a while drawing provisions; but
general Harrison halted the foot troops about 12 miles
in advance, whilst the mounted men came up and took
their place in front, in which order the army pushed
forward, the governor frequently observing "If we
desire to overtake the enemy, we must do more than
he does, by early and forced marches."   The bridges
across the ravines and creeks which empty into lake
St. Clair, had all been left unimpaired, which seemed
to prove that the enemy did not expect to be pursued
on that route.   About 20 miles up the road, six British
deserters met the regiment of mounted men, who said
they had left Procter with his army about 15 miles up
the Thames, at 1 o'clock on the preceding day, and
that he had between 6 and 700 regulars, some dragoons,
and about 1200 Indians.   This information infused

new life into the troops, and they pushed on with increased ardor till dark, having travelled about 25 miles the first day. On the 2nd day of the pursuit, an early and forced march was made, which soon brought the army to the mouth of the river Thames, below which a small party of dragoons were discovered by the spies under major Suggett, who pursued and captured them, together with a lieutenant and 8 privates of the infantry, who had just begun to destroy a bridge over a creek, a small distance above the mouth of the river. Captain Berry of the spies made five of them surrender, and bring back their boat, after they had crossed the Thames. All the men were captured; but one of the horses belonging to the dragoons made his escape, and went up to the British army, from which circumstance general Procter received the first hint of the near approach of his enemy. This little affair, the first fruits of the pursuit, had a very great effect in animating the pursuers.*

---

* The campaign was not without auspicious omens, which in the superstitious times of ancient history, would have had a more powerful effect on the minds of both officers and men, than the circumstance of capturing a small detachment of the enemy. When the army arrived at the mouth of the Thames, an eagle was seen hovering over it, which general Harrison observed was a presage of success, as it was our tutelary bird. Commodore Perry who had condescended to act as volunteer aid to the general, remarked that a similar circumstance had occurred to the fleet, on the morning of the 10th of September.

There was another singular occurrence in the animal creation. A sow shoat had followed a company of mounted volunteers from the interior of Kentucky. As she kept constantly with the army, she became generally known to the soldiers, who called her the governor's pig, and were careful to protect her, as they deemed her conduct an auspicious omen. At the margin of the lake she embarked with the troops and went as far as Bass island. She was there offered a passage into Canada, but obstinately refused to embark the second time. Some of the men attributed her conduct to *constitutional scruples*, and observed that she knew it was contrary to the constitution to force a *militia pig* over the line. In consequence of this remark, they gave her leave to stay, and return to the regiment at Portage.

About 250 yards above the first bridge, where the little party of infantry was taken, there was another bridge, of which the front guard took possession, and in a few minutes were informed by a guide, on whom the general relied for information respecting the country, that he had discovered a party of British and Indians coming down to the bridge. The mounted regiment immediately formed in order of battle, but no enemy appeared, and the bridge being repaired by the infantry, the army passed over and proceeded on their march. The vessels with the baggage had kept up with the army, and now crossed the bar at the mouth of the Thames, and sailed up that river. In passing the bridge, the mounted regiment was thrown in the rear, in which place it continued a few miles, till the spies in front were fired on by a few dragoons of the enemy. The regiment was then ordered by general Harrison to the front, with instructions to march briskly, but to be careful not to fall into an ambuscade. For several miles the dragoons continued to skirmish with the front guard, till night came on, and the army encamped about ten miles from the mouth of the Thames. Next morning the march was resumed at daylight in full confidence that the enemy would be overtaken on that day. The order of march was altered in some respects. The front guard and foot troops were permitted to march in the road near the river, while the balance of the mounted regiment marched about a mile distant on the right flank, in a succession of prairies, which run parallel to the river. Some skirmishing presently occurred between the spies, and the rear parties of the British; the mounted regiment several times formed the line of battle, and while in this situation a Canadian woman came to the front line, and informed lieutenant colonel Johnson, that the main body of the Indians were at the forks of the river, about 3 miles in advance, where she supposed they intended to give us battle. The march was resumed, and the skirmishing continued, till the spies reached the bridge at the fork of the river. The planks had been torn off the bridge, and some of the spies having attempted to cross on the naked sills, a heavy fire was opened upon them from an adjacent wood, and from the opposite bank of the main river. Major Wood was ordered up, with two 6 pounders, and the foot troops began to form the line of battle, as it was expected that an obstinate resistance would be made at this place.

The fork on the right, which the army had to cross, is much the smallest stream. There were two bridges over it, one at the mouth, and the other about a mile higher up. The Indians were posted in the fork near the lower bridge, with their left wing extending to the upper bridge; and also on the opposite side of the main stream. While the army was forming, and the artillery was playing on the Indians at the mouth of the river, colonel Johnson was directed to secure the bridge above. He brought up his troops in order of battle to that place, and had a warm skirmish with the Indians across the stream. They soon fled however from all points, having previously torn off the planks of the bridge, and set fire to M'Gregor's mill which was near it. The regiment lost 2 men killed, and 6 or 7 wounded—among the latter were captain Craig and lieutenant Griffith. The Indians had 13 killed and a considerable number wounded. Nor was this all the loss their ranks sustained on this day. The Wyandot chief, Walk-in-the-water, had left them in the morning with 60 of his warriors. He had visited general Harrison on the preceding day with a flag, desiring to make peace. The general told him he had no time then to make treaties, and that if he wanted peace he must abandon Tecumseh, and get out of the way of the American army; and with these terms he had hastened to comply.

The bridges were soon repaired, the lower one under the immediate superintendence of the governor and general Cass, and the other under the direction of lieutenant colonel Johnson; and in two hours from the time the skirmish commenced, the whole army had crossed. About half a mile above the forks, the British had set fire to a schooner freighted with military stores; and a house just below it was saved from the flames, in which there were near a thousand stand of arms. After marching about 5 miles farther, our troops were obliged to encamp another night, without having over-taken the British army. But certain intelligence was now received, that the enemy were only a few miles in advance.

Opposite to the place of encampment, there was another vessel and a large distillery in flames, which contained ordnance and naval stores to an immense amount. Two 24 pounders, with a large quantity of shells and balls were also taken at this place. A breastwork was formed round the encampment, and general Harrison continued on horseback till 10 o'clock, superintending and inspecting all the arrangements of the camp. During the night general Procter and Tecumseh came down the river and reconnoitred the encampment, with the intention of making an attack before day; but on seeing its strength and size they were discouraged, and abandoned the scheme. During the night governor Shelby was also on the alert, going round every part of his lines to see that proper vigil-ance was preserved, till exhausted with fatigue he took up his lodging in that part of the camp nearest the enemy, where he shared the blanket of one of his soldiers.

In the morning on the 5th of October, the troops were raised very early, and as the day dawned the whole army was put in motion. The mounted regi-ment took the front, with general Harrison and his staff at its head, and the infantry followed after as expedi-tiously as possible under the command of governor Shelby. By 9 o'clock the advance reached a mill, near which there is a rapid in the river, where it is practicable to ford it on horseback; and at this place general Harrison intended to cross, that he might reach the enemy who were known to be on the north side. Two gun boats and several batteaux, laden with military stores and other property, together with several prisoners, had already been captured this morning; and at the mill a lieutenant and 8 privates were taken, from whom information was received, that the enemy had determined to give us battle at no great distance from that place. The infantry in a few minutes came up with the mounted men; and the passage of the river was effected by 12 o'clock. Each horseman took up one of the infantry behind him, and the balance crossed in canoes, some of which were found at that place, and the others caught floating down the river. As soon as the whole were over, the line of march was resumed in the former order, and at every place where the road touched a bend of the river, boats and canoes were found, with military stores, clothing, and provisions, which the enemy had abandoned in the precipitation of their retreat. After advancing about 8 miles, an encampment was discovered, where colonel Warburton had lain the night before, with a part of the British troops; and it was ascertained, that general Procter had reached the Moravian town, 4 miles from this place, with a detachment on the preceding day. As it was now certain, that the enemy was nearly overtaken, the general directed the advance of the mounted regiment to hasten their march, with a view to procure the necessary information for regulating the movements of the main body. When they had proceeded about 2 miles, they captured a British wagoner, who informed them, that the enemy were lying in order of battle about 300 yards before them, waiting for the arrival of our army. Colonel Johnson, with major Suggett and his spies, immediately advanced within sight of their lines, and acquired by his own observation, as well as from the statements of the wagoner, every information that was attainable, respecting the place and order in which the enemy were posted, all of which was communicated without delay to general Harrison, agreeably to his directions. The regiment at the same time was halted and formed in order of battle.

The place selected by general Procter, to resist the progress of our army, was well calculated for his purpose. The ground along the margin of the river, through which the road passed, was covered chiefly with beech, intermixed with sugartree and oak timber, and tolerably free from undergrowth. At a small distance there was a marsh, running nearly parallel with the river about 2 miles, the distance between them becoming less as you proceed up the river. Where the enemy was posted, there was a narrow swamp, between 2 and 300 yards from the river, after which there was some solid ground, before the main swamp commenced. The British regulars were formed in two lines, with their left on the river, and their right extending to the first swamp, their artillery being planted in the road near the bank of the river. The Indians were all posted beyond the first swamp. Their left, where Tecumseh commanded in person, occupied the isthmus between the swamps, on which the undergrowth was tolerably thick; and their right extended a considerable distance down the main marsh, the margin of which at this place receded very fast from the river, and formed a very obtuse angle with the lines of the army.

The mounted regiment in its present order of battle, occupied the ground between the river and the first swamp. General Harrison immediately came up to it, on being informed that the enemy was discovered, and having satisfied himself as to the situation and views of his adversary, he directed colonel Johnson when the infantry approached, to take ground to the left, and forming his regiment on that flank, to endeavor to turn the right of the Indians. He then returned to give orders for the formation of the infantry, who were but a short distance in the rear of the horsemen when the enemy was first discovered. While engaged in this business, he was informed by major Wood, that he had approached very near the lines of the enemy and discovered that his regulars were drawn up in open order. This information, with the suggestion of colonel Johnson, that the thickets and swampiness of the ground on the left, would render it impracticable for his mounted men to act efficiently in that direction, immediately induced the general to change his plan of attack. He determined to refuse his left to the Indians, and to try the novel experiment of breaking the British lines at once, by a charge of mounted infantry. He therefore directed the mounted regiment to be formed in two charging columns in short lines, and on receiving the enemy's fire, to charge through his ranks, form in his rear, and act as circumstances might require.

The kind of enemy to be fought rendered it necessary, that the rear and flanks should be well secured against his attacks. The foot troops, consisting of five brigades, which averaged but little more than 300 men each, were therefore disposed in the following order. The brigade commanded by Trotter constituted the front line, at a convenient distance in the rear of the mounted regiment, with its right on the river and its left extending a short distance over the first swamp. The brigade of general King formed the second line, 150 yards in the rear of the former; and that of general Chiles was posted in the road, and still further in the rear, to act as a corps of reserve. These three brigades formed the command of general Henry. The division of general Desha, consisting of the brigades of Allen and Caldwell and the regiment of colonel Simrall, was formed on the left, in a line fronting the outer swamp, to protect the left flank against the In-

dians in that quarter. The right of this line joined
the left of the front line under Trotter, with which it
formed an obtuse angle or crotchet between the two
swamps, whilst it extended on the left to a considerable distance parallel with the margin of the swamp.
A small corps of regulars under colonel Paul, about
120 strong, was posted between the road and the river,
for the purpose of advancing in concert with a few Indians under the bank, and seizing the artillery of the
enemy.

The governor of Kentucky was directed to take his
position at the angle between the swamp, which was
considered as a very important point in these arrangements for the contest. General Harrison placed himself at the head of the front line, from which he would
be able to observe the charge of the horsemen, and to
give them any support which might be required.

When colonel Johnson proceeded to form his regiment, agreeably to the orders of general Harrison, he
found there was not room for all his men to act against
the British between the river and the nearest swamp ;
and having ascertained that he could cross the latter,
he concluded to exercise the discretion which had been
given him, and to carry his second battalion through
the swamp to attack the Indians. The first battalion
was therefore formed, according to orders, by lieutenant colonel J. Johnson and major Payne, opposite to
the British lines, in four columns of double files, with
major Suggett and his spies in front. Its right was
placed about fifty yards on the left of the road, that it
might be in some measure out of the immediate range
of the British artillery. The second battalion was
marched through the swamp, and formed in two columns on horseback, with a company on foot in front,
the right column being headed by colonel Johnson and
the left by major Thompson. These columns of course
were immediately in front of the angle where govern-
or Shelby was stationed.

Every thing being in readiness for the onset, the whole army advanced in the order now described, until the front of the first battalion received a distant fire from the British lines : this somewhat frightened the horses, and caused a little confusion, at the heads of the columns, and thus retarded the charge, giving the enemy time to prepare for a second fire, which soon followed the first. But the columns in a moment were completely in motion, and rushed upon the British with irresistable impetuosity. Their front line immediately broke in every direction, and their second about thirty paces in its rear, after giving us a fire, was also broken and thrown into confusion. Our columns having passed through, wheeled to the right and left, and began to pour a destructive fire on the rear of their disordered ranks—but in a moment the contest was over. No sooner had our horsemen charged through their lines and gained their rear, than they began to surrender as fast as they could throw down their arms. And thus in a moment, the whole British force, *upwards of eight hundred strong*, was totally vanquished and the greater part of it captured, by the first battalion of the mounted regiment, under lieutenant colonel James Johnson, before the front line of our infantry had got fairly in view of them. General Procter however made his escape, escorted by a small party of dragoons and mounted Indians, who were immediately pursued as far as the Moravian town, by a party of the mounted regiment consisting chiefly of officers.

The contest with the Indians on the left was more obstinate. They reserved their fire, till the heads of the columns, and the front line on foot, had approached within a few paces of their position. A very destructive fire was then commenced by them, about the time the firing ceased between the British and the first battalion. Colonel Johnson finding his advanced guard, composing the head of his column, nearly all cut down by the first fire, and himself severely wounded, immediately ordered his columns to dismount and come up in line before the enemy, the ground which they occupied being unfavorable for operations on horseback. The line was promptly formed on foot, and a fierce conflict was then maintained for seven or eight minutes, with considerable execution on both sides; but the Indians had not sufficient firmness to sustain very long, a fire which was close, and warm, and severely destructive. They gave way and fled through the brush into the outer swamp, not however before they had learnt the total discomfiture of their allies, and had lost by the fall of Tecumseh, a chief in whom were united the prowess of Achilles and authority of Agamemnon.

As soon as the firing commenced between the Indians and the second battalion, governor Shelby who was posted at the crotchet in its rear, immediately ordered that part of the front line of infantry, which lay between the first swamp and the crotchet, being a part of colonel Donelson's regiment, to march up briskly to the aid of the mounted men. They rushed up accordingly into colonel Johnson's lines, and participated in the contest at that point. This was the only portion of the infantry which had an opportunity of engaging in any part of the battle. The governor also dispatched general Adair, his aid de camp, to bring up the brigade of general King to the front line; but before this could be accomplished, the enemy had fled from colonel Johnson, and a scattering, running fire, had commenced along the swamp, in front of general Desha's division, between the retiring Indians and the mounted men in pursuit, who were now commanded by major Thompson alone, colonel Johnson having retired in consequence of his wounds. This firing in the swamp continued, with occasional remissions, for nearly half an hour, during which time the contest was gallantly maintained by major Thompson and his men, who were still pressing forward on the Indians. Governor

Shelby in the mean time rode down to the left of general Desha's division, and ordered the regiment of colonel Simrall, which was posted on the extreme left, to march up on the right flank of the enemy in aid of major Thompson; but before this reinforcement could reach the scene of action, the Indians had given up the contest.

Soon after the British force had surrendered, and it was discovered that the Indians were yielding on the left, general Harrison ordered major Payne to pursue general Procter with a part of his battalion; which was promptly done, and the pursuit continued, by the greater part of the detachment, to the distance of six miles beyond the Moravian town, some Indians being killed, and a considerable number of prisoners, with a large quantity of plunder, being captured in their progress. Majors Payne, Wood, Todd and Chambers, captain Langham, and lieutenants Scrogin and Bell, with three privates, continued the pursuit several miles further till night came upon them—but Procter was not to be taken. His guilty conscience had told him, that his only chance for safety from the vengeance of those whose countrymen he had murdered, lay in the celerity of his flight. The pursuers however at last pressed him so closely, that he was obliged to abandon the road, and his carriage and sword were captured by the gallant major Wood. The prisoners about 50 in number, were brought back to the Moravian town, where they were left in charge of captain M'Afee with 100 mounted men, until major Gano arrived about midnight with a reinforcement of 150 infantry. At the head of the town, six pieces of brass artillery were taken, three of which had been captured in the revolution at Saratoga and York, and surrendered again by Hull in Detroit.

The exact loss which either side sustained in this battle, has never been correctly known. According to the best information however which has been received, the total loss of the mounted regiment on that day, was 17 killed and 30 wounded. The loss of the infantry was much less, though considerable also, at the point where they reinforced colonel Johnson, which was the principal theatre of our losses. The Indians left thirty three dead on the battle ground, and had ten or twelve killed in different places by their pursuers. The British had 18 killed and 26 wounded, besides 600 prisoners captured, including 25 officers. Among our killed was colonel Whitley, a veteran who had been a distinguished soldier in former Indian wars, and had been no less conspicuous and serviceable in the present campaign, in which he accompanied colonel Johnson. Captain Craig and lieutenant Logan died of their wounds a few days after the battle. Colonel Johnson and captains Davison and Short were also wounded severely, but recovered. The colonel was shot through his thigh and in his hip, by the first fire of the Indians; and shortly afterwards he was shot through his left hand, by a ball which ranged up his arm, but did not enter his body. He continued however in front of his men, gallantly fighting the enemy, as long as the action lasted at that place. The white mare on which he rode, was also shot so severely, that she fell and expired soon after she had carried her rider within the lines of the infantry.

Tecumseh was found among the dead, at the point where colonel Johnson had charged upon the enemy in person; and it is generally believed, that this celebrated chief fell by the hand of the colonel. It is certain that the latter killed the Indian with his pistol, who shot him through his hand, at the very spot where Tecumseh lay: but another dead body lay at the same place, and Mr. King, a soldier in captain Davidson's company, had the honor of killing one of them.

From the best information that has been received, it appears that there was no material difference in the strength of the two armies in this battle. The troops under Harrison had been greatly reduced in number, by detachments left as guards and for other purposes, and by those who were sick and otherwise unable to keep up on forced marches. The distance from Sandwich to the Moravian town is upwards of eighty miles, which our army marched in three days and a half, though frequently harrassed by skirmishing and forming in order of battle, and delayed by repairing bridges and procuring supplies. A body of undisciplined militia, urged along and regulated alone by their patriotism and military ardor, would necessarily be much reduced by such a journey. The whole of the regulars had been left behind, except the small fragment of a regiment under colonel Paul. The brigade of general M'Arthur had been left at Detroit to protect the inhabitants against the Indians; and that of general Cass had been left at Sandwich, waiting for the baggage of the men, which delayed them so long that they were unable to come up with the army before the battle had been fought. The whole way from Sandwich to the battle ground was filled with scattering parties of the militia. Hence our force at the place of action was believed to be less than 2500 men, which was very little more than the force actually engaged on the part of the enemy. The British part of that force appears to have been about 845 strong. Its loss in killed, wounded and captured was 645; and the adjutant general of the British forces soon afterwards officially acknowledged, that 204 of those who escaped, had assembled at Ancaster on the 17th of October. This calculation is also confirmed by the official return of the troops at Malden on the 10th of September, which made them 944 in number—affording an excess of 100 above our estimate, to meet the losses experienced on the retreat before the battle. As for the amount of their Indian force, when it is shewn by their own official papers captured with the army, that 14,000 rations were issued daily to the Indians before the retreat, and that the

greater part of them accompanied Procter up the
Thames, it is certainly a reasonable calculation to estimate them at 15, 18, or even 20 hundred warriors in
the battle. The whole force of the allies must hence
have been at least considerably above 2000—yet a large
portion of that force was captured, and the balance entirely driven off, by the single regiment under Johnson, aided at one point only by a portion of the infantry, and making altogether, it is believed, much less
than half the army. But had our force been greatly
superior, the nature of the ground, and position of the
enemy, would have rendered its superiority useless ;
for a larger force than his, could not have been brought
efficiently into action, had his resistance been so great
as to render it necessary. The mounted regiment had
but 950 men in the battle—hence the force of the first
battalion, which was led into action by lieutenant colonel James Johnson, could not have been much more
than half as great as the British force, which it shattered in a moment by its impetuous charge.

Our important and glorious victory, it is evident was
principally achieved by the novel expedient of charging
through the British lines with mounted infantry. "The
measure, says general Harrison, who conceived it at the
moment for its execution, was not sanctioned by any
thing I had seen or heard, but I was fully convinced
that it would succeed. The American backwoodsmen
ride better in the woods than any other people. A
musket or rifle is no impediment to them, being accustomed to carry it on horseback from their earliest youth.
I was persuaded too, that the enemy would be quite
unprepared for the shock, and that they could not resist it." The shock was indeed so unexpected and impetuous, that all the resistance they were able to make
amounted to nothing. Two or three killed and a few
more wounded, was all the execution done by upwards
of eight hundred veterans, many of whom surrendered
without giving a second fire. "It is really a novel

thing, says colonel Wood, that raw militia stuck upon horses, with muskets in their hands instead of sabres, should be able to pierce British lines with such complete effect, as did Johnson's men in the affair upon the Thames; and perhaps the only circumstance which could justify that deviation from the long established rules of the art military, is the complete success of the result.   Great generals are authorised to step aside occasionally—especially when they know, that their errors will not be noticed by the adversary."

The preservation of the following testimony of general Harrison, to the merits of his officers on this occasion, will doubtless be gratifying to many persons who will read this history.   It is an extract from his letter to the secretary of war.

"In communicating to the President through you sir, my opinion of the conduct of the officers, who served under my command, I am at a loss how to mention that of governor Shelby, being convinced that no eulogium of mine can reach his merits.   The governor of an independent state, greatly my superior in years, in experience, and in military fame, he placed himself under my command, and was not more remarkable for his zeal and activity, than for the promptitude and cheerfulness with which he obeyed my orders.   The major generals, Henry and Desha, and the brigadiers, Allen, Caldwell, King, Chiles and Trotter, all of the Kentucky volunteer militia, manifested great zeal and activity.   Of governor Shelby's staff, his adjutant general, colonel M'Dowell, and his quarter master general, colonel Walker, rendered great services; as did his aids de camp, general Adair, and majors Barry and Crittenden.   The military skill of the former was of great service to us, and the activity of the two latter gentlemen could not be surpassed.   Illness deprived me of the talents of my adjutant general, colonel Gaines, who was left at Sandwich.   His duties however were ably performed by the assistant adjutant general, captain Butler. My aids de camp, lieutenant O'Fallon and captain Todd of the line, and my volunteer aids, John S. Smith and John Chambers, Esqrs. have rendered me the most important services from the opening of the campaign. I have already stated that general Cass and commodore Perry assisted me in forming the troops for action. The former is an officer of the highest merit, and the appearance of the brave commodore cheered and animated every breast. It would be useless sir, after stating the circumstances of the action, to pass encomiums on colonel Johnson and his regiment. Veterans could not have manifested more firmness. The colonel's numerous wounds prove that he was in the post of danger. The lieutenant colonel, James Johnson, and the majors Payne and Thompson, were equally active, though more fortunate. Major Wood of the engineers, already distinguished by his conduct at fort Meigs, attended the army with two six pounders. Having no use for them in the action, he joined in the pursuit of the enemy," &c. *Harrison.*

It has already been stated that only a small detachment of regular troops under colonel Paul were in the action, the balance of the brigade under Cass, which was composed of the regiments of Paul and Owings, and the battalion of light infantry under lieutenant colonel Ball, having been left behind waiting for their baggage. They were about 30 miles in the rear at the time of the battle, and were much mortified at not having an opportunity to come in contact with the enemy and participate in the glory of the victory. Their officers had made great exertions to discipline them, for which they had received the highest encomiums of general Harrison; and the gallant Perry had expressed his admiration of the skill and promptitude with which they performed their evolutions, particularly in debarking from the boats and forming the order of battle.

The merit of furnishing the means by which this important victory was achieved, belongs almost exclu-

sively to Kentucky.   Without her resources, under the
skilful management of governor Shelby, it is highly
probable, that the general government would not have
brought the campaign to a successful issue, although they
had obtained the command of lake Erie. The small force
of regulars, with which they had been able to furnish
general Harrison, was wholly incompetent to the invasion of Upper Canada : and it was so late in the season,
before they authorized him to call on the militia, that
the time usually consumed in drafting and marching
foot troops, including the delays unavoidable in procuring the supplies and transportation they would require, must have thrown him once more into the difficulties of a winter campaign. By raising mounted
volunteers, governor Shelby not only furnished the
necessary number of men with promptness, but he also
furnished in their horses the means of transportation,
by which they were enabled to reach the lake in good
time : and when the government had carried them over
the lake, they proceeded again upon their own resources and those of the enemy, without much assistance
from the government through the balance of the campaign. The unauthorized, but judicious and successful
course, pursued by governor Shelby in this instance
however, was afterwards approved not only by the
legislature of Kentucky, but also by the executive of
the Union and the voice of the nation.

On the 6th our troops continued to occupy the battle
ground, and the Moravian town about 2 miles above
it, being employed in burying the dead and collecting
the public property of the enemy, of which a considerable quantity was found in different places. In addition
to the artillery already mentioned, and a great variety
of military stores, there were at least 5000 stand of
small arms captured by our troops and destroyed by
the enemy on this expedition. A large proportion of
them had been taken from us at the surrender of Detroit, the massacre of the river Raisin, and the defeat

of colonel Dudley. Early on the 7th general Harrison
left the army under the immediate command of governor Shelby and returned to Detroit; and in the course
of the same day the different corps commenced their
return home, having embarked the greater part of the
property they had captured in boats on the Thames, and
set fire to the Moravian town, which was a very inconsiderable village, occupied chiefly by Delaware Indians, who professed to be of the Moravian sect of religion. On the 10th all the troops arrived with their
prisoners at Sandwich. It had now began to snow,
and the weather was extremely cold and stormy. For
two or three days the wind blew down the strait with
such violence, that it was impracticable to cross it, and
the vessels bringing down the public property, were
greatly endangered, and much of it was lost.

In the mean time an armistice was concluded by
general Harrison with the Indians. Before he marched
in pursuit of the British, a deputation of the Ottawas
and Chippewas had sued for peace, which he had promised them on condition that they would bring in their
families, and raise the tomahawk against the British.
To these terms they had readily acceded; and before
his return the Miamies and Potawatamies had solicited
a cessation of hostilities from general M'Arthur on the
same conditions. Even the ferocious and inveterate
Maipock of the Potawatamies now tendered his submission, and an armistice was concluded with seven of
the hostile tribes, which was to continue till the pleasure of the president was known. They agreed to
deliver up all their prisoners at fort Wayne, and to
leave hostages in security for their good behaviour.
Separated from their allies, by our victories on the lake
and the Thames, from whom they had received subsistence and council, they were now glad to accept our
friendship on any terms, which would save them from
extermination by famine and the sword.

On the 12th the storm had so far abated, that the
mounted regiment crossed over the strait to Spring

Wells; and on the next day the Kentucky infantry crossed at the mouth of the river Rouge. Some dissatisfaction and complaint now prevailed among the latter, at not being furnished with water transportation to carry them back to Portage; but general Harrison came into their camp, and in a public address assured them, that the vessels of the fleet were required for other important services. This satisfied and reconciled most of them to return on foot along the lake shore. The greater part of the fleet was still in lake St. Clair, many of the boats were lost, and commodore Perry had positive orders from the government, to carry an expedition in the fleet against Macinaw, which general Harrison was now preparing to execute with the regulars.

The foot troops arrived at the river Raisin on the 15th, where they found the bones of their massacred countrymen still bleaching in the village of Frenchtown and its environs. Governor Shelby directed the regiment of colonel Simrall to collect and bury them; but they were so numerous and widely scattered, that he found it necessary to employ the brigade of general King in the same business. They collected 65 skeletons, which were interred with the honors due to them by their brethren, returning from the conquest of their murderers, over whom they had triumphed more signally in honor and humanity than in arms. On the next day they continued their march, and arrived at the Miami bay, where they received a very seasonable supply of provisions, which were sent down to them by major Trigg from fort Meigs. On the 19th they arrived at Portage where their horses had been left, having performed a hard and laborious march of seven days, since they crossed the strait, in which they suffered greatly from hunger, fatigue and cold. The beach along the edge of the water afforded them a good road for a considerable portion of the way; but they had often to wade through deep waters in passing creeks and arms of the lake, and to penetrate through horrible swamps and difficult thickets. The care of the prisoners had greatly added to the difficulties, which his excellency, the governor, had to encounter, in superintending the homeward march, until the army arrived at Sandwich : at that place general Trotter voluntarily took charge of them, and notwithstanding the extreme difficulties of the journey thence to Portage, his management was so judicious and vigilant, that he was able at the latter place to account for every man who had been confided to his care.

The horses were collected from the enclosure in which they had been left, by forming a line of 1500 men across the lower end of the peninsula, before which they were driven up on the isthmus, and each delivered to its proper owner. Colonel Hife had not only taken good care of the horses, but he had also built a fort at Portage, and had opened and bridged a road to Lower Sandusky, for which he received the thanks of his returning countrymen. On the 20th a general order was issued, directing the return of the troops to Kentucky in detachments, passing by Franklinton where they were to deposit their arms. The governor concluded this order by observing—"although in the course of this campaign, you necessarily encountered many difficulties and privations, yet they were met with that cheerfulness and sustained with that manly fortitude which the occasion required. The uninterrupted good fortune which has attended us, is a source of the most pleasing reflection, and cannot fail to excite the warmest feelings of gratitude towards the Divine Being, who has been pleased in a peculiar manner to favor us, and to crown with success the exertions we have made for our country.

"In the course of the very active operations which we have performed, it is possible that expressions may have dropped, tending to irritate and wound the feelings of some who were engaged in them. The commanding general hopes, that with the campaign will and every unpleasant sensation, which may have arisen from that source, and that we shall return home united as a band of brothers, with the sweet solace of having served our country from the purest motives, and with the best of our abilities."

In pursuance of this order the troops returned to Kentucky, and were discharged by major Trigg at Limestone on the 4th of November. The mounted regiment was detained a few days at Detroit, till the Indians had dispersed after the armistice, and then returned home without any remarkable occurrence. Its colonel was left at Detroit in consequence of his wounds, where he was attended by his brother, the lieutenant colonel, who brought him a few days afterwards over the lake in a boat to Lower Sandusky. He was thence carried in a wagon to Cincinnati, where he met his own carriage coming for him. After he had arrived at home, he was confined to his bed several months; he was able however to resume his seat in congress about the middle of February. Though at last recovered of his wounds, they have left a permanent lameness behind them.

The expedition against Macinaw, for which general Harrison and commodore Perry were preparing, when the Kentuckians left them, was soon afterwards abandoned. They intended to have sailed on the 12th, but the weather was then so stormy, that they could not venture to embark; nor had they yet received a supply of provisions and baggage, which they were expecting up the lake for the expedition. Those supplies were on board the schooners Chippewa and Ohio, the former from Bass island, and the latter from Cleveland. They had arrived at the mouth of the strait, when they were met by the storm, by which they were so greatly distressed, that the mariners threw all the baggage and provisions overboard. The vessels were then driven down the lake, and finally run aground near Buffaloe. Some of the baggage being found on shore near the upper end of the lake, it was believed at head quarters that the schooners were entirely lost. A consultation was then held by general Harrison, with M'Arthur and Cass of the army, and Perry and Elliott of the fleet, at which it was determined unanimously, that the season was then so far advanced that the expedition ought not to be undertaken, unless it could sail immediately; and that it would be impossible to procure the necessary supplies for a considerable length of time. It was also believed that general Procter had ordered the commanding officer at Macinaw, to destroy that post and retreat by the way of Grand river. The enterprise was therefore abandoned without hesitation.

The Indians being subdued, and the expedition to Macinaw abandoned, general Harrison determined to proceed down the lake in the fleet, with general M'Arthur's brigade and a battalion of regular riflemen under colonel Smith. He had not for several months received any instructions from the war department, and knew not what the government wished him to do, on the close of the campaign in the northwest. Believing however that general Cass would be able with his brigade, to keep the Indians in subjection, and hold our conquests in that quarter, he left him in command at Detroit, and sailed down the lake with the rest of the troops. Orders to this effect had been sent from the war department by captain Brown, who was in one of the schooners, and was lost when she grounded at the lower end of the lake.

The secretary of war was at Sackett's harbor, when he received the first intelligence of Perry's victory, and on the 22nd of September had despatched captain Brown with orders for general Harrison to secure Malden, proceed down the lake with his forces, and throw himself in the rear of De Rottenburg, who was then investing fort George. A reinforcement of 3000 men, on both sides of the Niagara, was to be ready to join him on his arrival, and he was then expected to drive the enemy from the country between lakes Erie and Ontario.

On the 22nd of October general Harrison arrived at Erie where the fleet had been built, and soon pursued his voyage again to Buffaloe, where he arrived on the 24th, with an aggregate of 1300 men, which afforded however but 1000 effectives. He had still received no communication from the war department, and was entirely uninformed as to the situation of affairs where he was going. He determined however to proceed down the Niagara to fort George. De Rottenburg had long since abandoned that place, and retired to Burlington bay. General M'Clure of the New York militia was commanding at the fort when general Harrison arrived; and as the enemy was still at Burlington, they determined to march against him and drive him from that position. The troops in the mean time were marched down by the falls and stationed at Newark. A communication was now opened with the secretary of war at Sackett's harbor, and to obtain a sufficient force for the intended enterprise, a call was made on the militia of the adjoining counties. But before an adequate force could be collected, and the necessary arrangements made, a letter was received by general Harrison from the secretary, informing him that the brigade of M'Arthur was required at Sackett's harbor, and that he would be permitted to make a visit to his family; which he understood as an order to retire to his own district. The letter was dated on the 3rd of November, and on the 16th of that month, commodore Chauncey arrived at Newark, the head quarters of general Harrison, with vessels to transport his troops to the harbor. The troops were accordingly embarked, and the general set out immediately for Washington city, which he included in his route on the visit to his family at Cincinnati. On his journey he received all those marks and demonstrations of public confidence and gratitude, with which the American people were accustomed to greet their distinguished defenders; and as the campaign on the northern frontier soon terminated in a copious harvest of disgrace to all the generals immediately concerned in it, general Harrison soon had the additional satisfaction of being designated by public opinion, for the chief command on that frontier in the campaign of the ensuing summer. The judgment of the war department however, was at variance with the expectations of the people on this subject. Early in January the general arrived at Cincinnati, which continued to be his head quarters as long as he thought proper to retain his commission in the army.

General Cass being required to attend the trial of general Hull at Albany, the command at Detroit devolved on colonel Butler; and the former before his return to the western country was appointed governor of the Michigan territory. The greater part of the fleet was stationed for the winter in the harbor of Erie, some of the larger vessels being left in Put-in-Bay— and the necessary precautions were taken to guard the whole against any enterprise for their destruction by the enemy.

The campaign on the northern frontier, under the immediate superintendence of Armstrong, Wilkinson and Hampton, having terminated very unfavorably to our cause, apprehensions were entertained by the government in December, that the British thus encouraged, would make great exertions to reestablish their affairs in the northwest, and particularly to regain the friendship of the Indians, and perpetuate their influence among them. With the latter views, it was ascertained, that Dickson had been sent up from York with a large quantity of goods. Our government hence determined to take the most effectual and rigorous measures to counteract these designs of the enemy. Instructions were therefore sent after general Harrison on his return home, that the settlements on the Thames, which would afford the enemy the means of advancing towards Detroit, and intermeddling with the Indians, must be entirely destroyed and converted into a desert; that peace must be made with the Indians on the most liberal terms, supplying all their wants and allowing them to retain all the lands they had held before the war; and that they must be engaged to take up arms on our side, and let loose on the British frontier early in the spring, so as to drive away every British settler to be found on the west of Kingston. "A question may occur," says the secretary of war, "under what restrictions, as to their mode of warfare, we ought to employ them? The question has in it no difficulty. Under what justification do we employ them at all? The example of the enemy. It was not our choice but theirs, and is but an appeal made to their fears, after having unsuccessfully made many to their justice. The experiment should therefore have fair play. All the horrors brought to our firesides, ought to be carried to theirs. Nor is this a policy of mere retaliation. The settlements in Upper Canada abandoned, their posts cannot be supported, and will of course also be abandoned." When these instructions were issued, the cruelties of the savages, now threatened to be renewed, were not the only atrocities which merited this retaliation. The enemy had recently crossed into our settlements on the Niagara frontier, and laid the whole country in ruins, destroying every thing before them in the most wanton and barbarous manner. The humanity of the president however, would not permit him to persist in the rigorous measures he had authorized. The instructions from the secretary were speedily countermanded, and the general was merely authorized—"to make prisoners, and remove to our settlements, so many of the male British settlers as might be most disposed to do us harm."

It appears however, from a correspondence between general Harrison and the British generals Procter and Vincent, after the battle on the Thames, that the former had firmly resolved to take upon himself the responsibility of a rigorous retaliation, should a renewal of Indian barbarities render it necessary. Immediately after the battle of the Thames, Procter sent a flag with a letter to general Harrison, requesting that the private property and papers, which had been captured with the army, might be respected and restored to their proper owners. As general Harrison was on the eve of sailing down the lake, when he received the letter, he declined answering it until he had arrived at fort George, and then directed his reply to general Vincent, the senior officer at Burlington heights. As for his treatment of the prisoners, and his disposition of private papers and property, he referred general Vincent to the accompanying letters from the captured officers for information; at the same time assuring him, that his conduct had proceeded from motives of humanity alone, and not from any claim which the enemy could make on the score of reciprocity of treatment; for, of the American prisoners, who had fallen into the hands of Procter, those who escaped from the tomahawk, had suffered all the indignities and deprivations which human nature was capable of enduring. *There was not a single instance, in which the private property of the officers had been respected.* After enumerating many instances, in which families, comprising men, women, and children, had been most inhumanly butchered by Indians, who came direct from the British camp and returned to it; and after assuring general Vincent, that "The savages who had sued for mercy, would gladly have shewn their claims to it, by reacting on the Thames the bloody scenes of Sandusky and Cold creek"—that "a single sign of approbation would have been sufficient to pour upon the subjects of the king their whole fury—" he concludes his letter with the following paragraph—

"I deprecate most sincerely, the dreadful alternative which will be offered to me, should those barbarities be continued; but I solemnly declare, that if the Indians who remain under the influence of the British government, are suffered to commit any depredations on the citizens, within the district that is committed to my protection, I will remove the restrictions which have been imposed on those who have offered their services to the United States, and direct them to carry on the war in their own way. I have never heard a single excuse for the employment of the savages by your government, unless we may credit the story of some British officers having dared to assert, that "as we employed the Kentuckians, you had a right to make use of the Indians." If such injurious sentiments have really prevailed, to the prejudice of a brave, well informed and virtuous people, they will be removed by the representations of your officers, who were lately taken upon the river Thames. They will inform you sir, that so far from offering any violence to the persons of their prisoners, *these savages* would not permit a word to escape them, which was calculated to wound or insult their feelings—and this too, with the sufferings of their friends and relatives at the rivers Raisin and Miami fresh in their recollection."—*Harrison.*

General Vincent promised in his reply, that "no effort of his should ever be wanting to diminish the evils of a state of warfare, as far as might be consistent with the *duties,* which were due to his *king* and country"—a promise which portended butcheries and devastation without measure, as the history of "his majesty's reign over his *dutiful* subjects" most amply demonstrates. But fortunately the progress of the war did not afford an opportunity again for the performance of those duties.

3 D

CHAPTER X.

Expedition of captain Holmes—resignation of general Harrison—expedition to Macinaw—treaty with the Indians—affair of Prairie du Chien—expedition of general M'Arthur.

ALTHOUGH the enemy did not think proper during the winter, to send up any formidable force to the northwest, yet colonel Butler the commanding officer at Detroit, was scarcely in a condition to contend with their advanced posts, and the individuals of the militia who were disposed to be troublesome. The brigade of general Cass which was left at Detroit, was originally very weak, and during the month of December it suffered extremely from a violent epidemic, which resisted all the skill of its physicians. At one time its whole effective force did not amount to 300 men. Small corps of the Ohio and Pennsylvania militia, were hence kept in service through the winter, to assist in garrisoning the different posts, and in protecting the vessels of the fleet.

About the first of January, the enemy posted a corps of observation at Delaware on the Thames, thirty miles above the Moravian town, under the command of captain Stewart, who frequently sent foraging and reconnoitring parties down the Thames, and into the vicinity of Sandwich. Colonel Butler was hence induced to place a corps for similar purposes, and as a check to the movements of the enemy, on the Thames at Dobson's some distance below the Moravian town. It consisted of 30 men under the command of lieutenant Lowell. The British being apprised of the situation of this corps, descended the Thames from Delaware and surprised it in the night, capturing the whole party without much loss in killed and wounded on either side. The colonel did not think proper to reestablish the post, but occasionally sent reconnoitring and foraging parties up the Thames; one of which under captain Lee, who commanded a company of Michigan rangers, captured and brought away colonel Baby, captain Springer, and several others of the Canadian militia, who were the most active in the cause of the enemy. Captain Springer was a native of the United States, having been born near Albany in New York, and had been naturalized by the British and made a magistrate as well as a militia officer. Captain Lee some time afterwards caught major Townsley, a native of Connecticut, who had been the most active and vindictive partizan of the British in Upper Canada.

In February colonel Butler determined to make a stroke at some of the advanced posts of the enemy. The execution of the enterprise was confided to captain Holmes, with a detachment of regulars and some Michigan rangers and militia. He was directed to march against a small post called fort Talbot, situate about 100 miles down the lake below Malden; or if he should deem it more eligible to make an attack on the enemy at Delaware, he was authorised to change his destination to that place. He marched from Malden about the 20th of February, with two six pounders in his train; but he soon found it impossible to proceed down the lake with artillery, he was so much obstructed by fallen timber, thickets, and swamps. He was obliged to leave them and depend on his small arms. Captain Gill who had pursued some Canadian militia up the Thames, with a small company of rangers, was to cross the country and form a junction with Holmes. After this had been effected, the route down the lake was found to be so difficult that captain Holmes determined to leave it and go to the Thames, with a view either to attack the enemy at Delaware, or to intercept any detachment that might be sent down the river. He struck the Thames below the Moravian town, and immediately marched towards the enemy's post. When he had arrived within fifteen miles of it, he learnt that a detachment about 300 strong was coming to meet him. As the force which he commanded was much weaker, he determined to retreat till he could find a strong position to resist them. He fell back five miles to 20 mile creek, a stream which runs into the Thames from the north. Having crossed it on a bridge, he posted his men on the summit of an adjoining height, and began to strengthen his position with a breastwork. The enemy soon appeared on the opposite heights over the creek. The captain now called a council of officers, to determine whether they should endeavor to maintain their position, or retreat still further. On this question there was much difference of opinion. Many of the detachment had suffered so much from cold and fatigue, that they were now unfit for duty; and others had been permitted from the same causes to return home; so that the whole effective force did not exceed 160, while the force of the enemy was believed to be double that number. Captain Holmes and his adjutant, ensign Heard, a grandson of the celebrated general Morgan, were strenuously opposed to a retreat, and it was at last determined, that they would perish or triumph in their present position.

The enemy did not pretend to annoy them that evening; but early in the morning a party of British regulars came to the bank of the creek, fired a few times at the camp and then retired. After waiting some time for a more formidable attack, captain Holmes sent out lieutenant Knox with some of the rangers to reconnoitre. He returned in a few minutes and reported, that the enemy had fled with precipitation, leaving their baggage scattered along the road; and that they did not appear to have been more than seventy in number. Mortified at the idea of having retreated from such a diminutive force, captain Holmes immediately pursued them, with a determination to attack their position at Delaware next morning. Having pursued them about five miles, captain Lee of the advanced guard reported, that he had come up with the enemy in considerable force, and that they were forming in order of battle. Captain Holmes now apprehended, that they had retreated to draw him from his position, with a view to gain his rear with a superior force, which would compel him to advance towards their post at Delaware, or to cross the wilderness towards fort Talbot without forage or provisions. It was not their plan however to intercept his retreat, and in a short time he regained the position he had left on 20 mile creek.

Some of his officers again insisted on a retreat, but the captain determined to wait at this place for an attack from the enemy. He continued to strengthen his camp which was a hollow square, and posted his regulars on the north side, and on the brow of the hill without breastwork. His rangers and militia were posted on the west and south, the horses and baggage being placed in the centre. Late in the evening the enemy appeared again on the opposite heights, upwards of 300 strong, under the command of captain Basden. Their militia and Indians immediately crossed the creek above the road, surrounded the camp, and commenced an attack on the north, west, and south. Their regulars crossed on the bridge, and charged up the hill within 20 paces of our front line, which had been ordered to kneel so as to be effectually protected by the brow of the hill. The fire of that line was now opened with such effect, that the front section of the enemy was immediately cut down, and those which followed were very much injured. He then displayed his column along the hill side, and took open distance behind trees, in which order a warm contest was maintained for a considerable time. On the other lines the militia and Indians fought behind trees at a more respectful distance, but were also much thinned by the deliberate fire of our men. Finding it impossible to make much impression on the camp, the enemy at length retreated under cover of the night, having lost in the action, according to their own account, no less than sixty seven killed and wounded: but in the opinion of captain Holmes their loss was between eighty and ninety. Captain Basden and lieutenant M'Donald were wounded; and captain Johnson and lieutenant Graham were killed. The loss on our side was but seven in killed and wounded.

The brave detachment under Holmes received much applause for this victory, which formed a fine counterpart to the brilliant affair of Sandusky. The commanding officer, who was always remarkable for his zeal, activity, and knowledge of his duty, was immediately promoted to the rank of major, for his singular gallantry and good conduct on this occasion.

Soon after this affair colonel Butler obtained leave to return to Kentucky, chiefly with a view to superintend the recruiting of his own regiment in that state; and the command at Detroit devolved on lieutenant colonel Croghan.

As the government still expected, that the British would make considerable exertions in the approaching summer to regain the ground they had lost in the northwest, and particularly to reestablish their connexions and influence with the Indians, a plan of counteracting operations was adopted early in April, and commodore Sinclair and major Holmes were selected to carry it into execution. The views of the government will be best understood by the following extract of a communication from the commodore to colonel Croghan.

"Erie, 28th April, 1814.
" SIR—The government having thought proper, to separate the command of the upper lakes from that of Ontario, they have appointed me to the former; and in my instructions I am directed to open a communication with the commanding officer at Detroit. That you may be better informed of their views, I

give you the following extract from the instructions of the honorable secretary of the navy on this subject.

EXTRACT——'*April 15th,* 1814.

'You will immediately on your arrival at Erie, open a communication with the military commander at Detroit, asking of him all the information he may possess, relative to the passage into and navigation of lake Huron, and all the circumstances connected with your expedition, the nature and extent of which you will explain to him. You will also request him to have in readiness to join your force, a body of 300 hardy, intrepid volunteers, one half of which should be riflemen; for which I have no doubt the secretary of war will have directed the necessary measures to be taken.

'The information we possess, relative to the designs and movements of the enemy, rests upon report, and is rather probable than certain. There is however reason to believe, that the enemy have sent two small detachments of seamen, and perhaps mechanics, to lake Huron, where they are constructing some sort of naval force—rumor says, *two brigs;* but if the fact is so, they must be of small force. They are also said to be building a number of boats on lake Simcoe, and have recently transported considerable quantities of naval and ordnance stores to York, the distance from which to lake Simcoe is not above 40 miles over a good road. The boats are doubtless intended to convey those stores, through the waters emptying from lake Simcoe into lake Huron at Gloucester bay, on the southeast extremity of lake Huron. It is on the shores of this bay they are constructing their naval force. For this place you will make a prompt and vigorous push, destroy or capture whatever they may have prepared, and proceed, before the alarm can be extended, to St. Josephs at the mouth of French river, which place it is expected you may readily reduce, and get possession of all the property and stores deposited there; and leaving a force to protect that post if tenable, or not likely to be attacked by a superior force, you will thence proceed to Macinaw, with which the communication of the enemy being entirely cut off, and the place being destitute of provisions, it will doubtless prove an easy conquest. Having accomplished these objects, you will be governed by the season, the state of your provisions, and the information you may receive, whether to leave a small garrison at that place, and a part of your squadron on that lake, during the ensuing winter, or return to Erie with the whole.' "

After requesting colonel Croghan to despatch some active spies, to ascertain the situation and forces of the enemy; and also to secure a passage into lake Huron, by erecting a military post in some eligible situation on the strait between lakes St. Clair and Huron; the commodore proceeds—"It appears to me, that the military force mentioned by the secretary of the navy is by no means adequate, as my ships will be badly manned, owing to the great difficulty of procuring seamen; and if I am not misinformed, the land force will have in every instance to cooperate on shore, as their batteries are so situated as not to be reduced by the shipping." *Sinclair.*

About the time these instructions were communicated to the commodore, the secretary of war thought proper to send a corresponding order directly to major Holmes, entirely passing by colonel Croghan the commandant at Detroit, and merely notifying general Harrison the commander of the district, through whom the arrangements for the expedition should have been made. This course of the secretary was a violation not only of military etiquette, but also of the most important military principles—which require, that the commander of a district, or of a separate post, especially when situated on a distant frontier, should have the supreme direction of minor matters, within the sphere of his command. The interference of the government in such matters, must inevitably derange his plans, and produce confusion and disaster in the service. The general should be furnished with the object and outlines of the campaign or expedition, and with the necessary supplies of men, money, and munitions, for accomplishing that object; and then be made responsible for their proper management. But the secretary in this instance, issued his orders to major Holmes under the nose of his colonel, whereby the rank and authority of the latter were superceded, and the resources of his post were to be clandestinely withdrawn from his power. This was highly resented by colonel Croghan, who communicated his sentiments on this subject without reserve to commodore St. Clair and general Harrison. He assured the commodore, that he had already taken every means to reconnoitre the upper lakes and country, with a view to obtain such information as he requested, and that he would be happy to cooperate and assist him in the enterprise, but could not pledge himself in the present state of his resources, to furnish any important assistance. To the general he wrote—" Major Holmes has been notified by the war department, that he is chosen to command the land troops, which are intended to cooperate with the fleet, against the enemy's force on the upper lakes. So soon as I may be directed by you, to order major Holmes on that command, and to furnish him with the necessary troops, I shall do so; but not till then, shall he or any other part of my force leave the sod." *Croghan.*

In answer to a second letter from the commodore, written in the latter part of May, he proceeds : " I much fear sir, that in your expectation of being joined at this place by a battalion, or corps of regulars under major Holmes, you will be disappointed. Major Holmes it is true has been notified by the war department, that he is selected to command the land troops on the expedition up the lakes. But this notification, even did it amount to a positive order to the major, could not be considered as an order to me; nor can I deem it in itself sufficient to justify me in weakening the present reduced strength of my command. My objection to cooperate with you at this time, is not I assure you, moved by any thing like chagrin at this departure from military etiquette, but is bottomed on a thorough conviction, that nothing less than a positive order could justify or excuse my detaching a part of the small force under my command, from the *immediate* defence of this frontier. I agree with you, that the premised force under major Holmes appears too weak to effect the desired end. I cannot speak *positively* on the subject, as my knowledge even of the geographical situation of

3 E

that country is but limited; yet my belief is, that if resistance be made at all, it will prove too stout for 1000 men. The position of Macinaw is a strong one, and should the enemy have determined on holding it, he has had time enough to throw in reinforcements. The Engages in the employ of the N. W. Company, generally get down to Macinaw from their wintering grounds, about the last of May in every year. Will those hardy fellows, whose force exceeds 1000, be permitted to be idle? Will it not be the interest of the N. W. Company to exert all its means, in the defence of those posts, in which it is so immediately concerned? I send you a few queries on this subject, with the answers as given by an intelligent gentleman, formerly an agent to the N. W. Company, and well acquainted with the geographical situation of that country. Every arrangement is made for securing the entrance into lake Huron. I am under no solicitude about the passage up the strait." *Croghan.*

Although the colonel appears to consider the order to Holmes, as a mere notification of his appointment, yet it was certainly intended by the secretary, to be sufficiently positive and ample to put the expedition in motion, without any other communication from the war department, except the instructions to the commodore. Soon after the above was written, the colonel addressed another letter to general Harrison, from which the following is an extract. "I know not how to account for the secretary of war's assuming to himself, the right of designating major Holmes for this command to Macinaw. My ideas on the subject may not be correct, yet for the sake of the principle, were I a general commanding a district, I would be very far from suffering the secretary of war, or any other authority, to interfere with my internal police.

"I have not yet been able, even by three attempts, to ascertain whether the enemy is building boats at Mackedash (Gloucester bay.) None of my spies would venture far enough, being either frightened at the *view* of lake Huron, or alarmed at the probability of meeting hostile Indians." *Croghan.*

This letter was written in the latter part of May. General Harrison actuated by similar sentiments had already resigned his commission of major general in the army, which he had received about the time his appointment in the Kentucky militia had expired. He believed that the secretary of war disliked him, and had intentionally encroached on the prerogatives of his rank to insult him, by corresponding with the officers under his command, and giving them orders direct, which ought, at least, to have been communicated indirectly, through the commander in chief of the district. He had remonstrated in a spirited manner against this interference, and finding it again renewed in the present case, he resigned his commission by the following letters to the secretary and president.

'*Head Quarters, Cincinnati, 11th May, 1814.*

'SIR—I have the honor through you, to request the president to accept my resignation of the appointment of major general in the army, with which he has honored me.

'Lest the public service should suffer, before a successor can be nominated, I shall continue to act until the 31st instant, by which time I hope to be relieved.

'Having some reasons to believe, that the most malicious insinuations have been made against me at Washington, it was my intention to have requested an inquiry into my conduct, from the commencement of my command. Further reflection has however determined me, to decline the application—because, from the proud consciousness of having *palpably* done my duty, I cannot believe that it is necessary either for the satisfaction of the government or the people, that I should pay so much respect to the suggestions of malice and envy.

'It is necessary however, that I should assure you sir, that I subscribe implicitly to the opinion, that military officers are responsible for their conduct, and amenable to the decisions of a court martial, after they have left the service, for any improper act committed in it.

'The principle was established in England, in the case of lord George Sackville after the battle of Minden ; it was known and recognized by all the ancient republics; and is particularly applicable I think to a government like ours. I therefore pledge myself to answer before a court martial, at any future period, to any charge which may be brought against me.

' I have the honor &c.

' HARRISON.

' The Hon. J. Armstrong &c.'

(same date.)

' Dear Sir—I have this day forwarded to the secretary of war, my resignation of the commission I hold in the army.

' This measure has not been determined on, without a reference to all the reasons which should influence a citizen, who is sincerely attached to the honor and interests of his country; who believes that the war in which we are engaged is just and necessary; and that the crisis requires the sacrifice of every private consideration, which could stand in opposition to the public good. But after giving the subject the most mature consideration, I am perfectly convinced, that my retiring from the army is as compatible with the claims of patriotism, as it is with those of my family, and a proper regard for my own feelings and honor.

' I have no other motive for writing this letter, than to assure you, that my resignation was not produced by any diminution of the interest, which I have always taken in the success of your administration, or of respect and attachment for your person. The former can only take place, when I forget the republican principles in which I have been educated; and the latter when I shall cease to regard those feelings, which must actuate every honest man, who is conscious of favors that it is out of his power to repay.

' Allow me, &c.

' HARRISON.

' James Madison esq. president U. S. A.'

When commodore Sinclair had made every preparation to sail from Erie on the expedition up the lakes, and was waiting only for more men in which he was still deficient, he received on the 1st of June, a despatch from the secretary of the navy, countermanding the intended enterprise. This determination of the government was produced by a belief, founded on the intelligence they had received, that the enemy were not making much exertion to reestablish their affairs in the northwest. The plan of our operations in that quarter,

was therefore now to be substituted by that, which is developed in the following letter from the secretary at war to the president.

'*War Department, April 30th,* 1814.

'SIR—So long as we had reason to believe, that the enemy intended, and was in a condition to reestablish himself on the Thames, and open anew his intercourse with the Indian tribes of the west, it was no doubt proper to give our naval means a direction, which would best obstruct and defeat such movements and designs. An order was accordingly given by the navy department, to employ the flotilla in scouring the shores of the western lakes, destroying the enemy's trading establishment at St. Josephs, and in recapturing fort Macinaw. As however our last advices show, that the enemy has no efficient force westward of Burlington bay, and that he has suffered the season of easy and rapid transportation to escape him, it is evident that he means to strengthen himself on the peninsula, and make fort Erie, which he is now repairing, the western extremity of his line of operations. Under this new state of things it is respectfully suggested, whether another and a better use cannot be made of our flotilla.

'In explaining myself it is necessary to premise, that the garrisons of Detroit and Malden included, it will be practicable to assemble on the shores and navigable waters of lake Erie, 5000 regular troops, and 3000 volunteers and militia, and that measures have been taken to produce this result by the 10th day of June next. Without however naval means, this force will be necessarily dispersed, and comparatively inoperative—with their aid, competent to great objects.

'Lake Erie on which our dominion is indisputable, furnishes a way scarcely less convenient for approaching the heart of Upper Canada, than lake Ontario. Eight or even six thousand men, landed in the bay between Point Aubino and fort Erie, and operating either on the line of the Niagara, or more directly, if a more direct route is to be found, against the British post at the head of Burlington bay, would induce the enemy so to weaken his more eastern posts, as to bring them within our means at Sackett's Harbor and Plattsburg.

'In choosing between this object, and that to which the flotilla is now destined, there cannot I think be much hesitation. Our attack carried to Burlington and York, interposes a barrier, which completely protects Malden and Detroit, makes doubtful and hazardous the enemy's intercourse with the western Indians, reduces Macinaw to a possession perfectly useless, renders probable the abandonment of fort Niagara, and takes from the enemy half his motives for continuing the conflict on lake Ontario. On the other hand, take Macinaw, and what is gained but Macinaw itself? If this plan is adopted, no time should be lost in countermanding the execution of the other.

'I have the honor &c.

'J. ARMSTRONG.

' The PRESIDENT.'

The adoption of this plan for the campaign of 1814, was not however to produce a total abandonment of the expedition up the lakes. Commodore Sinclair was instructed to send a small detachment of the fleet in that direction, not exceeding three small vessels, to be accompanied by a cooperating force of 150 men from Detroit. He accordingly despatched that number under lieutenant Woodhouse to Detroit, where he was to receive the land forces and then proceed up the strait. On the very day however, that the order for abandoning the original expedition into the upper lakes, was received by commodore Sinclair, the government determined again to carry it into execution in its full extent. This change was produced by news of a more alarming complexion, respecting the naval preparations of the enemy on lake Huron; and in part perhaps by a conviction, that the army of 8000, to be drawn from the western country, would be found greatly deficient in the field. It is believed, that a report of great naval preparations being made on lake Huron, was propagated by the enemy on purpose to draw our flotilla in that direction.

However, commodore Sinclair was informed by a letter from the navy department, dated on the 1st of June, that the expedition to lake Huron, agreeably to the original design, must proceed without delay; and that the war office would direct colonel Croghan to accompany him, with as many troops as he could accommodate on board his squadron. The war department addressed colonel Croghan as follows—

"Information has been received, that the enemy is making a new establishment at Mackedash on lake

Huron, and that from 500 to 1000 seamen, mechanics, and others are now employed there, in the construction of armed vessels &c. This establishment must be broken up. The safety of Detroit, the command of the lakes, the general security of that frontier depends upon it. Captain Sinclair will accordingly receive orders to pass into lake Huron, with part of the flotilla, and to carry such troops as may be destined to coope- rate with the fleet, in the reduction of this and other places. His means of transportation will probably not accommodate more than 800; but the safest rule will be to embark as many as can be accommodated, taking yourself the command, and leaving behind you a com- petent force, to guard against Indian attacks, which at present are alone to be feared. If on reaching and reducing the place, it be found to be important, as I believe it will, it ought to be fortified and garrisoned, and become the left of a new line of operations, extend- ing by the way of lake Simcoe from Gloucester bay on lake Huron, to York on lake Ontario. In this last view of the subject, supplies of cannon, ammunition, and provisions ought to be carried with you." *Arm- strong*.

While on the subject of *plans* for the operations of the campaign in the present year, it will perhaps be interesting to some readers, to see the following full exhibition of the present views of the government, by the pen of Mr. secretary Armstrong, in a letter to gen- eral Izard.

‘ *War Department, June 10th, 1814.*

‘ Sir—I avail myself of the return of colonel Snelling, to communicate to you the general objects of the campaign.

‘ Captain Sinclair will repair to Detroit with a part of the fleet under his command. He will there embark colonel Croghan and as large a number of troops, with the necessary supplies of ammunition and provisions, as his vessels will accommodate. He will then enter lake Huron, and proceed to Gloucester bay, where the troops will debark, attack and carry the enemy's new establishment at Mackedash, fortify and garrison that place, and open a communication with general Brown, if another part of the plan, to be next detailed, shall have succeeded. This effected, the fleet will go on to the mouth of St. Josephs and to Macinaw &c.

'What remains of the fleet at Buffaloe, will be put under orders to transport general Brown's division to the Canada shore. The place of landing will be selected by the discretion of the general, under the best information of which he may be possessed. Burlington Heights will be his first object. There he will fortify, and as soon as commodore Chauncey will be in a condition to cooperate with him, say the first of July, he will proceed to attack the enemy's posts on the peninsula in succession &c.

'A number of armed gallies, such as those employed on lake Champlain, will be immediately constructed at Sackett's Harbor; and while we have the ascendency on lake Ontario, these will be pushed into the St. Lawrence, with orders to occupy the rapids of that river, and thus intercept the water communication between Montreal and Kingston. The better to effect this object, a post will be established on the south bank of the St. Lawrence, strongly fortified and garrisoned by a competent force, say 1500 men, and sustained by the 1st division of the right. The moment for beginning this establishment will be that which opens to us the command of lake Ontario. An engineer will be employed by the war department to select the site.

'Another post on lake Champlain, adapted to the purposes of cooperating with and covering our fleet on that lake, and of excluding the enemy's flotilla therefrom, will be immediately selected, established, and garrisoned. This post you will please to select.

'ARMSTRONG.'

That portion only of these various plans, which was to be executed by Sinclair and Croghan on the upper lakes, is embraced within the limits prescribed for this history. As soon as commodore Sinclair received his instructions on the 9th of June, he despatched a messenger after lieutenant Woodhouse to arrest his progress with the detachment under his command, and immediately prepared to sail with his whole squadron. He was soon able to proceed, and arrived at Detroit after the 20th of that month. Colonel Croghan had been making the most vigorous preparations on his part, and was ready to embark about the first of July. The expedition however was disapproved by him, and still more the manner in which the secretary had ordered it, having passed by general M'Arthur, on whom the command of the district had devolved since the resignation of general Harrison. The following is an extract from his letter to general M'Arthur on this subject, dated on the 3rd of July.

"You will have heard, that an expedition commanded by myself, against the enemy's posts on the upper lakes, is on the eve of sailing. The order for this expedition was issued by the secretary of war on the 2nd ultimo, most probably without advising you of the step. I could wish for many reasons, that this order had passed through the regular channel. This manner of interfering with the internal police of officers commanding districts, will sooner or later prove as destructive as it now appears unmilitary. To enable me to meet the wishes of the secretary of war, I was forced to take upon myself the responsibility of doing many things, to be justified *only* on the score of necessity. I ordered on from Lower Sandusky, a point without my limits, captain Sanders and lieutenant Scott of the 17th infantry, with their respective commands. I have also organized a company of Canadians 120 in number, to act until the return of the expedition, *pledging myself* to have them paid at the rate of one dollar per day each. I hope you will approve this step. I am enabled *by acting thus*, to embark 500 regulars and 250 militia. My troops are all on board, and part of the fleet is now under way. I disapprove the expedition against Macinaw, because *if it be taken*, we are not at all benefited." *Croghan.*

The fleet advanced but slowly through lake St. Clair, which is so shallow, that there was some difficulty in finding a channel deep enough for the largest vessels. It was the 12th, before they had passed fort Gratiot, on the west side of the river St. Clair, at the entrance into lake Huron. That fort had recently been built by captain Gratiot, who had been sent up by colonel Croghan on that service, with a few regulars early in May, and had afterwards been joined by colonel Cotgrove with a small regiment of Ohio militia, on whom the completion and maintenance of the post had devolved. Colonel Cotgrove now embarked with a few of his men in the expedition under Croghan.

Having entered lake Huron, the fleet agreeably to the instructions of the government, steered directly for Mackedash or Gloucester bay, which communicates through lake Simcoe, with York the capital of Upper Canada. The entrance of the bay is closed by a chain of islands, through which our commodore had no pilot to conduct him, and the navigation is extremely difficult and dangerous. A whole week was spent in searching for a channel, through which the fleet could safely reach the establishment of the enemy, the destruction of which was the principal object of the expedition ; but no such channel could be found, and the commander was at last compelled to proceed without visiting the place against which the government had principally sent him. This failure however was in reality unimportant, for the enemy had no such establishment at Mackedash, as the expedition was intended to destroy.

The fleet now sailed to St. Josephs, where they arrived on the 20th of July. That post had been evacuated by the enemy, apparently several months ago. A detachment was sent on shore to burn the fort. Major Holmes was then detached with two small vessels under lieutenant Turner of the navy, and a small force of regulars and artillery, to visit the strait of St. Marys which forms the communication between lakes Huron and Superior, for the purpose of destroying a trading establishment belonging to the enemy at that place. The balance of the fleet steered for Macinaw. Major Holmes reached his destination in two days, and immediately attacked the trading house of the northwest company. It was easily taken, for the agent and the Indians immediately fled into the wilderness. They had previously carried a great quantity of their goods into the woods, as soon as they had been apprized of our approach: those goods however were soon found by our men. They were deposited within the limits of our territory, and were claimed as American property, by a fellow who had been a citizen and magistrate of the Michigan territory, but was now in the service of the company, for whom he was thus endeavoring by false pretexts to save their property. Major Holmes however was not to be gulled in this manner. A schooner was also found above the fort, which the enemy had abandoned and set on fire. She was saved from the flames by lieutenant Turner, but in bringing her through the rapids, she bilged and was then voluntarily destroyed.

The fleet arrived off Macinaw on the 26th of July, and some prisoners being taken, from whom information was obtained, that the schooner Nancy, a vessel which the enemy had kept on the upper lakes, was daily expected from the Natawasauga river, commodore Sinclair immediately stationed his vessels in a manner to intercept her. On the next day colonel Croghan made a demonstration towards a landing on Round island, about three quarters of a mile from Macinaw. This being observed by the enemy, two batteaux of British regulars, and 20 or 30 canoes filled with Indians were immediately sent to the island; and a number of other boats were held in readiness at the beach to reinforce this detachment, should it become necessary. As commodore Sinclair did not think it prudent to station his vessels, so as to cut off the communication between the islands, on account of the difficult anchorage which he would have to occupy, the attempt to land was abandoned. From every appearance in these manœuvres, and from the best information that could be obtained, it was believed, that the force of the enemy was at least 1000 including Indians,

and that he had determined on making an obstinate
resistance.   It was ascertained that the garrison had
lately been reinforced by colonel R. M'Dowell, who
had strengthened the fort and occupied the heights
which command it, with a strong fortification.   Colonel
Croghan hence determined to postpone any further
operations, until major Holmes should arrive with the
detachment under his command, which happened on
the next day after the attempt to land.

Colonel Croghan now resolved to effect a landing on
the island of Macinaw, and to seize some strong position and fortify it, from which he could annoy the fort.
He was in hopes, that the enemy would be tempted to
meet him and risk a battle in the open plain; or provoked by the annoyance, and anxious to terminate the
siege, that he would be induced at last to make a sortie
and attack our entrenchments.   Without some fortunate occurrence of this kind, our commanders had but
little hope of succeeding, against a superior force strongly fortified.   A landing on the east end of the island
would have been preferred, as being near the position
of the enemy; but the height of the bank was there so
great, the batteries of the enemy being upwards of 100
feet above the water, that no material advantage could
be derived from the guns of the fleet at that place.   It
was therefore determined to sail round the island and
land on the west side, where the ground was so low
that the debarkation could be effectually covered by
the fleet.   Having ascertained, that a strong position
could be had for a camp in that quarter, the commodore
sailed round the island in the night, and on the morning of the 4th of August, a landing was effected without opposition.   The troops were formed in two lines
with a corps of reserve.   The front was composed of
the militia 250 strong, formed in open order under
colonel Cotgrove.   A battalion of regulars 420 in number formed the second line under major Holmes.   The
reserve consisted of 80 regulars and marines posted

on the rear of the flanks. In this order our troops advanced towards a small field, about three quarters of a mile from the place of landing; but before they had proceeded far, colonel Croghan ascertained, that the enemy were waiting for us in order of battle, at the opposite side of the field, in the edge of the woods. A fire was soon afterwards opened upon us from a battery, covered by a temporary breastwork, in front of their line, which extended the whole length of the field. Colonel Cotgrove returned their fire with a 4 pounder, which was attached to his line, as soon as he could uncover it in the edge of the field : and colonel Croghan now determined to push forward the battalion of regulars on the right under cover of the woods, and while Cotgrove amused the enemy in front, to turn their left flank with the regulars, or by a sudden charge break through it, and thus gain their rear. Major Holmes was gallantly advancing in the execution of this plan, when a fire from an advanced party of the enemy unfortunately killed him, and at the same moment wounded captain Desha, the second in command. This unlucky occurrence produced a halt, and caused some confusion in the line : but captain Desha, not being disabled by his wound, soon had his men again in motion; and finding the woods impenetrably thick on the left of the enemy, he immediately charged them in front with great bravery, and drove them from their position. Being exposed to the fire of the enemy for some time in advancing upon them, while they lay secure behind their breastwork, we necessarily sustained some loss, which we had not an opportunity to retaliate. Though driven from their position, they still kept up a warm fire for some time in the woods, and particularly on our left, till they were driven in that quarter by a piece of artillery under lieutenant Morgan.

Being in complete possession of the ground, colonel Croghan immediately examined the advantages of the position, and found it so weak, that he deemed it imprudent to attempt to occupy it for any length of time. The heights which he first intended to occupy, were yet two miles in advance, and were only to be reached by marching through a thick wood, over ground with which he was entirely unacquainted. In performing such a march, the enemy would annoy him excessively, and perhaps be able to defeat him, and even capture his whole force. He therefore prudently determined to retire to the fleet, and abandon an enterprise in which there was so little prospect of final success. Preparatory for the retreat, the militia were formed on the route towards the shipping; and the battalion of regulars under captain Sanders, the severity of his wound having forced captain Desha to retire, was then ordered to fall back through the field in line, and as it reached the woods to file off to the rear through the militia by the heads of divisions, the intervals between which were to be covered on the rear by the militia, who retreated in line. In this order colonel Croghan safely withdrew his forces, in the face of an enemy superior in numbers, and embarked them again without molestation. Two of our wounded, and the body of major Holmes, were unfortunately left on the ground. Our total loss was 12 killed and 38 wounded. The loss of the enemy was much less.

On the next morning after the battle, colonel Croghan sent captain Gratiot with a flag to the garrison, to ascertain the situation of the wounded, who had been left on the island, and to request the body of major Holmes. The following is an extract from the answer of colonel M'Dowell.—" The wounded of the U. States troops, left upon the field of battle yesterday, have been brought into the garrison, where they have received the requisite medical assistance, and every possible attention and comfort, which their respective cases required. I had flattered myself that you had been enabled to carry off the body of major Holmes, and regret exceedingly to add, that in consequence of his being stripped by the

Indians (a circumstance, however unpleasant to my feelings, it was out of my power to prevent) his rank was not discovered, which unfortunately prevented his being interred with those military honors, which were so peculiarly due to his rank and character. I personally superintended the decent interment of the dead previous to my quitting the field.

" I beg leave to send you some of our latest papers. I should have been happy to have accompanied them with such little luxuries as might have been acceptable in your situation; but fruit and vegetables being the principal we have to offer, captain Gratiot informs me you are already supplied with them." Such conduct and complaisance, as are indicated in this letter, would have been a great novelty in the British northwestern service, and would have signally illustrated the name of colonel M'Dowell, amid the host of British barbarians who served in that quarter, had not the letter been a piece of gross hypocrisy and misrepresentation. It was afterwards ascertained, that the Indians in this case, were permitted in the presence of the British officers, to eat the hearts of the Americans who fell in the battle; and that one of the prisoners was actually murdered by a militia man, who was screened from punishment by the authority of M'Dowell.

In his letter to the war department, colonel Croghan bears the following testimony to the merits of his officers and men on this occasion. " This affair has cost us many valuable lives, and leaves us to lament the fall of that gallant officer major Holmes, whose character is so well known to the war department. Captain Vanhorne of the 19th, and lieutenant Jackson of the 24th, both brave intrepid young officers, fell mortally wounded at the head of their respective commands. The conduct of all my officers merits my approbation. Captain Desha of the 24th, though severely wounded, continued with his command, till forced to retire, by faintness from loss of blood. Captains Sanders, Haw-

kins, and Sturgus, with every officer of that battalion,
acted in the most exemplary manner. Ensign Bryan
acting adjutant of the battalion, actively forwarded the
orders of the commanding officer. Lieutenants Hickman of the 28th, and Hyde of the marines, who commanded the reserve, merit my particular thanks for
keeping their commands in readiness to meet any exigency. Lieutenant Morgan was active, and his two
asssistants, lieutenant Pickett and Mr. Peters, deserve
the name of good officers. The militia were wanting
in no part of their duty. Colonel Cotgrove, his officers and soldiers, deserve the warmest approbation.
My acting assistant adjutant general, captain N. H.
Moore of the 28th, with volunteer adjutant M'Comb,
were prompt in delivering my orders. Captain Gratiot of the engineers who volunteered as adjutant on
the occasion gave me valuable assistance." *Croghan.*

Every idea of continuing the operations against
Macinaw was now abandoned; and the commandants
of the expedition determined, to discharge the militia
and send them home in some of the vessels, together
with a portion of the regulars, who were to proceed
down lake Erie to join the army under general Brown.
The Lawrence and Caledonia were despatched on this
business under lieutenant Dexter; and colonel Croghan
with commodore Sinclair and the remainder of the fleet
and regulars, proceeded towards the mouth of the Natawasauga river, in search of the schooner Nancy,
which was freighted with supplies for Macinaw. Immediately after the arrival of our flotilla off Macinaw,
colonel M'Dowell had sent an express, a single individual in a canoe, who made his escape in the night,
to meet the Nancy and apprize her of the blockade,
which induced her to return within the mouth of the
Natawasauga river. On the 13th commodore Sinclair
anchored off its mouth, and the troops were immediately landed on the peninsula formed between the
river and the lake, for the purpose of forming an en-

campment. On reconnoitring up the river, a blockhouse was discovered with the schooner Nancy under
its guns. As it was late in the evening and none but
4 pounders had yet been landed from the fleet, colonel
Croghan determined to wait till morning before he
would commence an attack.

Early in the morning commodore Sinclair opened the
fire of the fleet on the blockhouse; but a few hours
experience proved, that the object was too distant, and
too much covered by the timber on shore, to be much
affected in this way. Two large howitzers were then
landed, and placed in a position selected by captain
Gratiot. They were fired but a few times before a
shell was thrown into the magazine of the blockhouse,
which immediately blew it up, and set the schooner on
fire. The enemy then fled precipitately, and commodore Sinclair despatched several boats to extinguish
the flames of the vessel; but several explosions took
place on board, which prevented the sailors from approaching her. A supply of flour with various other
stores, sufficient to subsist the garrison of Macinaw for
six months was thus consumed. Before the explosion
of the magazine, lieutenant Worsley who commanded
the enemy, resisted the attack with great spirit; and
the Indians occasionally fired at our men from the opposite side of the river, which was a narrow stream,
with a forest almost impenetrable on its banks. Several articles of property were found on the premises,
and among them the desk of lieutenant Worsley with
all his papers, from the contents of which it appeared,
that the garrison at Macinaw were so scarce of provisions, that the supplies on board the Nancy were
deemed of the utmost importance. Two 24 pounders
were taken in the blockhouse, together with a 6 pounder; and a new boat large enough to carry a 24 pound
carronade was found in the river.

The communication from York into lake Huron, lies
through lake Simcoe and the Natawasauga river, the

mouth of which is immediately below Mackedash, or Gloucester bay, on which colonel Croghan had received discretionary instructions to establish a post, with a view to form a new line of operations from that place to York, as soon as the enemy could be driven from all the peninsula above such a line. The colonel was not of the opinion however, that it would be advisable at this time to establish such a post; for the distance to York was so short, and the communication so easy, that while the latter remained in the possession of the enemy, they would be able to seize a favorable moment, and capture any garrison he could establish without much difficulty. He determined however to leave a part of the squadron at the mouth of the river, to cut off the communication between York and Macinaw during the present season. As the garrison of Macinaw were already short of provisions, and their expected supply in the Nancy was now destroyed, it was not doubted but that a blockade of the pass through which their supplies must be brought, until its navigation was closed by the winter season, would certainly produce the evacuation or surrender of Macinaw. Lieutenant Turner was therefore left at this place with two of the smaller vessels, and with instructions to keep up a rigid blockade of the river, not suffering a boat nor canoe to pass, until the inclemency of the season should render it unsafe to remain any longer. Trees were felled into the river to interrupt its navigation; and the lieutenant was cautioned to watch the coast for some distance on both sides, and to guard particularly against a surprise.

The troops being again embarked, the fleet sailed down the lake for fort Gratiot; but it was overtaken by a heavy gale, by which it was greatly endangered. All the boats, including the commodore's launch, and the new gun boat lately taken from the enemy, were entirely lost; and the Niagara with 450 men on board was for several hours in the most imminent danger: the commodore was compelled to throw some of his guns overboard, and at last was saved by a sudden change of the wind. " There is nothing, says commodore Sinclair, like anchorage in lake Huron, except in the mouths of rivers, the whole coast being a steep perpendicular rock. In this extremely dangerous navigation, entirely unknown to our pilots except direct to Macinaw, I have several times been in danger of total loss, by suddenly falling from no sounding into three fathom water, and twice into less over a craggy rock. Those dangers might be avoided from the transparency of the water, were it not for the continued thick fogs, which prevail almost as constantly as on the Grand Bank." On the 21st of August they reached fort Gratiot, and in two days more arrived at Detroit. Without any unnecessary delay at that place, commodore Sinclair proceeded to Erie, and thence sent several of his vessels to Buffaloe, to render any assistance which might be practicable, to the army of general Brown at that time besieging fort Erie.

Lieutenant Turner continued to blockade the mouth of the river agreeably to his instructions, for a week or more after the departure of the fleet, and then made several excursions in one of his vessels, as he had been authorised to do, among the islands along the northwest coast of the lake. Lieutenant Worsley and the crew of the Nancy, about 20 in number, after their escape from the block house, had fortunately found a boat on the lake shore, probably one of ours which had been lost in the storm, in which they crossed the lake in safety to Macinaw. Colonel M'Dowell in the mean time had closely watched the movements of the fleet under commodore Sinclair, and was well apprised of the situation and objects of the detachment under Turner. On the arrival of Worsley at Macinaw, an expedition was therefore immediately planned, and the execution entrusted to him, for the capture of that detachment. To open the communication with York immediately, was an object of so much importance, that the most intrepid and hazardous exertions would be made to effect it. Lieutenant Worsley with his marines, and 60 or 70 men from the Newfoundland regiment, accordingly embarked at Macinaw on the first of September, in four batteaux each commanded by a lieutenant. Having received information, that one of our vessels, the Tigress, was then lying off St. Josephs, near a place called the Detour, he steered directly for that place and arrived near it on the evening of the third. A reconnoitring party was sent in advance, by which the precise situation of the Tigress was ascertained. The night came on cloudy and dark, and about nine o'clock lieutenant Worsley brought up his batteaux against her with the utmost silence. Her commander, sailing master Champlain, did not discover them until they had arrived within a few yards of his vessel. He then called all his men to their quarters, and for a considerable time repelled the attempts of the enemy to board, until himself and all his officers being wounded, and his men greatly overpowered by numbers, he was compelled to give up the contest. The Tigress carried a 24 pounder, and had 30 men on board. Three of her men were killed, and several more wounded—the enemy had two killed and seven or eight wounded. Dickson, the celebrated emissary of the British among the Indians, was a volunteer under Worsley in this affair.

Next day lieutenant Worsley sailed down the lake in the Tigress, to look for the Scorpion, the vessel in which lieutenant Turner was embarked. The latter carried a long twelve in addition to her 24 pounder; yet Worsley determined to risk an attack upon her in the Tigress alone. Having descried her on the evening of the 5th, he came to anchor at a considerable distance from her without passing signals, it being then too late to make an attack before night, in which he did not wish to engage her. Early in the morning he got under way, and ran down along side of the Scor-

pion, when there were but four or five men on deck.
As he came up close, he fired into her, and immediately boarded her, before the crew could get to their quarters, so as to make any efficient resistance.   And thus
lieutenant Turner and his two gun boats fell, an easy
prey, into the hands of the enemy, both being captured
by surprise, and without much fighting.   In a few days
lieutenant Worsley arrived in triumph at Macinaw, to
the great joy of the allied forces at that place.   To
them it was an important victory, for it opened at once
their communication with York, and furnished them
vessels for the safe transportation of supplies across the
lake.   The British also made it a very great affair *on
paper*—when officially announced by adjutant general
Baynes, he stated that the captured vessels " *had crews
of three hundred men each.*"   He only exaggerated 570,
in stating the forces of two gun boats—such is the *royal*
contempt for truth, which is constantly observed in the
British officials.   In this instance however the exaggeration was excusable; for John Bull was in great
need of something to raise his spirits, after the severe
drubbings he had recently received on the Niagara
frontier and at Plattsburg.

And thus terminated the operations on the upper
lakes with the results decidedly in favor of the enemy.
Colonel Croghan and commodore Sinclair however
conducted the expedition, as far as it depended on them,
with great prudence, skill, and bravery, effecting every thing which it was possible to effect with the forces
under their command : and had lieutenant Turner
managed the business on which he was left, with equal
prudence and good fortune, the result of the whole
would have been greatly in our favor ; for the communication with Macinaw being cut off, that post must
have fallen in the winter, or early in the spring, for
the want of adequate supplies.

It is now time we should notice a treaty with the Indians, which was negociated about the time colonel
Croghan sailed on his expedition from Detroit.

Some time in June, the President constituted a commission to treat with the northwestern Indians at Greenville : it consisted of general Harrison, governor Shelby, and colonel Johnson. The two latter declined the appointment, and generals Cass and Adair were nominated to succeed them, but at a period too late for the latter to attend. The treaty was expected to commence on the 20th of June; and at that time the Indians began to assemble, and continued to arrive until the first of July. The greater part of those tribes who had been engaged in the war, made their appearance at the council, or were amply represented by their deputies. A large portion of the Potawatamies, Winebagoes, and Chippewas however, preferred to adhere to the British and continued hostile. The whole number present, men, women, and children, was about 4000—of whom not more than a fourth were warriors. The negotiation was opened early in July, and eventuated about the middle of that month, in a renewal of the treaty of Greenville, a treaty concluded at the same place with general Wayne in '95 ; and an engagement on the part of the Indians, to take up the tomahawk against the British. To the latter condition two of the Miami chiefs objected. They were then reminded, that at the commencement of the war the American government had used its best endeavors to prevail upon them to remain neutral ; and as they had then refused to do so, and had joined the British, they could not now be indulged in an equivocal course. They at last agreed to engage on our side ; and the treaty being signed, the assemblage broke up in a war dance. A considerable portion of the warriors were detained, till the pleasure of the war department was known, in relation to their employment in our service. Some of them were then carried to Detroit by governor Cass, with a view to employ them against the enemy, should a suitable opportunity occur.

The pacification thus confirmed at Greenville, did not however entirely relieve us from Indian hostility,

as we have already seen in detailing the occurrences
of the expedition under Croghan.   The savages residing to the northwest beyond lakes Huron and Michigan; and those still more westwardly beyond the Illinois river who had not felt the force of our arms; and
who were still accessible to the intrigues of the British
from their posts on lake Huron, continued to oppose us
wherever they had an opportunity to strike.   Even
many of those residing within the Michigan territory,
on the borders of lakes Huron and Michigan, also continued hostile.

After their defeat on the Thames, a number of their
chiefs had visited Quebec, where they received the
most conciliating treatment, and in return gave assur-
ance in their speeches to the governor general, that the
British might still rely on their friendship.   Dickson
was soon afterwards sent up, loaded with presents for
them, and instructed to carry his intrigues to the westward.   He went to Macinaw in the winter and thence
among the western Indians about Prairie du Chien,
from which place he brought reinforcements for the defence of Macinaw in the spring.   Governor Edwards
being apprised that he was among the Indians in that
quarter, was again exceedingly alarmed for the safety
of his territory; but the British emissary once more
disappointed him, and conducted his recruits to a more
northern theatre.

Early in the spring governor Clarke of the Missouri
territory was instructed by the war department, to ascend the Mississippi to Prairie du Chien, and establish a garrison at that place.   He left St. Louis about
the first of May, and proceeded up the river in several
armed boats, with 200 men under captains Yeiser and
Sullivan, and lieutenant Perkins.   He reached his destination without difficulty, all the Indians he met being
friendly, or at least not disposed to engage him.   Captain Drace of the British service, had been posted at
the village of Prairie du Chien with an inconsiderable

corps, with which he fled on the approach of governor Clarke. The Indians most disposed to fight, had gone about a month before with Dickson to Macinaw, and those who remained would not agree to fight for Drace. The inhabitants of the village, mostly French people, also fled from their homes, but were soon induced to return. Lieutenant Perkins with 60 regulars took possession of the house formerly occupied by the British Macinaw company, and immediately began to build a fort, about 200 yards from the bank of the river, which was called fort Shelby, as soon as the post was tolerably strengthened, governor Clarke returned to St. Louis, leaving captains Yeiser and Sullivan with a gun boat and an armed barge, and a crew of 100 men, to co-operate with lieutenant Perkins in maintaining the post. Captain Sullivan's company in the barge, and a part of the crew belonging to the gun boat, were militia who had engaged only for sixty days. When their time expired they returned home in the barge, leaving about 100 men at the Prairie. No indications of hostility had yet appeared; but early in July lieutenant Perkins was informed, that preparations for an attack were in progress among the Indians.

As soon as the British at Macinaw received intelligence, that governor Clarke had occupied the post of Prairie du Chien, colonel M'Dowell determined to send an expedition against it. He was uncertain at that time, whether an attack would be made on his own post, and ventured to detach colonel M'Kay with 120 men, and some light pieces of artillery on this enterprise. They proceeded in boats by the way of Green bay; and having dragged their watercraft and artillery across the portage to the Ouisconsin river, they embarked again and continued their voyage down that river for fort Shelby. On their way they were able to engage upwards of a thousand Indians in the enterprise. With this force the colonel made his appearance before the fort about the middle of July. Lieutenant Perkins had made every practicable arrangement for a formidable resistance. Captain Yeiser had anchored the gun boat in the river opposite to the fort. As soon as colonel M'Kay's forces had surrounded the fort, and he had planted his artillery in a situation to play upon the gun boat, he sent in a flag to demand a surrender. This was promptly refused by lieutenant Perkins, who assured his adversary that he was prepared to defend himself to the last extremity.

A general attack now commenced with the artillery and small arms, the former being directed at the gun boat, but at so great a distance that no execution was done. Having changed their position, they compelled captain Yeiser to change his also, by going higher up the river, opposite the upper end of the village. From a contiguous island which was thickly covered with timber, and from the houses of the village, the Indians now annoyed his crew in safety. Hence he was induced to retreat down the river, which he effected under a heavy fire on both sides for several miles. His loss however was very inconsiderable.

Lieutenant Perkins was now left with 60 regulars, to oppose the combined forces of the enemy, amounting at least to 1200 men. A brisk fire was kept up on both sides, but with very little effect, as the garrison were protected by their walls, and the enemy by the houses in the village. The British began to approach the fort by regular entrenchments, and in two or three days had made very considerable progress, having reached within 150 yards of the pickets. Ammunition by this time had also become very scarce in the garrison. Lieutenant Perkins was hence induced to call a council of his officers to consult on their critical situation. Satisfied that it would be impossible to maintain the post much longer, a capitulation was advised under a belief, that the chance to escape a massacre was better if they surrendered, than it would be if they were captured. A flag was accordingly sent to colonel M'Kay, with whom the terms of capitulation were soon settled. He agreed that private property should be respected, that the Americans should be protected against the Indians, and that they should be sent down the river to the nearest American post, not to serve till regularly exchanged. However incredible it may appear to our readers, we can assure them that these terms were honorably fulfilled on the part of colonel M'Kay!!! Though a *British* officer, and acting in concert *as usual* with a great body of Indians, yet he would not suffer them, however anxious they might be, to murder a single prisoner, nor to maltreat them in any manner!! With a degree of firmness and humanity, which would have been honorable to a Kentuckian, he restrained the savages and fulfilled his engagements! With pleasure we record the solitary instance.

After governor Clarke had arrived at home, general Howard, who had just returned to St. Louis from a visit to Kentucky, thought it advisable to send up a reinforcement with supplies to the garrison at fort Shelby. Lieutenant Campbell with 42 regulars, and 66 rangers under the command of two other subaltern officers, were accordingly embarked in three boats, with a fourth in company belonging to the contractor's department, and including in the whole upwards of one hundred and thirty souls. When they had reached near the head of the rapids, and not expecting any hostility, were at a considerable distance apart, a furious attack was made by the Indians on the near boat under lieutenant Campbell, which was then grounded on a lee shore. As soon as the others were apprized of the attack, they came down to her assistance, and gallantly defended themselves for several hours. But by this time five or six hundred savages had collected on the banks, and concealed themselves behind trees and other objects, from which they could fire at the boats in safety. The boat first attacked had also taken fire, and was abandoned by her crew. Under these circumstances a retreat was commenced, after sustaining a loss in the whole of 12 killed and 20 or 30 wounded.

At the time of the battle, captain Yeiser in the gun boat from fort Shelby, had arrived at the head of the rapids, where he met the contractor's boat still in advance, and was fired on by the Indians, while lying at anchor near the shore in consequence of an unfavorable wind. The attack of the Indians induced him to haul off, and anchor beyond the reach of their small arms, where he lay till the next morning. Having in the mean time ascertained the defeat of the other boats, he now proceeded down the river also, and arrived soon after them at St. Louis. And thus terminated in defeat, the expedition to Prairie du Chien, which was commenced with flattering prospects of success. It failed through the inadequacy of our resources, and chiefly for the want of men—the great cause of all our failures in the war. Wherever the American forces had an equal chance, in point of numbers and equipment, the victory was almost invariably on their side. In a few instances, the fortune of the day was turned against us, by the base cowardice, or gross stupidity of an unworthy commander; but in general, when the difficulty of bringing an adequate number of men into the field had been surmounted, Heaven crowned the invincible bravery of the freeborn American and the justice of his cause with success.

After the expedition of Prairie du Chien had failed, the Indians continued to commit depredations on the frontiers of our territories. Success encouraged and rendered them insolent and daring. To keep them in check, several small expeditions were sent out against them, on the Missouri and Mississippi rivers, and several skirmishes were fought with them, in which a good many lives were lost on both sides. It would be too tedious to enter into details—we therefore hasten to the mounted expedition, led into Upper Canada by general M'Arthur in the fall of this year, with which the operations of the war in the northwest were finally closed.

It being conclusively ascertained by the treaty of Greenville, that the Potawatamies residing on the borders of lake Michigan, had determined to adhere to the British, our government immediately resolved to send an expedition to chastise them into peace. The following order was therefore issued to general M'Arthur from the war department on the 2nd of August.

'SIR—The president has determined to carry an expedition of mounted men and friendly Indians, against the Potawatamie tribe inhabiting the country on both sides of lake Michigan. It is his wish also, that you should take command of the expedition. With these views, you are authorized to raise a body of 1000 mounted men, within the district now under your command. The auxiliary Indian force will be seen in the enclosed extract of a letter from generals Harrison and Cass. Besides destroying the towns and crops of this hostile tribe, it is desirable to establish a post, and raise one or more blockhouses, at such place near the mouth of St. Josephs, as may be best calculated for covering during the winter, the whole or a part of the fleet under the command of commodore Sinclair.

'ARMSTRONG.'

The latter part of the order was penned in the expectation, that colonel Croghan would succeed completely in his expedition on lake Huron. As soon as general M'Arthur received the order, he called on the governors of Ohio and Kentucky to furnish 500 mounted men each, to rendezvous at Urbana on the 20th of September. It was the 20th of August before the requisition was received by the governor of Kentucky, but such was the patriotism and zeal of that state, that seven volunteer companies were raised and marched to the place of rendezvous in due time. Similar exertions were attended with equal success in the state of Ohio. Their destination was still left to conjecture. In the mean time the failure of the expedition under Croghan was ascertained; and general M'Arthur then determined to abandon that, which he was directed to lead against the Indians. An order for disbanding the volunteer militia was accordingly issued on the 17th of August. Those from Kentucky however, forming a battalion under the command of major Peter Dudley, continued their march and reached Urbana on the 20th, without having received the order; and on the same day general M'Arthur received a despatch from governor Cass at Detroit, informing him that the Indians had committed several murders in the vicinity of that place, and requesting assistance to chastise them. The general was induced by these occurrences to countermand his order for disbanding the volunteers, and sent expresses in different directions to recal the Ohio companies which had returned home. Many of them had dispersed, and having given up the idea of going, could not be induced to come forward again. A small battalion of three companies, and some fragments of companies, were all that appeared; so that the whole force collected did not exceed 640 men, of whom about two thirds were Kentuckians. In a few days the whole was properly organized and prepared to march. Major Charles S. Todd, assistant inspector general of the United States army, accompanied the detachment as adjutant general, and captain William Bradford of the 17th, as brigade major—both gallant young officers, zealously devoted to the cause of their country.

On the 28th they arrived in the open plains above Upper Sandusky, where a portion of the day was spent by major Todd, and adjutants Berry and Wood, in training the troops. On the next day the detachment was left under major Todd, with orders to move down slowly below Sandusky, occasionally training the men, while general M'Arthur, captain Bradford and doctor Turner visited old Tahe, the Wyandot sachem, to pro-

cure some of his warriors for the expedition. That
venerable chief agreed, that as many of his young men
as could be mounted, might join our standard ; and 74
Shawanese, Delawares, Wyandots &c. were accordingly equipped under their chiefs Lewis, Wolf, and
Civil John.

Some delay having taken place about Lower Sandusky, for the purpose of resting the horses &c. it was
the 5th of October before the detachment arrived at the
river Raisin. In the mean time general M'Arthur
had twice received despatches from governor Cass, informing him that the Indians continued to commit depredations and murders in the vicinity of Detroit. At
the river Raisin the general was informed by some of
the inhabitants, that a body of 3 or 400 Potawatamies
were assembled at an old trading house on the river
Huron, about 45 miles distant, near which it was said
there was a village of that tribe. With a view to
attack them, and destroy the village, the detachment
was marched up the river Raisin some distance, and
then conducted across the country to the place where
the enemy was expected ; but there was no appearance
at the old trading house, of any large number of Indians
in that quarter ; and on searching up the river no village could be found. Some prisoners were captured,
consisting chiefly of squaws, who contradicted the statements received at the river Raisin. The general then
marched his men directly towards Detroit, at which
place he arrived on the 9th of October.

The critical situation of the army under general
Brown at fort Erie, now induced general M'Arthur to
change his destination, and march towards Burlington
Heights at the head of lake Ontario, with a view to form
a junction with general Brown, or at least to make a
diversion in his favor, by destroying the mills in the
neighborhood of Grand river, from which general Drummond drew the principal support of his troops. To
accomplish such an enterprise, secrecy and despatch

were required; but before it could be commenced, it was necessary to refresh the horses by a few days rest. In the mean time, to prevent intelligence of the intended movement from being conveyed to the British by traitorous citizens in Detroit, and to prevent even the apprehension of such an enterprise from being excited in the enemy, the real object was concealed and a report was circulated as a secret, that an expedition was to be carried against an Indian village on the Saganaw river, which empties into lake Huron on the southwest side, about 120 miles above Detroit. In a general order the troops were entreated "to take special care of their horses, and to prepare for a short, rapid, and it is believed a brilliant expedition—one which may be attended with some danger, and may require all their fortitude to produce a successful issue."

On the 22nd, the preparations for the enterprise were deemed sufficient, and on that day five pieces of artillery were sent up the river in boats, under the pretence that they were intended to batter a fortification, which the Indians had erected on the Saganaw river. The Kentucky ba'talion also marched up the west side of the river Detroit, and on the next day was followed by the other, under the command of captain M'Cormick of the rangers, who had joined the expedition with his company and a few Michigan volunteers. The whole force was now estimated at 720 men. On the 26th, after encountering many difficulties in crossing swamps, rivers, and arms of lake St. Clair, the whole detachment arrived about 6 miles up the river St. Clair, where the general intended to cross into Canada and proceed direct on his enterprise. The object of the expedition was now explained to the troops, together with the necessity of taking this route, to prevent intelligence of their march from being sent to the enemy, by their friends in Detroit and Sandwich. The boats with the artillery having arrived, the troops proceeded to cross the strait, which was completed next morning; and on the same day they marched up to the Belldoon settlement, on the north side of Bear creek.   This settlement is a little colony of 75 Scotch families, which was planted here in 1806 by lord Selkirk.   They were supplied with horses, and a stock of merino sheep which rapidly increased, while the people and horses were gradually diminishing.   The boats having ascended Bear creek, and set the troops across it at this place, were now dismissed and returned home with the artillery, one only being retained to carry the ammunition up the creek; and that one was unfortunately lost on the following day.

The detachment now marched rapidly on their way towards the Moravian town, Delaware &c. through which they intended to pass.   Above the Moravian town, the front guard fortunately captured a British sergeant, who was proceeding with intelligence of the expedition directly to Burlington Heights.   A detachment of the rangers was then sent forward under lieutenant Rayburn, to get in the rear of Delaware and guard every pass, to prevent intelligence from being sent forward from that place; which he effectually accomplished.   When the troops reached the lower end of the Delaware settlement, where it became necessary to cross the Thames to the north side, they were detained a considerable portion of two days in effecting its passage, which they accomplished with great difficulty in consequence of its being raised by late rains.

On the 4th of November the detachment entered the village of Oxford, very much to the astonishment of the inhabitants, who had received no credible information of its approach.   The general promised the inhabitants protection, and paroled the militia of the place after having disarmed them.   He threatened destruction however to the property of any person, who should send forward intelligence of his advance. But two militia men, who had been paroled, were not

to be deterred in this way from carrying the news to
Burford, where a body of the militia had collected and
were constructing a breastwork.   The escape of those
fellows from Oxford being ascertained, their property
was instantly destroyed agreeably to promise.   On the
5th the troops proceeded to Burford, from which the
militia fled precipitately a few hours before their arrival, spreading consternation through the country.   The
inhabitants believed, that general M'Arthur had a force
of 2000 men at least; for they could not conceive, that
he would dare to venture so far into their country,
with less than that number.

The general had information that a body of militia
were collecting to oppose him at Malcolm's mill, about
12 miles from Burford ; but he determined to push on
for Burlington, without paying any attention to them.
When he arrived near the crossing of Grand river with
these views, he was informed that a force of some Indians, militia and dragoons, were posted on the opposite heights to contest the passage of the river ; and as
soon as the advance of the rangers entered the open
ground on the bank of that stream, the enemy began to
fire upon them from the opposite side.   Some of our
men crept up behind the ferryhouse, and returned the
fire with so much effect, that the Indians were compelled to fall back.   During the skirmish general M'Arthur
was consulting what course should be taken, when a
prisoner was fortunately captured, from whom he ascertained, that major Muir had crossed the river that
morning, on his way from Kentucky to join the British
army, having recently been exchanged and sent home
after his capture on the Thames ; and that a large body
of Indians with some regulars and three pieces of
artillery, were stationed at a very dangerous defile on
the road to Burlington, and but a few miles from the
river.   The distance to Burlington was 25 miles.
This information combined with the difficulty of crossing the river, determined the general to turn down the

3 I

Long Point road, for the purpose of attacking the militia at Malcolm's mill. The project of joining general Brown was now obviously visionary, and was left entirely out of his calculations. A plan was conceived, to mask his design from the enemy at Grand river. Only a few of his troops had come up so close to the river, as to be seen from the opposite side : the balance remained concealed by the woods in the rear. Captain Wickliffe was therefore directed to remain on the ground with 100 men, and to make as great a shew of encamping as possible, while the main body was secretly marched off towards Malcolm's mill, in which direction he was to pursue them, after remaining two hours at Grand river. This manœuvre had the desired effect. A part of the men left on the ground kept up a galling and efficient fire on the Indians from the ferryhouse, while the others pretended to be forming an encampment, by which means the enemy were kept from pursuing and harrassing the main body.

General M'Arthur arrived in sight of the enemy near Malcolm's mill about 4 o'clock in the evening. They were about 550 strong, under the command of colonels Ryason and Bostwick; and were well posted in a fortified camp on a hill, before which there was a deep and rapid creek about 120 yards from their breastwork. The mill pond effectually secured their left, and in front the only chance to cross was on the frame of a narrow bridge from which the planks had been torn. From two prisoners who were taken, the force of the enemy was ascertained, together with the practicability of fording the creek some distance below. The detachment was now dismounted, and their horses placed in the rear under the protection of a guard. The general determined to cross the creek below with the Ohio battalion, surround the camp of the enemy, and attack it in the rear; while major Dudley crossed with the Kentuckians on the bridge, and attacked it in front at the same moment. The Ohio battalion was accordingly marched off by the rear, undiscovered by the enemy, and taking a circuit through the woods arrived at the creek, where it still appeared too deep to be forded. General M'Arthur being at the head of the line on foot, immediately plunged into the water, which in a few steps came up to his shoulders, and convinced him that his men could not cross there, and keep their ammunition dry. Further down a pile of driftwood was discovered, which reached quite across the stream, and on that the battalion soon crossed in safety. In a few minutes more the rear of the enemy was gained, where he had but slightly fortified his camp. Our Indians had crossed with the general, and as soon as they came in sight of the enemy they raised their usual hideous yell, which produced such a panic in the Canadians, that the whole of them fled in confusion at the first fire. On hearing the approach of our troops in the rear the Kentuckians crossed the bridge with the utmost expedition, to attack the enemy in front; but before this could be effected, and the breastwork gained, there was no enemy to be seen. General M'Arthur pursued them, and captured a considerable number, but their escape was favored by the approach of the night. Their total loss was one captain and 17 privates killed, and 9 privates wounded who were taken—3 captains, 5 subalterns, and 123 privates, taken prisoners. General M'Arthur lost one killed and 6 wounded.

The detachment recrossed the creek, and encamped near it for the night, taking care to place out strong pickets. The wounded of the enemy were brought to camp and well attended by our surgeons. In the morning captain Murray was sent two miles back to burn a mill, which he promptly accomplished; and Malcolm's mill being also set on fire, the march was commenced at 8 o'clock in pursuit of the enemy, towards Dover. At Savareen's mill, 65 of the militia, who had again collected after their dispersion last night, surrendered

themselves and were paroled. All their arms were
destroyed and the mill burnt. In the evening the detachment encamped in the neighborhood of Dover, having captured and paroled thirty more of the militia,
and burnt two other merchant mills, which were employed in manufacturing flour for the army under
Drummond. The detachment had drawn no flour until this day, since they left Beldoon.

Authentic information was now received, that general Izard had abandoned fort Erie and retired to
Buffaloe. The situation of the detachment had become extremely critical. It was now 225 miles within the enemy's country, and was entirely destitute of
provisions for the men and forage for the horses. It
might also be expected, that the enemy would make
the most vigorous exertions to effect its destruction.
Such circumstances were calculated to damp the ardor
of the most undaunted spirits : but the volunteers under M'Arthur were possessed of too much firmness and
enterprise to be discouraged by common difficulties and
dangers. A retrograde movement was now made, leaving Dover a short distance on the left, and keeping
parallel with the shore of lake Erie. The country
was barren and destitute of resources. A few sheep
furnished a scanty subsistence for the troops. A journey of 18 miles was performed this day from the encampment near Dover. In the mean time the enemy
was in pursuit, and this night a regiment of 1100 regulars encamped on the ground which was occupied last
night by the mounted volunteers. The pursuit however was continued no further.

On the 12th the troops arrived, after a fatiguing
march through the settlements of the enemy and a portion of wilderness, at the river Thames opposite an old
Indian village called Muncey town, where rafts were
constructed and the sick placed upon them in the care
of the Indians. The march was again resumed, and
on the 17th the troops reached Sandwich, where they

were honorably discharged on the 18th and returned home. And thus terminated an expedition, which was not surpassed during the war, in the boldness of its design, and the address with which it was conducted. It was attended with the loss of one man only on our part, while that of the enemy was considerable in men, as well as in the injury done to his resources. It was with great difficulty that general Drummond could subsist his troops, with the aid of all the mills in his vicinity; and without them, his difficulties must have been greatly increased.

General M'Arthur who conceived and conducted the expedition, displayed great bravery and military skill. No one could have managed his resources with more prudence and effect. His officers and men were also entitled to the praises and gratitude of the country, for their firmness in danger, and the cheerfulness and fortitude with which they obeyed his orders, and endured the greatest hardships. Major Todd was particularly distinguished. "I have the support of all the troops, says general M'Arthur, in assuring you, that to the military talents, activity and intelligence of major Todd, who acted as my adjutant general, much of the fortunate progress and issue of the expedition is attributable; and I cheerfully embrace this occasion to acknowledge the important services, which he has at all times rendered me, whilst in command of the district. His various merits justly entitle him to the notice of the government." *M'Arthur.*

Major Dudley and captain Bradford were also highly commended by the general for their zeal, activity, and intelligence; together with most of the other officers who served on the expedition.

CHAPTER XI.

The war with the Creek Indians in the south.

HAVING brought our detail of the operations in the northwest to a conclusion, we propose in the last place to give some account of those transactions in the southwest, in which the militia from the states of Tennessee and Kentucky were chiefly concerned.

We have seen in the early part of this history, that the intrigues of the British before the war, were not confined to the northwestern Indians alone, but were also extended to those residing south of Tennessee and west of Georgia, in the Mississippi territory and the Floridas. When the battle of Tippecanoe was fought, Tecumseh was absent from his own country on a journey of intrigue among the southern Indians, for the purpose of engaging them in the British interest. It is probable that but few of the British agents in Canada were so enterprising as to traverse our extensive frontier from the northern lakes to the Mexican gulf in person; but they did not fail for many years before the war, and during its whole continuance, to keep up a constant intercourse from the northwest, with the Creeks and other nations in the south, through the medium of the most active and influential chiefs in their employment. These intrigues however, were attended with but very partial success. The Chickasaws, Cherokees, and Choctaws remained friendly through the whole war; and only a few individuals the most abandoned and vicious, of the Creek nation, could be induced at an early period to take up the tomahawk against us.

In the spring of 1812, a party of 5 Creeks attacked and massacred two families, in the frontier settlements near the Tennessee river, and made their escape unmolested. Several other depredations were also committed in all the southern country, during the same season by other lawless renegadoes of the same nation; and much apprehension was felt by our people, lest these murders and barbarities by scattering and inconsiderable parties, should be the prelude to general hostilities; and preparations to meet such an event and avenge our wrongs were anxiously desired. The continuance of the evil at last excited the utmost indignation in the people of Tennessee, and their legislature in the month of October, had under consideration a preamble and resolutions on this subject, from which the following are extracted.

" *Resolved*, That the governor of this state be directed to order into service on the frontiers, 10,000 of the militia of this state, viz. 5,000 on the frontier of West, and 5,000 on the frontier of East Tennessee, for the purpose of preventing a repetition of those horrid scenes of savage barbarity; and to punish with death the savage foe who dare make the attempt.

" *Resolved*, That the governor be directed to send a messenger to the Creek nation forthwith, and demand a prompt surrender of all the murderers of the citizens of Tennessee; and if not delivered within 20 days after the return of said messenger, to order out a sufficient force *to exterminate the Creek nation.*"

It was not deemed necessary however to carry these exterminating resolutions into effect. About the time they were under consideration a grand national council was held by the creeks, in which nearly all their tribes were amply represented. It terminated in a resolution to punish those who had committed hostilities upon us, together with an address of the most pacific character to colonel Hawkins, the agent for the United States in the Creek nation. A considerable number of the murderers accordingly suffered for their crimes, some of them being executed and others punished in different ways. About the same time also an expedition upon a small scale, was conducted by colonel

Newman of Georgia, against some of the Seminole Indians, residing further to the south, who are not considered by the Creeks as an intimate part of their nation. The colonel was successful in his enterprise, having beaten the enemy in several skirmishes, in which they lost about 50 of their warriors. It was the opinion of colonel Hawkins, and also of general Hampton, who passed through the Creek country during these transactions, that we might now safely rely on the peaceful conduct, and friendship of all the Creeks, with the exception only of the Seminoles.

Late in the fall, a detachment of 1500 militia infantry, and 600 mounted volunteers, were marched from West Tennessee, by order of the war department, for the defence of the lower country. The foot troops descended the river in boats under the immediate command of major general Andrew Jackson of the Tennessee militia, whilst the mounted men under colonel Coffee marched by land to Natchez, where both parties arrived and formed a junction early in February 1813. In the latter part of the following month, they commenced their march home again, no occasion for their services having occurred in that quarter. Another small detachment of Tennessee volunteers in the mean time, had marched under colonel Williams of East Tennessee, in search of adventures on the frontiers of Georgia. This party was 200 strong, and marched early in December from Knoxville. Having reached St. Marys, and formed a junction with a corps of 200 mounted men in that place under colonel Smith, the whole marched in February against the nearest towns of the Seminole Indians, who still continued hostile. Their expedition was completely successful. In three successive battles the enemy were defeated, with the loss of 38 warriors killed, and a considerable number in wounded and prisoners. The houses of their towns were burnt, all their corn was destroyed, and about 400 horses with an equal number of cattle were brought away : nor did the detachment leave their country as long as an enemy could be found, or any property remained which could be useful to reinstate their shattered fortunes.

The Spanish provinces of East and West Florida having for some years past been in a revolutionary insurrectional state; and the government of Spain being unable from its embarrassments in Europe to maintain its authority over them; the American government now determined to occupy the town of Mobile, to which it had acquired a title by the purchase of Louisiana, but which still remained in the possession of the Spanish authorities. On the same grounds, that part of West Florida which lies on the Mississippi river and lake Ponchartrain, had already been taken, and incorporated with the state of Louisiana. To seize upon the balance of our rightful property by force had now become a necessary measure of precaution, lest that important place should fall into the hands of the British. Accordingly general Wilkinson, who still commanded at New Orleans, was ordered about the first of March 1813, to wrest Mobile from the Spanish garrison at that place, unless its commandant should voluntarily surrender it to us. Preparations were immediately made for an expedition against it, which was carried into execution with so much address, that the fort was invested about the middle of April, before the Spanish commandant had received any intimation of our approach. The general had taken with him a detachment of troops from New Orleans, in our flotilla under commodore Shaw, and on the bay of Mobile had formed a junction with another detachment, under lieutenant colonel Bowyer from fort Stoddart. With these he intended to take measures for reducing the fort, while commodore Shaw was to prevent with his gun boats the approach of reinforcements by water from Pensacola. A summons to evacuate the place was immediately sent to the Spanish commandant, with

3 K

which he thought it most prudent to comply. About the same time a small Spanish garrison was driven from the Perdido by colonel Carson, which placed the most eastern extremity of the purchased territory in our possession.

It would doubtless have been good policy on the part of the American government, and it would certainly have been a justifiable course, to have seized and occupied the whole of the Floridas during the war; for as the British were closely allied with the Spaniards, for whom they were then fighting against the French on the Spanish peninsula, the officers of Spain in the Floridas very amicably afforded every assistance in their power to our enemies. In many instances, they departed in the most flagrant manner, from the character of a friendly neutral, even going so far as to embody their militia to fight with the enemy against us. But that of which we had most to complain, was their instrumentality in exciting the Creek Indians to hostility. Although the British agents in Upper Canada were unable, through the medium of the northwestern Indians, to excite those of the south to take up the tomahawk; yet the Spaniards in the Floridas, co-operating with the British agents in that quarter, were able at last to bring nearly the whole of the powerful Creek nation into the field against us. Whenever the British and Spaniards began to enforce their intrigues, by presents of arms and ammunition, and such articles of merchandise, as either pleased the fancy, or gratified the wants of the savage, they soon became successful. Finding from their experience in the early part of the war, that this would be the only effectual course with the southern Indians, they did not hesitate long in resorting to it. Had there been no other inducement, the mere gratification of that savage ferocity, which is such a conspicuous feature in the character of the modern British, would have impelled them to adopt it. The gold of that degenerate people is now always lavished freely, as the price of innocent blood. But by employing the Creek Indians, they doubtless expected also, to derive much benefit from drawing our troops and resources into the wilderness, and producing a diversion in favor of any expedition, which might be attempted against the southern section of the Union.

At the very time of Wilkinson's expedition to occupy Mobile, the Spanish governor was intriguing with the Indians, and proffering them supplies for engaging in the war with the British. A considerable number of Seminoles and chiefs of the Creek nation, were collected at Pensacola in April, for the avowed purpose of receiving arms from the Spanish authority ; but the governor being anxious, to extend his influence over a greater number, and to effect a more formidable combination, informed them that he had been instructed to arm the whole nation, and could not therefore supply those who were present, until a majority of the nation could be induced to join them. The chiefs were then immediately despatched to the different towns, with instructions to hold councils with the other chiefs and warriors on this subject, and to induce them if possible to accept the proffered bribe, which was at once the price and the means of committing barbarities on the American people. The emissaries were but too successful. A large proportion of the Creeks agreed to accept the tempting boon, and were accordingly supplied as speedily as practicable, with arms and ammunition from the British stores at Pensacola. A very powerful minority however, still continued friendly to the United States, and refused to have any participation with the British and their partizans. This led, in the present season, to a civil war in the Creek nation, and no doubt delayed the perpetration of barbarities on the American frontiers, for which they were now effectually excited by the British and Spaniards.

Having witnessed the powerful effects of fanaticism on the northwestern Indians, under the management of that miserable vagabond, the Wabash Prophet, the British agents from Canada had already been careful to *inspire* some of the Creek worthies, with prophetic and miraculous powers. These prophets were now the leaders of the war party, being the most active and influential partizans of the British; while those chiefs who had been the most active, in procuring the punishment of the renegadoes, who had murdered the American citizens, were at the head of the party, which was for peace in the nation and friendship with the United States. Colonel Hawkins, our agent, in conjunction with these chiefs, made every effort in their power for the preservation of peace : but it was all in vain : the most ferocious of the nation had accepted the British price, and the implements, for shedding the blood of their best friends ; and nothing but the carnage of a bloody war could now satiate their fury. Skirmishes and murders ensued among themselves ; and the friendly party, which was much the weakest, implored the aid of the American arms, to protect them and subdue their opponents. " If we are destroyed," said their chiefs to colonel Hawkins, " before you aid us, you will then have the work to do yourselves, which will be bloody and attended with difficulties, as you do not know as well as we do, the swamps and hiding places of those hatchers of mischief."

The information given and the requests made by the friendly chiefs, were not disregarded by the American people. As soon as the proper authorities in the neighboring states and territories, and the government of the Union, were apprized of the advancing hostility, preparations were made to meet the storm, and if possible to allay it, before it had burst on our defenceless frontiers. But sufficient time was not left to perfect our arrangements, and march to their towns, before the dreadful havoc had commenced in the settlements of the Mobile country. The settlers in that quarter, well apprized of the British and Spanish intrigues, and of the supplies which the Indians had received from Pensacola, as well as of the progress of public sentiment and of hostile movements in the Creek nation, had prepared themselves for the storm, by collecting together and establishing temporary forts for their protection, according to the long established custom of our people, on every frontier exposed to savage incursions. Not less than 20 of those forts had been erected in the settlements above fort Stoddart, on the Tombigby and Alabama rivers. But from their number, many of them were necessarily weak; and the people in the latter part of the summer, had so long expected an incursion into their settlements, that they began to be less apprehensive and vigilant; nor were they to be roused from this apathy by the most definite intelligence of approaching danger.

About the 20th of August 1813, the Choctaw Indians brought information to the forts, that within ten days, attacks would be made, by three separate parties of Creek Indians, on fort Mims in the Tensaw settlement, which lies on the east side of the Alabama, nearly opposite to fort Stoddart; on the forts situated in the forks, between the Tombigby and Alabama rivers; and on the forts situated more immediately on the Tombigby. Fort Mims however, in which there was a great number of people, and a large amount of property collected, appears to have been the primary object of attack. It contained about 24 families, and upwards of 130 volunteer militia of the Mississippi territory, under the command of major Beasley—making altogether about 400 souls, including nearly 100 negroes and some half-breed Indians. Notwithstanding the intelligence communicated by the Choctaws, and the frequent discovery of Indians, in the neighborhood of the fort a few days before the attack, by negroes who were sent out on business; yet an unpardonable and most unaccountable degree of negligence prevailed in the garrison. The commanding officer disbelieved the

reports of the negroes, and probably had but little faith
in the information given by the Choctaws. To his
incredulity and supineness must the success of the enemy be chiefly attributed.

On Monday morning about 11 o'clock, the enemy
had approached in a body through an open field, within
30 paces of the gate, which was standing wide open,
before they were discovered by the garrison. A sentry then gave the alarm, and the Indians raising their
hideous warwhoop rushed in at the gate without opposition. Major Beasley was near the place of entrance,
and was immediately shot through the body. He was
still able however, to give orders to his men, to retire
into the houses and secure their ammunition; and then
retired himself, and either died of his wound, or was
destroyed in the devastation, which ultimately closed
the scene. By entering the gate, the enemy had not
completely gained the interior of the fort. Its limits
had lately been extended, by erecting a new line of
pickets on one side, about fifty feet in advance of the
old one, which was still standing, with the former gateway through it unclosed. By entering at the gate, the
Indians got possession only of the outer court, enclosed
by the new pickets, and then fired through the gateway
and port holes of the old pickets, on our people who
held possession of the interior. On the other sides of
the fort, the volunteers held the port holes, and fired
on the Indians who still remained on the outside. In
this manner a fierce and bloody contest was maintained
for several hours. The enemy in the mean time gained
the summit of a blockhouse at one corner, but our
troops succeeded in dislodging them, before they could
effect any thing important. At last however they succeeded in firing a house, which stood near the pickets;
and from that, the flames were successively communicated to the other buildings in the fort. Despair now
seized on the stoutest hearts; destruction by the tomahawk or the flames seemed inevitable; the only possi-

bility of escape, lay in the project of cutting an opening through the pickets, rushing through the ranks of the enemy, and securing safety by celerity of flight. This hopeless project was accordingly undertaken by the remains of the garrison, and was executed with so much gallantly and vigor, that upwards of 20 succeeded in saving their lives. The rest of the people in the fort all perished by the flames and the tomahawk, except a few of the negroes and half-breed Indians. Most of the women and children had taken refuge in the upper story of the principal dwelling house, where they were consumed in the conflagration, to the great joy of the savage spectators. The whole number of persons destroyed was considerably upwards of 300.

The force of the enemy was not less than 5, and was probably as high as 700. It has rarely happened however, in the annals of savage warfare, that a force of that superiority has succeeded in capturing any fort, where the works and the garrison had only a tolerable degree of strength and perseverance. The advantages, gained by the surprise at the onset, no doubt contributed essentially to their success; yet with all those advantages in their favor, it required a degree of bravery and perseverance to succeed, which have rarely been displayed by savages in any similar attack. They fought closely and desperately for about 4 hours, and sustained a loss it is believed of near 200 warriors. Such conduct could proceed only from their inordinate thirst for British presents, a furious fanaticism excited by their prophets, and a sanguine hope of success inspired by the surprise they effected at the commencement of the attack. After the fall of the fort, they roamed through the settlement, destroying the houses and farms, and carrying off all the moveable property of the inhabitants, to which their means of transportation were competent.

In the mean time the preparations for marching into the Creek country were actively progressing in the states of Georgia and Tennessee. From the former the confines of the enemy were entered, about the middle of September, by an army upwards of 3000 strong, consisting chiefly of militia infantry under the command of general Floyd : from the latter an army still stronger, and chiefly composed of volunteers, soon afterwards entered their country in two divisions, one from West Tennessee under major general Jackson, and the other from East Tennessee under major general John Cocke. The legislature of Tennessee was in session, when the news of the massacre at fort Mims reached that state ; and a law was immediately passed, authorizing the governor to detach a corps of 3500 men for the Creek campaign, in addition to those who had been detached under the authority of the general government. It was thus that so large a force was sent into the field from that patriotic state. Measures were also taken in the Mississippi territory after the massacre at fort Mims, to assemble a more formidable force in the Mobile country ; and about 1500 men were accordingly collected at fort Stoddart as speedily as practicable, consisting chiefly of the local militia and two regiments of volunteers from other parts of the territory—all under the command of brigadier general Flournoy of the U. S. army. The Choctaw Indians also declared war against the Creeks, and tendered their services to cooperate with us in the commencing campaign.

Early in November general Jackson had arrived and encamped with his army, at a place called the Ten Islands, on the Coosa river. Here he despatched general Coffee, with 900 men from his brigade of cavalry and mounted riflemen, to destroy the Tallushatche towns about 8 miles distant, at which place he had ascertained there was a collection of hostile Creeks. On the morning of the 3rd of November, general Coffee arrived within a mile and a half of the principal town where the enemy were posted, and divided his command into two columns, the right being cavalry under colonel Allcorn, and the left mounted riflemen under colonel Cannon. The former was ordered to cross a creek which run before them, and to march up, on the right of the town, so as to encircle it on that side; while the latter was to perform a similar movement on the left, until the heads of the columns had joined on the opposite side of the town, which would thus be completely enclosed within our lines. This plan was executed correctly, each column keeping at such a distance from the town, which was situated in the woods, as not to be immediately discovered by the enemy. However the Indians soon ascertained that our troops were approaching, and with drums beating, and the warwhoop resounding prepared themselves for action; which was brought on in a few minutes by captain Hammond, who had been sent within the circle of alignment to draw them from their houses. As soon as the captain had shewn his detachment near the town, and had given the savages a distant fire, they rushed out againt him in a furious manner. Retiring agreeably to the plan of battle adopted by the general, he soon led them out to the right column, which gave them a general fire, charged upon them, and drove them back into their town. They now found themselves completely overpowered, and cut off from the possibility of retreat; yet they still bravely maintained the contest with desperate valor. "They made all the resistance that an overpowered soldier could do—*they fought as long as one existed*—but their destruction was very soon completed. Our men rushed up to the doors of their houses, and in a few minutes killed the last warrior." They "met death with all its horrors, without shrinking—*not one asked to be spared*, but fought as long as they could stand, *or sit*. In consequence of their flying to their houses, and mixing with their families, our men in killing the males, without intention killed and wounded a few of the squaws and children, which was regretted by every officer and

3 L

soldier of the detachment, but which could not be avoided." *Coffee.*

It was believed, that not one who was in the town, escaped to carry the news of their signal defeat to their friends in other places. The whole number killed and *counted* was 186—but there was probably as many more killed, and not found in the weeds, as would make up the number of 200. The squaws and children captured, amounted to 84, many of whom were wounded. The loss in general Coffee's detachment was 5 killed and 41 wounded, none of them mortally. The Indians fought a considerable part of the battle with the bow and arrow, each warrior being provided with arms of that description, which he used after discharging his gun, till a favorable opportunity for reloading occurred.

This destruction at the Tallushatche town was considered, and not without reason, as a retaliation for the massacre at fort Mims. The result in this instance was more complete however, and accompanied with much less barbarity in the execution, than in the former case where the enemy triumphed. There is also this striking difference between them, that at the Tallushatche the enemy compelled us to the unsparing carnage, by the obstinacy and the manner of his resistance. No warrior was saved, because none would accept life at our hands; but all the women and children were spared as far as it was practicable. Not so at fort Mims—indiscriminate massacre and conflagration was there the universal doom.

In five days after the affair of Tallushatche, the enemy received another signal chastisement from the hands of general Jackson. On the evening of the 7th, the general was informed by a friendly Indian, who was sent express from Talladega, a fortified establishment of our friends, about 30 miles below the camp at Ten Islands, that a large collection of hostile Creeks were encamped near that place. and were momently

expected to attack and destroy it. The general immediately determined, to march that night with all his
disposable force, and to give them battle as quick as
possible. Leaving every thing in his camp, which
could retard the rapidity of his march, he crossed the
Coosa at Ten Islands, and moved with such celerity,
that he was able to encamp in the night, and give his
men some rest and refreshment, within 6 miles of the
fort which he was marching to relieve. Before day
the march was again resumed, and about sunrise the
army was within half a mile of the hostile encampment.
The order of battle was now formed: the infantry
were disposed in three lines, the militia on the left, and
the volunteers on the right: the cavalry formed the
extreme wings, thrown forward in a curve, with instructions to keep the rear of their columns, or interior
end of their lines, connected with the flanks of the infantry, with a view to encircle and destroy the whole
force of the enemy. A corps of cavalry was also held
in reserve under lieutenant colonel Dyer. In this
order the troops proceeded leisurely towards the enemy,
while the advanced guard was pushed forward to engage them, and by retiring to draw them within the
wings of our army. The advance performed its duties
in an excellent manner, engaging the enemy very bravely, and giving them four or five destructive rounds before it began to retreat. This had the desired effect;
the Indians no doubt believed, from the intrepidity of
the attack, that the main part of our force was before
them, and they pursued it with alacrity and vigor.
The front line was now ordered to advance briskly and
meet them; but a few companies of the militia in that
line preferred the backward movement and began to
retreat. The general to supply the vacancy, immediately ordered the reserve to dismount and form in
that line, which was executed with much promptitude
and effect. The retiring companies, finding the progress of the enemy thus arrested, were emboldened to

rally and return to the onset. The fire soon became general, along the whole of the front line, and the contiguous portions of the wings. Our force however was too strong, and our fire too effectual, for the contest to be long maintained by the savages; they soon began to retreat, though they found but little safety in such a measure. In their flight they were met at every turn, and pursued in every direction. The right wing chased them with a most destructive fire to the mountains, at the distance of three miles; and it was the opinion of the general, that if he had not been compelled to dismount his reserve, scarcely one of the enemy could have escaped destruction. The victory however was very decisive: 290 dead bodies were counted, and no doubt many more were killed, who were not discovered. Our loss was 15 killed and about the same number wounded.

General Jackson now marched back without delay to his camp at Ten Islands, lest the enemy should discover its weakness in his absence, and destroy his baggage, which he had left entirely unprotected. At the time of marching from that place, he had momently expected the arrival of a detachment under general White, from the division of East Tennessee commanded by major general Cocke. It was originally intended, that the two divisions from Tennessee should form a junction in the Creek country, and act together under the immediate direction of general Jackson; and a detachment from the eastern division had arrived near the camp at Ten Islands with this view, and had apprized general Jackson of its near approach. On the evening of the 7th, relying on its advance, the general sent an express to inform its commandant, general White, of the intended movement, and to order him to come on by a forced march for the protection of the baggage. This order was received; but soon after it another arrived from general Cocke, ordering the detachment back to his head quarters. General White thought proper to obey the latter, and immediately sent an express to inform general Jackson of this determination.

The object of general Cocke in recalling White, was to send a detachment under that officer against the Hillabee towns of the hostile Creeks. On the 11th of November, general White was accordingly detached on this enterprise, with a regiment of mounted infantry under the command of colonel Burch, a battalion of cavalry under major Porter, and 300 Cherokee Indians commanded by colonel Morgan. He had to march upwards of 100 miles through a very rough country, to reach the object of his destination. On the way he passed three towns belonging to the hostile Creeks, which were now evacuated—two of them he burnt, and preserved the other in the expectation that it might be useful in the further operations of the army. Having arrived on the 17th, within 6 miles of the Hillabee town, where there was an assemblage of the enemy, the detachment was halted and arrangements made for the attack. Colonel Burch, with a considerable portion of the troops dismounted, and accompanied by colonel Morgan with the Cherokee Indians, was sent forward in the night, with instructions to surround the town before day, and as soon as the light appeared, to commence the attack upon it. The night however was so extremely dark, that this detachment did not reach the town before daylight: yet they succeeded so completely in surprising and surrounding it, that the whole assemblage it contained was killed and captured by the troops on foot alone, without losing a drop of blood on their part. About 60 warriors were killed; and 250 warriors, squaws, and children were captured. General White arrived with the mounted reserve, in time to have decided or improved the victory, had the resistance or flight of the enemy rendered his co-operation necessary. The troops subsisted themselves and their horses, on the supplies procured in the country of the enemy, during the greater part of this expedition, which lasted about two weeks.

In the latter part of this month, a fourth victory was obtained over the Creeks, by the army of Georgia under the command of general Floyd. Having obtained information, that a considerable force of the hostile Creeks were assembled at the town of Au-tos-see, on the south bank of the Talapoosa river, about 20 miles above its junction with the Coosa, general Floyd proceeded against them in the latter part of September, with a corps of 950 militia, and about 400 friendly Indians. He arrived on the 28th near the town, and the dawn of the 29th found his army arrayed in order of battle before the town, which was situated at the mouth of Caulebee creek. His plan had been, to surround the town completely, by extending his right to the creek above it, and his left to the river below it, while the friendly Indians occupied the opposite bank of the Talapoosa. For this purpose, the corps of Indians had been detached with instructions to cross the river above, and fall down so as to occupy the bank opposite the town, when the attack was made at daylight. But owing to the difficulty of crossing, and the coldness of the season, this part of the plan was not executed; and when the day dawned, another town was discovered, about 500 yards below that which the army was prepared to attack, which still further disconcerted the arrangements originally made. A portion of the troops were now detached against the lower town, and the friendly Indians were sent over the creek, to prevent a retreat up the river. A vigorous attack was then made on the upper town, which was resisted with desperate bravery by its inhabitants. The deluded fanatics had been taught by their prophets to believe, that Au-tos-see was a sacred spot, on which no white man could assail them without inevitable destruction. They were now soon convinced however, by the fire of our artillery and the points of our bayonets, that their sacred houses, with the utmost bravery they could display in their defence, would be wholly unavailing. They accordingly began to fly in every direction, where there was any prospect of escape. By 9 o'clock they were completely driven from the plain, and both of their towns enveloped in flames. The exact amount of their killed was not ascertained, but it was believed to be about 200. On our part there was 11 killed and 54 wounded—among the latter, general Floyd severely, and his adjutant general Newman slightly. As there were many other populous towns in this vicinity, which could send into the field a large number of warriors, general Floyd thought it most advisable to retire again to the Chatahouchie.

After these signal defeats of the enemy in the month of September, the operations against the hostile Creeks experienced a temporary suspension. This was owing in a great measure, to the reduction of the Tennessee troops, by the citizens of that state returning home as their terms of service expired. The intrepid Jackson endeavored in vain to keep up a formidable force in the hostile country—his fellow citizens who were with him in the field, would not volunteer the second time and join him in a winter campaign. He still however, kept a sufficient force together to maintain his position and hold the barbarians in check: and exertions were soon made with success by the patriots of Tennessee, to reinforce him with new levies of volunteers. Before the middle of January, he was joined by a brigade of 800 mounted infantry, which enabled him again to commence active operations. But in the mean time an affair occurred in the Mobile country, and another with the army under Floyd, which it will be proper to notice in this place.

About the middle of December general Claiborne of the Mississippi volunteers, marched up the Alabama from fort Claiborne, on an expedition against a new town, which had lately been built upwards of 100 miles above him on that river by Witherford, a chief who commanded at the massacre of fort Mims. The force of general Claiborne was composed of regulars, volunteers, militia, and some Choctaw Indians. Having arrived near the town, he prepared to attack it on the morning of the 23rd, with his troops divided into three columns. The enemy were apprized of his approach, and had chosen a position in advance of their town to give him battle. As our troops came in sight of their houses, they made a vigorous attack on the right column, consisting of volunteers under the command of colonel Carson. The centre was ordered to support the right, but before it could reach the point of action, the volunteers had gallantly driven the enemy from their position. Flying in every direction through the swamps and deep ravines, by which the town was environed, they soon completely eluded their pursuers, and gained the opposite side of the Alabama, where they had secreted their women and children on the first intelligence of our approach. They had left all their property however in the town, which contained about 200 houses—the whole was now committed to the flames. In the house of Witherford, a letter was found, from the Spanish governor at Pensacola to the heroes of fort Mims, in which they were congratulated on their success in destroying the fort, and assured that he had used his best endeavors to procure more arms and ammunition for them from the Havanna. The enemy left 30 killed. Our loss was 1 killed and 6 wounded.

The Creeks in the eastern section of the nation at last conceived themselves sufficiently strong to commence offensive operations against the troops under general Floyd. On the 27th of January, a formidable attack was made before day on his camp, about 50 miles west of the Chatahouchie, by a large assemblage of warriors. They stole up near the sentinels, fired upon them, and then rushed furiously against the lines of the camp. In a few minutes the action became general on the front and flanks, which were closely pressed by the savages, who boldly approached within thirty paces of the artillery. They were unable however to make any serious impression, and were soon compelled, by the well directed fire of the artillery and riflemen, followed at daylight by a charge of the bayonet, to fly in every direction for safety. The cavalry pursued them, and destroyed many in their flight. Thirty-seven dead bodies were found, and a great number of wounded made their escape. General Floyd lost seventeen killed, and one hundred and thirty-two wounded.

When general Jackson was joined by the new brigade of volunteers from Tennessee, he immediately prepared himself for an excursion against the enemy. The volunteers combined with the force which had remained in the field, the most efficient part of which was an artillery company with a 6 pounder, and a company of officers commanded by general Coffee, who had remained in service after their men had left them, amounted in the whole to 930 exclusive of Indians. The general had received intelligence, that the hostile towns on the Tallapoosa, were collecting their forces into one body, to make an attack on fort Armstrong, where the remains of the eastern division were stationed ; and he now determined to anticipate them by marching into their country, and giving them battle on their own ground.   Having previously crossed the Coosa, he marched from the vicinity of Ten Islands on the 17th of January 1814, and on the next day reached his old battle ground at Talladega, where he was joined by a reinforcement of 300 Indians, chiefly of the friendly Creeks.   Understanding that the enemy were concentrated, to the amount of 900, in a bend of the Tallapoosa, near a creek called Emucfau, he directed his march without delay for that place.   On the evening of the 21st, he arrived in the vicinity of Emuc-

3 M

fau, and having discovered several Indian paths, that had lately been much travelled, from which he knew there must be a large force of the enemy in his neighborhood, he determined to encamp and reconnoitre the country in the night. A strong position was selected, and an encampment formed in a hollow square, with every necessary arrangement to receive a night attack. Spies were sent out, who returned about 11 o'clock in the night with information, that they had discovered a large encampment of the enemy at the distance of 3 miles; that from their whooping and dancing they seemed to be apprized of our approach; and that in the opinion of an Indian spy, who saw them conveying away their women and children, they intended either to attack our camp or make their escape before day. Prepared either to receive an attack, or to commence an early pursuit if the enemy retreated, our men had nothing to do but await the result of their determination. Of this they were apprized about 6 o'clock in the morning, by a vigorous attack on the left flank. Our troops maintained their ground with much firmness, and effectually repelled the onset of the savages. General Coffee, the adjutant general colonel Sittler, and the inspector general colonel Carroll, were particularly active in encouraging the men to the performance of their duties. The battle raged on the left flank and left of the rear for half an hour, when the dawn of day enabled the general to prepare for a charge, which was gallantly led by general Coffee, and colonels Carroll and Higgins. The enemy were completely routed at every point, and the friendly Indians having joined in the pursuit, they were chased about two miles with great slaughter.

The pursuit being over, general Coffee was detached with 400 men and the friendly Indians, to destroy the encampment of the enemy, unless he should find it so strongly fortified, as to render it necessary to carry the 6 pounder against it. On examining its strength, he concluded that the latter would be the most prudent course, and accordingly returned for that purpose. But he had been in camp but a short time, when the enemy appeared in some force on the right flank, and began to fire on a party, who were looking for dead bodies, where some Indians had engaged them on guard in the night. General Coffee was immediately authorized at his request, to take 200 men and turn their left flank; he was followed however by no more than 54, chiefly officers of the disbanded volunteers. With these he bravely attacked the left of the enemy; and 200 of the friendly Indians were ordered at the same time to assail them on their right. It was now discovered however, that this attack was a feint on the part of the enemy, by which they designed to draw our attention and troops to the right, while their main force attacked the camp on the left, where they expected of course to find nothing but weakness and confusion; but general Jackson anticipating their scheme, had ordered the left flank to remain prepared in its place, and as soon as the alarm was given, he repaired to that quarter himself with a reinforcement. The whole line received the enemy with astonishing firmness, and after giving them a few fires were ordered to the charge, which was gallantly executed under the direction of colonels Carroll and Higgins. The Indians now fled precipitately, and were pursued to a considerable distance with a close and destructive fire.

The friendly Indians who had been ordered to co-operate with general Coffee on the right, had returned to the left when the attack commenced in that quarter; and the general was still contending with his 50 men, against a very superior force of the enemy, after the main contest had terminated. A hundred of our Indians were then sent to reinforce him, with which he was able to charge the foe, and route them completely with very considerable destruction. General Coffee was wounded, and his aid with 3 others was killed.

The balance of this day was spent in burying the dead, taking care of the wounded, and fortifying the camp, lest another and more formidable night attack should be made : and general Jackson now determined to return the next day towards his former position on the Coosa river. "Many causes concurred," says the general. "to make such a measure necessary. As I had not set out prepared, or with a view, to make a permanent establishment, I considered it worse than useless to advance and destroy an empty encampment. I had indeed hoped to meet the enemy there; but having met and beaten them a little sooner, I did not think it necessary, or prudent, to proceed any further—not necessary. because I had accomplished all I could expect to effect by marching to their encampment; and because if it was proper to contend with, and weaken their forces still further, this object would be more certainly attained by commencing a return, which having to them the appearance of a retreat, would inspire them to pursue me—not prudent, because of the number of my wounded; of the reinforcements from below, which the enemy might be expected to receive; of the starving condition of my horses, they having had neither corn nor cane for two days and nights; of the scarcity of supplies for my men, the Indians who joined me at Talladega having drawn none, and being wholly destitute : and because, if the enemy pursued me, as it was likely they would, the diversion in favor of general Floyd would be the more complete and effectual."

The return was accordingly commenced the next day, and at night the camp was again fortified. On the morning of the 24th an attack was expected, not only from the occurrences of the night, but because there was a dangerous defile not far from the camp, at the Enotachopco creek on the route on which the army was marching. The general hence determined to cross the creek at a different place, where it was clear of reeds except immediately on its margin. Having issued a general order, prescribing the manner in which the men should be formed, in the event of an attack on the front, rear, or flanks; and having formed the front and rear guards, as well as the right and left columns; the general moved off, his troops in regular order from the encampment. The creek was reached; the front guard with part of the flank columns had crossed, the wounded in the centre were over, and the artillery was entering the water, when the alarm gun was heard in the rear. Confidently relying on the firmness of his troops, the general heard it with pleasure. Colonel Carroll was at the head of the centre column of the rear guard; its right column was commanded by colonel Perkins, and its left by colonel Stump. Having selected the ground on which he was attacked, the general expected he would be able to cut off the assailants completely, by wheeling the flank columns on their pivots, re-crossing the creek above and below, and falling upon the flanks and rear of the enemy. But when the order was given by colonel Carroll, for the rear guard to halt and form, and the enemy began to fire upon it, instead of forming, it fled precipitately into the centre of the army, carrying consternation and confusion into the flank columns, and leaving but 25 men with colonel Carroll to arrest the progress of the pursuers. The militia appeared, as well as the enemy, to have considered the return of the army as a retreat from a superior conquering foe, with whom it was dangerous to contend. The confusion was not easily restored to order; but in the mean time colonel Carroll with his handful of men bravely maintained their post, as long as it was possible to resist such superior numbers; and being then joined by lieutenant Armstrong with the artillery, and captain Russell with a company of spies, the contest was still continued with success. They now advanced to the top of the hill, in the rear of the creek, amidst a most galling fire from their numerous enemies, and maintained that commanding position, till the 6 pounder was dragged up, and discharged a few rounds of grape shot on the opposing host. The impression thus made, was followed by a charge, which put the enemy to flight; and by this time the frightened militia, having regained their spirits, had recrossed the creek in considerable numbers, and were ready to join in the pursuit, which was vigorously pressed for the distance of two miles. The Indians appeared in their turn to have experienced a panic, for they fled in great precipitation, throwing away whatever might retard their flight. Too much praise cannot be bestowed on the brave little band of heroes, who arrested their progress and actually defeated them, after the main body had fled over the creek in confusion. Lieutenant Armstrong fell mortally wounded immediately after the first fire from the 6 pounder. "My brave fellows," he exclaimed as he lay, "some of you may fall, but you must save the cannon." Several of them did fall at the same spot, covered with glory like their brave commander.

The rest of the return march of the army, was effected without molestation. Although the signal success which attended every prior descent upon the enemy, was not experienced in this instance, yet the general had the satisfaction to know, that he had accomplished in substance the principal objects of the expedition. The attack on fort Armstrong was averted, a diversion was produced in favor of the Georgia troops, the numbers of the enemy were reduced, and they were taught that the ardor and perseverance of Jackson, would give them no respite from the toils of war, not even in the dead of winter, until they were totally subdued to peace and tranquillity On the whole expedition, Jackson lost 24 men killed, and 71 wounded. The loss of the enemy was not exactly known, but it was ascertained that 189 warriors at least were killed.

This excursion in January, was in fact but the precursor of another, and more decisive expedition to the same place, which was executed in the latter part of March. After the return of the general to the Coosa river, he was joined by large reinforcements from Tennessee, consisting of two brigades of volunteer militia under the command of generals Dougherty and Johnson, and a regiment of regulars under the command of colonel Williams, besides several other smaller corps of different descriptions. With these, combined with his former forces, general Jackson found himself in a condition to advance against his enemy about the 20th of March. Having changed his position since the former expedition, he now proceeded by a new route, and of course had a new road to open, upwards of 50 miles over the hills between the two rivers.

On the morning of the 27th he reached the bend of the Tallapoosa where the enemy were stationed, and which had before been the object of his destination. It is but 3 miles from the ground on which the battle was fought on the 22nd of January. The bend is in the form of a *horse shoe*, and has received that appellation from our people. The situation is remarkably strong by nature, and the savages had fortified it with a degree of skill and industry, which were not to be expected from the untutored sons of the forest. Across the neck of the bend, where it opens towards the north, they had erected a breastwork of logs from 5 to 8 feet high, possessing great compactness and strength, and extending to the river on both sides. Through this they had cut two ranges of port holes, suitable for the small arms with which they had to defend themselves. The direction of this wall had also been so contrived that an army could not approach it, without being exposed to a cross fire from the enemy lying in safety behind it. The enclosure contained about 80 acres of ground, and in the furthest extremity of the bend, there was a village of a moderate size. From the breastwork on the neck, a ridge of high land extended about half way to the village. the summit of which was com-

paratively open ground : but on its sides, and on the
flat ground along the margin of the river, there had
been a heavy forest, the large trees of which were now
felled in such a manner, that every one formed a breastwork, from which the Indians could in safety assail
their enemies in crossing the river, which was upwards of 100 yards wide and very deep ; so that on
every side, the position strong by nature, was rendered still stronger by art.

Within this fortification the enemy had collected all
their warriors from six towns on the Tallapoosa river,
amounting in the whole to 1000 men. Among them
were several of the greatest prophets and chiefs in the
nation, who had been the principal instigators of the
war. Relying on the strength of their position, their
strength in numbers, and the prophetic assurances of
success, which their fanatic leaders had liberally giv-
en them, they entertained no doubt of repulsing our
army with the utmost ease. The large force with general Jackson, and the spirit which animated his men,
inspired him with an equal and better founded confidence, that he would be able to give them a signal
defeat.

Before the army reached the *consecrated* spot, general Coffee was detached with 700 mounted men and
600 Indians mostly Cherokees under the command of
colonel Morgan, with instructions to cross the river at
a ford about three miles below, and coming up on the
opposite side, to surround the bend in such a manner,
as to prevent any of the enemy from escaping over the
river. General Jackson with the balance of the army,
then advanced slowly down the declining ground which
led to the breastwork, and at half past 10 o'clock, was
ready to commence the attack. Two small pieces of
cannon, a 6 and a 3 pounder, under the direction of
captain Bradford, who had already distinguished himself in the northwest, were planted on a small eminence, within eighty yards of the breastwork at the

nearest point, and 250 at the most distant. The infantry were also formed for action, and a brisk fire commenced which was continued for two hours with but little intermission and not much effect. The artillery was directed at the breastwork, and the infantry fired upon the Indians, wherever they ventured to expose themselves to view; but the artillery was too light to batter down the works, and the insidious foe was too prudent to expose himself to unnecessary destruction.

General Coffee had nearly completed the circuit, which he had been directed to take, when the firing commenced at the breastwork. He had already sent forward his Indians under colonel Morgan to occupy the bank of the river, and now halted his mounted men about a quarter of a mile of the bend, with a view to intercept a reinforcement, which he expected would be sent up from the Oakfuskee village, about eight miles down the river. This precaution however was unnecessary, for all the warriors of Oakfuskee were already in the bend. The Indians under Morgan occupied the whole extent of the exterior bank, in a few minutes after the first gun was fired, so as to render it impossible for an enemy to cross the river in safety. All the cowardly fugitives, who attempted it at this stage of the battle, met with certain destruction.

In the village which was situated in the remotest part of the bend from the breastwork, about 100 warriors were stationed, apparently to protect the women and children, and to prevent the passage of the river at that exposed point. Our Cherokees who occupied the opposite bank in view of them, at last became so impatient to engage them, and to participate in the thundering combat, that some of them plunged into the water, swam over, and returned with the canoes of the village, while their companions covered the enterprise, by firing over the river so as to keep off the enemy. The first who crossed in the canoes, remained under

3 N

cover of the bank, till others had joined them to the amount of 200, colonel Morgan and captain Russell with the spies being of the number. They marched up then to the high ground in the middle of the fortification, where they were assailed on every quarter but their rear, and that was kept open only by hard fighting, and the constant approach of reinforcements, which were still crossing the river at the village. By this lodgment of the Cherokees, in the camp of the enemy, a considerable portion of the river being left unguarded, general Coffee ordered up a sufficient number of his men, to preserve the chain unbroken round the bend. Captain Hammond with a company of rangers occupied the upper side, while lieutenant Bean with 40 men took possession of an island on the lower side, where many of the enemy had sought refuge when their hopes of success had fled.

The battle having raged about two hours, without much execution being done at the breastwork by the artillery and infantry; and the river being now effectually guarded by the Cherokees and mounted men; general Jackson at last determined to carry the breastwork by storm. This determination was received with acclaim by the troops, by whom it was to be executed. They had entreated to be led to the charge with the most pressing importunity, and received the order which was now given with the strongest demonstrations of joy. The result was such as this temper of mind foretold. The regular troops, led on by their intrepid and skilful commander colonel Williams, and the gallant major Montgomery, were soon in possession of the outside of the breastwork: to which they were accompanied by the militia, with an intrepidity and firmness which could not have been excelled, and which have seldom been equalled by troops of any description. An obstinate contest was now maintained for a few minutes through the port holes, with muzzle to muzzle, in which many balls of the enemy were welded to the bayonets of our muskets. Our troops at last bravely mounted over the breastwork, and took possession of the opposite side. The event was no longer doubtful. A dreadful carnage and slaughter of the enemy ensued in every direction. Though many of them defended themselves with that bravery which desperation inspires, yet they were all at last entirely routed and cut to pieces. The whole margin of the river which surrounds the peninsula, was strewed with the dead bodies of those who fled there, in hopes they could effect their escape. But all who attempted to cross met inevitable destruction—"not one escaped, says general Coffee; very few ever reached the bank, and those few were killed the instant they landed." It was believed by those who had the best opportunities of knowing the fact, that not more than 20 escaped during the whole battle. Five hundred and fifty seven dead bodies were counted—and general Coffee estimated the number killed in the water to be at least 250, and probably near 300. These calculations however do not account for the number 1000, which was declared by the prisoners, to have been the number of warriors on the peninsula. It appears to be certain, that upwards of 800 were killed; and it is probable that the whole number present was less than 1000, and that more than 20 of them escaped. The slaughter continued till dark, for many concealed themselves in hiding places and were not immediately found by our men—even on the following morning, 16 were hunted up and destroyed—from which it is extremely probable, that a considerable number made their escape in the night. Three of their prophets, and one of them the most revered in the nation, were among the slain; and about 300 women and children with a few warriors were made prisoners. Such was the signal destruction, which the British had bribed and instigated these deluded fanatics, to bring upon themselves from the Americans, who had for many years endeavored, with much labor, expense, and trouble to promote civilization among them. We cannot forbear to compassionate their misfortunes, while we execrate with indignation, the brutal barbarism of the British, whose cold blooded policy could doom this nation to inevitable ruin, merely in the hope that it would produce some temporary and inconsiderable benefit to the unhallowed cause in which they were engaged.

Our loss in the battle of the Horse Shoe, was 26 white men killed, and 107 wounded—of whom 17 of the killed, and 55 of the wounded were regulars, major Montgomery being among the former. Our Cherokee friends lost 18 killed and 36 wounded—and the friendly Creeks, 5 killed and 11 wounded—total, 49 killed and 154 wounded

This decisive battle effectually broke the power of the hostile Creeks, and convinced them that it was in vain to persist any longer in the war. Many of their chiefs soon afterwards came in voluntarily and surrendered themselves to general Jackson, supplicating peace on any terms, which the United States might please to grant them. Among those who surrendered was the celebrated Witherford, whose name has already been mentioned. In an interview with general Jackson, he boldly addressed him in the following terms : "I fought at fort Mims; I fought the Georgia army; I did you all the injury I could. Had I been supported as I was promised, I would have done you much more : but my warriors are all killed; I can fight you no longer. I look back with sorrow, that I have brought destruction on my nation. I am in your power, do with me as you please—I am a soldie ."

While the chiefs were thus supplicating peace, the greater part of the remaining warriors fled to their friends in the Floridas, where they were soon afterwards met by an arrival of some British troops, the number not known, with a fresh supply of arms and ammunition, which were distributed among them. Every artifice and means of excitation were then-used by the British and Spanish agents, to reanimate the fugitives and induce them to continue the war: but all their diabolical labors and expenditures were in vain: they could do nothing more, than to preserve a spirit of hostility in those who remained there, and excite them occasionally to trivial depredations on the nearest of our settlements. The hostile party indeed *felt* themselves too weak, to continue formally at war as a nation, unless a more powerful co-operating British force had joined them. It is believed that all the hostile towns were now unable to raise 1000 fighting men.

After the battle general Jackson returned with his army to the Coosa river, and soon afterwards went down to the junction of the Coosa with the Talapoosa, and was joined by major general Pinkney of the United States' army, the commandant of the southern district, who had exercised a general superintendence of the Creek wars. As it was now evident, from the shattered condition of the enemy, and the number of their principal chiefs who had surrendered and been captured, that no effective hostility could be continued on their part, general Jackson was permitted to return home with his troops, merely leaving a few to garrison the forts he had built on the Coosa, and to preserve a line of safe communication with the nearest settlements of Tennessee. Corps of militia had lately been marched into the Creek country from the Carolinas, and on them alone general Pinkney now relied to keep the country in subjection during the period of their service. Through colonel Hawkins the Creek agent, general Pinkney soon communicated to the Indians, the terms on which the United States would grant them peace. Those terms were, that our government would retain as much of the conquered territory, as would be a just indemnity for the expenses of the war, and for the injuries and losses experienced by our citizens and the friendly Creeks: that it would reserve the right of establishing such military posts, trading houses, and roads in their country, as might be deemed necessary, together with the right of navigating all their waters; and that on their part they must surrender their prophets and other instigators of the war, and submit to such restrictions on their trade with foreign nations as our government might dictate.

The hostile chiefs without much difficulty, agreed to meet commissioners on the part of the United States in a grand council, to embody these conditions in a treaty of peace. In the mean time a corps of 1000 militia was raised in West Tennessee, and sent into the Creek country, to relieve those who had been left in the garrisons, and more effectually to overawe the hostile feelings of the enemy; and general Jackson was sent back by the government, as a commissioner to dictate the intended treaty. It was ultimately concluded on such terms as he thought proper to prescribe, nearly all the country through which our troops had marched being retained to the United States.

Within seven months from the massacre of fort Mims, which may be considered as the commencement of the war, the Creek nation was thus completely subdued and their power broken forever, in their final battle with general Jackson at the Horse Shoe. Many causes contributed to the rapid progress and decisive termination of the contest. In the first place, the enemy was completely overpowered by numbers, In almost every engagement, it is obvious that the American arms had an overwhelming superiority in this respect. The only instance, in which the Indians had any thing like an equal chance, was in the battle fought on the 22nd of January in the neighborhood of the Horse Shoe. The force under Jackson in that case was about 1200; and as the enemy soon afterwards mustered 1000 warriors near the same place, it is not to be doubted, but that their force on that occasion was nearly equal to ours. We had also as great a superiority, in the aggregate of our troops in every quarter, over the whole number of the enemy, as we had in any single engagement. Immediately after the commencement of hostilities, we had probably not less than 10,000 men in arms, including the troops from Tennessee, Georgia, and the Mississippi territory, together with the Cherokees, Choctaws and Creeks who joined our standard ; whilst the whole number of hostile warriors according to the best accounts did not exceed three thousand. It was believed that not less than one fourth of the Creek nation continued friendly.

In the Indian wars of the northwest we had to oppose a much more formidable foe. In the south, 1000 warriors was the largest force ever collected in one place ; in the northwest it was believed by general Harrison, from the best information he could collect, that Proctor had assembled nearly five thousand warriors for the siege of fort Meigs ; and before that renowned barbarian ran away from Malden, he was issuing 14,000 rations daily to his savage associates. Among the American people, who double their numbers every 20 years by natural propagation, the proportion of men able to bear arms appears to be about one sixth of the whole population. Among the Indians, who instead of increasing are rapidly diminishing in number, the proportion of fighting men to the women and children must be much greater—at least one fourth of the whole. Hence the assemblage at Malden afforded probably about 4000 warriors. In the northwest also, when the nearest tribes were destroyed or thinned, the British had a boundless range of tribes more remote, from which they could bring in fresh recruits. The Creek Indians on the contrary were surrounded on all sides of the interior by enemies, and had no outlet of unmolested country, to furnish them allies and recruit their wasted strength.

A second circumstance which contributed to their speedy subjugation, was the neglect of their British instigators to furnish them with adequate supplies and efficient co-operation. They had to fight all the battles by themselves, without the aid of artillery, and in many instances with the bow and arrow as a part of their armour. The northwestern Indians had constantly with them, a strong co-operating force of British regulars and Canadian militia, well supplied with artillery and all the necessary munitions of war; and they were themselves not only supplied with arms of the best quality, but they also regularly drew rations for their whole families from the British stores.

A third disadvantage on the part of the Creeks, was their imprudent manner of conducting the war. They suffered themselves to be repeatedly surprised, surrounded, and cut to pieces in small parties at their towns; and their rule neither to give nor receive quarter, produced the annihilation of every corps, which came within the grasp of our army. They should have concentrated their forces in larger bodies, have carefully guarded against surprise, and have thus never suffered a defeat to be the annihilation of the corps. Knowing their inferiority of numbers, and their determination never to surrender, it was madness and folly to expose themselves to the possibility of having their retreat cut off. Their proper course would have been, to harrass our troops on their march, and by attacks in the night, so as to worry out the patience of our militia, and protract the war till the British were ready to give them more efficient assistance. Tecumseh knew better how to manage his affairs in the northwest.

A fourth cause which hastened the termination of the war, is to be found in the character of the principal general, who was employed in conducting it. The combining skill, the persevering energy, and the intrepid bravery of general Jackson, probably contributed more than any other circumstance to the speedy success of our arms in that quarter. The reader must already have remarked and admired, the clear and comprehensive views and skilful plans, which guided every movement to the most successful result; but what has been detailed, displays not half the merits of the man. His military skill and intrepidity in the field, were less important and honorable to the general, than the unrelenting perseverance and irresistible energy, with which he struggled against difficulties, insuperable to any other person, in keeping and supplying an imposing force in the country of the enemy, from the moment the war commenced to the period of its termination. The want of an accurate knowledge of details, prevents us from doing justice to general Jackson in this respect.

CHAPTER XII.

Military operations at Mobile and New Orleans.

WHILE the treaty with the Creeks was on hand general Jackson despatched a messenger to the Spanish governor at Pensacola, to demand two of the hostile chiefs, Francis and M'Queen, who had taken refuge in the Spanish territory; and to know why the governor, who was the functionary of a neutral power, had presumed to aid and abet the Indians, and to afford them a sanctuary in his dominions. The governor seemed to be highly exasperated at the demand, affected to know nothing of the hostile chiefs, and returned a verbal answer of an ambiguous but rather menacing character. The treaty being at last concluded, and general Jackson in the mean time having been appointed a major general in the army of the United States, and invested with the command of the 7th military district, he determined early in August, to fix his head quarters immediately at Mobile, and concentrate at that place, all the disposable force of his district, where he would be convenient to the remaining enemies of the United States, and ready to meet any irruption which the British might attempt from the gulf of Mexico. He had not been long at Mobile, where he had concentrated nearly 2000 men, chiefly regulars, when he received information by a citizen of Pensacola, that on the 25th of August three large British armed vessels had arrived at that place with a large quantity of arms, ammunition &c. that they had been permitted to take possession of the Spanish fort, in which they had placed 2 or 300 men under the command of colonel Nichols, and that 13 sail of the line with a large number of transports and 10,000 troops, were expected soon to arrive. A number of other reports of an alarming character, but not so well authenticated were also received, from all which it appeared evident, that the enemy had determined to make a formidable invasion with a view to the conquest of Louisiana.

This information was immediately communicated by the general to governor Blount of Tennessee, with a request that he would without delay cause to be brought into the field, all the militia of that state which the gov. ernment had authorized to be detached for actual service.   Corresponding intelligence of the intended expedition of the enemy, was about the same time received in the United States, from a variety of other sources ; and the government itself was advised on the subject by its commissioners, who had been sent to Europe to negociate a treaty of peace with Great Britain.   The governor of Tennessee immediately complied with the request of general Jackson ; and an additional body of 2000 mounted volunteers, were also raised in that patriotic state, and marched for Mobile under the command of general Coffee.   The war department, taking the formidable preparations of the enemy into consideration, also ordered for the defence of the lower countries, 2500 of the detached militia of Kentucky, an equal number from the state of Georgia, and an additional draft of 500 men from the state of Tennessee. The whole number thus ordered and volunteering for the service, in Tennessee, Kentucky and Georgia, amounted to more than 12,000 men, which constituted, with the regulars now under Jackson, and the militia resources of Louisiana and the Mississippi territory, the whole force with which he had to meet the approaching storm and repel the haughty, plundering, and barbarous invader.

The force of the enemy which had already arrived, at Pensacola, appears to have been a corps of observation, sent forward to take possession of certain important points on the coast and islands of the gulf, to foster the hostility of the Creeks and Spaniards in the Floridas, and to feel the public sentiment in the state of Louisiana. Colonel Nichols after taking possession of the fortress with the approbation of the Spanish governor, immediately commenced his intrigues with the Indians, and supplied them with munitions of war and a variety of other presents. He met with but poor success however in enlisting them in his service. The remnant of the Creeks remembered too well the dreadful exterminating chastisement, which they had so recently received from general Jackson, as well as the base perfidy with which the British had left them to their fate, after exciting them to war and promising them an effectual support.

On the day after his landing, this *renowned and brave* colonel issued a general order to his troops, intended however less for them than *for the world*, in which he spoke in as pompous swaggering terms of the duties and prospects of the expedition, as if he had been at the head of an invincible army, with which he was just going to overrun the whole Union. Yet this, like his diminutive force of two or three hundred British, and about as many Indians, was but the vanguard, the mere precursor of an act of more consummate extravagance and folly. On the 29th of August he issued a proclamation to the people of Louisiana *and Kentucky*, calling upon them to join his standard. To the former he said "Natives of Louisiana! on you the first call is made, to assist in liberating from a faithless and imbecile government, your paternal soil. The American *usurpation* in this country must be abolished, and the lawful owners put in possession. I am at the head of a *large body* of Indians well armed, disciplined and commanded by British officers; and a good train of artillery with every requisite, seconded by the powerful aid of a numerous British and Spanish squadron of ships and vessels of war" &c. His appeal to the Kentuckians was consummately ridiculous. "Inhabitants

of Kentucky! You have too long borne with grievous
impositions. The whole brunt of the war has fallen
on your brave sons; be imposed on no longer; but
either range yourselves under the standard of your fore-
fathers, or observe a strict neutrality. If you comply
with either of these offers, whatever provision you
send down the river will be paid for in dollars, and
the safety of the persons bringing it, as well as the free
navigation of the Mississippi guaranteed to you.   Men
of Kentucky! let me call to your view, and I trust to
your abhorrence, the conduct of those factions, which
hurried you into this cruel, unjust, and unnatural war,
at a time when Great Britain was straining every nerve
in defence of her own, and *the liberties of the world;*
when the bravest of her sons were fighting and bleeding in so sacred a cause; when she was spending mil-
lions of her treasure in endeavoring to pull down one
of the most formidable and dangerous tyrants that ever
disgraced the form of man &c. . . . .   After the experience of 21 years, can you any longer support those
brawlers for liberty, who call it freedom and know not
when themselves are free? Be no longer their dupes;
accept my offer; every thing I have promised in this
paper, I guarantee to you on *the sacred honor of a British officer* (a thing well understood in Kentucky)."
That any man of common sense and information,
should have addressed such nonsense to the Kentuckians, is truly astonishing.   He had some grounds however, for making his call on the people of Louisiana—
for there were British spies, partizans, and traitors in
New Orleans, who did not fail to communicate every
possible information to the enemy, and to assure them
that the *people* of Louisiana were dissatisfied with the
government, and ready at a-moments' warning to come
under the British yoke. How much they were deceived
in the great majority of that people, and how glorious
for them the contrast between the northeast and southwest was visibly displayed in the sequel.

But the armed negociators at Pensacola, who were sent in advance of the expedition, to seduce the people of Louisiana from their allegiance, and to fan the embers of the Creek war, and if possible procure a few more scalps of women and children, had still another and more degrading task to perform for their master— *to solicit an alliance with a nest of pirates* on the island of Barrataria, situated to the west of New Orleans. The British being themselves nothing more than a great nest of pirates on a large island, found no difficulty nor felt the least degradation in stooping to this measure. On the last day of August, captain Lockyer of the navy, and captain M·Williams of the army, were despatched on this embassy in the brig Sophia, with letters from both colonel Nichols and sir William H. Percy, the naval commander, to Lafite the captain of the pirates, in which they solicited him to join the British cause with his armed vessels and troops, and tendered him the rank of captain in the British service, together with a bounty in land to all his followers on the return of peace. They had the mortification however to meet with a refusal. Lafite disdained to associate himself with the British marauders against his adopted country, although he had raised his rebellious hands to rob and murder her citizens.

The assemblage at Barrataria was composed of renegadoes from all nations, who had established themselves on that island, and robbed the commerce of the gulf for several years past, smuggling their plundered goods into New Orleans, where they had many friends and associates. Their commander Lafite, was originally a captain in the French service, and their whole force at this time was about 800 men, and twenty pieces of cannon, mounted in 8 or 10 small vessels. Immediately after the British overture, the whole establishment was broken up, by an expedition sent against it from New Orleans, under commodore Patterson and colonel Ross, which sailed from the Balize about the

middle of September, in the schooner Carolina and 8
gun vessels, and succeeded in capturing the greater
part of the pirates with their armed and unarmed vessels, dispersing the balance and destroying their little
village on the island, without the loss of a man on
our part.

The capture and possession of Mobile, appears from
the instructions of commodore Percy to his plenipoten-
tiary at the court of Barrataria, to have been one of the
primary objects of the British van at Pensacola. They
deferred the attack however until the result of the mission to Barrataria was known, as they expected to derive, from the alliance of the pirates, very important
assistance in the enterprise. Disappointed in this expectation, and apprized that general Jackson was at
Mobile with a considerable force, their prospect of success was very much darkened. They determined
however to make an attack on fort Bowyer at Mobile
point, a fortress well calculated for the defence of the
town and country of Mobile, against invasion by a naval force. It was built, when general Wilkinson took
possession of the country in 1813, by lieutenant colonel
Bowyer, on the neck of land which bounds the entrance
of the bay on the east side, and commands the only
channel through which large vessels can pass into the
bay. The town of Mobile is situated near the head of
the bay, 30 miles from its entrance. When general
Flournoy was in command on that frontier, he had ordered fort Bowyer to be evacuated; but on the arrival
of general Jackson it was immediately reoccupied and
repaired by major Lawrence.

On the evening of the 15th of September, a combined
attack was made on the fort by the land and naval
forces of the allies. The naval armament consisted of
2 ships, carrying each from twenty-four to twenty-eight
32 pound carronades; 2 brigs carrying from sixteen
to eighteen 24 pound carronades; and 3 tenders—all
under the command of commodore sir William Henry

Percy.   The land forces consisted of 100 marines, 2 or 300 Indians under the British captain Woodbine, and a small corps of artillerists with a 12 pounder and howitzer.   The force of the garrison was but 160 men. As soon as the foremost ship, the Hermes with commodore Percy on board, had arrived within the range of our guns, the fire of our batteries was opened upon her, which was returned by the whole of the squadron, as fast as they could come into action.   At half past 4 o'clock the action became general, not only with the squadron but also with the land forces in the rear of the fort, where the 12 pounder and howitzer were brought into play.   The allies under Woodbine however were soon put to flight and their battery silenced by a few discharges of grape and cannister from the fort.   The Hermes anchored nearest to the fort, and was soon so much disabled, that her cable being cut by our shot, she drifted on shore within 600 yards of our battery.   About sunset the others were compelled to cut their cables and make off, under a very destructive fire from our guns.   The Hermes being now the only object in view, our fire was concentrated upon her, and at 10 o'clock her magazine was inflamed and blew her up.

The loss of the enemy in this attack was very great. The Hermes with the whole of her crew, 170 in number, were totally destroyed, excepting only the commodore and 20 men, who made a timely escape in the boats of the other vessels, which were sent to their relief.   On board the other ship called the Charon there was 85 killed and wounded.   The loss in the smaller vessels was not ascertained, but it was also very considerable.   The brig Sophia, captain Lockyer, was particularly observed to be very much damaged. Our loss was 4 killed and 5 wounded.   Every officer and soldier in the garrison performed his duty well, and acted with the most determined courage, coolness and intrepidity.   For his admirable and gallant defence, major Lawrence was promoted to the rank of lieutenant colonel by the president of the U. States.

The expedition against fort Bowyer having sailed directly from Pensacola, and returned again immediately to that place; and the conduct of the Spanish governor having at last become intolerable, in harboring and aiding the British with their red allies, and encouraging their depredations on the nearest American settlements; general Jackson at length determined to return the compliment of their visit at Mobile, by giving them a call at Pensacola, as soon as the advance of reinforcements would authorize him to move. He accordingly marched for that place in the latter part of October, with all his disposable force, consisting of the 3rd and detachments of the 39th and 44th United States regiments, about 500 Tennessee militia, major Hinds's squadron of Mississippi dragoons, and a few Choctaws; and was joined on his march by general Coffee, with a part of the new brigade of mounted volunteers from Tennessee, which rendered his effective force about 3500 strong. On the evening of the 6th of November, he arrived at Pensacola, and sent major Peire with a flag, to communicate the object of his visit to the Spanish governor. As the flag approached the fort, it was fired on by the guns of the fort and obliged to return. The British no doubt dreaded the consequences of a communication being opened between Jackson and the governor, and warmly promoted this wanton act of hostility, with a view to involve us in an unrelenting war with the Spaniards. It appeared by the issue however, that the combustible materials of the governor were consumed by a flash, and that he wanted firmness to persist in the decisive part he had now taken. General Jackson immediately reconnoitred the fort in person, and finding it defended by British and Spanish troops, he retired with a determination to storm the town in the morning, for which every necessary arrangement was made during the night. In approach-

3 P

ing Pensacola, captain Kempt with his troop of Mississippi dragoons had captured a small Spanish guard about ten miles from the town. General Jackson being anxious, notwithstanding the perfidy of the Spaniard, to prevent bloodshed, liberated one of the prisoners with a letter to the governor, reproaching him for having violated the rules of war in refusing a flag, and requesting that a negociation might be opened. A Spanish officer arrived in the American camp about midnight with a communication from the governor. Major Peire was then admitted into the town and to a conference with the commandant, who refused to capitulate on the terms proposed.

Being encamped on the west of the town, the general supposed that the enemy would expect the assault in that direction, and be prepared to rake his advancing columns from the fort and British armed vessels in the bay. To encourage such an expectation, he ordered a portion of the mounted men to shew themselves on the west, while he marched with his main force undiscovered, round the rear of the fort to the east side of the town. At the distance of a mile on that side, his troops came in full view of the destined theatre as they supposed of a bloody conflict. They advanced however with the most undaunted firmness and bravery. On the right there was a strong fort ready to assail them; on the left, 7 British armed vessels; and in front before the town, strong blockhouses and batteries of cannon. Though possessed of these commanding advantages, the allies did not think proper to interrupt the firm and steady pace of our advancing columns, until the town was entered. The centre column composed of the regulars, was then assailed by a battery mounting two pieces of cannon, and a shower of musketry from the houses and gardens. The battery was immediately carried by captain Levall's company assisted by the column of regulars, and the musketry soon silenced by their steady and well directed fire. The Spanish governor now resorted himself to a flag, the sanctity of which he had so recently violated, and approached colonels Williamson and Smith at the head of the dismounted volunteers, begging for mercy and tendering an unconditional surrender of the town and fort. Mercy was granted by the general, and the citizens protected in their persons and property; yet the treacherous Spaniard withheld the possession of the fort till midnight. It had been evacuated on the night before by colonel Nichols, who fled with captain Woodbine and their red allies to the shipping and to the south side of the bay for safety, after our army had appeared before the town in the evening.

At the mouth of the bay, there was a fortress called the Barancas, which commanded the entrance to the harbor of Pensacola. On the morning of the 8th, general Jackson prepared to march against it, with a view to carry it by storm; but his march was prevented by tremendous explosions, which announced the destruction of that place. The British had obtained possession of that, as well as of the fortress at the town, and now blew it up to prevent its being turned upon them. Had general Jackson obtained possession while their ships remained in the harbor, he would have been able greatly to injure, if not to destroy them entirely in attempting to escape; but the Barancas being destroyed they proceeded to sea unmolested. The loss of their fortress was not the only injury which the Spaniards sustained from their retiring friends. The British very honestly and honorably carried off a number of negroes, with a variety of other property, and behaved to the inhabitants in a very insolent manner. While Jackson occupied the town, the exemplary conduct of his troops, and his liberal and generous treatment of its inhabitants, formed a perfect contrast to the British, and drew from the deluded Spaniards an acknowledgement, that even his Choctaws were more civilized than the British. After remaining a few days in the town, the British and

Indians being driven off, and the Spaniards very favorably impressed with our friendly intentions and honorable deportment, the general delivered up every thing again into the hands of the lawful Spanish authority, except the cannon of the battery that opposed the entrance of the regulars, and then evacuated the place. Having returned to Mobile, he immediately made arrangements for marching to New Orleans, the destined theatre of the approaching contest.

Before we detail the immediate operations of the contending armies, in the attempt of the enemy to get possession of New Orleans and subdue the state of Louisiana, it will be proper to take a preliminary view of the preceding situation of our affairs in that quarter, and of the preparations on foot both to make and to meet the invasion.

The late pacification in Europe had placed at the disposal of the British government, a large body of their choicest troops. Animated by their extraordinary success in subjugating France, and in capturing Washington City, where with Gothic barbarism they burnt and destroyed our capitol, our national library, and every other monument of the civic arts; and having not only prepared a powerful land and naval armament for the expedition, but also placed it under their most able and experienced commanders; they expected to give new tone to the war in America, and calculated with the utmost confidence on the conquest of Louisiana. According to the advices from our commissioners in Europe, a large armament was to sail from Great Britain in September, carrying out from 12 to 15,000 troops for the intended conquest. The armament which had captured Washington City was also now directing its course to the south, where its rapacious commanders were allured by the spoil of a rich and luxurious city, and favored in their designs by the climate, the season, and situation of our affairs. We had no army of veterans led by long experienced generals to oppose them in that quarter. The indispensible munitions of war, and the militia men destined to use them, were still in the arsenals and at their houses, more than a thousand miles distant, on the route they had to traverse to the scene of action.

It hence became the duty of our government and its military functionaries, to make the most active preparations for a vigorous defence : nor was the pressure of this duty in the least alleviated, by adverting to the internal condition of Louisiana, both in regard of its population and the facility with which it could be invaded from the ocean. Its situation in the union was remote in the extreme; its coasts were intersected by numerous bays, lakes, rivers and bayous, through which the enemy could penetrate to the interior in his small vessels; the banks of those avenues being marshy and uninhabited, they could not with any facility be guarded by our militia; and the population in general was composed of Frenchmen and Spaniards, who had, whether foreigners or natives, been bred under the most despotic forms of government, and had not yet become familiar with our institutions, and completely assimilated in their sentiments and views to the American people. The militia of the country had on a late occasion, refused to comply with the requisitions of the governor; and a great many European Frenchmen had entered their adhesions to Louis XVIII, and through the medium of the French consul, claimed exemption from military service. Local jealousies, national prejudices, and political factions, dividing and distracting the people, prevented that union and zeal in the common cause, which the safety of the country demanded. Hence there was a general despondency and want of preparation for the approaching crisis. The disaffected and traitorous however were on the alert, and carefully communicating the earliest intelligence, and every species of useful information respecting the country to the British. - The legislature was

protracting its session to an unusual length, withou.
adopting such measures as the alarming situation of the
state required. It was represented as being politically
rotten; and particularly, that in the house of representatives, the idea had been advanced, advocated, and
favorably heard, that a considerable portion of the state
belonged of right to the Spanish government—and that
too, at a time when the co-operation of the Spaniards
with the British in the expected invasion was the prevailing opinion.

Such was the character of the population, and the
situation of our affairs at New Orleans, as represented
by the highest authority, to the government and the
commander of the district.   A vast majority of the peo.
however, consisting of the natives of that country, and
emigrants to it from other parts of the union, were
well disposed to our cause, and willing to acquiesce
and co-operate in the necessary measures of defence.
By these general Jackson was hailed, on his arrival
at New Orleans, with acclamations of unbounded joy,
as a deliverer sent by Heaven to save their country
from approaching ruin.

In the mean time the militia from Tennessee, Kentucky, and Georgia were in motion. The orders of
the war department were received by the respective
governors about the 20th of October, and about one
month afterwards the militia of Kentucky and Tennessee were embarked in flats and ready to descend to
New Orleans. The Kentucky detachment of 2500
men, was commanded by major general John Thomas,
who was accompanied by general John Adair as adjutant general to the division, an officer of tried valor
and known military talents. Three thousand of the
Tennessee militia were sent down the river, under the
command of major general William Carroll, and brigadier Byrd Smith, the former having recently been elected to succeed general Jackson in the militia, when he
was translated into the regular service. The other

2000 of the Tennessee draft, were sent towards Mobile under the command of general Taylor; and the Georgia detachment were ordered for the same place, under the command of major general John M'Intosh, and brigadier general Blackshear. Artillery, musketry, and ammunition were also embarked at Pittsburg and other points on the Ohio, for the use of these troops and the fortifications at New Orleans, the greater portion of which did not arrive until the contest terminated.

Before general Jackson left Mobile, he made arrangements for transferring nearly the whole of his troops in that quarter to New Orleans. The corps of the army brought from that quarter were the mounted brigade of Tennessee volunteers, two companies of the 44th United States' regiment and Hinds's squadron of dragoons. About the first of December general Jackson arrived with his infantry at the city, and immediately commenced the most active preparations for defence. His lofty character as an energetic, intrepid, and skilful general had gone before him, and having secured him the unbounded confidence of the people, enabled him to exercise an unlimited influence over them. The governor had ordered the militia of his state en masse, to hold themselves in readiness to march at a moment's warning, and several corps were already in actual service.

To guard the different avenues through which the enemy could approach the city, so as to prevent a surprise and be ready at every point to meet them, was an object of primary importance. The general hence immediately reconnoitred the country in person, to ascertain the places at which it was most necessary that guards should be posted. He accordingly stationed a detachment of regulars on the bayou Bienvenu, which led from lake Borgne into the plantation of general Villere, on the bank of the Mississippi about six miles below the city. A guard was also posted on the Chef

Mentiere, a bayou which leads from lake Borgne into lake Ponchartrain. The enemy would be able to come up these natural canals in their boats, and on foot along their banks, which would greatly facilitate their approach, all the country around Orleans, except where there is a pass of this description, being an impenetrable morass. Strong batteries and a garrison were at the mouth of the bayou St. John, which forms the chief communication, and common highway from the city into lake Ponchartrain. Between the latter and lake Borgne, which lies below it, there is a communication called the Rigolets, through which vessels of some burthen can pass; on which was a fortification on an island, called the Petit Coquille. The general also visited and strengthened the old fortress on the Mississippi below New Orleans, called fort Plaquemine or St. Phillip. A flotilla commanded by lieutenant Jones, and consisting of 5 gun boats, a schooner and a sloop, was stationed at the bay of St. Louis, about 50 or 60 miles east of New Orleans.

On the 12th of December intelligence was received at the city, that the hostile fleet had made its appearance in the gulf, between the Balize and Mobile point, to the number of 35 or 40 sail. Having selected Ship Island off the bay of St. Louis, as a place of rendezvous, they began to concentrate at that place, and on the 12th they had arrived there in such force that lieutenant Jones thought it most prudent to retire from their vicinity to the Malhereux islands at the entrance of lake Borgne, from which he could again retire if necessary to the Petit Coquille, and dispute the passage into lake Ponchartrain. On the morning of the 13th, he discovered a large flotilla of barges leaving the fleet and steering westward, obviously with the intention of attacking his gun vessels. He had that morning sent the schooner into the bay of St. Louis, to bring away the public stores from the position he had evacuated. The enemy having discovered her, sent three barges against her, which were driven back by a few discharges of grape shot, until they were joined by four others : a sharp contest was then maintained for half an hour, when they were again forced to withdraw with considerable loss. But the commander of the schooner, Mr. Johnson, finding it impossible to escape with his vessel, now blew her up, set fire to the store house on shore, and escaped with his crew by land.

Lieutenant Jones in the mean time had got under sail with the intention of retiring to the Petit Coquille, but the water being unusually low in those shallow bays, lakes, and passes, and the wind and tide being unfavorable, neither the pursuers nor the pursued could make much progress. At midnight the gun boats came to anchor at the west end of the Malhereux pass ; and in the morning of the 14th the enemy's barges were discovered within a few miles of them. A calm with a strong current against him, now obliged lieutenant Jones to prepare for action, though the force of the enemy was vastly superior. They had 42 launches and barges, with three gigs, carrying 42 carronades, 12, 18, and 24 pounders, and 1200 men, all commanded by captain Lockyer, the ex-minister at the court of Barrataria. Our five gun vessels carried 23 guns and 182 men—the sloop carried only one 4 pounder and 8 men.

The enemy came up in line of battle, and at 11 o'clock the action had become general, warm, and destructive on both sides. Three barges presently made an attempt to carry the nearest gun boat by boarding, and were repulsed with dreadful slaughter, two of them being sunk. The attempt was renewed by four others with nearly the same result. The enemy however persevered, and finally succeeded in capturing the whole, having carried most of them by boarding. The action lasted about two hours and was uncommonly severe and bloody. The loss of the enemy was estimated at 300 killed and wounded, and several barges sunk. Our loss in killed and wounded was comparatively

3 R

very small, being only five killed and 30 wounded.
Both Jones and Lockyer were wounded severely. A
resistance so obstinate, and destructive to the enemy
against a force so superior, reflects the highest honor
on the American officers and seamen. They had formerly been under the command of captain Porter, who
immortalized Valparaiso, by the obstinate and desperate resistance, which he made at that place against a
superior force of the enemy ; and they now proved
themselves worthy pupils of that invincible naval hero.

On the day after the battle, intelligence of the result
was brought to New Orleans by the commander of the
schooner, who had escaped by land from the bay of
St. Louis. The city already alarmed, distracted, and
despairing, was thrown into consternation and confusion by the event. A powerful, well disciplined, and
well appointed army was on the coast, and the only
feeble barrier which prevented its approach through
the lakes, within a few miles of the city, was now entirely swept away. The whole force under Jackson,
on which the salvation of the state depended, did not
exceed 4000, of which only 1000 were regulars. The
greater part of this force was kept at the city, that it
might be ready to meet the invaders in any pass, which
they might select for their approach. The mounted volunteers under Coffee had not yet arrived from
Mobile.

At such a crisis and in such circumstances, the utmost
exertions of every patriot, and the most rigorous and efficient measures for the public security became indispensible. The general had not forgotten the representations
which he had previously received from the highest authority, concerning the general character of the population, the number of disaffected persons in the city, and
particularly the want of confidence in the legislative representatives of the people, which their conduct in the
present session had inspired. With a view therefore, to
supercede such civil powers, as in their operation might

interfere with those, which he would be obliged to exercise, in pursuing the best measures for the safety of the country; and under a solemn conviction, after consulting with the best patriots in the place, that the measure was proper and required by the situation of our affairs; he determined to place, and on the 16th did proclaim, "the city and environs of New Orleans *under strict martial law.*" This decisive measure received the approbation and cordial acquiescence of every friend to the safety of the country. It was accompanied by suitable regulations, which required every person entering the city, to report himself at the office of the adjutant general, and every person or vessel leaving it, to procure a passport from the general, one of his staff, or the commanding naval officer. The street lamps were to be extinguished at 9 in the night, and every person afterwards found abroad without permission in writing, was to be apprehended as a spy. The whole of the citizens, sojourners, passengers, and persons of every description, who were capable of bearing arms, were pressed into the land and naval service.

The general at the same time published the following address to the people.

'The major general commanding has learnt, with astonishment and regret, that great consternation and alarm pervade your city. It is true the enemy is on our coast, and threatens an invasion of our territory; but it is equally true, that with union, energy, and the approbation of heaven, we will beat him at every point, where his temerity may induce him to set foot on our soil.

'The general with still greater astonishment has heard, that British emissaries have been permitted to propagate a seditious report amongst you, that the threatened invasion is with a view of restoring the country to Spain, from a supposition that some of you would be willing to return to your ancient government— believe no such incredible tales—your government is at peace with Spain. It is the vital enemy of your country, the common enemy of mankind, the highway robber of the world, who threatens you, and has sent his hirelings amongst you with this false report, to put you off your guard, that you may fall an easy prey to his rapacity. Then look to your liberties, your property, and the chastity of your wives and daughters. Take a retrospect of the conduct of the British army at Hampton, and other places where it entered our country—and every bosom which glows with patriotism and virtue, will be inspired with indignation, and pant for the arrival of the hour, when we shall meet the enemy and revenge these outrages against the laws of civilization and humanity.

‘The general calls upon the inhabitants of the city, to trace this unfounded report to its source, and bring the propagator to condign punishment. The rules and articles of war annex the punishment of death, to the crime of holding secret correspondence with the enemy, supplying him with provisions, or creating false alarms; and the general announces his unalterable determination, rigidly to execute the martial law, in all cases which may come within his province.

‘The safety of the district entrusted to the protection of the general, must and will be maintained with the best blood of the country; and he is confident that all good citizens will be found at their posts with arms in their hands, determined to dispute every inch of ground with the enemy, and that unanimity will pervade the whole country. But should the general be disappointed in this expectation, *he will separate our enemies from our friends. Those who are not for us are against us, and will be dealt with accordingly.*

‘TH: L BUTLER, *A. D. C.*’

The traitors well knew, from the character of general Jackson, that the threatening parts of this proclamation were not mere sound and fury, but that they would be carried into execution with the utmost rigor and promptitude. Disaffection was thus awed into silence, and the friends of the country were inspired with unbounded confidence, harmony, and enthusiasm. The militia of the city and all its environs were armed, accoutred, and drilled twice every day. On the 18th an address from the general was read to those of the city, by his volunteer aid Mr. Livingston, the following extract from which will exhibit the spirit of the times.

“The general commanding in chief, would not do justice to the noble ardor that has animated you, in the hour of danger—he would not do justice to his own feelings—if he suffered the example you have shewn to pass without public notice. Inhabitants of an opulent and commercial town, you have by a spontaneous effort, shaken off the habits which are created by wealth, and shewn that you are resolved to deserve the blessings of fortune by bravely defending them. Long strangers to the perils of war, you have embodied yourselves to face them with the cool countenance of veterans—and with motives to disunion, that might operate on weak minds, you have forgotten the difference of language, and the prejudices o, national pride, and united with a cordiality that does honor to your understandings, as well as to your patriotism."

Information was now received that the enemy, after the capture of our brave flotilla, was pressing to the westward, through the islands and passes of lake Borgne, in his boats and light vessels; but the point at which he would attempt to debark, or the pass through which he would endeavor to reach the city, was still unknown. With a view to greater security, in guarding the numerous bayous and canals, which lead from the lake through the swampy district, to the high land on the margin of the river, the superintendence of that service was entrusted to major general Villere, who commanded the militia between the river and the lake, and who being a native of the country was presumed to be best acquainted with its topography. He kept a picket guard stationed at the mouth of the bayou Bienvenue, which led into his own plantation on the bank of the river; but contrary to the orders of general Jackson, he left the navigation of the bayou unobstructed. On the 23rd of December, the enemy having selected this pass for their approach, succeeded in surprising the guard at the mouth of the bayou, and in capturing a company of militia, stationed on the plantation of general Villere. Their troops were then conveyed up the bayou to the amount of 3000, and an encampment formed between the river and the marsh, on the premises of major Lacoste. The intelligence of their approach was brought to head quar-

ters at the city about 1 o'clock on that day, and general Jackson immediately determined to attack them
without delay in their first position.

In the mean time general Coffee had arrived with
his brigade of mounted men from Mobile; and also
general Carroll with part of his division of militia infantry from West Tennessee. The latter had descended the rivers with a degree of celerity unparalleled in the history of military movements. His troops
had embarked on the 24th ultimo at Nashville, and on
the evening of the 22nd instant, it being the 29th day
of their voyage, they arrived *very opportunely* near the
city of New Orleans. They were now encamped with
the mounted men, who had also recently arrived, about
4 miles above the city, and were all immediately ordered down by general Jackson, to superinduce the
dangers of the battle on the toils of the march. The
general expected that the troops which the enemy were
debarking by the pass of Bienvenue, did not constitute
their principal, or at least their only force, but that a
simultaneous attack would be made by the way of Chef
Mentire. He therefore posted the division of general
Carroll, with the city militia, on the Gentilly road leading to Chef Mentire, to meet such an event; and at 5
o'clock he was ready to march down against the enemy,
with the rest of his troops, consisting of general Coffee's brigade, a corps of dragoons under major Hinds,
a battalion of uniformed volunteers under major Plau-
che, 200 men of color under major Daquin, a detachment of artillery with two 6 pounders under the direction of colonel M'Rea, and parts of the 7th and 44th
regiments of regulars under major Peire and captain
Baker. The whole force was very much inferior to
that of the enemy, which was commanded by major
general Keane.

About 7 o'clock, general Jackson arrived near the
British encampment, where all was quiet, his advance
upon them being concealed under cover of the night,

while their fires in the camp fully exposed them to his
view. Their right extended to the swamp, and their
left which was the strongest part of their lines, rested
on the bank of the river. Arrangements were immediately made for the attack : general Coffee was ordered
to turn their right, whilst Jackson with the regulars attacked their strongest position on the left. Commodore
Patterson had been ordered to drop down the river in
the schooner Carolina, and commence a fire on their
camp, which was to be the signal for a general charge.

At half past 8 the commodore opened his fire, and
general Coffee's troops then rushed upon the right of
the enemy, with great impetuosity, and entered their
camp, while Jackson engaged their left with equal ardor, supported by the fire of the schooner and the two
field pieces. The action soon became general, and was
obstinately contested on both sides, the hostile troops
being frequently intermixed with each other in the conflict. About 10 o'clock, after the battle had raged more
than an hour, a thick fog came over them, which caused
some confusion among our troops, and rendered it necessary in the opinion of our general, to desist from the
contest. Had it not been for this unfortunate occurrence, he would no doubt have gained a decisive victory, and have blasted at once the presumptuous hopes
of the rapacious invader. He lay on the field of battle
in the face of the enemy, till 4 o'clock in the morning,
and then withdrew his army with so much address, as
to elude their vigilance, and conceal the weakness of
the force by which they had been so boldly attacked.
Having retired up the river about two miles, he encamped his troops, on the firm open ground between
the river and the swamp, at a narrow point between the
enemy and the city, where their progress could be arrested with less labor and fewer troops, than at any
other position he could have selected.

When general Keane first reached the banks of the
Mississippi, he felt supinely confident, that the conquest

of the city would be an easy achievement for his *Wellington invincibles ;* but the uncivil greeting, which he received the first evening on our shores, convinced him of his error, taught him to respect our prowess and enterprise, and made him contented with maintaining his first position, till the commander in chief of the expedition, the lieutenant general sir Edward Packenham, could arrive with the balance of the forces. The most important advantages were thus derived to our cause, by this bold, decisive, and judicious movement of our general. The progress of the enemy was arrested, which gave us time to fortify and entrench our lines, in the most eligible position for defence ; and our success in the battle inspired our troops with the confidence of veterans. The loss of the enemy was computed at 100 killed, 230 wounded, and 70 prisoners captured, including among them one major, and several other officers of less rank. Our loss was 24 killed, 115 wounded, and 74 missing. Among the dead were lieutenant colonel Lauderdale of the Tennessee mounted men, and lieutenant M'Clelland of the 7th infantry ; and several other officers were wounded.

General Jackson now determined to fortify his position, act on the defensive, and wait the arrival of the Kentucky detachment. The interests committed to his care were too important, to be exposed to any unnecessary hazard by offensive and premature operations against the enemy. The care of Chef Mentire pass being entrusted to colonel Morgan of the city militia, the division of general Carroll was brought down to the lines, and the fortifications commenced with the utmost vigor and despatch. They consisted of a straight line of works extending from the river on the right of our troops to the swamp on their left. A breastwork was thrown up, from 4 to 5 feet high, with a wet ditch close in front, about 4 feet deep and 8 feet wide. Several heavy pieces of artillery were mounted on the works, with their embrasures lined with bales of cotton.

On the right the works terminated in a bastion, with a battery calculated for raking the ditch. Such were the fortifications now completed with the utmost expedition in the power of our troops, aided by the labor of a number of negroes from the plantations. The opening of the ditch was also facilitated by the presence of an old canal, which had been dug to convey the water of the river, *down* to a mill at the edge of the swamp.

On the 26th the ship Louisiana, commodore Patterson, and the schooner Carolina, captain Henley, dropped down the river, took a position near the enemy's camp, and opened a brisk, destructive fire upon them, from the severity of which they were glad to shelter themselves by retiring into the swamp. In the night however they erected a furnace and battery at a convenient distance on shore, and were ready at daylight on the 27th, to commence a fire of red hot shot on the assailing vessels. The ship was out of their reach, but the schooner being becalmed within the range of their guns, and prevented from ascending by the strength of the current, captain Henley was compelled to abandon her, and she soon afterwards took fire and was blown up.

Sir Edward Packenham, lieutenant general and commander in chief, having now arrived and brought up large reinforcements to the British camp, they resolved on making a demonstration against our works, with a view to effect something important and decisive. On the 28th they advanced with their whole force, and commenced a tremendous cannonade and bombardment of our lines. Balls, shells, and congreve rockets were thrown in showers on the breastwork, and over the heads of our troops; and their columns were formed and brought up, apparently with the intention of storming our works on the left. But their fire was returned with great spirit and vivacity by our batteries, which compelled them, after three hours of incessant cannonading, and fruitless exposure of their lives, to retire with disappointment and mortification to their camp. Their expectations appeared to be, that their tremendous cannonade, and great quantity of combustibles thrown on our works, would frighten away the militia, or throw them into confusion, and thus afford a favorable opportunity for making an assault. But the firmness and cool intrepidity of our troops, combined with the destructive fire of our batteries, kept them at a respectful distance, and at last compelled them to abandon the enterprise. Their loss on this occasion was considerable—not less than 120 killed: whilst ours was but 7 killed, and 8 wounded. Lieutenant colonel Henderson of the Tennessee militia was among the slain. For several days after this affair, nothing important occurred. Skirmishes occasionally took place between the picket guards, and the enemy's camp was sometimes annoyed by the ship Louisiana.

Though disappointed in their expectations on the 28th, they did not abandon the project of forcing our lines, but prepared for a more formidable attack on Sunday morning the 1st of January. Admiral Cochrane, the naval commander, had sent us word on his arrival off the coast, that he would eat his Christmas dinner in New Orleans; and general Packenham now resolved at least to spend his Newyear in the city. Under cover of the night, and a heavy fog which continued till 8 o'clock in the morning, the enemy advanced within 600 yards of our works, being considerably nigher than they had come before, and there erected three different batteries, mounting in all fifteen guns, from 6 to 32 pounders; and as soon as the fog had cleared away in the morning, they commenced a heavy and incessant fire, throwing shot, bombs, and rockets in showers at our works. They also essayed again to advance to the assault in column, but the steady and skilful fire of our batteries, soon arrested their progress and put them to flight. An incessant cannonading however was continued through the day, till late in the evening, when our balls had dismounted and silenced nearly all of their guns; and under cover of the night, they again withdrew from the unprofitable contest. Our loss on this day was 11 killed and 23 wounded, whilst that of the enemy, from their very exposed situation, must have been extremely great.

The opposite side of the river, or the right bank, now became an object of attention with both armies. Commodore Patterson had landed some of the guns of the Louisiana, and erected a battery on the bank, opposite our main works on the left side, for the purpose of co-operating with the right of our lines, and flanking the enemy in his advance up the river to attack them. After the affair on the 1st of January, the battery was enlarged by landing and mounting more guns, and a furnace was prepared to heat shot, with a view to fire the houses between the two armies, which were occupied by the British. The Louisiana militia, and New Orleans contingent, were also stationed at that place under general D. B. Morgan, for the purpose of repelling any attack on the battery, or any attempt to move up, on that side, and annoy the city across the river, which the enemy might make. On the 4th general Morgan began to throw up a breastwork, and mounted three 12 pounders, for the defence of his troops. On the 4th also, the Kentucky detachment under general Thomas arrived at the city. Being nearly destitute of arms, for they had brought but few with them from home, and those which had been shipped in *trading boats* at Pittsburg had not yet arrived, they were ordered to encamp at the canal of Madame Piernass, one mile above the American lines, till they could be equipt for service. The city was now ransacked for arms to supply the Kentuckians, and by the 7th a sufficient number was collected and repaired, together with a loan obtained by general Adair from a corps of exempts, to arm the regiment commanded by colonel Slaughter, and the battalion under major Harrison.

These corps, 1000 strong, were then marched down to
the lines under the command of general Adair, major
general Thomas being unwell; and were posted immediately in the rear of general Carroll's division, to support the centre of our works.

The enemy in the mean time were engaged, on the
suggestion of admiral Cochrane, in enlarging a canal
which connected the Mississippi with the bayou Bienvenue, to enable them to draw their boats through it
into the river, and make an attack on our establishment
under Patterson and Morgan. On the 7th their operations were reconnoitred across the river by the commodore, who ascertained in the evening, that they had
nearly completed the undertaking, and immediately
communicated this information to Jackson, with a request that reinforcements might be sent over, to assist
in the defence of his position. The general accordingly ordered 400 of the unarmed Kentuckians, to go
up to the city where they would be supplied with arms,
and then come down on the opposite side to Morgan.
It was in the night when they marched, and a supply
of indifferent arms could be procured for no more than
200, who proceeded to their place of destination while
the balance returned to camp. About 1 o'clock in the
morning of the 8th, the commodore discovered that the
enemy had got their barges into the river, and that an
uncommon stir was prevailing in their camp, of which
the commanding general was duly notified.

No doubt now existed in the American camp, but
that another formidable attack was on the point of being
carried into execution on both sides of the river; and
as the enemy had already been twice repulsed, it was
reasonable to expect that his third attempt would be
desperate and bloody. Our main army however, was
well prepared to receive him, and anxious for an assault
to be made. The whole extent of our works, about
1800 yards from the river to the swamp, was well
finished, well manned with brave soldiers, and well

defended with artillery. The regulars with a part of the militia from Louisiana, occupied 600 yards on the right next the river; general Carroll's division occupied 800 yards in the centre; and general Coffee defended the balance of the works on the left. The Kentuckians formed in two lines, occupied 400 yards in the centre, close in the rear of general Carroll's command.

As soon as the dawn of day enabled us to see some distance in front of our lines, the enemy were discovered advancing in great force, formed in two powerful columns on the right and left, and prepared with fascines and scaling ladders to storm our works. Their left column which was the least, was led up the bank of the river by major general Keane; whilst their main column was conducted against the centre of our works by major general Gibbs. A third column was held in reserve under the command of major general Lambert. The ground over which they had to march to the assault was a perfect level, beautifully overgrown with clover, and without any intervening obstruction whatever. The signal for the onset was the discharge of a rocket from the head of their column next the river, when their whole force rent the air with a shout, and advanced briskly to the charge. A tremendous cannonade was at the same time opened on our works from their mortars and field artillery, and from a battery of six 18 pounders, which they had erected within 500 yards of our lines.

Their attack was received by our troops with the utmost firmness and bravery, and their fire immediately returned by the artillery on our works, under the direction of deliberate and skilful officers, who tore their columns, as they approached, with a frightful carnage: and as soon as the heads of their columns had arrived within the range of our small arms, they were assailed in a manner still more destructive, by the steady, deliberate, well aimed fire of our rifles and musketry. Though they advanced under this havoc with aston-

ishing firmness and intrepidity, yet ere they could
reach our works they were thrown into confusion and
repulsed : but the brave officers who led them, soon
rallied their flying troops, reformed their shattered columns, and led them the second time to the charge,
with renovated vigor and fury. In vain was their
bravery—in vain the utmost exertion of their powers—
they only renewed the charge to suffer a new repulse
with redoubled carnage.   Their principal column advancing against the centre of our works, was opposed
by the strongest part of our lines, consisting of Tennessee and Kentucky marksmen, at least six men deep,
who literally poured forth a sheet of fire, which cut
down the ranks of the enemy, like grass by the scythe
of a mower.   Yet their heavy columns pressed on with
such force and desperation, that many of their men at
last entered the ditch in front of our breastwork, where
they were shot down in heaps at the very muzzles of
our guns.   Slaughtered, shattered and disordered, they
were again forced to retire.   Their leaders however,
apparently resolved on victory or total destruction,
again rallied and brought them up a third time to the
charge ; but their principal officers being now slain
and disabled, and their strength greatly broken and
spent, this last effort was less successful than the former, and they were soon forced to fall back in disorder on their column of reserve, with which they pursued a precipitate and disorderly retreat to their camp,
under a galling fire from our batteries, leaving the field
literally covered with the dying and the dead.   Lieutenant general Packenham was killed, and major generals Keane and Gibbs were both severely wounded,
the latter of whom died a few days afterwards.   Colonel Rannie was also killed—a brave and intrepid officer, who in the second charge entered the bastion on
our right, at the head of his men, but was immediately
slain and his followers repulsed by our brave regulars
and Beale's company of city riflemen.   The action

lasted about an hour, and terminated in a decisive and total defeat of the enemy.

On the other side of the river our arms experienced a reverse. The battery erected by commodore Patterson, was constructed for annoying the enemy across the river, and raking the front of our works on the left side; and during the attack this morning it was employed in that way with considerable effect. But before the action ceased on the left, an attack was also made on the right bank. The 85th regiment with some seamen and marines, having crossed the river opposite the British camp, and led by colonel Thornton advanced under cover of some field pieces, and put to flight a corps commanded by major Arno, who had been sent down to oppose their landing. Continuing their march up the river, they next attacked the 200 Kentuckians under colonel Davis, who had been sent half a mile in front of our works to oppose them. After a sharp skirmish, colonel Davis retreated by order of general Morgan, with the loss of about 30 men, in killed, wounded, and missing; and having reached the entrenchment, he was ordered to post his men on the right of the Louisiana militia. The guns in the battery could not be employed against colonel Thornton, until they were turned in their embrasures, which was not undertaken till it was too late to accomplish it before the charge was made. General Morgan had 500 Louisiana militia, safely posted behind a finished breastwork, which extended 200 yards from the battery, at right angles to the river, and was defended by 3 pieces of artillery. The 170 remaining Kentuckians on his right, were scattered along a ditch 300 yards in extent; and still further on the right there was several hundred yards of open ground entirely undefended.

In this situation of things, the enemy with steady pace continued advancing to the charge in two columns under the cover of a shower of rockets. Their right column advancing next the river, was thrown into disorder, and driven back by Morgan's artillery : the other advancing against the Kentuckians, was resisted by their small arms, till a party of the assailants had turned their right flank, and commenced a fire on their rear. Overpowered by numbers in front, assailed in their rear, and unsupported by their companions in arms, they were at last compelled to retreat from their untenable position. The Louisiana militia then retreated also from their breastwork and artillery, before they had felt the pressure of the enemy. Commodore Patterson perceiving how the contest would issue, spiked his cannon and was ready to join in the retreat with his marines. The enemy pursued them some distance up the river, and then returned to destroy the battery and other works.

Patterson and Morgan, conscious that they had acted badly, the former in not turning his guns in time, and the latter in leaving his right flank weak, uncovered, and unsupported, whilst his main force was uselessly concentrated behind the breastwork, determined to throw the whole blame of the defeat on the handful of Kentuckians, who had the misfortune to be present, and to do all the fighting that was done, except a few discharges from the artillery. They induced general Jackson to tell the war department, that "the Kentucky reinforcements *ingloriously fled*, drawing after them by their example, the *remainder* of the forces"—and the commodore in his report to the navy department, stigmatized them in terms still more offensive. A court of enquiry was demanded by colonel Davis, before which the facts were proven as above detailed. The court however merely pronounced the Kentuckians *excusable :* which being deemed unsatisfactory, general Adair again pressed the subject on the commander in chief, and at last obtained a dry, reluctant sentence of *justification.* The detachment did all, at least, that could be expected from brave men, if it was not entitled to the praise of uncommon gallantry.

Our victory on the left bank of the river was very complete and decisive. The inequality of loss in the opposing armies, was probably unparalleled in the annals of warfare—ours being only six killed and seven wounded in the main battle, while that of the enemy was estimated at *two thousand six hundred*, in killed, wounded and prisoners. Immediately after the action an armistice for a few hours was craved and obtained by the enemy, for the purpose of burying their dead, and taking care of their wounded. A line was then designated across the field of battle, to which they were allowed to come; and between that line and the breastwork 482 dead bodies were counted and carried out, while it was estimated that upwards of 200 lay on the out side of it; the killed was therefore set down at 700; and supposing as usual, that twice that number were wounded, the whole killed and wounded would be 2100; and 500 prisoners were captured—making a total of 2600. Lieutenant general Packenham who was killed was an officer of great distinction. He was brother-in-law to the celebrated lord Wellington, under whom he had been trained; and most of the troops he commanded, had also fought and signalized themselves under that commander in Spain. Our effective force engaged at the works, according to the official returns, was a little upwards of 4000—of which about 2000 were Tennessee militia, 1000 Kentucky militia, and upwards of 1000 regulars and Louisiana militia. The force engaged on the part of the enemy was not known; but his whole force present was believed to be between 8 and 10 thousand—the original force of the expedition having been much above that number.

Though the enemy succeeded in their enterprise on the right bank of the river, yet they met with a considerable loss on that side also—their killed and wounded in that affair being about 97, among the latter colonel Thornton severely; whilst our loss was comparatively small, perhaps not half that number

After setting fire, not only to the platform and carriages of the battery, but to all the private dwelling houses, and destroying all the private property they could find, for several miles along the river, the detachment retreated over to their main camp, carrying with them 2 field pieces and a brass howitzer. The object of the enterprise was to wrest the battery from Patterson, before the main attack was made, with a view to employ it in raking Jackson's lines, instead of flanking their own columns; but from some cause the detachment did not get over the river as soon as they intended, and of course did not prevent the battery from answering the purpose for which it had been erected. Morgan and Patterson immediately re-occupied their old position, when the enemy retreated; began to drill the cannon and repair the works; and in a few days were again ready for efficient service.

On the day after the great battle, an attack was made by the enemy on fort St. Philip, commanded by major Walter H. Overton, with a view to bring their armed vessels up the river, to co-operate with the land forces in the capture of the city. Major Overton received intelligence of their intentions as early as the 1st of January, and was well prepared to sustain the attack. They doubtless had intended to carry the fort, and get up the river in time for the main contest, but were prevented by the difficulty of ascending the river. On the 9th two bomb vessels, a brig, a sloop and a schooner, came to anchor about two miles below the fort, and commenced an attack with sea mortars of ten and thirteen inches calibre, which they continued nine days without intermission, and without molestation, for their position was beyond the range of the guns in the fort. In this period they threw upwards of 1000 large shells; besides a great many small ones, with round and grape shot, from boats under cover of the night. A large mortar in the mean time was sent down to the fort, and in the evening of the 17th was brought to bear upon their vessels, which induced them to withdraw at day light next morning. All the loss in the fort was 2 killed and 7 wounded—so judicious had been the preparations and police of major Overton to meet the attack.

As soon as intelligence of the attack had been brought to head quarters, a battery mounting 4 twenty four pounders, with a furnace to heat shot, had been erected to burn the shipping of the enemy, should they succeed in capturing the fort, or in passing it with their armed vessels.

Preparations were now making by general Lambert and admiral Cochrane for a retreat. An exchange of prisoners took place on the 18th, by which all our men who had been captured and not sent to the shipping, were recovered and restored to their country; and in the night of that day, the enemy made good their retreat from the banks of the Mississippi to their boats and small vessels, and commenced embarking their troops and baggage for their large vessels, still lying off Ship Island in the gulf of Mexico. In their camp they left 14 pieces of heavy artillery, a quantity of shot, and eighty of their wounded with a surgeon to attend them, all of whom had been so disabled in their limbs, that a recovery from their wounds would not render them fit for service. The retreat was not accomplished without molestation. Such was the situation of the ground which they abandoned, and through which they passed, protected by canals, redoubts, entrenchments and swamps, that general Jackson did not think proper to press upon them in the rear with his whole force; but an enterprise was successfully conducted against their light vessels on the lake by Mr. Shields, the purser of the navy. After the battle of the gun boats " Mr. Shields had been sent down under a flag of truce to ascertain the fate of our officers and men, with power to negotiate an exchange, especially for the wounded. But the enemy would make no terms—they treated the flag with contempt, and himself and the surgeon who was with him as prisoners." Before they retreated however, "they lowered their their tone, and begged the exchange that we had offered. Defeat had thus humbled the arrogance of an enemy, *who had promised his soldiers 48 hours of pillage and rapine in the city of New Orleans.*" When the intention of the enemy to retreat was discovered, Mr. Shields was sent out through Pass Chef Mentire, in 5 armed boats and a gig, manned with 50 sailors and militia, to annoy their transports on lake Borgne, a service which he undertook with great alacrity, as he was anxious to avenge the personal insults and injuries he had experienced. He succeeded without loss on his part in capturing and destroying a transport brig and two boats, and bringing in 78 prisoners, besides capturing several other boats and a number of prisoners whom he was obliged to parole.

And thus the projected conquest of Louisiana, and the siege of New Orleans, which were vigorously prosecuted for 27 days by a powerful army, terminated in the total discomfiture of that army, and a most complete victory for the American arms, which illuminated the closing scenes of the war with a blaze of American glory. So confident had the British government been, that the expedition would be successful—that they would be able to take and to hold Louisiana—that Sir Edward Packenham was provided with a special commission as governor of the province, and was accompanied by all the necessary civil magistrates, custom house officers, &c. &c. to make a permanent governmental establishment in the city of New Orleans; and that no excitement to the most desperate exertions, might be wanting among the soldiers, to make them secure such a valuable prize for Sir Edward, he promised them an unrestrained pillage of the city; and as a memento and confirmation of his promise, gave them *beauty and booty* for a watchword on the morning of the great battle. How mistaken were the calculations of the government! and how greatly disappointed the hopes of its Vandal army! Instead of enjoying the beauty and booty of a rich commercial city, they experienced the severest privations and hardships, and met the most signal and ignominious defeat. From the time they arrived in that quarter till they retreated, their loss was not less than 4000 by the sword and the privations they endured; for they were sometimes scarce of suitable provisions, and the season was the most cold and inclement which had been known in that country for ages.

The enemy being entirely driven from our soil, the lines which had been maintained with such astonishing success were broken up, and the different corps composing the army, after receiving the thanks of the general in the most lively and expressive terms, were distributed and encamped in such places as were most convenient for the comfort of the troops and the safety of the country. Strict discipline however was still preserved, and martial law enforced with all its rigors; and no exertions were omitted to keep suitable guards on the different passes to the city, and to watch every movement of the enemy. The general moved his head quarters to the town, where he was received with the greatest marks of attention, respect, and gratitude by its inhabitants, by whom he was universally acknowledged as the saviour of their city. As a testimony of their respect, and of the high sense they entertained of his great and distinguished exertions, in defence of their persons and property, their rights and liberties, their wives and their daughters, against a rapacious and mercenary soldiery, whose avowed intention was *beauty and booty*, they crowned their adored general with laurels—an honor never conferred on any chieftain in this county since the similar coronation of the illustrious Washington at Princeton. The ceremony was attended by a numerous concourse of people, and conducted in a very splendid manner.

There were many citizens in New Orleans however, and still more in many other parts of the Union, who condemned this regal pomp, as inconsistent with that republican simplicity, which ought always to be preserved in our country, and as tending to corrupt the minds of our citizens, by inspiring them with sentiments of false glory and sinister schemes of ambition.

When our country was invaded, the pirates of Barrataria, as well those who had escaped as those who had been captured, requested to be employed in defence of the city, against "the common enemy of mankind, the highway robber of the world—" and were accordingly posted on our lines, where they acted with great fidelity and courage—in consideration of which, and at the intercession of the legislature of Louisiana, they obtained a free and full pardon, for all their piratical offences, from the president of the United States; who declared in his proclamation, that "Offenders who had refused to become the associates of the enemy in the war, upon the most seducing terms of invitation; and who had aided to repel his hostile invasion of the territory of the United States; could no longer be considered as objects of punishment, but as objects of a generous forgiveness."

During the operations at New Orleans, the British under the famous Cockburn, who was a full match on the Atlantic frontier for Procter in the interior, took possession of Cumberland Island off the coast of Georgia near the Florida line, from whence they landed and plundered the town of St. Marys in Georgia, of every article of value belonging to that place, which they could carry away, and destroyed much of that which was immoveable. Only a part of the armament, which had burnt Washington City, and robbed Alexandria, had joined the expedition under sir E. Packenham, and the balance was thus employed in robbing every as-

sailable town and farm house on the southern coast.
By a parcel of letters found on board the schooner St.
Lawrence, captured by the privateer Chasseur of Baltimore, on her passage from Cumberland to the British
fleet off New Orleans, which purported to be a correspondence between the officers of rear admiral Cockburn's fleet and those under vice admiral Cochrane,
their rapacious conduct and meanness of spirit was
exhibited in glowing terms, in which they congratulated
one another on their success in plundering and their
shares of prize money, and seemed to be intent on nothing but the dirty gains of an infamous pillage. The
enemy in their retreat from New Orleans, also carried
away a number of negroes, and a variety of other property; and Mr. Edward Livingston, volunteer aid to
general Jackson, being sent after them with a flag, to
demand redress and reparation for such injuries, inflicted on private persons contrary to the rules of honorable warfare, he was detained in their fleet while
they prepared and executed an expedition against
Mobile.

General Winchester who had lately been exchanged,
and returned home from Canada, was now entrusted
with the command at Mobile, for the protection of
which he had an ample force, consisting of the Georgia
militia, the Tennessee militia under Taylor, and several other smaller corps. On the 8th of February the
enemy invested fort Bowyer, with a formidable armament by land and water, under the immediate command of Cochrane and Lambert. They made regular
approaches by land, and had advanced within 30 yards
of its ditches, when colonel Lawrence by the advice of
his officers determined to capitulate, as there was no possibility of maintaining the post much longer. Though
he obtained highly honorable terms for his troops, and
was perfectly justifiable in making the surrender, yet
such an event was painful to a gallant soldier who had
been accustomed to victory. General Winchester was

much blamed for the result; for although he had a sufficiency of soldiers at the town of Mobile, and had been
apprized of the intentions of the enemy previous to
their landing, yet he delayed to send a reinforcement
to Lawrence until the siege had commenced. A detachment was then passed over the bay and sent to his
assistance, but it did not arrive until 24 hours after the
capitulation. Winchester soon afterwards resigned his
commission in the army, and the command at Mobile
devolved on general M'Intosh of Georgia. Our loss
in the surrender was 360 prisoners; and the loss of the
enemy in capturing the fort was between 30 and 40 in
killed and wounded.

Mr. Livingston now returned from the enemy, and
arrived at New Orleans on the 20th of February, bringing with him a rumor, that a treaty of peace had been
signed by the commissioners at Ghent, the ratification
of which by both governments was expected to follow.
This intelligence, though not official, had an astonishing effect on the militia troops at New Orleans. Inspired by their unparalleled success, with great confidence in the safety of that country, which was defended
by their prowess, and believing that peace was at hand,
the discipline of the camp became irksome, and they
began to murmur at the hardships of military duty.
They began to consider of their rights as freemen, and
to complain against the rigors of martial law. General
Jackson however supposed, that this report of peace
might have been invented by the enemy to put us off
our guard, and give them a chance to effect by stratagem and surprise, what they could not effect by force—
or although the intelligence might be true, yet that such
barbarians, if an opportunity should offer, would probably make a sudden incursion to the city, and burn it
through mere wantonness and revenge—he therefore
determined to continue and strictly enforce all his measures of vigilance and precaution, until peace should be

officially announced, or the British fleet had entirely
gone from that quarter.

The desire of relaxation on the other hand, became
so great in some of the corps, as even to excite apprehensions of mutiny. Two points at which it was necessary that guards should be stationed, were actually
deserted by the city militia. The spirit of insubordination was most apparent and formidable among the
European Frenchmen, who had entered their adhesions
to Louis XVIII, in the consular books of the chevalier
De Tousard. General Jackson hence determined, by
a rigorous measure in relation to them, to put a stop to
the progress of discontent, and ensure that strict discipline and vigilance which he still deemed necessary.
All French subjects whose foreign citizenship had been
regularly authenticated, were therefore ordered to leave
the city before the 3rd of March, and to proceed to the
interior at least as far as Baton Rouge. This order
instead of suppressing discontent and silencing opposition, had rather a contrary tendency. It was deemed
tyrannical and unnecessarily rigorous. The French
troops and citizens could not see, or would not acknowledge the necessity of remaining *in statu quo*, as
long as the war continued and a formidable hostile fleet
was hovering on the coast. Several unpleasant acts
ensued, the motives and propriety of which we shall
not stop to discuss as we briefly mention them.

On the day fixed for the departure of the French
aliens for the interior, a piece was published in a news-
paper, in which the course of the general was censured,
and the services of those persons during the siege highly
extolled. Viewing this piece as intended to counteract
the execution of the order, and excite mutiny among
the troops, general Jackson demanded of the printer,
the name of the author, who proved to be Mr. Louillier,
a member of the house of representatives from Opelou-
sas. He had him arrested and confined in the barracks. On the petition of Mr. Morel, attorney at law,

in behalf of Mr. Louillier, judge Hall of the United States' district court, granted a writ of habeas corpus for the enlargement of the prisoner.   On the same evening Hall was also arrested and carried to the barracks. Mr. Dick, the attorney of the United States for the district, then applied to judge Lewis of the Louisiana district court, for a writ in favor of judge Hall, and was himself immediately taken into custody by the military. Lewis however issued the writ, and was threatened but not arrested for doing it.   Another general order was now issued, in which it was enjoined on all officers and soldiers, to arrest forthwith, all persons whatever, who had infringed the former respecting the aliens, or were in any manner concerned in seditious practices.   A general court martial, of which major general Gaines was president, was ordered to try Mr. Louillier, the jurisdiction of which he denied, and would not plead before it.   The court however proceeded to try him as if he had plead not guilty; and after examining witnesses, and deliberating on the subject, they gave a sentence of not guilty, which was disapproved by general Jackson.   Mr. Louillier was however liberated; judge Hall and the French consul were sent a few leagues up the coast; and Mr. Dick was permitted to walk the streets.

In this state of things, the news of peace was officially announced.   A national salute was fired from fort St. Charles, followed by a federal salute from the dock yard.   A very splendid illumination of the city took place in the evening, diversified by the discharge of sky rockets, and enlivened by the shouts of the populace, proclaiming "peace on earth, and good will towards men."   Martial law was now annulled, and a free pardon of all prisoners proclaimed.   The glorious intelligence, with the measures it produced, came very opportunely to allay all the discontents prevailing among the people of the town and the troops of the army.

Judge Hall having resumed the functions of his office, cited general Jackson to appear before him, for an alleged contempt in refusing to obey the process of his court, in the case of the writ of habeas corpus in favor of Mr. Louillier. The general accordingly appeared, attended by his counsel, and tendered a written defence, in which he excepted to the proceedings against him as illegal, unconstitutional, and informal; relied on the existence of martial law for his justification; and gave the reasons which had induced him to proclaim it. The judge being apprized of the nature of the defence, decided that part which related to martial law to be inadmissible, and refused to hear it read. The general on his part refused to make any other; and the judge then told him, that for the contempt he had shewn the civil authority, he must pay a fine of $1000; which was immediately done.

Although there was a strong faction opposed to the general, and the mass of the people had been uneasy under the restrictions he had imposed, yet on the return of peace, and more particularly when judge Hall undertook to punish him for his military measures, it was found that there was an immense majority of the people who approved his conduct, and were grateful for his services. No one who knew the state of the country, and the situation of our affairs, when martial law was proclaimed, could doubt the propriety of that measure; and as long as the same state of things continued without much alteration, the general was certainly not to blame for continuing the measure; and as long as it was necessary to continue it, he was certainly justifiable in taking care that it should be enforced. With a little more address and temporizing however, its rigors might have been rendered more palatable, and many unpleasant circumstances have been avoided; but such a course did not suit the temper of general Jackson. In the case of the prosecution against him in the district court, his cause was so popular in New Or-

leans, that the check on the bank, with which he paid
his fine to the marshal, was immediately redeemed by
the citizens, who limited the contribution for that purpose to one dollar from each individual, in order that a
greater number might be gratified with the honor of
bearing a part in the expense.

The general on the return of peace had the pleasure
of restoring to Tennessee, Kentucky, Louisiana, and
the Mississippi territory, those brave troops who had
acted such a distinguished part, in the close of a war
which terminated so honorably for the American arms.
The Tennessee and Kentucky troops commenced their
return to their respective states on the 18th of March.
They had a long, painful, and fatiguing journey to
perform, and were nearly destitute of the necessary
transportation for their baggage and provisions, of
which they had but a scanty supply on many parts of
their journey. The patriotism of the people of Tennessee was still conspicuous. They met the famished
soldiers far in the wilds of the Indian country, with
comfortable provisions for their sustenance and refreshment. The majority of the troops at last arrived in
their respective states in the latter part of April and
first of May, after having suffered incredible hardships
from disease and fatigue. Their sufferings and losses
from disease, after the termination of the war, were
much greater than those they experienced from the toils
and dangers of the tented field.

The following extract from the address of general
Jackson to the militia, before they left New Orleans,
will shew in what light he viewed, and in what manner their country ought to estimate, the services of those
patriotic men.

'In parting with those brave men whose destinies have been
so long united with his own, and in whose labors and glories it
is his happiness and his boast to have participated, the commanding general can neither suppress his feelings, nor give ut-
terance to them as he ought. In what terms can he bestow suita-

ble praise on merit so extraordinary, so unparalleled! Let him
in one burst of joy, gratitude and exultation, exclaim—" These
are the saviours of their country—these the patriot soldiers, who
triumphed over the invincibles of Wellington, and conquered the
conquerors of Europe!"

' With what patience did you submit to privations—with what
fortitude did you endure fatigue—what valor did you display in
the field of battle! You have secured to America, a proud
name among the nations of the earth—a glory which will never perish!

' Possessing those dispositions which equally adorn the citizen
and the soldier, the expectations of your country will be met in
peace, as her wishes have been gratified in war. Go then my
brave companions to your homes; to those tender connections
and those blissful scenes, which render life so dear—full of honor
and crowned with laurels which will never fade. With what
happiness will you not, when participating in the bosoms of your
families the enjoyments of peaceful life, look back to the toils
you have borne—to the dangers you have encountered! How
will all your past exposures be converted into sources of inex-
pressible delight! Who that never experienced your sufferings,
will be able to appreciate your joys? The man who slumbered
ingloriously at home, during your painful marches, your nights
of watchfulness and your days of toil, will envy you the happiness which these recollections will afford—still more will he
envy the gratitude of that country, which you have so eminently
contributed to save.

' Continue fellow soldiers, on your passage to your several
destinations, to preserve that subordination, that dignified and
manly deportment, which have so ennobled your character.

' While the commanding general is thus giving indulgence to
his feelings towards those brave companions, who accompanied
him through difficulties and dangers, he cannot permit the names
of Blount, of Shelby, and Holmes to pass unnoticed. With
what a generous ardor of patriotism have these distinguished
governors contributed all their exertions to provide the means of
victory. The memory of these exertions, and of the success
with which they were attended, will be to them a reward more
grateful, than any which the pomp of title or the splendor of
wealth could bestow.

' What a happiness it is to the commanding general, that
while danger was before us, he was on no occasion compelled
to use, towards his companions in arms, either severity or re-
buke. If after the enemy had retired, improper passions began
to shew their empire in a few unworthy bosoms, and rendered
a resort to energetic measures necessary for their suppression,
the commanding general has not confounded the innocent with

the guilty—the seduced with the seducers. Towards you fellow soldiers, the most cheering recollections exist, blended alas! with regret, that disease and war should have ravished from us so many worthy companions. But the memory of the cause in which they perished, and of the virtues which animated them while living, must occupy the place where sorrow would claim to dwell.

'Farewell, fellow soldiers! The expression of your general's thanks is feeble; but the gratitude of a country of freemen is yours—yours the applause of an admiring world!"

THE END

☞ THE PUBLISHERS of the preceding History, having sent that part of it to general Winchester, which relates to his operations in the northwest, have been requested by him to give publicity in this edition to the following

NOTE.

GENERAL WINCHESTER has read, with injured feelings, that part of the History of the late War in the Western Country, which relates to the left wing of the northwestern army. He avers that material facts have been omitted, and others misstated, which, if they had been incorporated in the work, would have given a different cast to public opinion. These errors in the history, he attributes, not to any wish in the historian to do him injustice, but to a want of full and impartial information on that subject.

A concise exposition of facts, with a few observations upon them, is now in preparation, and will be published for the satisfaction of those, who seek for truth.

Crag font, Tenn. 5th Sept. 1846.

PRINTED
BY WORSLEY & SMITH,
Reporter Office. Lexington, K.